Engagement
&Change

Exploring Management, Economic and Finance Implications of a Globalising Enviroment

edited by

Parikshit Basu • Grant O'Neill • Antonio Travaglione

AUSTRALIAN ACADEMIC PRESS
Brisbane

First published in 2007
Australian Academic Press
32 Jeays Street
Bowen Hills Qld 4006
Australia
www.australianacademicpress.com.au

National Library of Australia
Cataloguing-in-Publication data:

>Engagement and change : exploring management, economic and
>finance implications of a globalising environment /
>editors, Parikshit K. Basu ; Antonio Travaglione ; Grant
>O'Neill.

1st ed.

Bowen Hills, Qld. : Australian Academic Press, 2007.

ISBN: 9781875378883 (pbk.)

International business enterprises--Management.
Globalization--Economic aspects.
International economic relations.

Basu, Parikshit K.
Travaglione, Antonio.
O'Neill, Grant.

658.049

Contents

continued over

Part 3
Financial and Accounting Issues in a Globalised World

Part 4
Cultural Change and Its Effects on Management and Workplace Performance

Exploring the Impact of Globalisation on Contemporary Business

Grant O'Neill

Parikshit Basu

Antonio Travaglione

Globalisation and Business Practice

While globalisation became a phenomenon of major interest in the 1990s, it is increasingly recognised as having a powerful influence upon business, governments and societies across the globe. As globalisation impacts all areas of modern life, any review of the literature on globalisation and its imputed effects will demonstrate that its conceptualisation and effects are contested (see, e.g., Beck, 1999; Bhagwati, 2004; Hirst & Thompson, 1996; Giddens, 2000; Stiglitz, 2006). Following Beck (1999), we hold that globalisation should be understood as something more than growing interconnectedness of economies, people and processes between nation-states. For while nation-states and businesses have long experienced deep global interconnections, it is apparent the transcendence of space and time (Giddens, 2000) associated with 'transnationalism' differentiates globalisation from past movements of goods, services, capital, people, processes and ideas. Indeed, globalisation has witnessed complex and multiple processes that are often linked to a decline in the power of nation-states, even their 'transcendence', and the emergence and growth of 'transnational' actors, and flows of capital, products, people and information that are unprecedented in history. Interregional trade and financial cooperation are currently increasing rapidly (Ahn & Cheong, 2007) and the consequences of this are far-reaching.

Major drivers and effects of globalisation include:

- increased international trade
- economic competition, changes in economic policies, including deregulation and tax reform
- transnational economic agreements
- technological advancements, including sophisticated communications and IT
- increased movement of businesses in search of lower costs of production and lower tax regimes.

However, despite the existence of transnational actors and increasing flows of capital, goods, services, people, ideas and information, it is clear that globalisation is variously having fragmenting, uneven and homogenising effects (see, e.g., Bauman, 1998; Held, McGrew, Goldblatt, & Perraton, 1999; Olds, Dicken, Kelly, & Wai-Chung, 1999; Sirgy, Lee, Miller, & Littlefield, 2004). Globalisation is having an uneven impact upon the economies, governments and societies of the world. Businesses and organisations encounter variable pressures and effects, and new opportunities are not equally accessible. While it is not our intention to address the numerous theories and accounts of cultural, economic and political globalisation in detail, given the focus and content of subsequent chapters in this book, we do wish to focus attention upon the critical importance of globalisation for businesses and other organisations in the Asia–Oceania region (comprising countries in the region including Australia, China, Hong Kong, India, Japan, Indonesia, New Zealand, Philippines, Singapore, Taiwan, Thailand).

At the most general level, the greater cross-national flows of capital, goods, services and people mean that organisations and populations within Asia–Oceania are exposed to increasing competition. Survey research among senior executives around the world (Bandyopadhyay, 2006) shows that this trend is likely to result in the need for more complex risk management, and continuing development of markets with unequal stages of maturity and varying customer knowledge and expectations in the region. The recent trend in financial globalisation has also created political tensions between those who welcome the associated changes and those who perceive the change negatively.

At the regional level, the increased flow of investment has resulted in significant improvement in economic efficiency and growth (Bandyopadhyay, 2006). It has also been observed that increased economic 'freedom', and associated increased flows of trade, is a significant and robust determinant of foreign investment flows in the Asia–Oceania region (Quazi, 2007).

Clearly, globalisation is affecting all businesses, even if only indirectly through its impact upon the policies and practices of governments. Indeed, government policies and practices have changed in response to globalisation and businesses in many countries are being freed from past levels responsibility vis-a-vis taxation, wages and employment conditions for workers. Arguably, the power of governments has diminished in the face of businesses that are increasingly able to move operations, funds and profits to locations around the globe that are deemed more desirable because of such factors as lower costs of production, greater government support, proximity to major markets and lower taxation.

At a range of levels, globalisation is variously associated with internationalisation, the decline of barriers to trade and capital movements, the rise of supranational bodies such as the International Monetary Fund, the World Trade Organization, and the World Bank, and westernisation of ideas and practices. There is a greater connectedness across the globe that is productive of, and produced by, the intensification of social and economic relationships that are uncoupled from particularities of territory. There is also notable resistance to change in the face of the decline of local tradition, culture and practice in the face of universalising forces. Indeed, such resistance can stimulate a strengthening of local tradition and even the rise of fundamentalist thinking. That said, despite resistance and uneven effects across populations, globalisation has seen marketisation continue its ascendancy at an intellectual and practical level in many nations, especially developing nations. There are potential costs as well as benefits, but businesses, organisations and nations can ill afford to eschew globalisation and so be excluded from its many benefits.

Asia–Oceania: A Key Site of Globalisation

As noted above, the impact of globalisation and the associated changes are critical to the success of businesses all over the world, and this is no less the case within the Asia–Oceania region. The impact of globalisation is evident in, and illustrated through, the changing ways of doing business across the region. The current pace of change in the region is unprecedented and there is a strong compulsion to remain current with new practices and processes or risk marginal status within the region. The harsh reality is that the socially marginal, within and across nations, are at greatest risk from the negative effects of globalisation. It is highly desirable for nations to support their populations moving up the international division of labour, yet this is no simple task within this increasingly competitive region. Nations and their businesses must be increasingly competitive within, and beyond, the Asia–Oceania region.

The chapters that follow represent a response to the need for businesses and organisations to understand their context of operations, learn and change so that they, and the various populations across the region, may fully benefit and prosper from the opportunities of globalisation. Organisations and governments within the region must develop sound strategies to respond to globalisation and the opportunities it offers, for they can ill afford to restrict their thinking and action to the local. In so many respects, this is no longer even possible despite the fact that globalisation is always experienced in a local context.

Harnessing the potential benefits of globalisation is more important now than ever before. Ongoing change and innovation are critically important in a context where competition from overseas and domestic competitors continues to grow, and capital, goods and services move ever more freely across national borders. We hold that there is no real choice but to engage with the rest of the region and the world. Businesses and other organisations with the region must address globalisation and respond to change in an informed and timely manner. Economic growth, even survival, compels businesses to expand their horizons.

Insights into Contemporary Business Practices

Developed from the best papers presented at the Third International Conference on Contemporary Business,[1] each of the chapters that follow make a contribution to the enhancement of understanding and practice of business in the Asia–Oceania region. The processes and issues addressed in each of the chapters are impacted by the multiple processes and flows we associate with globalisation. In terms of identity and identification, the significance of regionalism is rather limited beyond the existence of common space, but regionalism and increasing regional integration are evident in such initiatives as free trade agreements and common markets, are more important at the economic and political and level.

In subsequent chapters, when discussing the issues, processes, theories and practices that are addressed, globalisation is a key contextual issue. While not addressed at length, globalisation is accepted by each of the authors as a powerful force of change and opportunity for organisations operating within the Asia–Oceania region. Further, globalisation, be it cultural, political or economic, is recognised as a key contextual issue and driver of change in management, economics, accounting and finance theory and practice. While reflecting multiple disciplinary traditions, the chapters speak to the common theme of contemporary business experience in the region. Each offers academic critique, commentary and insight into issues of considerable importance to businesses in the Asia-Oceania region.

Overview of the Contents

As noted above, the contributions included in this book examine key issues facing business in the Asia–Oceania region and reflect the major discipline areas of business — management, economics, finance, accounting and marketing. Several chapters have multidisciplinary perspectives, and here the authors cross disciplinary boundaries in order to address the complex issues being discussed. The chapters are diverse in nature, with the aim of giving the reader a holistic view of the world of business in a global environment. Such complexities and fast-paced issues are brought into play through the phenomenon of globalisation and this complexity is reflected in the chapters collected herein. We trust that the readers will find each chapter insightful and thought provoking.

This book has been divided into four parts as per the major focus of chapters included. The first part deals with China — its role in the global market and Australia's relationship with China. The second part explores issues relating to Human Resource Management in a globalised workforce context. The third part deals with accounting and finance issues with Australian and international focus. The final section looks at cultural change and its effect on management and performance.

China, the emerging superpower of the new world market, is the focus of four chapters included in the first part of this compilation of chapters. The first two chapters deal with economic and business relationships with China. The first chapter by Tisdell provides a broad overview and examines the nature of China's economic globalisation. It also examines the importance of Australia's link with China in terms of merchandise trade, increasing importance of service trade and China's continuing reputation in the area of attracting foreign investment. In the second chapter, Basu, Sappey and Hicks attempts to assess the possibilities of future benefits to Australia of Chinese growth and associated risks in the long term. It argues that so long as the commodities boom continues, Australia benefits. However, any disruption to that boom may have severe consequences for the Australian economy. At the same time, the continuation of the boom may be distracting Australia from other potential opportunities that exist in China. Both chapters argue that Australia needs to take advantage of new opportunities in China, particularly in the service sector.

Still within the first part of the book, the focus then shifts from financial and economic relationships to the subject of culture. Hutchings deals with the practical issue of multicultural management. There is no doubt that China is a major economic force in the current global climate. However, the ability of an organisation to be successful in China can significantly depend on knowledge of the cultural nuances that define the culture. The level of cultural awareness of senior managers from within or outside China can significantly influence major deals, depending on their knowledge and understanding of the different ways their cultures work. Hutching argues that cultural intelligence of senior managers play a very important role in success of business ventures in China. In the last chapter in this section, Tierney examines a similar issue in more specific surroundings and identifies a negative aspect of globalisation. The chapter attempts to establish the relationship between immigration and racism in Taiwan by analysing the guest worker program, where divergent nationalities of guest workers are expected to engage in different kinds of work. Tierney argues that the product of this expectation is racism and stigmas. Guest workers are also found to be excluded from the mainstream society for being seen to be responsible for local unemployment.

Seven chapters in the second part of this book explore human resource management and the changes occurring in this field due to the ever-increasing integration of the global labour market. In the first chapter, Smith explores some assumptions that have been made about Australia's 'lacklustre' performance in providing training to staff. Traditionally, performances of Australian employers have not been considered as satisfactory in this area compared to other nations. This chapter challenges this belief and argues that unreliable comparative data might have caused this view. In reality, Australian employers are possibly not shirking their responsibilities in relation to training. Siemionow's chapter deals with one of the most debatable areas in Australia at present — workplace relations. It analyses the perceptions of senior executive officers of the Australian Public Service in their transition to individual contracts under Australian Workplace Agreements (AWAs). It observes that Senior Executive Service AWAs were implemented with high degrees of coercion on template-based one-size-fits-all approaches.

Some challenges for the university sector are explored in the next three chapters. Bone looks at the relationship between universities and industry, in particular, exploring the demand from industry for 'work-ready' graduates. The role of universities in producing profitably employable graduates is assessed. With increasing competition at global, national and local levels, industries have developed very specific needs. The chapter argues that universities must produce graduates with the right skills and attributes to meet these needs. The next chapter by Krivokapic-Skoko, O'Neill, Travaglione and Foundling explores the impact of the psychological contract between academics and their employers. It explains the nature of the psychological contract in detail, focusing on one faculty in an Australian university. Still within the same area, the next chapter by Tipples and Verry analyses the situation in New Zealand. It deals with the question on how research on this topic developed, how the contract provides useful guidelines for managers, and the implications for the newly individualised employment situation in Australian universities.

Hosie, Sevastos and Travaglione attempt to establish a link between job satisfaction and performance of managers. Although a strong relationship exists in theory, empirical evidence seems to be inadequate. Using quantitative methods the chapter provides an empirical support to the theory. The World Trade Organization Agreement on Trade-Related Intellectual Property Rights (TRIPS) has created a new world legal order concerning intellectual property as part of world trade. The purpose of Ardagh's chapter is to stimulate further debate on intellectual property criteria and standards and on improvements for restructuring the TRIPS legal environment. Ardagh argues that it is necessary to achieve a better balance between the needs of developed and developing countries.

The third part of this volume includes five chapters relating to finance and accounting issues. In the first chapter, Calitz discusses the economic or resources approach of financial management involving the issues of stability, efficiency and equity. It also explains the dynamics within the organisation in relation to their role in shaping its financial management. In a more focused area, Gupta explains the size and volatility of equity capital flows to emerging markets from Australia, especially into Asia. Hoque explores the plight of developing countries and the role of development banks. The chapter argues that persistent loan default can be reduced significantly if the development banks adopt a development role with a paternalistic approach.

Bowrey, Murphy, Smark and Watts describe the establishment and later repeal of the *Public Accountants Registration Act*, and its replacement with a self-regulating accounting profession as an example of the regulatory capture theory. The chapter also illustrates the possible dangers faced by accountants and the public operating in a nonregulated framework. Duncan developed a model to explain why we may observe regulatory structures cycling between periods of increasing complexity toward periods of reform. It also explains changes in regulatory structures over time.

Seven chapters in the last section of the book look at various social and relationship issues that managers should consider. Diversified issues such as cultural and generational differences, change and its effect on workplace performance, impacts of innovation, ethics, and employee engagement and performance are considered in this section of the book.

The first chapter by Herkenhoff argues that the arrival of the iGeneration in the workplace has resulted in new issues for those who plan to lead them. It observes that successful leaders require both cognitive and emotional capabilities. In the next chapter, English discusses the Innovation Development Early Assessment System (IDEAS) as a means of applying a consistent methodology to the early assessment and planned development of a new product, process or service idea. The complex area of moral decision-making in management is the focus of Macklin's chapter. It argues that ethical judgments require managers to use practical reasoning when applying normative criteria to the inevitably unique circumstances of any case. Sharkie's chapter explains that employees' perceptions of the level of organisational support given to them will be a significant determinant of their willingness to reciprocate and engage in discretionary extra-role behaviour to assist the organisation to reach its objectives. How the employees view the organisations' acknowledgment of their contributions and the organisations' care and concern for its employees' wellbeing plays a large part in how the level of organisational support is perceived.

In the next chapter, Frost and Crockett highlight the potential benefits of industry-based collaboration to promote sustainable regional development of industry collaboration in regional settings, particularly in terms of marketing, economies of scale related to production and in lobbying. It is based on a pilot study within the mining and engineering industry sector in the Central-West region of New South Wales in Australia. The value and use of mentoring and the current concerns associated with the increasingly difficult challenge of achieving work–life balance is discussed in the next chapter by Mathews and Jenkins. The use of mentoring and the achievement of work–life balance are viewed as effective means of enhancing performance. This chapter argues that bringing the two together may prove to be much more beneficial for an organisation.

The qualities of international marketing managers have been linked to effective export marketing information and, more generally, to the international success of companies. The last chapter of this book, by Williams and Heffernen, explains the results of an investigation into the backgrounds and marketing intelligence behaviour of export managers in small- and medium-sized enterprises (SMEs). It observes that the experience of living and working overseas has a greater effect on information-gathering and decision-making than linguistic ability, while experience with exporting has the least effect.

Endnote

1 The conference theme was 'Engagement and Change: Exploring Management, Economic and Finance Implications of a Globalising Environment'.

References

Ahn, C., & Cheong, I. (2007). A search for closer economic relations in east Asia. *Japanese Economic Review, 58*(2), 173–90.

Bandyopadhyay, D. (2006). How financial development caused economic growth in APEC countries: Financial integration with FDI or privatization without FDI. *Asia–Pacific Development Journal, 13*(1), 75–100.

Bauman, Z. (1998). *Globalization: The human consequences.* Cambridge: Polity Press.

Beck, U. (1999). *What is Globalization?* Cambridge: Polity Press

Bhagwati, J.E. (2004). *In defense of globalization.* Oxford: Oxford University Press.

Giddens, A. (2000). *Runaway world: How globalisation is reshaping our lives.* New York: Routledge.

Held, D., McGrew, A., Goldblatt, D., & Perraton, J. (1999). *Global Transformations: Politics, economics and culture.* Cambridge: Polity Press.

Hirst, P., & Thompson, G. (1996). *Globalisation in question: The international economy and the possibilities of governance.* Cambridge: Polity Press.

Olds, K., Dicken, P.F., Kelly, L., & Wai-Chung, Y. (1999). (Eds.), *Globalisation and the Asia–Pacific: contested territories.* London: Routledge.

Quazi, R. (2007). Economic freedom and foreign direct investment in east Asia. *Journal of the Asia–Pacific Economy, 12*(3), 329–344.

Stiglitz, J.E. (2006). *Making globalization work: The next steps to global justice.* Melbourne, Australia: Allen Lane.

Sirgy, M.J., Lee, D.-J., Miller, C., & Littlefield, J.E. (2004). The impact of globalization on a country's quality of life: Toward an integrated model. *Social Indicators Research, 68*(3), 251–298.

Part 1

China in the Global Market Environment

Economic and Business Relations Between China and Australia: Insights Into China's Global Economic Footprint

Clem Tisdell

Since the opening up of China to the outside world, following its decision in 1978 to start its economic reforms, economic and business exchange between Australia and China has developed rapidly (Tisdell, 1993; Wen & Tisdell, 2002). According to the Economic Analytical Unit (EAU) of the Australian Department of Foreign Affairs and Trade (DFAT, 2006), Australia's commercial relations with China have boomed in the last decade or so. It states:

> Australia's dynamic commercial relationship with China, based predominantly on trade, boomed over the last decade. Australian exports to China grew very rapidly, in line with China's strong growth and industrialisation; this relationship is likely to grow and broaden over the coming decade, with Australian exports widening to include more manufactured goods and services. Australian FDI, while much smaller, also is likely to increase, especially in the liberalising services sector. Chinese exports to Australia also are growing strongly and Chinese investment in Australia, particularly in resource projects, continues to grow. (Economic Analytical Unit, 2002, p. 60)

Since that was written, China's imports from Australia have continued to grow strongly but there has not been a boom in China's investment in Australia.

This chapter provides an overview of trends and features of the merchandise trade between Australia and China, as well as the nonmerchandise trade between the two countries, and considers patterns of foreign direct investment by China in Australia and of Australia in China. Subsequently, the pattern of economic relationships that have emerged between the two countries is assessed and their future economic business prospects considered.

Australia's Overall Merchandise Trade with China: Trends and Relative Value

In just over 2 decades or so, China has gone from being a very minor trading partner of Australia to being a major trading partner. Table 1 indicates the relative importance of China as a market for the export of Australian merchandise and as a source of Australia's imports. Before the 1990s, China was an unimportant trading partner for Australia but by the early 1990s, it was amongst Australia's top ten trading partners and its relative importance has continued to rise rapidly. By 2005, China was Australia's second most important trading partner on a country basis. By 2005–2006, China had displaced the United States (US) as the main single country source of Australia's imports of merchandise.

In considering the relative importance of the geographical direction of Australian trade, much depends on how this is determined geographically. For example, if the European Union (EU), with 25 countries, is considered as one geographical unit, then the EU is much more important than the US as an outlet for Australia's exports and in 2005–06, took slightly more by value of Australia's exports than mainland China. However, Japan was by far the major outlet for Australian exports, even though Australian exports were relatively diversified by destination countries. Table 2 ranks the relative importance of Australia's major destinations of exports by countries, assuming that the EU is one entity. On this basis, it can be seen that the EU emerges as one of Australia's most important trading partners and is of much greater importance in this respect than the US. Nevertheless, China still remains of high importance to Australia as a trading partner. On a total trade basis, in 2005–2006, the EU had the largest amount of trade with Australia (A$54,807m), followed by Japan (A$48,319m), with China in third place (A$41,095m and China with Hong Kong, A$45,643), followed well back in fourth place by the US (A$32,557m). In fact, in recent times, the US has declined in relative importance as a trading partner of Australia whereas China's relative position has risen.

Table 1

The Relative Importance of China as an Outlet for Australia's Merchandise Exports and a Source of Australia's Merchandise Imports, 1970–71 to 2005–06

Year	Exports to China		Imports from China	
	Rank by country	% of Australian exports	Rank by country	% of Australian imports
1970–71	Very low	1.4	Very low	0.76
1980–81	Low	3.5	Low	1.68
1990–91	10	2.37	8	3.07
2000–01	5	5.7	3	8.3
2005	2	11.6	2	13.7
2005–06	2	11.8	1	14.28

Source: Based on Department of Foreign Affairs and Trade, (February, 2002). Direction of Trade Time Series and DFAT, (2006) China Fact Sheet.

Table 2

Major Destinations of Australia's Exports and Sources of Imports, 2005–2006, Ranked by Value (A$ in Millions)

Rank	Export destination	A$ (million)	Rank	Source of imports	A$ (million)
1	Japan	30,982	1	EU (25 countries)	36,266
2ª	China + Hong Kong	20,785	2ᵇ	China + Hong Kong	24,858
3	EU (25 countries)	18,541	3	US	22,776
4	Republic of Korea	11,691	4	Japan	17,337
5	United States	9,781	—ᶜ	Republic of Korea	6,491

Note: ª For top export destinations, the breakdown of the value of exports for China and Hong Kong respectively are A$17,889 million and A$2,896 million. China ranks third if Hong Kong is excluded.
ᵇ For top sources of imports, the breakdown of the value of imports for China and Hong Kong respectively are A$23,206 million and A$1,652 million.
ᶜ Not in the top five.
Source: As for Table 1.

It can be seen from Table 2 that Australia has a trade deficit with the EU, China and the US but surpluses with Japan and the Republic of Korea. However, Australia's trade deficit with China is much more moderate than that with the EU and the US. China's trade deficits with Japan and South Korea help balance multilateral trade involving Australia.

The pie diagrams shown in Figures 1 and 2 highlight the relative importance of Australia's major trading partners.

The Comparative Importance of Australia for China's International Merchandise Trade

If the relative value of merchandise trade is used as an indicator, then Australia is a less important trading partner for China than China is for Australia. According

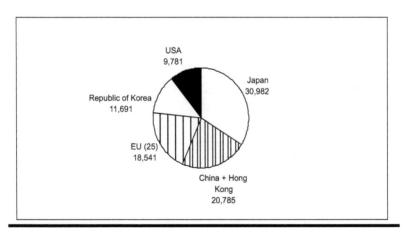

Figure 1

Australia's main export destinations and export values in millions of A$, 2005–2006.

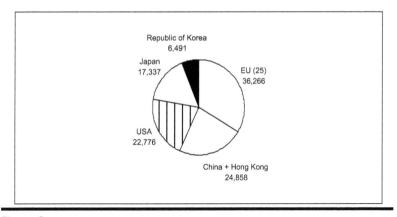

Figure 2
Australia's main sources of imports and import values in millions of A$, 2005–2006.

to DFAT (2006), Australia ranked 14th as an export destination for China in 2005 and accounted for 1.5% of China's total exports by value. Australia reached 9th place as an import source for China and accounted for 2.4% of China's imports by value in 2005. However, Chinese statistics rank Australia as 8th as an import source (The US–China Business Council, n.d.).

China's top export destinations in 2005 (see Table 3) were (1) US, (2) Hong Kong, (3) Japan, (4) South Korea and (5) Germany. However, exports to the EU exceeded those to Japan. China's top import suppliers (see Table 4) in the same year were (1) Japan, (2) South Korea, (3) Taiwan, (4) US and (5) Germany (US–China Business Council, n.d.). China's imports of supplies from the EU appear to exceed those from the US. It can be seen that other East Asian countries are the prime trading partners of China, particularly as import suppliers. Much of China's imports from these countries are of components to be used in manufacturing in China (Prasad & Wei, 2005).

The Composition of Australia's and China's Merchandise Trade

Australia's exports of merchandise consist predominantly of primary products and its imports are mainly of manufactured goods, even though Australia's exports of manufactured goods have risen in recent times. Interestingly, the major portion of both China's imports and exports of merchandise consist of manufactured goods, even though its imports of minerals and fuels are important.

In 2005, Australia's main exports to China were iron ore (A$5721m); wool (A$1327m); copper ore (A$628m) and coal (A$531m). Thus iron ore dominates Australia's exports to China and China buys the lion's share of Australian wool. In

Table 3

China's Top Export Destinations (US$ million) 2005

Rank	Country/region	$US million
1	United States	162,899.6
2	Hong Kong	124,481.1
3	Japan	83,992.1
4	South Korea	35,109.3
5	Germany	32,527.6
6	Netherlands	25,876.8
7	United Kingdom	18,977.0
8	Singapore	16,632.6
9	Taiwan	16,549.6
10	Russia	13,212.2

Source: PRC General Administration of Customs, China's Custom's Statistics.

the future, Australia's export to China of liquefied natural gas will also become important.

Australia's main imports of merchandise from China in 2005 were clothing (A$3,055m); computers (A$2,406m); toys, games and sporting equipment (A$1,095m and telecommunication equipment (A$1073m). The types of manufactured goods that Australia is importing from China have become more sophisticated and have increased in range in recent years. There has been a noticeable increase in household electrical appliances supplied by China to Australia.

Table 5 lists the main merchandise exports of China by type and Table 6 sets out its main imports by type. It can be seen that China's top 10 categories of exports consist mostly of manufactured products. Half of the categories of China's top ten imports also consist of manufactures with the remainder being primary or near-primary products. The former exceed the latter in value. Thus, while China's imports are more primary-intensive than its exports, China's imports are also relatively concentrated on manufactured goods. Several cate-

Table 4

China's Top Import Suppliers (US$ million), 2005

Rank	Country/region	$US million
1	Japan	100,451.6
2	South Korea	76,822.0
3	Taiwan	74,684.4
4	United States	48,726.3
5	Germany	30,724.4
6	Malaysia	20,096.2
7	Singapore	16,516.4
8	Australia	16,186.5
9	Russia	15,890.9
10	Thailand	13,991.9

Source: PRC General Administration of Customs, China's Custom's Statistics.

Table 5

China's Top Exports ($US million), 2005

Rank	Commodity description	$US million
1	Electrical machinery and equipment	172,320.8
2	Power generation equipment	149,715.5
3	Apparel	65,904.1
4	Iron and steel	34,123.7
5	Optics and medical equipment	25,478.0
6	Furniture and bedding	22,363.5
7	Toys and games	19,123.6
8	Inorganic and organic chemicals	19,064.0
9	Footwear and parts thereof	19,052.9
10	Plastics	17,783.3

Source: PRC General Administration of Customs, China's Custom's Statistics.

gories of the same manufactured goods appear in both Tables 5 and 6. One reason for this is that manufactured components and parts are imported to China for use in the assembly and further manufacture of products in China, many of which are subsequently exported.

China requires both imports of manufactures and of primary products for its current phase of industrialisation and economic growth. China's imports of capital equipment and machinery are also important as are, in many cases, its imports of components for manufactured goods. The latter imports may be fostered partly by foreign direct investment (FDI) by multinational companies in China. Thus, a Japanese multinational with manufacturing plants both in Japan and China may source some of its components from Japan and others from China and locate the more labour-intensive parts of its manufacturing in China. Thus, a supply chain, like that shown in Figure 3, may emerge. As China's manufacturing industry develops, it may try to reduce its dependence on imported components to be used in its manufacture of final products.

Table 6

China's Top Imports ($US million), 2005

Rank	Commodity description	$US million
1	Electrical machinery and equipment	174,839.8
2	Power generation equipment	96,374.8
3	Mineral fuel and oil	64,098.6
4	Optical and medical equipment	49,972.2
5	Plastics and articles thereof	33,323.5
6	Inorganic and organic chemicals	32,836.1
7	Iron and steel	31,905.2
8	Ore, slag and ash	26,014.3
9	Copper and articles thereof	12,895.8
10	Vehicle and parts other than rail	12,312.8

Source: PRC General Administration of Customs, China's Custom's Statistics.

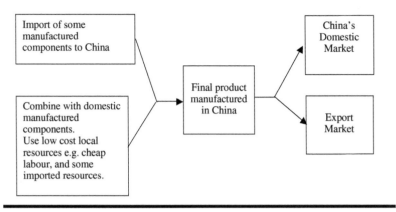

Figure 3
A frequent supply chain for products manufactured in China.

This pattern may be quite common for multinational companies with foreign direct investment in manufacturing plants in China which also have plants in other countries, for example, Japan.

Australia's Trade in Services With China

International trade in services (nonmerchandise trading) is becoming increasingly important as a component of international exchange. In 2005–06, 20% of Australia's earnings on its current trade account (total export income) was from services and 19% of its total expenditure on its current trade account was for services.

In 2005, sales of services by Australia to China equalled 13.44% of Australia's total current account earnings from China, and services purchased from China amounted to 4.97% of Australia's payments in its current trade account. Consequently, Australia's trade in services with China was less intense than Australia's general trade in services; and the balance was in Australia's favour.

In 2005, Australia's exports of services to China amounted to A$2,494m and its imports of services from China were A$1,177m., giving Australia a favourable trade balance on services of A$1,317m. Education was the major source of service income for Australia from China. In 2005, Australia earned A$1,633m from this component; more than from its wool exports to China. After iron ore, provision of education was the largest income-earner for Australia from exchange with China.[1] The second most important source of income from services sold by Australia to China was for travel (tourism). The numbers of Chinese visitors (travellers) to Australia have increased considerably in recent years and now they constitute a significant segment of the Australian inbound tourist market.[2]

China's main sales of services to Australia are for transportation, for example shipping (A$430m in 2005) and for tourism (personal travel)[3] (A$362m in 2005). Consequently, there was a slight deficit for Australia on its tourism account with China.

China's Investment in Australia and Vice Versa

China continues to be the destination for a large amount of foreign investment globally as well as the source of much investment abroad. However, Australia is a relatively minor outlet for Chinese foreign investment and is also a minor source of investment in China. Again, from Australia's perspective, China is not a major source of foreign funds invested in Australia, nor is China a major outlet for Australian funds invested abroad. This is clear from Tables 7 and 8.

From the tables, it can be seen that together the US and the UK accounted for the lion's share of foreign investment in Australia (87.6%) and 79.2% of Australia's investment abroad was in these two countries in 2005. The US and the UK have traditionally dominated foreign direct investment in Australia and Australia's strong trading relationships with Asia have not altered this position. After the US and UK, Japan holds third place as an investor in Australia and China (if combined with Hong Kong) is in fourth place. However, the level of China's plus Hong Kong's investment is quite small compared to that of the US and the UK. After the US and the UK, New Zealand and Japan are Australia's major outlets for investment abroad. Australia's comparative level of investment in China is very small, even if China and Hong Kong are combined. Thus, historical and continuing cultural connections still seem to dominate the sources of foreign investment in Australia and Australian foreign investment abroad.

In recent years, China's investment in Australia has shown little growth. It may have even declined, particularly in recent times (see Table 9). Furthermore, Australian investment in China has remained very low, although its level was up in mainland China in 2005 compared with previous years (see Table 9). Australia's combined investment in mainland China and Hong Kong appears to be waning. It

Table 7
The Top Four Countries Investing in Australia in 2005

Rank	Country	A$ (million)	%
1	US	325,294	46.0
2	UK	294,693	41.7
3	Japan	53,349	7.5
4[a]	China + Hong Kong	33,535	4.7
	TOTAL	706,871	100.0

Note: [a] Investment by China and Hong Kong separately are, respectively, A$2,275 million and A$31,260 million.
Source: Based on Australian Bureau of Statistics (2006).

Table 8

Australia's Investment Abroad in 2005 by Top Four Destination Countries, Plus China and Hong Kong

Rank	Country	A$ (million)	%
1	US	290,974	41.2
2	UK	96,132	13.6
3	New Zealand	58,862	8.3
4	Japan	31,597	4.5
[a]	China + Hong Kong	12,331	1.7
	TOTAL	489,896	69.3

Note: [a] Australia's investment in PR China was A$2,043 million and in Hong Kong A$10,288 million.
Source: Based on Australian Bureau of Statistics (2006).

can also be seen that China's investment in Australia exceeds Australia's investment in China, particularly so if China and Hong Kong are considered as one unit. According to the Economic and Analytical Unit (2002, p. 75):

> China's largest and highest profile Australian investments are in the resources sector. Real estate, including hotels in major metropolitan centres, farming and agricultural processing ventures and a variety of general manufacturing plants are other destinations for Chinese investment in Australia (Invest Australia, 2002).

The Economic and Analytical Unit (2002, p. 69) also reported that:

> A recent survey of Australian companies operating in China showed business numbers were reasonably evenly split between three areas: manufacturing; property and business services; and a diverse range of 'other sectors' including wholesale and retail trade, mining, finance and insurance, construction, education, information services and energy supply (Maitland & Nicholas, 1999).

Discussion

China is now Australia's main single-country source of merchandise imports and the second largest single-country outlet for Australia's merchandise exports.

Table 9

China's Investment in Australia and Australia's Investment in China 2001–2005, A$million

	2001	2002	2003	2004	2005
China's investment in Australia					
P.R. of China	3,132	2,843	2,987	2,287	2,275
Hong Kong (HK)	31,974	35,565	27,829	29,363	31,250
P.R. China and HK	35,106	38,408	30,816	31,650	33,525
Australia's investment in China					
P.R. of China	1,885	1,233	1,349	1,270	2,043
HK	12,534	12,986	13,623	12,698	10,288
P.R. China and HK	14,419	14,219	14,972	13,968	12,331

Source: Based on Australian Bureau of Statistics, (2006). Cat. No. 5352.0 International Investment Position, Australia. Supplementary Country Statistics 2005.

However, if the EU is considered as one unit, then the EU outranks China as a source of Australia's imports. Furthermore, Japan, the main destination of Australia's exports, buys much more Australian merchandise than either the EU or China. In practice, Australian exports remain quite diversified by destination and although China is an important customer for Australia it does not dominate Australia's trade.

Nevertheless, trade with China seems more important for the Australian economy than China's trade with Australia is for China's economy. Australia ranks about 14th as the most important destination for China's exports, whereas China is the 2nd or 3rd largest outlet for Australian exports. Australia is placed about 8th as a source of imports for China, whereas China is the prime or second most important source of imports for Australia, depending upon whether the EU is considered as one unit. Given the increased degree of openness of the global economy, both countries have alternative (substitute) sources of supplies of imports and export possibilities. Therefore, the market power of each is limited.

China's exports of merchandise consist mainly of manufactures and Australia mostly imports manufactures from China, whereas the bulk of Australia's merchandise exports to China consist of primary products, of which minerals are the most prominent. However, the bulk of China's imports do not consist of primary products. More than half of China's imports appear to consist of manufactured goods (e.g., components) to be used in further manufacturing in China. Many of the manufactures subsequently produced and then exported by China. According to Rumbaugh and Blancher (2004, p. 4), 'imports for processing are estimated to be embodied in over 40% of China's exports'.

The major direction of China's trade is with the industrialised world. 'China's share in world markets is growing rapidly and the penetration of China's exports into industrial country markets has been equally dramatic' (Rumbaugh & Blancher, 2004, p. 5) and it is expected that China will maintain substantial export growth for some time to come (Rumbaugh & Blancher, 2004, p. 4).

China's exports of manufactures have also become more diversified and sophisticated (Economic and Analytical Unit, 2002; Rumbaugh & Blancher, 2004, p. 4). Chinese policy-makers will, no doubt, wish to strengthen this trend.

Trade in services (nonmerchandise) has assumed growing importance in international exchange, and Australian trade in services with China is expanding. While Australia has a deficit in its trade in merchandise with China, it has a surplus on its trade in services with China. A major reason for this surplus is the high level of enrolment of Chinese students at Australian educational institutions. In 2005, more students from China were enrolled in Australia's educational institutions than from any other country and they constituted almost 25% of total overseas student enrolments. While the numbers of Chinese students in Australia may grow for some time, the rate of growth of these numbers is declining. As China progresses economically, there will be less need for it to send its students abroad for training and it may increasingly become an exporter of educational services. There has also been a substantial rise in Australia's earnings from Chinese travellers (tourists) to Australia which has helped boost Australia's nonmerchandise exports to China. Expenditure by Australian tourists in China is now not substantially in excess of tourist expenditure by Chinese in Australia. Considerable scope exists for expanding inbound tourism to Australia from China.. Nevertheless, it should be noted that both education and tourism are vulnerable export industries because they rely on visitors to Australia. Demand for visits is vulnerable to factors such as political disturbances, war, health risks, or terrorism.

It is well known that China has 'become a magnet for foreign direct investment (FDI) overtaking the United States (in 2003) as the number one destination for FDI' (Prasad & Wei, 2005, p. 3). The main sources of FDI in China are from five Asian economies; Hong Kong, Special Administrative Region (SAR); Japan; Korea; Taiwan; and Singapore. Even allowing for 'round-tripping' of funds between mainland China and Hong Kong SAR, the level of FDI by the US and EU combined, while important, is estimated to account for not more than 30% of FDI in China (Prasad & Wei, 2005, p. 6). By comparison, Australia's FDI in China is miniscule. However, just as cultural barriers may limit Australia's investment in China, they also seem to have had some dampening effect on FDI in China by the US and the EU compared to East Asian countries. Nevertheless, proportionately, China has been less of a magnet for Australian FDI than for the US and the EU.

While cultural affinity may help to explain the pattern of sources of FDI in China, it is probably not the only important influence. Given the international product cycle (Vernon, 1966, 1979) and the global pattern of development of manufacturing industries, China's economic development comes at a stage when Japan and several Asian Newly Industrialising Countries (NICs) find it economic to relocate their mature industries or mature parts of some of their industries (such as the production of television sets) offshore. China is well placed in that regard.

China's FDI is increasing and about 8% of its FDI has been to the US with a much larger percentage going to Asia. According to Prasad and Wei (2005, p. 7), 'the Chinese government has recently encouraged FDI outflows to countries in Asia and Latin America in order to ensure more reliable sources of raw materials (for instance, by purchasing mining operations) and importing products for processing in China'. It is possible, however, that the focus of China's FDI will alter as its economy becomes more mature. It may have to invest increasingly in securing markets for its finished products abroad as these products become more sophisticated. Chinese exports have already become more sophisticated and diverse and China itself is likely to become more involved in establishing offshore manufacturing industries, as it has already done in television set production (Gao & Tisdell, 2005). Given the continuing small size of the Australian market, Australia may not be a high priority for such investment.

A downward trend in China's FDI in Australia has been noted, but its significance is difficult to determine. One reason could be that China has been able to make more favourable natural resource investments in Latin America, Asia and Africa than in Australia. It may also want to diversity its source of supply of raw materials. Again, there could be a growing realisation in China that it really does not need to own natural resources to secure its supply in a competitive international economy. In fact, it is likely to become strategically more important for China to undertake FDI to secure its overseas markets for its processed products and ensure that these increasingly incorporate up-to-date technologies (Gao & Tisdell, 2004; Tisdell, 2006).

Conclusion

In the space of about 15 years, China has gone from being a negligible trading partner of Australia to being one of its most important trading partners. After Japan and the EU, China is the most important destination for Australian exports, and after the EU it is the main source of Australia's imports. Given that China's economy continues to grow at a rapid rate, it has the second largest economy in the world in terms of purchasing power and is highly trade-oriented, trade between China and Australia (both in merchandise and services) can be expected to continue to grow. China may eventually surpass Japan and the EU as a destination for Australian exports, and it is likely to move closer to the EU as a source of Australia's imports.

Nevertheless, despite the importance of China as a trading partner, China does not have a dominating trade position in relation to Australia. This is likely to continue in the foreseeable future because China appears to be diversifying its trade both by direction and by types of commodities.

China's FDI in Australia is relatively small and Australia's FDI in China is very small. The bulk of FDI in Australia comes from countries with which Australia has had traditional ties — the US and the UK. These countries have also been the main outlets for Australian investment abroad. There is no indication that China will become a major outlet for Australian foreign investment in the near future,[4] nor that China will replace either the US or the UK as a major investor in Australia, notwithstanding a possible free trade agreement (FTA) between Australia and China.

Australia's and China's leaders agreed in April 2005 to begin negotiations on a free trade agreement. The Australian Department of Foreign Affairs and Trade (DFAT) states that a joint study concluded that an FTA between Australia and China would result in considerable economic benefits for both countries such as 'higher economic growth, more jobs and higher living standards' (DFAT, 2006). Nevertheless, it also states that 'even without FTA, our [Australia's] trade and investment relationship with China will continue to grow because of complementarities between our economies' (DFAT, 2006). Consequently, DFAT says that Australia will not be rushed in negotiating a free trade agreement with China and will be seeking a comprehensive agreement. This agreement is still pending.

Nevertheless, the Australian case helps illustrate China's growing global economic footprint.[5]

Acknowledgments

I wish to thank Dr Glyn Edwards and Hemanath Swarna Nantha for their research assistance and Dr. PK Basu for asking me to present this paper (now revised) at the 3rd ICCB.

Endnotes

1   For several years, China has been the main source of foreign students enrolled in Australia. Almost 3.4 million international students were enrolled in Australia in 2005 and 23.5% of these were from China. Furthermore, the number of Chinese students enrolled has continued to rise, albeit with a reduced rate of growth. India, with about 265,000 enrolments in 2005, was in second place as Australia's main source of international students. It was well behind the number of enrolments from China, about 794,000, in the same year. (Source: Australian Government Australian Education International Website, http://aei.dest.gov.au/AEI/MIP/statistics/StudentEnrolmentAndVisaStatistics/2006/Default.htm#pivot)

2   According to Tourism Australia (data from Australian Bureau of Statistics, 2006. *Overseas Arrivals and Departures*, Cat. No. 3401.0), Australia received about 5.4 million overseas visitors in 2005 and just under 5.5 million in 2006, a slight increase only in 2006 compared to 2005. New Zealand was the largest source of supply in 2006 (over 1 million), then the UK (0.71 million) with Japan in third place (0.67 million), with the US in fourth place (0.51 million) followed by China in fifth place (0.29 million). With continuing economic growth in China, one can expect considerable growth in the numbers of Chinese visitors to Australia. Within a few years, it is likely that China will become the major Asian source of visitors to Australia.

3   Particularly in relation to its population, Australia is a significant source of foreign tourists to China. It accounted for more Chinese visitors than each of Germany, France or Italy in 2005 and almost as many from the UK. The China National Tourist Office reports 482,968 visitor arrivals from Australia for 2005 (Source: China National Tourist Office, 2006. Retrieved July 19, 2006, from http://www.cnto.org/chinastats.asp). In the same year, the number of visitors from China to Australia was 274,100 according to the source given in Note 2. Therefore, the number of Chinese visitors to Australia is still well below the number of Australians visiting China. China has had a large surplus on its international tourism account and tourism has played a significant role in China's economic development (Wen & Tisdell, 2002). Pressure has mounted on China to liberalise its restrictions on Chinese citizens travelling abroad and China has made considerable progress in this respect. In a few decades China has risen to be the world's second most important tourist destination and it is expected to be number one soon.

4   The hesitancy with which Australian firms approach investment in China appears to be reflected in the following comments by the Economic and Analytical Unit (2002, p. xi) of DFAT:

> Australian companies are taking advantage of services liberalisation in China and are positioning themselves to gain access to China's rapidly expanding services markets. Despite the improved environment, Australian firms still face major challenges from entrenched domestic players, high capital requirements and a lack of transparency in a rapidly changing regulatory and administrative situation. China has to be viewed as a

long-term market. Before entering the China market, businesses need to assess the risks along with the opportunities.

5   The original source for data in Tables 3–6 is indicated but the data were taken from a secondary source, The US–China Business Council (undated) document.

References

Australian Bureau of Statistics. (2006). *Overseas Arrivals and Departures* (Cat. No. 3401.0).

Australian Government Australian Education International Website. (2006). Retrieved from http://aei.dest.gov.au/AEI/MIP/statistics/StudentEnrolmentAndVisaStatistics/2006/Default. htm#pivot

Australian Bureau of Statistics. (2006). *International Investment Position, Australia. Supplementary Country Statistics, 2005* (Cat. No. 5352.0). Canberra, Australia: Australian Bureau of Statistics.

Australian Department of Foreign Affairs and Trade. (2006). *Australia–China Free Trade Agreement negotiations.* Retrieved August 18, 2006, from http://www.dfat.gov.au/geo/china/fta

China National Tourist Office. (2006). Retrieved July 19, 2006, from http://www.cnto.org/china-stats.asp

Economic and Analytical Unit. (2005). *Unlocking China's service sector.* Canberra, Australia: Department of Foreign Affairs and Trade.

Economic and Analytical Unit. (2002). *China embraces the world market.* Canberra, Australia: Department of Foreign Affairs and Trade.

Gao, Z., & Tisdell, C. (2004). China's reformed science and technology system: An overview and assessment. *Prometheus, 22,* 311–331.

Gao, Z., & Tisdell, C. (2005). Foreign Investment and Asia's, particularly China's, rise in the television industry: The international product cycle reconsidered. *Journal of Asia-Pacific Business, 6*(3), 37–61.

Maitland, E., & Nicholas, S. (1999). *Australian multicultural enterprises in China: Motivations, technology transfer and operations.* Melbourne: Australian Centre for International Business, University of Melbourne.

Prasad, E., & Wei, S.J. (2005). The Chinese approach to capital inflows: Patterns and possible explanations. *NBER Working Paper* (11306). Cambridge, MA: National Bureau of Economic Research.

Rumbaugh, T., & Blancher, N. (2004). *China: International Trade and WTO Accession* (IMF Working Paper, WP/04/36). Washington, DC: International Monetary Fund.

The US–China Business Council (n.d.). *US–China trade statistics and China's world trade statistics.* Retrieved August 8, 2006, from http://www.usChina.org/statistics/tradetable.html

Tisdell, C. (2006). China's economic performance and transition in relation to globalisation: From isolation to centre stage? *Economic Theory, Applications and Issues* (Working Paper No. 40). Brisbane, Australia: School of Economics, The University of Queensland.

Tisdell, C. (1993). *Economic development in the context of China: Policy issues and analysis.* London: Macmillan.

Vernon, R. (1979). The product cycle hypothesis in a new international environment. *Oxford Bulletin of Economics and Statistics, 41,* 255–267.

Vernon, R. (1966). International investment and international trade in the product cycle. *Quarterly Journal of Economics, 80,* 190–207.

Wen, J.J., & Tisdell, C.A. (2002). *Tourism and China's development: policies, regional growth and ecotourism.* Singapore: World Scientific.

How Can Australia Benefit From China's Economic Reforms?

Parikshit Basu

John Hicks

Richard B. Sappey

Australia–China trade and business relationships have been growing significantly in recent years but still have only limited coverage of the Chinese economy. This chapter attempts to assess the future benefits to Australia of Chinese growth and the associated long-term risks for Australia. While the commodities boom continues, Australia benefits — however, any disruption to that boom may have severe consequences for the Australian economy. At the same time, the continuation of the boom may be distracting Australia from other potential opportunities that exist in China. As a country that seeks to have balanced economic growth, there are arguments in favour of spreading the risk and to position Australia to take advantage of new opportunities, particularly in the services sector.

There have been many remarkable events of economic significance in the last 2 decades of the 20th century. The demise of almost all socialist regimes has been possibly the most significant. Within this context, economic reform in China is notable because it happened without any apparent economic crisis and because it has largely been considered successful (Naughton, 1995; Pyle, 1997; Shen, 2000). In 1979, after 3 decades of an authoritative central planning system (and just a few years after the death of its architect, Mao Ze Dong), the Chinese authorities decided to gradually (and to some extent methodically) open up the economy to the influence of domestic and international market forces (Pyle, 1997; Shen, 2000).

In recent years, Australia's trade and business relationship with China has been growing steadily. China was ranked as Australia's second-largest partner (only after Japan) in merchandise trade in 2005–2006 — compared to 10th in the mid-1990s (Australian Bureau of Statistics [ABS], 2007). This bilateral relationship is expected to be closer in the foreseeable future. The primary objective of this chapter is to assess the future benefits of Chinese growth and associated long-term risks for Australia. In more specific terms, there are three principal questions addressed in this chapter. First, to what extent has Australia benefited from economic reform in China? Second, what are the future benefits of economic change in China that might accrue to Australia and, will they be ongoing or temporary? Finally, what are the major risks to Australia in its economic relationship with China?

Opportunities and Threats From an Australian Perspective

China's integration into the world economy appears to have had little impact on Australia until relatively recently. Australia mainly exports natural resources and agricultural products to China and imports manufactured goods from China. The impact on the export of metal ores and coal is illustrated in Figure 1, which shows the sharp jump in the export of these commodities following the increase in demand from China. Indeed, Weemaes (2005) reports that Australia was China's largest source of imported coal, iron ore and nickel ore in 2005. However, the surge in the export of these commodities is said to underpin much of Australia's sustained economic performance since 2000 and national expectations of future prosperity. The questions arise, therefore, as to whether the mining export boom to China can be maintained and is it all that China has to offer us? We consider each of these two issues in turn.

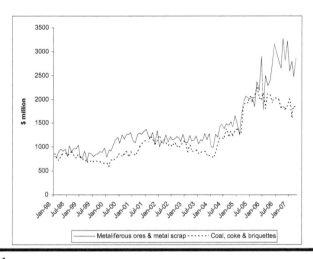

Figure 1

Australia's exports of ores and coals 1998–2006.

Source: ABS Time Series Statistics Plus — June 2007. dXdata. Melbourne: EconData Pty Ltd.

The Export Commodity Boom

There can be no question that the mining industry in Australia has benefited significantly from developments in China. It is also reasonable to expect that demand for Australian ore and coal will remain strong into the foreseeable future. This is notwithstanding some potential risks. These include (a) the risk of a cyclical economic downturn in China, (b) a risk of a decline in China's demand for resources as the resource-intensive phase of China's economic development wanes, (c) a risk that the government of China will move away from the development of a market economy and (d) the risk of a political upheaval which debilitates the Chinese economy for some years

Cyclical Risk

Capitalist or market economies are subject to periodic swings. While China is currently booming it is accepted that a downturn will eventually arrive. Evidence from the past (Figure 2) clearly shows that China has not been immune to swings in economic activity and prices. The pattern apparent throughout most of the period in which China has been developing its market economy (since 1978) is one of periodic accelerating inflation that has been severely and effectively contained by the advent of sharp downturns in the rate of economic growth (although negative growth has been avoided). The downturns in the rate of growth of economic activity have usually resulted from the application of relatively crude instruments of monetary policy or direct regulatory intervention (Economist Intelligence Unit [EIU], 2007).

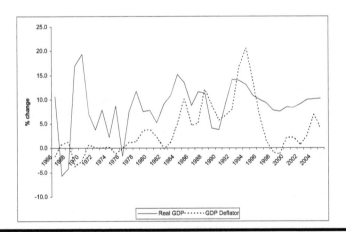

Figure 2

China: Percentage changes in output and prices 1966–2004.

Source: World Bank World Tables — July 2225. dXdata. Melbourne: EconData Pty Ltd.

The Chinese government has never been able to apply macroeconomic policy in order to avoid wide swings in economic activity in the ways practiced in the West. This is because China lacked the prerequisites of sophisticated monetary and fiscal policy weapons. The People's Bank of China (PBC), China's central bank, is not an independent institution. It operates under the guidance of the state (Shen, 2000) and can only offer token resistance if the policies of the PBC conflict with the policies of the various levels of government (Yusuf, 1994). Throughout most of the post-reform period, the PBC has been hamstrung by an exchange rate regime in which the RMB (official currency in the mainland of the People's Republic of China [PRC]) has been pegged to the US dollar (Ma, 2000; Shen, 2000).

For much of the reform period, the Chinese government has been unable to implement conventional monetary policy through intervention impacting on interest rates because of its fixed exchange rate policy (EIU, 2007). Rather, monetary policy was administered through the management of credit. When government wished to run a contractionary monetary policy, government simply instructed the state-owned banks to cease making loans. Since most of the loans by state-owned banks were to state-owned enterprises (SOEs) the activity of the SOE sector was almost immediately curtailed, resulting in significant economic disruption to a single sector of the economy. Fortunately, the need for the continuation of this type of monetary control is receding. In July 2005, the RMB was permitted to begin to appreciate, slowly, against the US dollar, signalling a move towards a more flexible exchange rate regime (EIU, 2007). Research by Basu, Hicks and Sappey (2006a) indicated that young Chinese tended to support a floating exchange rate and although the older Chinese supported a pegged system their influence on policy can be expected to gradually wane.

More effective macroeconomic management is also presaged by the development of more effective tax regimes. Allsop (1995) has noted that pre-reform, fiscal policy was an unsuitable instrument for economic management in China. This was because its main function was to allocate resources to ensure that the central plan's targets were achieved in each sector. Taxation was unimportant, as the government derived its income from the transfer of revenue from SOEs. Moreover, government expenditure consisted primarily of the allocation of funds to expenditure units in accordance with the dictates of the central plan (Allsop, 1995). Under such a system taxation, in the western sense, was hardly necessary and government expenditure primarily reflected the Central Government's control over the economy's resources (Xu, 1996).

Changes in the structure of taxes in China were not seen as a reform priority until well into the 1990s. Prior to this time, only minor ad hoc measures designed to support the agricultural and industrial reforms were implemented. There was no comprehensive or long-term reform (Ma, 2000). 'True' tax reform took place during the third phase of China's economic reform from the mid-1990s. The objective of this reform was 'unifying the tax code, simplifying the tax system and its administration, and strengthening the macrocontrol capability of the central government ...' (Xu, 1996, p. 375). The reform of the tax system saw the establishment of four principal tax bases — taxes on transactions, income, property and resources (Wang, 2000, pp. 30–31). Of these, taxes on transactions (including a value added tax) were the most important (Wang, 2000, Xu, 1996).

While the tax structure was a problem, commentators generally agree that the pre-reform system of tax administration (and expenditure authorities) was an even greater issue. Indeed, both Ma (2000) and Xu (1996) argue that reform to the tax administration and collection procedures has had a greater impact on post-reform China than the changes in the taxes themselves.

Unfortunately, in the early stage of economic reform, and notwithstanding the reform of the tax system, state sector revenues in China actually decreased. This was due to, and coincided with, the decline in the importance of SOEs and was compounded by the fact that, despite the new taxes, the taxation system remained undeveloped, inefficient and subjected to abuse (Ma, 2000). However, the EIU (2007) argues that the government is increasingly bringing these problems under control. Of more importance to the EIU are the constraints placed on fiscal policy by the inability to bring under control off-budget expenditure items such as defence, a large implicit pension debt resulting from an unfunded defined-benefits pension system and support to the SOEs in the form of 'soft loans' issued by the state-owned banks. Nevertheless, the EIU (2007) concede that the authorities were able to successfully conduct an expansionary fiscal policy to support gross domestic product (GDP) growth at the time of the Asian financial crisis — something they could not have implemented ten years earlier.

These developments in fiscal and monetary policies cannot ensure that the Chinese economy will not again be plunged into recession in order to stem an inflationary surge, but it does make it less likely. To the extent that a recession in China may occur, the impact on Australia is likely to be significant if Australia continues to rely on a booming minerals sector to sustain its economic performance.

Risk of a Fall in the Demand for Resources

The inevitable cyclical nature of economic activity and the variable ability of governments to deal with fluctuations aside, is it likely that China's economic development will bring the country to a point where China's demand will move away from the resources of oil and coal? In our view, this is unlikely in the next 20 to 30 years.

There remains great diversity on a regional basis in China. For every region that is booming there are others that have yet to experience the benefits of economic reform. Indeed, data reported by EIU (2007) from the *China Statistical Yearbook* (NBSC; 2006) enables us to calculate that in 2005 annual income per head in Shanghai was over RMB 51,000, whilst it was just over RMB 5,000 in another part, Quizhou. The mean provincial income per head was just over RMB

16,000. There are continuing inequalities in development that have been created in the process of reform (Basu, Hick, & Sappey, 2006b).

This economic inequality is not something that is simply accepted by the Chinese people. While Shanghai is not China, the people of Shanghai are, to some extent, a reflection of the aspirations of people throughout China. Basu et al. (2006a) observed that even the older Chinese have begun to see that the concentration of development in the coastal areas has become a problem and tend to look to the government to resolve the resulting inequality. By contrast, the younger generation, while recognising the inequality, are far more confident that it can be resolved through the application of market principles rather than government intervention. Interestingly, these findings were consistent between the developed and underdeveloped areas of the country. The inhabitants of poorer areas (e.g., Changchun) were found to be as inspirational as their counterparts in developed cities (e.g., Tianjin; Basu et al., 2006b).

There is no question that the Chinese government has responded to the call for action in the development of the inland provinces. Addressing the issues of regional inequality was declared a priority of the 11th 5-year plan for 2006–2010 (EIU, 2007). While it is not expected that the reduction of the existing inequality can occur quickly and while there are many problems to be overcome, the process will undoubtedly ensure China's long-term continuation of the demand for the resources Australia currently provides. This view is reinforced by Edey (2007) who notes that China's income levels have not yet attained the same levels as Japan, even when its growth rate slowed. He concludes that until such levels are attained China will continue growing at a round 10% per annum.

Risk of Movement Away From the Market

With respect to the third issue, it is true that China is not a democracy and probably will never be a democracy in a western sense. However, this does not mean that the government of China is not pursuing the development of a market economy that will make China a global economic power. It is very unlikely that China will turn away from its attempts to build a strong market economy. China is actively expanding its bilateral and multilateral relationships with a wide range of nations and groups of nations. Asia Pulse (2005) reported that China was pursuing 23 free trade agreements (FTAs). China had reportedly notified the WTO of the signing of four agreements in June 2006 (WorldTradeLaw.net, 2006). These include a framework agreement with the Association of South East Asian Nations (ASEAN) in July 2003 which will result in an FTA by 2010 (EIU, 2007); with the original members of the Bangkok Agreement (Bangladesh, India, the Lao People's Democratic Republic, the Republic of Korea and Sri Lanka) in January 2002, which provides for the introduction of trade concessions; with Hong Kong in January 2004; and with Macao, also in January 2004. All were in pursuit of closer economic relations. China is also seeking to enter a FTA with

Australia (Basu, Hicks, & Sappey, 2005, 2006a). In addition, China is a member of Asia Pacific Economic Cooperation and founded the Shanghai Cooperation Organisation (SCO) with Russia, Kazakhstan, the Kyrgyz Republic and Tajikistan in 1996 — a move aimed at boosting regional trade.

Further evidence of China's ongoing commitment to a market economy is found in its espoused compliance with the requirements of the World Trade Organization (WTO). The EIU (2007) argues that entry into the WTO changed the way China managed its economic reform process, moving it from ad hoc changes to a strict timetable for implementing market reforms. China's apparent adherence to this timetable and its compliance with WTO requirements has provided more confidence amongst western trading economies than would have been the case had China not succumbed to WTO membership.

Moreover, there has been a clear recognition of the market system within China — both politically and constitutionally. In 2002, the Communist Party of China (CCP) formally adopted the ideology of what is known as the 'Theory of the Three Represents'. This refers to the CCP developing a justification for moving towards capitalism, including accepting entrepreneurs as CCP members (EIU, 2007). In 2004, this ideology was also written into the constitution and amendments made to guarantee private property rights (EIU, 2007). Most recently, the National Party Congress of 2007 passed the property law to come into effect on October 1 and it is reported that 'property of the state, the collective and the individual is protected by law, and no unit or individuals may infringe upon it' (Callick, 2007, p. 11).

Research by Basu et al. (2005, 2006a) found a trend in favour of the market. Younger Chinese, in particular, were very supportive of freeing up markets and were more open and outward-looking than older Chinese, and wished to encourage higher levels of capital inflow and the associated access to new technology. However, both young and old acknowledged the importance of China's entry into the WTO and were convinced of China's sincerity in pursuing its obligations under WTO. In sum, they were eager to be involved in the global economy and convinced that China could compete under a market system.

The Risk of Political Turmoil

Unfortunately, the risk of an extremely disruptive political change continues to exist in China. In the past, the apparent mechanism for dealing with dissent was repression — as exemplified by the deaths in Tiananmen Square in 1989. However, the authorities do seem to have learned some lessons from this period and have demonstrated a willingness to adapt. There can be no question that increased economic freedom brought with it increased demands for political freedom, with the latter being harshly managed. More recently, the extension of economic freedom has continued, but the country's style of leadership has changed. The EIU (2007) reports that there is a far greater level of collective decision-making based on compromise among senior authorities than had been evident in the past.

Perhaps the leadership has recognised that totalitarianism would lead to further disasters. It has certainly recognised that China is a very unequal society and that perhaps the most difficult issue confronting authorities is how to deal with the displacement of the so-called 'rural workers'. The authorities are certainly pursuing vigorous policies designed to address the economic development of rural areas and the raising of health and education standards. However, that has not reduced number the protests — with the official number rising from 10,000 in 1994 to 87,000 in 2005 (EIU, 2007). Failure to deal appropriately with this problem could have very disruptive political and economic consequences.

Opportunities not to be Missed

In all likelihood Australia's export commodity boom, fuelled by demand from China, will continue for some time yet. However, there appears to be little evidence that Australian industry is fully grasping the opportunities presented by China's economic reforms.

Australia is a major producer of food. A trend observed in China has been the rise in the importation of food as a result of the reduction in agricultural tariffs following entry into the WTO (EIU, 2006). This is an area where Australia has failed to fully seize the opportunity. The Australian Bureau of Agricultural and Resource Economics (ABARE; 2006) reports that there are significant changes taking place in the demand for food in China largely because increased affluence has given rise to the demand for a range of agricultural products, which China's farmers are unlikely to be able to supply because of the pressures being felt by water constraints and land degradation. These changes have enhanced the potential for developing a greater export trade in food to China. In 2004–2005, exports of grain to China grew by 160% helping Australian food exports to China grow by 85% (*Australian Food News*, 2006). As a result, Australia's food exports to China grew from 3% of total food exports in 1990–91 to 5% in 2004–05 (*Australian Food News*, 2006). However, such growth, from a relatively low base, only serves to underscore the potential that remains.

With respect to manufacturing exports, Basu et al. (2005) canvassed some of the negative attitudes that arose in the context of discussion over a FTA with China. However, although dire predictions of Australian job losses are still being put forward by opponents of the FTA, some more positive statements on the prospects for the development of our trading relationship with China are beginning to appear. This is to be expected. In manufacturing, China's comparative advantage is in the mass manufacture of labour-intensive products. However, while domestic capacity is certainly growing, China tends to import more complex and sophisticated manufactured goods to meet the needs of the domestic market and to support its own industrial expansion (Weemaes, 2005). Pickworth (2007) reports that nearly 4000 small to medium sized manufacturers from Australia are exporting heavily to China — usually into selective niche markets. *The Age* newspaper article ('Gumboot on the other foot', 2007) also supports the prospect of niche marketing of manufactured goods to China and points to the need for automotive parts — China has the world's highest sales growth for cars and will be the world's second biggest automobile market by 2010 (Weemaes, 2005). This is true despite that fact that automotive parts manufacturers are resisting tariff reduction in Australia and fear the FTA because of cheap Chinese parts being imported into Australia. The concern is generally with basic components of little technical sophistication, yet, even with these there is an opportunity for Australian automotive parts manufacturers to move to China, manufacture there and then import into Australia. With respect to products that require sophisticated manufacturing, there remains substantial opportunities for Australian manufacturers in Australia, as Australian companies have developed considerable expertise in this area. Edey (2007) also points to recent successes in high value areas like pharmaceuticals, professional and scientific equipment and industrial machinery as showing the way for Australian manufacturers.

A number of reports highlight education and tourism as being amongst Australia's largest export earners in services trade with China ('Gumboot on the other foot', 2007; Tisdell, 2006; Weemaes, 2005). However, the potential for trade in services with China is much greater than the trade represented by these two areas and Australia's Minister for Trade has recognised that this potential is often overlooked (Langdon-Orr, 2006). Langdon-Orr (2006), commenting on information contained in Department of Foreign Affairs and Trade (DFAT; 2005), points out that the proportion of the economy represented by services in China is not just low in comparison with Australia (and other OECD countries), it is also low when compared with economies that have a similar per capita income to China. The explanation reported by Langdon-Orr is that the former communist model emphasised the production of industrial goods at the expense of services. China, therefore, has considerable catching up to do in the development of its services sector.

To some extent, this 'catch up' has begun as the services sector has been rising faster in China than in most other countries. Much of this growth is the result of government policy following the announcement in the 10th Five-Year Plan (2001–2005) to develop the services sector (DFAT, 2005). During this process of catch up, considerable opportunities are likely to be created for countries like Australia to export services to China. For example, architects, environmental designers and town planners are in demand in China (Weemaes, 2005) as are investment bankers, lawyers and professionals in port and recreation services ('Gumboot on the other foot', 2007). In the short term, this development may be stimulated by the export of services and foreign direct investment in the Chinese service sector to meet growing domestic Chinese demand.

While there is a great deal of potential for the delivery of Australian service industries in China there are also some significant problems. DFAT (2005) has identified that notwithstanding China's entry into the WTO, China continues to apply restrictions on ownership, business scope and geographical coverage of the service sector in China. The Chinese authorities continue to apply an 'opaque' regulatory process and licensing arrangements. Service providers are frustrated by operating requirements, lack of legal transparency and a failure to apply laws consistently and to enforce laws on intellectual property rights.

Conclusions

China began its economic reform process in 1979, progressing steadily towards a market economy. The old structures of state-owned enterprises were retained but increasingly a private sector was allowed to emerge and become the dominant means of growth. This resulted in an inflow of funds from abroad — largely from other Asian economies — seeking to take advantage of China's relatively cheap labour. Joint ventures were established which were largely oriented to export and China, which had previously had little involvement in international trade, began to emerge as a significant trading nation.

Under the reform approach, China's economy continued to grow and the rising incomes of the Chinese people generated an increasing demand for consumer goods which had been relatively unknown. As well as importing these goods, companies began to expand domestic production to meet the rising domestic demand. This, in turn, gave rise to the need for basic products (such as steel) which China had little capacity to produce. However, from the late 1990s basic processing capacity expanded, giving rise to a significant increase in demand for commodities such as ore and coal. This continues today and Australia, to this point, has been one of the chief beneficiaries.

In all likelihood, the commodities export expansion in Australia will continue for some years — however, a number of risks are apparent. China, like all economies, is prone to cyclical swings in economic activity. This can be a major problem in the case of China as their weapons of macroeconomic control are not well developed and may not serve to avoid swings in activity that could prove damaging. Fortunately, in recent years, changes in both fiscal and monetary policy have taken place, but it is still to be seen whether such policy weapons will be able to cope when put under pressure, particularly from rapid expansion which generates inflation.

Because China is starting from such a low market base and because many areas of China are still substantially underdeveloped, the risk of a downturn, or even a flattening, in the growth trend appears remote. Cyclical swings aside, the underlying demand for resources will continue. A factor that has been of some concern is the potential for China to regress from the pursuit of developing a market economy. However, the evidence is that the authorities are pursuing the extension of market principles. A far more worrying issue is the widening regional and personal income inequalities in recent years. Along with deteriorating public support in basic areas such as health and education, expanding inequality can create significant discontent among the population. With its primarily centralised political system China might face a difficult task in controlling any major sociopolitical challenge to government authority. The history of other nations suggests that if violent change does occur, the economy will be one of the first victims.

In the current situation, Australia is confronted by both opportunities and threats. To the extent that the commodities boom continues, Australia will benefit — but anything that disrupts that boom will have severe consequences for Australia. In addition, the continuation of the boom may be distracting Australians from other potential opportunities that exist in China. As a country that seeks to have balanced economic growth, policies that target the spreading of risk and taking advantage of an expanding services sector may better serve Australia's future economic prospects in conducting trade and investment with China.

References

ABARE (2005). *Rapid economic growth transforming China's food consumption.* Retrieved March 20, 2007, from http://bureau-index.funnelback.com/search/cache.cgi?collection=abare&doc=http/www.abareconomics.com/corporate/media/2005_releases/14july_05.html

ABARE (2006). *Economic growth and urbanisation driving changes in China's agriculture.* Retrieved March 20, 2007, from http://bureau-index.funnelback.com/search/cache.cgi?collection=abare&doc=http/www.abareconomics.com/corporate/media/2006_releases/6march_06.html

Allsop, C. (1995). Macroeconomic control and reform in China. *Oxford Review of Economic Policy, Winter, 11,* 43–53.

Asia Pulse. (2005). *China moves on free trade negotiations.* Retrieved March 15, 2005, from http://au.news.yahoo.com/050308/3/teac.html

Australian Bureau of Statistics. (2007). *International trade in goods and services.* (Cat. no. 5368.0). Canberra: Australian Bureau of Statistics.

Australian Food News. (2006). Retrieved March 20, 2007, from http://www.ausfoodnews.com.au/flapa/flapa.php?nid=3219&tid=609

Basu, P.K., Hicks, J., & Sappey, R. (2005). Chinese attitudes to trade agreements in the context of the proposed Australia–China free trade agreement. *Economic Papers, 24*(4), 294–308.

Basu, P.K., Hicks, J., & Sappey, R. (2006a). Free trade agreements and investment: A Chinese perspective. *Agenda, 13*(2), 179–192.

Basu, P.K., Hicks, J., & Sappey, R. (2006b, July). *Potential for change in the unequal regional distribution of direct foreign investment in China?: Some implications for the proposed Australia–China Free Trade Agreement.* Conference Proceedings, 5th Global Conference on Business and Economics, Cambridge, England.

Callick, R. (2007, March 21). Chinese leaders' push for property law revealed. *The Australian,* p. 11.

Department of Foreign Affairs and Trade (DFAT). (2005). *Unlocking China's Services Sector.* DFAT, Economic Analysis Unit. Retrieved March 22, 2007, from http://www.defat.gov.au/publications/eau_unlocking_china_services.pdf

Economist Intelligence Unit (EIU). (2007). *China: Country Profile 2007.* London: The Economist Intelligence Unit Limited.

Edey, M. (2007). *Address to the Australia Industry Group*, Economy 2007. Retrieved March 21, 2007, from http://bureau-index.funnelback.com/search/cache.cgi?collection=abare&doc =http/www.abareconomics.com/corporate/media/2006_releases/6march_06.html

Gumboot on the other foot for China's currency. (2007, 16 March). *The Age*. Retrieved March 20, 2007, from http://www.theage.com.au/news/business/gumboot-on-the-other-foot-for-chinas-currency/2007/03/16/1173722748446.html?page=2#

International Bank for Reconstruction and Development (The World Bank) (n.d.). *World Tables*, Johns Hopkins University Press, December. Reproduced as World Bank World Tables Database by dX EconData.

Langdon-Orr, C. (2006, 9 February). *Report on Minister Vaile's speech at the launch of the Economic Analytical Unit Report*, Sydney. Retrieved March 22, 2007, from http://www.isoc-au.org.au/Events/ChinaServices.html

Ma, J. (2000). *The Chinese economy in the 1990s*. New York: Macmillan.

National Bureau of Statistics of China (NBSC). (2007). *China statistical yearbook 2006*. Beijing: China Statistics Press.

Naughton, B. (1995). *Growing out of the plan: Chinese economic reform, 1978–1993*. New York: Cambridge University Press.

Pickworth, C. (2007, March 18). Exporters still upbeat. *The Courier-Mail*. Retrieved March 21, 2007, from http://www.news.com.au/couriermail/story/0,23739,21402854–37574,00.html

Pyle, D.J. (1997). *China's economy: from revolution to reform*. Basingstoke, England: Macmillan.

Shen, R. (2000). *China's economic reform: An experience in pragmatic socialism*. Westport, CT: Praeger.

Tisdell, C. (2006, September). Economic and business relations between Australia and China: An overview and assessment. *Conference Proceedings, 3rd International Conference on Contemporary Business*. Leura, Australia.

Wang, Y-C. (2000). Current tax system and its future reform in the People's Republic of China. In G-H. Wan, G. MacAulay, Z-Y. Zhou, & J. Chudleigh (Eds), *Chinese economy towards the 21st century:* Vol. 2. Sydney, Australia: The University of Sydney.

Weemaes, H. (2005). *Australia's exports to China*. Retrieved March 22, 2007, from http://www.dfat.gov.au/trade/downloads/australia_exports__china_2005.pdf

WorldTradeLaw.net (2006). *Bilateral and regional agreements notified to the WTO*. Retrieved March 20, 2007, from http://www.worltradelaw.net/fta/ftadatabase/ftas.asp?f1001=&f1002= &f1003=China

Xu, Y.C. (1996). Deepening and widening the economic reform in China: From enterprise reform to macroeconomic stability. *The Journal of Developing Areas, 30*, 361–384.

Yusuf, S. (1994). China's macroeconomic performance and management during transition. *Journal of Economic Perspectives, 8*(2), 71–92.

There is Serious Money to be Made in China: Challenges and Lost Opportunities for Western Managers

Kate Hutchings

Since Deng's Open Door Policy of 1978, which opened China to the world for the first time since the early 1900s, western businesses have flocked to China, lured by the promise of big returns on investment through access to not only cheap labour and production but also a market almost a quarter of the size of the world's total population. During this 30-year period, China has undergone radical change, from having a population of which almost 98% lived in near poverty undertaking agricultural work with the majority employed in state-owned enterprises, to having a bourgeoning middle-class and a higher echelon whose personal wealth and purchasing capacity rivals that of the most well-to-do in New York, Paris and London. Indeed, the China success story rivals the post-war development of its near neighbour, Japan. Yet unlike Japan, that had rapid economic development, China has also undergone vast political and social adjustment during this short time period, with the inclusion of Hong Kong under its jurisdiction, creating 'one country, two systems' to characterise the existence of a Communist polit-bureau alongside capitalist market forces (for an interesting discussion of China's transition and its implications for international business, see Child & Tse, 2001). Western business has been attracted to a nation that has embarked upon a period of fast modernisation that has seen it shift from being vilified for its human rights record within its borders as well as in neighbouring countries, to a nation that in the early-2000s won entree into the World Trade Organisation (WTO) and the right to host the 2008 Olympics. China is second only to the United States (US) in attraction of foreign direct investment (FDI) (Yan, 2005) and its annual growth rate from 1979 to 2005 has averaged 9.7% (Morrison, 2006). China remains Australia's third-largest trade partner (Austrade, 2005) in imports and a major target market for exports in the wake of declining investment by traditional trade partners. Despite the potential value of China to the West, though, while undertaking research in Beijing in mid-2006 a western expatriate candidly suggested to me that, 'There is serious money to be made in China — and the Chinese are going to make it!'. His comment elucidated what many western business managers had been thinking for some time — that they had rather underestimated the challenges they faced in China, as well as the ability of the Chinese to capitalise on their own internationalisation, modernisation and industrialisation.

Over the course of 30 years China has shifted from a largely agrarian society to one that produced cheap, disposable goods for an international market, to being able to produce excellent copies of the best Italian and Scandinavian design. Yet, the transformation of China has not stopped there — while great imitators, western businesses have underestimated the ability of the Chinese also to innovate and to begin to take their place among the high technology producers on the international stage.

Some have questioned China's ability to innovate, arguing that the era of innovation stopped with the introduction of the printing press and development of suspension bridges. Yet, while it is true that China only holds about 1.4% of patents given internationally each year, they are also well represented in science and technology, having eighth position in the world as authors of science and technology papers, being 18% of those employed as science professors in the US (CLSA, 2006) — a major brain drain from China — and being well represented amongst the authors of articles in top US management journals. I do agree, though, that there are still problems with Chinese professors being expelled from leading Chinese universities like Tsinghua and Shanghai Jiao Tong for fraud and that China is held back by needing more reforms to education, lack of rule of law, fledgling accounting practices, and poor intellectual property protection (CLSA, 2006), but it is these systemic issues that are at fault, not a lack of innovation on the part of individuals.

Moreover, while many developing nations have invested into other developing nations, China is one of the first developing nations to actually engage in outward FDI into western markets, notably having established Chinese multinationals in the United Kingdom (UK) and North America (Wei & Lui, 2001). Though the Chinese have quickly learned to understand the West, the West's knowledge of China has remained somewhat trapped in the clichés provided in the ubiquitous guides with titles like 'Doing Business in China'. While such books have their place, and I have long advocated that any form of cross-cultural preparation and training is better than none, many such books have not kept pace with the changing business and management practices of China. Even such long-held traditions as the banquet are rapidly disappearing with modernisation. During the short 9 years that I have been primarily researching management of Australian businesses in China I have witnessed vast adjustments in the way that the Chinese go about their business. Indeed, just a leading Australian university lost a potentially strong university partner in China because, as the senior Chinese professor remarked, 'We are tired of having so many dinners and meetings without anything happening!' Like the long Australian business lunch that all but disappeared with the introduction of fringe benefits tax in the late 1980s, the day of the long banquet is certainly also well past for many large Chinese organisations who are quick to do business and quick to pass over those who take too long to come to an agreement.

While the Chinese have moved a long way towards western modes of business, the West has largely failed to keep pace with the sheer scale of economic, political and social change occurring in China. Anyone who has visited China on a regular basis over the last 10 years will have noted the plethora of new buildings and other physical development evident on each subsequent visit. Yet, the social transformation is just as dramatic. While the World Wide Web and the popular press is replete with examples of marketing failures that have occurred in international distribution of products through simple problems of language communication, still much less consideration is given to managerial and human resource management problems that result from crosscultural misunderstandings. If a company with the history and international exposure and experience of Fosters can lose an estimated $250 million in a few short years in China, it does not auger well for smaller players.

Taking Fosters as a case in point, it has been suggested that a myriad of factors were to blame for its failure in China, including Chinese dislike of the actual product, Chinese dislike of the colour of the packaging, lack of branding and customer service by poor performing local staff. Yet, there was also a key element in the lack of consistency of expatriate management which undermined morale of local staff, contributing to poor performance (Chung & Smith, 2006). Having established four breweries in China in Shanghai, Guangdong, Doumen and Tianjin, Fosters did not demonstrate longevity to local staff by the rapid turnover of expatriate managers — Shanghai alone had 6 general managers within an 11-year period. For Chinese who had not long stepped out of the 'iron rice bowl' the perceived lack of commitment by Fosters managers to China was quite threatening and was reinforced by lack of language skills and China knowledge of most of the Australian managers (Chung & Smith, 2006).

In this chapter I discuss some of the issues that I view as key to the problems that the West continues to face in China, and how a better understanding of Chinese culture, development and business management practices will stand it in much greater stead for harnessing the potential of this enormous market. Moreover, I proffer some suggestions about how western businesses can not only enhance their managerial effectiveness in their Chinese operations but also to transfer some of the best practices that they find China to their headquarters and other international operations.

Australian Business People in China: Expats, Local-Hire Foreign Managers, Gone-Native and Hearts-At-Home

My own interest in undertaking research in China arose from recognition of the strategic importance of China to Australian businesses and the necessity of those businesses to develop their international managers' China knowledge if they were to be successful in commercial dealings in China. Throughout eight research visits to China over the last 9 years, the most valuable lesson I have personally learned is the necessity to build networks, if one is to achieve some degree of ease in undertaking research. I rapidly became aware that not only was networking a ubiquitous part of daily life for Chinese, but that the Australian expatriate community also had its own form of *guanxi* (a Chinese term, loosely defined as interpersonal connections), and building and maintaining it was essential if one wanted to do research with this group of people. Indeed, I discovered that gaining access to expatriates and building their trust to elicit further information was dependent upon networking within this expatriate circle (for further details on the difficulties of undertaking research in China, see Adler, Campbell & Laurent, 1989; Roy et al., 2001). I also quickly came to realise that there were several distinct groups of expatriate Australian managers and businesspeople and the categories into which they fell had important implications for their ability to adjust to, and succeed in, China. The Australian managers and expatriates I have interviewed over the years have fallen into three main types. These types have been categorised as 'dual allegiance' expatriates, 'hearts at home' expatriates and 'gone native' expatriates (Black & Gregersen, 1992). For further discussion of my experiences with these expatriates, see Hutchings (2004).

What is most interesting about the Australian expatriates is their limited crosscultural training (CCT) and company support in contrast to their European and North American counterparts. My research suggests that the 'training' they receive is very much limited to relocation assistance and general briefings about the subsidiary operations with very little crosscultural training or language study provided. What this suggests is that adjustment is very much down to the individual and that those that manage to be most successful in China are those that 'go native' or seek out support from the extended expatriate community. Interestingly though, despite the reticence of Australian organisations to provide CCT and support, a substantive number of the Australian expatriates I have interviewed do have prior language and crosscultural knowledge skills and have completed other foreign postings. This suggests that while organisations are still not prepared to invest financial and time resources in preparing their expatriates, at least they are acknowledging the importance of acquiring individuals for expatriate assignments who already have some of the skills that contribute to crosscultural competency (Hutchings, 2005b). Further, within the expatriate community, there are clear divisions between those who can be characterised as traditional expatriates who are posted by their organisation to China and local-hire foreign managers (LHFM), or self-selected expatriates who are individuals who have voluntarily moved to China to undertake further language study or to seek work and are then headhunted within China by Australian and other western organisations (Hutchings, 2005b).

My research has found that expatriates who have been in China for 3 or more years (the majority of whom also speak Mandarin) suggest that language skills and increasing length of time in China increases adjustment and that understanding cultural practices decreases the likelihood of committing cultural faux pas. Indeed, individuals who have been in China longer than 5 years generally no longer regard themselves as expatriates, but suggest that they are now making a conscious choice to live in China and adapt to the society, that is as self-selected expatriates (Hutchings, 2005b). The expatriates who have been in China for a shorter time period highlight the importance of working to build relationships with local Chinese business partners if they are to improve their sensitivity to the Chinese culture and assist their own adaptation. Indeed, many individuals who operate small import–export businesses in China have recognised the value of local contacts and communication and have married local Chinese women who serve both as their business partner as well as translator and for entrée into local ministries (Hutchings, 2005b). While other research (Forster, 2000) concurs with mine that expatriates are younger and earlier in their careers than the expatriate of 20 years ago who had extensive work experience, there is evidence that while less established in their careers, more of the people working in China today are better culturally adjusted. Yet, as Australia has a limited history of internationalisation vis-a-vis Europe and North America and the majority of Australian companies in China are small-to-medium enterprises (SMEs), Australian expatriates do not have a large accumulated knowledge of crosscultural understanding within their organisations from which to draw (Hutchings, 2005b). This may place them at a disadvantage relative to international counterparts and suggests the need for greater attention to CCT if they are to maximise opportunities to be made in China.

Challenges of Managing in China: Culture, Modernisation and Diversity

Even with the most comprehensive, strategic CCT available, managers of international businesses, be they joint ventures or wholly-owned subsidiaries, face what would sometimes seem to be insurmountable obstacles in managing in China. While certainly foreign companies find that China may not afford them the logistics or communications (see Zapalaska & Edwards, 2001) to which they have grown accustomed in the West, such practicalities are often the least of their problems in contrast to the need to make local political contacts and work within the Chinese business and social culture. Yet for as many companies that make the mistake of not appreciating Chinese cultural practice and expecting that everything should be as it is 'at home', there are an equal number that go to great lengths to adapt to the 'textbook' culture and ignore the rapid changes that have occurred in Chinese business practice over the last decade.

In the context of such change, certain cultural practices have remained constant, although they have been modified by forces of modernisation and internationalisation. Core to Chinese culture is the concept of *guanxi* (Buttery & Wang, 1999; Luo, 2000). Whereas exchanges favoured in western society are sporadic and discrete in time, the Chinese focus on relationships created over long periods of time built on frequent exchanges (Michailova & Worm, 2003). Whereas in most western nations business and social positions are quite separate, in China interactions with another are viewed as part of a whole relationship. Hierarchical relationships in the workplace are replicated in a social setting.

Guanxi is a means of achieving status and moving from being an outsider to an insider (Buttery & Wang, 1999). Those who fall out of a personalised network are regarded as outsiders and do not share benefits of networking with insiders (Hutchings & Michailova, 2004). A Chinese individual with a problem, whether personal or organisational, naturally turns to his or her *guanxiwang*, or 'relationship network', for assistance. An individual is not limited to his or her own *guanxiwang*, but may tap into the networks of those with whom he or she has *guanxi*. Integrally tied to the existence of *guanxi* relationships is the prior development of *xinyong* (trust), which is established over a long period of time, as well as concepts of *mianzi* (face) and *renqing* (favours). Yet, while it has been suggested that such practices are declining in importance in an internationalised China (see Guthrie, 1998; Hutchings & Murray, 2002; Luo, 2000), as a result of the development of rule by law and adoption of international accounting practices, they still have their place, and western organisations ignore them at their peril.

Undoubtedly, some of the affluent young people who dominate the streets of the eastern seaboard provinces and major cities of Beijing, Guangzhou and Shanghai, sending SMS messages on their latest mobile phones and listening to western music on their I-Pods, do have different norms and are in the process of blending modern trends with traditional values. Further, the international movement of Chinese business people around the globe, increasing numbers of Chinese students who study abroad and greater numbers of average Chinese people who have moved out of poverty and into international travel, are having a dramatic impact on the view and knowledge that the Chinese have of the western world (Weir & Hutchings, 2006). Yet, while holding this picture in our minds, we must also be careful not to forget that the rather westernised business cities of China are in stark contrast to rural areas, particularly those in the far western and northern provinces, many of which have remained largely closed to the western world. So, the international businessperson needs to have one code of business for one part of China, but many other codes of business for other parts in this still very economically and socially diverse nation. Moreover, there is also need for international business to be cognisant of the fact that although China has opened its doors to supply and demand, it does still try to maintain high levels of political and social censorship, an increasing challenge for authorities in the face of the World Wide Web. In recent years, Chinese authorities have attempted to block flows of information about aspects of the SARS epidemic, Falun Gong, human rights' websites, some foreign news providers, people providing information in any way seen to be 'anti-government and as inciting the overthrow of the state' (Deibert, 2002; Kalathil, 2003; Yang, 2003).

Management and Knowledge Management in China

From knowledge management literature has developed a belief in the need for a broader management learning, in which information is also communicated from subsidiary or joint venture partners to the developed world in order to recognise that knowledge assets are also economic goods in their own right (Boisot, 1998). Yet, there has also been a tendency within the knowledge management literature to try to universalise concepts of knowledge. This has led to recent research suggesting that cross-culturally it may not be possible to have such universal understandings. Indeed, Glisby and Holden (2003) maintain that an approving silence has descended particularly upon Nonaka and Takeuchi's (1995) literature on knowledge management and claim that Nonaka and Takeuchi are guilty of what they critique, namely of objectifying knowledge overly focused on explicit manifestations. They argue that while Nonaka (1994) critiques the western approach to knowledge management, Nonaka analyses knowledge sharing through a Japanese lens, believing his findings to be universally applicable to an understanding of knowledge management. Glisby and Holden (2003) and Holden (2002) further proffer that there is need to understand how knowledge is constructed and constituted outside of Japan and the western world and that the literature on knowledge management in a crosscultural context is almost nonexistent. Weir and Hutchings (2005) have argued that Glisby and Holden (2003) may make the same mistake and suggest that while Nonaka and Takeuchi are not necessarily universal, there may be aspects of their model that do have application outside of Japan and the industrialised world and argue that in particular there are important synergies with knowledge management in China.

Weir and Hutchings (2005) point to the work of Hutchings and Michailova (2004) which emphasises that knowledge sharing is not as natural as often presented in the knowledge management literature, and Sbarcea (2001) who suggests that it is an ungrounded assumption that people will share the knowledge they possess with others or automatically tap into a collective corporate knowledge base. Weir and Hutchings (2005) submit that attitudes to knowledge sharing, as well as actual knowledge-sharing behaviour, depend on conditions that vary across institutional and cultural environments and that conditions under which individuals are prepared to share knowledge, either with other individuals or groups within the organisation or with individuals or groups external to the organisation, do differ between cultures.

After 6000 years of relying on informal networks, China's late 1970s shift towards a market economy has resulted in embryonic formal business groups, legally binding contracts, business (and to a lesser extent, government) accountability, and utilisation of many western management and human resource management (HRM) practices. Yet, it would be premature to suggest that institutions will completely take the place of cultural norms as China undertakes a gradualist reduction of central planning (Hutchings, 2005a). The management literature is full of articles detailing the difficulties that western companies have faced in trying to implement western HRM practices — such as rewards/incentives, group performance assessment, and managing upwards — in a business culture that was not yet prepared for them. These scenarios usually lead to exacerbation of the insider–outsider divide between foreign managers and local employee and often to complete business failure.

For western businesses in China this means the continued uncertainty of informal networks alongside new ways of thinking and managing. While one-way processes of knowledge transfer from international manager to Chinese employee may be achieved in the short term, the international organisation that seeks to achieve two-way management learning, and organisational cultural change, will need to be prepared to invest much greater time and resources, and to employ third party intermediaries who already have insider status until the international managers achieve such a relationship themselves (Hutchings, 2005a; see also Michailova & Hutchings, 2006).

Though shifting to a market economy China still faces a lot of discrepancies in terms of levels of development between rural and urban areas, indifferent technology in parts of the country, transport problems, poor infrastructure and limited educa-tion and training of much of the workforce — with those on the eastern seaboard likely to have familiarity with western practices yet those from more remote parts will have limited international knowledge. For international investors there are still problems with inadequate energy supply, bureaucratic red tape, nonconvertible currency, and Chinese partners' continuing inexperience in international concepts of accounting, taxation and law. Outdated communication tools and unreliability of new technologies, such as E-mail and mobile phone, where they exist, further stifle intercultural communication. While a huge market, China is still a difficult market and foreign investors are wise to take note of these problems and realise that being able to succeed in China means making a commitment to the long-term.

Child and Tse (2001) claim that the role of supranational institutions like the World Trade Organization (WTO) contribute to driving China's transition to fully fledged market economy and present a challenge to the influence of the central gov-ernment, just as fiscal and monetary international institutions have also influenced the decision-making of national governments in the industrialised nations. Yet, they caution that though the WTO will assume increasing relevance for trade and invest-ment and China's transition (Child & Tse, 2001), it will not immediately subsume the need for most businesses to cultivate provincial-level politicians. Many international businesses continue to operate on the edge, balancing between the reforms that have accompanied moves towards open trade and continuing the need to work within the boundaries of long-established networks (Hutchings, 2005a).

Though western businesses are bringing in their familiar practices and standards of accounting, production, and management, there is still difficulty in transferring these concepts to many potential employees who have spent lives working in the state-owned enterprises. Accordingly, the key necessity for international businesses is in building trust within their organisations if management learning is to occur — Chinese employees simply do not just unilaterally accept the largely-western concept that sharing is learning. Another challenge for international business is in creating organisational cultures in which employees see the value of applying decisions consistently across the board, rather than making arbitrary decisions based on established relationships. So, there is need for trust, but also trust that works within the confines of both Chinese and western standards. Factors that continue to work against such intra-organisational trust are the existence of provincial laws and national laws and confusion about jurisdiction; leftover remnants of a Communist era which discouraged sharing of information outside one's trusted inner circle, and a departmental rather than organisational-level of focus (Hutchings, 2005a; Hutchings & Michailova, 2004). The key message for western businesses is: Do your homework. Most businesspeople would not think of starting a business in Australia without a business plan, so why do they continue to believe that they can go into China, despite the enormity of the market but with the multitude of challenges it poses, and think that they can prosper without any forethought or preparation!

References

Adler, N.J., Campbell, N., & Laurent, A. (1989). In search of appropriate methodology: From outside the People's Republic of China looking in. *Journal of International Business Studies, Spring*, 61–74.

Austrade (Australian Trade Commission). (2005). *China profile*. Canberra, Australia: Australian Trade Commission, Commonwealth Government of Australia. Retrieved October 7, 2006, from http:www.Austrade.gov.au

Black, J.S., & Gregersen, H.B. (1992). Serving two masters: Managing the dual allegiance of expatriate employees. *Sloan Management Review, 33*(4). 61–71.

Boisot, M. (1998). *Knowledge assets: Securing competitive advantage in the information economy*. Oxford: Oxford University Press.

Buttery, E.A., & Wang, Y.H. (1999). The development of a guanxi framework. *Marketing Intelligence and Planning, 17*(3), 147–154.

Child, J., & Tse, D. (2001). China's transition and its implications for international business. *Journal of International Business Studies, 32*(5), 5–21.

Chung, M., & Smith, W. (2006, June). *The impact of cultural differences on an Australian firm doing business in China*. Conference Proceedings of Academy of International Business (AIB) Annual Conference, Beijing, China.

CLSA. (2006). Reinventing China: In search of an innovative economy. Hong Kong, PRC: CLSA Asia-Pacific Markets.

Deibert, R.J. (2002). Dark guests and great firewalls: The Internet and Chinese security policy. *Journal of Social Issues, 58*(1), 143–159.

Forster, N. (2000). Expatriates and the impact of cross-cultural training. *Human Resource Management Journal, 10*(3), 63–78.

Glisby, M., & Holden, N. (2003). Contextual constraints in knowledge management theory: The cultural embeddedness of Nonaka's knowledge-creating company. *Knowledge and Process Management, 10*(1), 29–36.

Guthrie, D. (1998). The declining significance of *guanxi* in China's economic transition. *The China Quarterly, 3*, 254–282.

Holden, N.J. (2002). *Cross-cultural management: A knowledge management perspective.* Harlow, England: Financial Times/Prentice Hall.

Hutchings, K. (2004). Behind the bamboo curtain: Problems and pitfalls in doing research with expatriates in China. In S. Michailova & E. Clark, (Eds.), *Fieldwork in transforming societies: understanding methodology from experience.* London: Palgrave.

Hutchings, K. (2005a). Examining the impacts of institutional change on knowledge sharing and management learning in China: Some challenges for international managers. *Thunderbird International Business Review, 47*(4), 447–468.

Hutchings, K. (2005b). Koalas in the land of the pandas: Reviewing Australian expatriates' China preparation. *International Journal of Human Resource Management, 16*(4), 553–566.

Hutchings, K., & Michailova, S. (2004). Facilitating knowledge sharing in Russian and Chinese subsidiaries: The role of personal networks. *Journal of Knowledge Management, 8*(2), 84–94.

Hutchings, K., & Murray, G. (2002). Australian expatriates' experiences in working behind the bamboo curtain: An examination of *guanxi* in post-communist China. *Asian Business Management, 1*, 1–21.

Kalathil, S. (2003). China's new media sector: Keeping the state in. *The Pacific Review, 16*(4), 489–501.

Luo, Y. (2000). *Guanxi and business.* Singapore: World Scientific.

Michailova, S., & Hutchings, K. (2006). National cultural influences on knowledge sharing in China and Russia. *Journal of Management Studies, 43*(3), 383–405.

Michailova, S., & Worm, V. (2003). Personal networking in Russia and China: Blat and Guanxi. *European Management Journal, 21*(4), 509–519.

Morrison, M.M. (2006). *C R S issue brief for Congress: China's economic conditions.* Retrieved 21 August 2006 from http://www.fas.org/sgp/crs/row/IB98014.pdf

Nonaka, I. (1994). A dynamic theory of organizational knowledge creation. *Organization Science, 5*(1), 14–37.

Nonaka, I., & Takeuchi, H. (1995). *The knowledge creating company.* Oxford: Oxford University Press.

Roy, A., Walters, P.G.P., & Luk, S.T.K. (2001). Chinese puzzles and paradoxes: Conducting business research in China. *Journal of Business Research, 52*, 203–210.

Sbarcea, K. (2001). The mystery of knowledge management. *New Zealand Management, 48*(19), 33–36.

Wei, Y., & Liu, X. (2001). *Foreign direct investment in China: Determinants and impact.* Cheltenham, UK: Edward Elgar.

Weir, D., & Hutchings, K. (2005). Cultural embeddedness of knowledge sharing in China and the Arab world. *Knowledge and Process Management, 12*(2), 89–98.

Weir, D., & Hutchings, K. (2006). Cultural filtering in the Arab world and China: Exploring the interrelationship of the technological knowledge age and traditional cultural networking and interpersonal connections. In S.G.M. van de Bunt-Kokhuis & M. Bolger (Eds.), *World wide work*, The Hague: Free University of the Netherlands.

Yan, Y. (2005). *Foreign investment and corporate governance in China,* New York: Palgrave MacMillan.

Yang, G. (2003). The Internet and civil society in China: A preliminary assessment. *Journal of Contemporary China, 12*(36), 453–475.

Zapalaska, A.M., & Edwards, W. (2001). Chinese Entrepreneurship in a cultural and economic perspective. *Journal of Small Business Management, 39*(3), 286–292.

Guest Workers in Taiwan: Experiences of Racialisation and Racism

Robert Tierney

Some Theoretical Considerations

Neo-liberalist theorists generally regard racism as a phenomenon logically antithetical to capitalism. For Bernstein (2005), only the unfettered market has the potential to eliminate the injustices of poverty and class, and to abolish racism. The key to the dissolution of racism, as typically claimed, is not the state but the workplace itself because capitalism impels employers to compete in markets which demand the rewarding of merit and the recognition of achievement. As Reisman (1982, p. 5) contends, for employers and managers 'race [sic: 'race'] is simply irrelevant. Any consideration of race means extra cost and less profit; it is bad business in the literal sense of the term.' Some specialising in the field of business ethics and human resource management argue along similar lines (see, e.g., Sintonen, 2006, p. 1).

The problem with neo-liberal treatises is that they ignore evidence that racism is not abating, despite the rapid rate of market deregulation, and may even be getting worse. Griffiths (2005, p. 160) has contended that 'Australia became a significantly more racist society' in the aftermath of the election of the Howard government in 1996 and that this racism has provided a means of deflecting working discontent away from the government's market reforms. The sources of racism are complex, irrespective of the country under study, but among the most significant institutions which create and reproduce racist tensions and violence in contemporary capitalism are capital and the state (Callinicos, 1993; Mahamdallie, 2002).

According to Griffiths (2005, p. 163), Australian racism has always served class interests:

> Governments and employers used racism as a *divide and rule* tactic to contain challenges to their authority. From the first, racism divided convicts from Aborigines. Later, prejudices against the Irish weakened a working class solidarity that mostly came from the British Isles. After World War II, southern Europeans and, more recently, immigrants from the Middle East and Asia have been the targets of this [*divide and rule*] racism.

The emphasis on class stratagems of *divide and conquer* has been an important element of Marxist analyses, dating back more than 30 years. In their seminal, though flawed, analysis of immigrants and class in western Europe, Castles and Kosack (1973) proposed the existence of racist and xenophobic aristocracies of western European labour, who were economically, socially and politically isolated from the mass of imported workers, who existed as an industrial reserve army of cheap labour — exploited for the benefit of capital accumulation and functional to the overall hegemony of capital over labour.

The positing of mutually causal relationships between capitalism and racism, however, is problematical because it depicts racism as something structurally and functionally orchestrated by the ruling class to secure the dominance of capital over labour, and because it portrays the working class as some kind of 'empty vassal into which has poured bourgeois ideas' (Miles, 1982, p. 85). It also offers little explanation about how racism originated (Miles, 1982). It is not only reductionist and functionalist (Solomos & Black, 1999) but can also be ahistorical.

It is true that divide and rule can be a powerful ruling class stratagem, but it can also create the opposite effect. Social isolation does not always diminish class conflict; it can also foster industrial militancy (Tierney, 1996, p. 105). Moreover, there is an abundance of evidence demonstrating that workers can resist and overcome divide and conquer strategies. Griffiths (2005, p. 168–172) himself is aware of this and goes to considerable lengths to explain interethnic solidarity in class struggle. In so doing, he eschews functionalism.

A more convincing framework than functionalism is one which identifies racism not as the direct outcome of capital accumulation but rather as an ideology 'structured by [capitalist] economic and political relations' (Miles, 1982, p. 85). Racism is not determined by class but is rather structured or grounded by it (Miles, 1982; Rath, 1999, pp. 148–149).

This perspective recognises that workers can be agents of antiracist struggle and change. It can also explain how workers themselves can be the authors of racism, though not under economic and social circumstances of their own choosing. Trade unions can embark on exclusionist practices against migrants in the 'interests'of local members. Although racist and xenophobic unions are rarely successful in abolishing immigration altogether, they are nevertheless able to force the state to limit intakes. Guest worker intakes in Taiwan have been the outcome of class compromises between capital and labour, brokered by the state

(Tierney, 2007). Whereas the racism of employers, managers and the state against foreign workers is the *racism of exploitation* designed to increase the expropriation of surplus value, the racism of organised labour is the *racism of exclusion*, emanating from trade unions' attempts to minimise foreign workers' presence in the job market in order to 'protect' local workers' job security and to prevent capital from pushing down the cost of labour power (Castles, 1996, pp. 26–27).

Furthermore, viewing racism as something structured by economic and political relations of production allows greater scope for recognising disparities in the victims' experiences of racism. There is no such thing as a homogeneous experience of migrants within any host country, partly because the state racialises migrants in divergent ways, incorporating them into different sites of production relations. Different migrant nationalities accordingly undergo divergent experiences of racism. The Canadian state's racialisation of foreign workers in the post World War II era, for instance, corresponded with their allocation to unequal positions in the labour market (Satzewich, 1990, 1991). The job market and broader experiences of permanent settlers were fundamentally different from Carribeans who arrived in the mid-1960s and who were locked into temporary jobs under lower pay and poorer working conditions. The concept 'mode of incorporation' facilitates the analysis of the multiple racialisations and of the heterogeneity of experiences of racism as it further eschews reductionist and functionalist problems associated with a singular set of foreign worker experiences (Satzewich, 1991, p. 35).

Racialisation, Racism, Thais and Filipinos

Cheng (2004) argues that Taiwan's domestic employers construct and naturalise the 'Otherness' of their female guest employees along an 'axis of difference', utilising imagined foreign national identities, nationally-based class differences and 'racial' characteristics, integral to their economic, political and social marginalisation in Taiwan. Taiwan's employers of domestic labour evoke images of the supposed superiority of their own 'race' and imagined national culture in order to define the class inferiority of their domestics, regardless of economic and social background, and this in turn legitimates the domestic helpers' low wages and often insufferable working conditions (Cheng, p. 56).

There is an element of Cheng's impressive study which makes the overall thesis less than convincing — her treatment of guest worker 'Otherness' as an all-pervasive subordinated experience.

The fact that Taiwan's domestic helpers labour under substantially similar conditions has contributed to Cheng's treatment of guest worker otherness. All guest workers earn the minimum monthly wage of NT$15,840. However, in early 2007, about 54% of them were employed outside the domestic help industry — in building and construction and in particular manufacturing (Council of Labor

Affairs, 2007a), and the ways in which these guest workers were racialised varied appreciably between nationalities as well as industries of employment.

Taiwan had some 342,000 legal guest workers in February 2007, 3.2% of the total workforce (Council of Labor Affairs, 2007a). Just over 53% of these migrants were Thais and Filipinos (a roughly equal number of each), 27% were Indonesians and 20% were Vietnamese (Council of Labor Affairs, 2007b). Manufacturing employed slightly less than 50% of the aggregate guest worker population. About 3.5% worked in building and construction (Council of Labor Affairs, 2007c).

The ethnic and gender divisions of labour revealed clear patterns. The vast majority of Indonesians and Vietnamese were women employed as domestic helpers, although there was also a large presence of Filipino women in this sector. In February 2007, Thais and Filipinos represented 47% and 34% respectively of guest worker jobs in manufacturing (Council of Labor Affairs, 2007c). The bulk of Thai factory workers, male and female alike, were concentrated in labour-intensive sectors, dominated by sweatshops producing textiles, leather and fur, pulp and paper, rubber products and so forth. Conversely, Filipinos — mostly men — greatly outnumbered the Thais in capital intensive manufacturing, comprising a large number of technologically advanced companies in electronic components and computer technology, radio and television production. About 82% of migrants in construction were Thais.

The 'ghettoisation' of Thai workers in small sweatshops intensifies their exposure to despotic management practices, to dirt and grime, and to the increased risk of injury and illness. However, the construction sector is even worse, as job opportunities are concentrated in the subcontracting sphere, which has a reputation of bypassing Taiwans' already weak occupational health and safety laws and of evading workers' compensation (Tierney, 2005). Thai building and construction workers suffer these problems disproportionately.

Thais are overwhelmingly drawn from their country's rural-based and economically underdeveloped north and north east regions, with fewer traditions of industrial activism than the Filipinos, who are largely derived from large industrial cities back home (Tierney, 2006). Employers and employees typically label Thai workers as 'buffalo', which conjures images of a greater preparedness to work long hours, while remaining timid in the face of unceasing calls for overtime, without due payment, and under dangerous conditions.

Anecdotal evidence suggests that employers and managers, as well as officials employed in the Council of Labour Affairs (the government instrumentality responsible for allocating jobs to foreign workers), began to apply the buffalo label at the very outset of the guest worker program in order to legitimate the concentration of Thais in sweatshops and building sites. Buffalo legitimates the Thais' incorporation into labour market sectors which other nationalities of guest workers, and the local Taiwanese, are unprepared to enter.

Guest workers can be repatriated to their home countries and this constitutes one of the most terrible forms of state violence against imported labour. Early repatriation can be made for any reason, and alleged inefficiency on the job is one. Oftentimes, accusations of inefficiency are accompanied by bullying, as a Thai process worker in a footwear plant explains:

> Supervisors really like[d] to give us a threat of deducting our salary or sending us back home. We were all scared to be sent back home, especially in the early period because we [had] not yet paid back all the [brokers'] debt yet. (Quoted in Yimprasert, 2000, p. 5)

Deportation is one of the reasons why guest workers infrequently resist oppressive practices in the labour process. It is also associated with and supported by racist images of 'inferior' social class backgrounds, of 'unsophisticated' foreign cultures, of darker and (by definition) 'repulsive' skin pigmentations, and of 'backward' nationalities (Tierney, 2006). Almost invariably, early repatriation follows police harassment and violence and is legitimated by reference to the 'national interest' — only the most compliant should be permitted to participate in this 'tiger' economy.

Many employers appreciate the Filipinos' English language skills, industrial experience and relatively high levels of education. However, they are also prepared to apply negative and demeaning labels to justify violence against them. Employers, foreign labour broker firms, politicians and civil servants share the perception that Filipinos tend to be 'complainers', 'whingers', and 'troublemakers' (Tierney, 2006). They believe that Filipinos are more willing to strike than any other foreign nationality (Tierney, 2002, pp. 151–152). These labels, in turn, legitimate police 'crackdowns' on Filipinos.

These crackdowns are supposed to rid Taiwan of illegal workers, who are somewhat evenly represented across nationalities. One would expect that all guest worker nationalities are evenly targeted in crackdowns. However, church-based groups in Taiwan contend that Filipinos disproportionately suffer from harassment in police raids — not because they are more heavily represented among illegals but because the state is prepared to resort to violence in order to intimidate a cohort deemed to be militant (Tierney, 2007). Corporate and state violence has always been fundamental to Taiwan's guest worker system and to ruling class expectations of compliance and docility. The existence of foreign troublemakers directly violates these expectations.

Racism of Exclusion

Much of the racism of migrant exclusion in Taiwan emanates from the labour unions' idea that the guest worker program has been a major cause of local unemployment (Tierney, 2007, pp. 211–213). In the second half of the 1990s, annual unemployment rates in Taiwan roughly accorded with the intake of imported labour. Between 2000 and 2005, unemployment rose from 3% to 4.3%. During this period, unemployment overtook guest worker intakes — in 2005 there were some

314,000 legal migrant workers and 429,000 unemployed locals. Labour unions have long accused employers of replacing local labour with cheaper foreign labour.

While there is some evidence of replacement of local labour by migrants (Chan, 1999), caution is recommended to those who make exaggerated claims that these problems have long been out of control. There is little indication that unemployed locals are prepared to reenter the types of jobs that they vacated to the migrants almost 2 decades ago. Wu Chun-ming (until 2003, Director of the Work Permit Division of the Council of Labour Affairs) has spoken publicly against perspectives linking the guest worker system to rising unemployment. At a policy conference on foreign workers, organised by the council in June 1999, Wu stated that the 'unemployed are those whose industries have closed. Foreign workers do not have anything to do with the unemployment problem' (Tierney, 2007, p. 212). In November 2000, Wu made a similar contention to the author, emphasising that there was little or no evidence that local workers were prepared to engage in the so-called 3-D (dirty, demeaning and dangerous) jobs and that the main source of unemployment was the outflow of manufacturing capital to cheaper labour countries in Asia (Wu Chun-ming, personal communication, November 29, 2000).[1]

Some union organisations have called for the abolition of the guest worker program altogether, as instanced in January 1998 when representatives and supporters of the Taiwan Labor Front, regarded as one of the principal organs of Democratic Progressive Party influence in the union movement, carried posters outside the Council of Labour Affairs headquarters in Taipei, calling for some kind of 'humane' repatriation, carrying banners stating: 'Send Back Immigrant Labour Now' (Tierney, 2007, p. 212).

The labour unions are rarely interested in recruiting guest workers (Tierney, 2007, p. 213). This estrangement of guest workers from organised labour has contributed to union leaders' and members' reluctance to extend support to guest workers in the event of corporate and police abuse. It has also brought about the absence or marginalisation of migrants at rallies. Migrants are welcomed at demonstrations only in so far as they bolster attendance figures (Reverend Alexander Doan, personal communication, January 7, 2001).[2]

Racism and Dysfunctionality

The application of differential racist stigmas and the indifference and hostility of the unions played a part in the 8-hour bloody protest between 200–300 guest workers at the Formosa Plastics sixth naptha cracker plant in Mailiao on September 5, 1999, in which Thai and Filipina men attacked each other, using pipes, rocks and petrol bombs as weapons (Kung, 1999). Twenty people were seriously injured. At the time, the plant employed some 18,000 guest workers, including some 8500 Thais, more than 7300 Filipinos and 1700 Indonesians (Yu Sen-Len, 1999).

The protest was sparked by claims about the monopolisation of public telephone facilities in the dormitories. Church groups and sympathetic local labour activists blamed high broker fees, the overcrowded work-based dormitory conditions, the lack of competent translators (one for every two hundred residents), speed-up pressures, bullying managerial styles and the compulsion to work under unsafe conditions (Lin, 1999; Shu, 1999).

These explanations, though plausible, may not have exhausted all of the causes. My interviews with Filipina and Thai workers in Chung-li, some twelve months after the riot, indicated Thai concentration in the worst jobs and of corresponding Thai perceptions of 'Filipina privilege' at the workplace. According to some interviewees, these factors played a part in the explosion of resentment against those reaping such privilege. However, this evidence was anecdotal and far from optimally reliable, sourced from guest workers who did not witness the riot as they were hundreds of kilometres distant from it and had only heard 'stories' about it. Unfortunately, the author was unable to interview Thais and Filipinos working at Mailiao because they feared the possibility of retribution by the employers (especially the major contractor, Formosa Plastics), by broker companies and by the police.

Some union leaders claimed that the event demonstrated that migrant 'violence' represented a threat to national security and called for either significant reductions in migrant intakes or the abolishment of the guest worker program altogether. The Council of Labour Affairs immediately deported three men — all Filipinos. This effectively absolved Formosa Plastics, the 44 subcontracting companies at the Mailiao site, together with the broker firms, of any responsibility. It also pardoned the Thai workers directly involved in the riot. The longstanding stigma of troublemakers was decisive in this response. Along with the horror of the violence, which thousands of people had been forced to witness — guest workers and locals alike, the council's hostility towards the Filipinos encouraged 531 employees at Formosa Plastics to return to their home country early — all Filipinos ('Foreign workers pack their bags', p. 2).

Although Formosa and its subcontractors were able to avoid any responsibility for the interethnic hostilities, they now experienced the unavailability of labour. The deported guest workers were not replaced by local workers because of the latter's desire to avoid 3-D jobs and Formosa found it difficult attract new guest workers. The labour shortfall endured for several months, which caused lengthy delays in meeting production targets and lower than normal profit rates.

Class Struggle and Interethnic Solidarity

Guest worker militancy against racism also has the potential to mobilise migrants across ethnic backgrounds and to unite guest and local workers in solidarity. Such demonstrations of militancy occurred during the long dispute at the Ching Yang factory in T'aoyuan in 1998 and more recently at the Formosa plant in Mailiao in March 2006.

In October 1998, local, Thai and Filipina workers employed at Ching Yang organised a demonstration to force their employer, who had closed down the establishment, to pay NT$6.8 million in wages that were owed. In response, the Council of Labour Affairs allegedly telephoned the Philippines de facto embassy in Taipei, threatening police arrests and deportation, on the grounds of national security (Minns & Tierney, 2005). This further strengthened unity between the Ching Yang workers and, on the 16th of that month, almost 100 foreigners and 80 locals 'stormed' the office of the Taipei Labour Affairs Bureau, demanding equal rights for all employees participating in demonstrations, irrespective of nationality (Minns & Tierney, 2005). The bureau permitted a meeting with elected employee representatives, locals and foreigners alike. They continued to demonstrate and not one was arrested. The bureau resolved to find employment for Ching Yang's guest workers for the duration of their visas.

The upshot was a greater preparedness of these and other guest workers to resist exploitation and repression. Guest workers represented about 15% of the aggregate demonstrators at a rally the following month for shorter working hours (far exceeding their relatively small presence in the Taipei job market). One of the Ching Yang migrants managed to address the rally — an unprecedented action (Minns & Tierney, 2005). The labour leaders may not have approved of the guest workers' interventions in the rally but the rank and file applauded them nonetheless.

Ever since the disastrous protests of Thais and Filipinos at Formosa Plastics in 1999, the site has comprised many migrant activists determined to foster interethnic solidarity. It would seem their efforts have been successful. On March 13 and 14, 2006, some 3000 Thais and Filipinos at Mailiao, representing 60% of the site's Filipina and Thai workforce, went on strike demanding that Formosa pay the broker fees in full, together with workplace insurance. Fearing a protracted battle, the company agreed to pay brokers NT$18,000 for each foreign worker employed at the site — an unusual position for a Taiwanese company which employed guest workers to find itself in. Several migrant lobbies were active in the dispute — as everyone expected — but so too were representatives of the Chinese Federation of Labour, the island's largest labour body. The federation has also intervened in the attempted deportation of a Filipina woman on who had close associations with the Catholic Rerum Novarum Labour Centre in Taipei (Huang, 2005).

Conclusion

The operations of the free market and of the capitalist state ensure not only the continuance of racism but also its intensification. This is due, in part, to the role the state plays in racialising imported labour. The racialisation of guest workers engenders the racism of exploitation, while the exclusionist practices of the labour unions create the racism of exclusion.

Taiwan's guest workers are concentrated in the lower echelons of the labour market and earn the lowest wages; however, their labour market experiences are not homogeneous. The divergent ways in which employers and the state have racialised foreign labour has meant that guest workers do not engage in substantially similar work. In manufacturing and building and construction, the workplace experiences of Filipina and Thai workers vary significantly and the construction of racist stigmas has legitimated their unequal sites of labour market incorporation. Racist stigmatisation reinforces widespread perceptions of docility (in the case of Thais) and legitimates state violence against those who are seen to be less likely to adhere to expectations of compliance (Filipinos).

Taiwan's employers and managers, together with state officials, may exploit racist hostility to divide the working class and to promote capital accumulation but they do so under economic and political risks. Formosa and its subsidiaries faced a protracted dearth of labour in the aftermath of 1999 protest at Mailiao and found it impossible to meet production targets for several months afterwards. Employers and managers discovered, during the 2006 dispute in Mailiao, that inter-ethnic hostilities between Thais and Filipinos had long ceased to exist, forcing the Formosa company into paying its guest workers' brokers' fees. Class struggle has also engendered solidarity between local and foreign workers, forcing at least some leaders of the Chinese Federation of Labour to abandon its exclusionist practices against guest workers. Though most union leaders are unwilling to follow suit, the evidence suggests that struggles by guest workers, supported by locals, may break down this racism of exclusion emanating from the union bureaucracy.

Endnotes

1   Place of interview: Council of Labour Affairs Head Office, Taipei, Work Permit Division. Translator: Ho Hseuh-cheng (MA Hons student, Institute of International Relations, National Chengchi University of Taiwan). Transcript held by the author.

2   Catholic Hope Workers' Centre, Chung-li Taiwan, interviewed January 7, 2001. No translator required. Transcript held by the author.

References

Bernstein, A. (2005). *The capitalist manifesto: The historic, economic and philosophic case for laissez-faire.* Lanham, MD: University Press of America.

Callinicos, A. (1993). *Race and class.* London: Bookmarks.

Castles, S., & Kosack, G. (1973). *Immigrant workers and class structure in western Europe.* Oxford: Oxford University Press.

Castles, S. (1996). The racisms of globalisation. In E. Vasta & S. Castles (Eds.), *The teeth are smiling: The persistence of racism in multicultural Australia* (pp. 17–45). Sydney, Australia: Allen and Unwin.

Chan, R. (1999). Taiwan's policy towards foreign workers. *Journal of Contemporary Asia, 29*(3), 383–400.

Cheng, S-J. A. (2004). Contextual politics of difference in transnational care: The rhetoric of Filipina domestics' employers in Taiwan. *Feminist Review, 77,* 46–64.

Council of Labor Affairs. (2007a). *Monthbook of Labor Statistics.* March. Tables 2–2 and 11–1. Retrieved April 9, 2007, from http://statdb.cla.gov.tw/html/mon/monehidx11.htm

Council of Labor Affairs. (2007b). *Monthbook of Labor Statistics*. March. Tables 11–1 and 11–2. Retrieved April 9, 2007, from http://statdb.cla.gov.tw/html/mon/c11010.htm

Council of Labor Affairs. (2007c). *Monthbook of Labor Statistics*. March. Table 11–3. Retrieved April 9, 2007, from http://statdb.cla.gov.tw/html/mon/monehidx11.htm

Foreign workers pack their bags. (1999, September 9). *Taipei Times*, p. 2.

Huang, J. (2005, August 29). Thugs, lies and anarchy mark domestic workers' lives. *Taipei Times*, p. 3.

Griffiths, P. (2005). Racism: Whitewashing the class divide. In R Kuhn (Ed.), *Class and struggle in Australia* (pp. 159–176). Sydney, Australia: Pearson.

Kung, L. (1999). Migrant workers are not scapegoats. *Migrants and Locals*, nos. 2–3. Retrieved July 16, 2006, from http://61.222.52.195/net/mars/index_03.htm

Lin, E. (1999, September). *Foreign labour changes the face of Taiwan*. Philippines Church Commission. Unpublished manuscript.

Mahamdallie, H. (2002). Racism: Myths and realities. *International Socialism Journal*, 95. Retrieved April 15, 2007, from http://pubs.socialistreviewindex.org.uk/isj95/mahamdallie.htm

Miles, R. (1982). *Racism and migrant labour*. London: Routledge and Kegan Paul.

Minns, J., & Tierney, R. (2005). Class and class struggle in Taiwan. *Bulletin of Labour Research*, 18, July, 79–117.

Rath, J. (1999). The Netherlands: A Dutch treat for anti-social families and immigrant ethnic minorities. In M. Cole & G. Dale (Eds.), *The European Union and migrant labour* (pp. 147–170). Oxford: Berg Publishers.

Reisman, G. (1982). *Capitalism: The cure for racism*, Jefferson School of Philosophy, Economics and Psychology. Retrieved April 11, 2007, from http://www.capitalism.net/excerpts/1-931089-07-8.pdf. Unpublished manuscript.

Satzewich, V. (1990). Rethinking post-1945 migration to Canada: Towards a political economy of labour migration. *International Migration*, 28(3), 327–346.

Satzewich, V. (1991). *Racism and the incorporation of foreign labour*. London: Routledge.

Shu, T. (1999, September). *About the conflict at Mailiao*. Labour Rights Association. Unpublished manuscript.

Sintonen, T. (2006). Racism and business ethics. *Electronic Journal of Business Ethics and Organization Studies*, 11(1), 1–5.

Solomos, J., & Black, L. (1999). Marxism, racism, and ethnicity. In R.D. Torres, L.F. Miron & J.X. Inda (Eds.), *Race, identity and citizenship: A reader* (pp. 65–78). Malden and Oxford: Blackwell.

Tierney, R. (1996). Migrants and class in postwar Australia. In R. Kuhn & T. O'Lincoln (Eds.), *Class and class conflict in Australia* (pp. 95–113). Melbourne, Australia: Longman.

Tierney, R. (2002). Foreign workers and capitalist class relations in Taiwan: A study of economic isolation and political exploitation. *Bulletin of Labour Research*, 12, 125–165.

Tierney, R. (2005). *Foreign workers and occupational health and safety concerns in Taiwan*. Unpublished manuscript.

Tierney, R. (2006). *Foreign workers and the construction of a racist nationalism in Taiwan*. Unpublished manuscript.

Tierney. R. (2007). The guest labour system in Taiwan: Labor market considerations, wage injustices and the politics of labor hire brokerage. *Critical Asian Studies*, 39(2), 205–228.

Yimprasert, J. (2000). *Taiwan shoemakers: Thai Workers*. Thai Labour Campaign, October. Retrieved April 11, 2007, from http://www.thailabour.org/docs/TaiwanShoes.html

Yu Sun-Len. (1999, September 8). Rioting ends, problems remain. *Taipei Times*, p. 2

Part 2

Human Management Issues in the Integrated World

The Evolution of Human Resource Development in Australian Firms: Towards a More Strategic Function

Andrew Smith

It is commonly assumed that Australian employers chronically under-invest in the training of their employees and show little inclination to increase their training effort in response to government initiatives (Smith, 1998, p. 10). Much of this belief is based on the results of successive surveys of employer training expenditure in Australia and some notoriously unreliable international comparative data. Since 1989 the Australian Bureau of Statistics (ABS) has conducted five surveys of employer training expenditure (ABS, 1990a, 1991, 1994a, 1997a, 2003). The original survey conducted as a pilot in 1989 indicated that only 22% of Australian employers carried out any form of training for their employees and that an average of 2.2% of payroll costs was invested in training activities with employees receiving, on average, 22 hours of training per annum.

This data, together with the results from some international comparisons of incentive schemes to promote higher levels of enterprise investment in training, provided a significant part of the case for the then federal Labor government enacting the Training Guarantee Scheme in 1990. This scheme operated from 1990 to 1996 (although it was technically suspended in 1994) and required Australian enterprises with payroll costs of over A$200,000 to spend at least 1.5% of their payroll on the provision of 'structured' training for their employees or pay an equivalent levy to the Australian Taxation Office. Assessments of the effectiveness of the Training Guarantee in raising the level of training expenditure in Australia vary, but it is generally accepted that the scheme failed to lift training provision for the majority of employees in any significant or lasting fashion (Teicher, 1995). Subsequent iterations of the Employer Training Expenditure survey (TES) have tended to confirm the original rather gloomy assessment of the state of enterprise training in Australia.

The data from the Training Expenditure surveys has also prompted commentators to draw the conclusion that Australian employer commitment to training has declined since the abolition of the Training Guarantee in the mid-1990s. For instance, in a paper for the Dusseldorp Skills Foundation, Hall, Buchanan, and Considine (2002) argue cogently that there has been a flight of employers from training since the repeal of the Training Guarantee Act in 1996. This, combined with Australia's poor comparative performance on investment in knowledge, education and the creation of high skill jobs, they argue, means that the Australian economy is in a low skills equilibrium (Finegold & Soskice, 1988) and there is little evidence of strong training culture amongst Australian employers.

However, these are very broad claims to be based on a selective interpretation of the employer training statistics. It is far from clear that this pessimistic view of the state of industry training in Australia is justified given the range of data now available on the incidence of enterprise training. Data from the 2002 survey of training expenditure (ABS, 2003), shows that the incidence of employer-sponsored training appears to be increasing. The proportion of Australian workers undertaking work related training grew from 30% of the workforce in 1993 to 45% in 2001. A total of 37% of workers completed at least one work-related training course in 2001 and the proportion of workers completing on-the-job training grew from 6% in 1996 to 69% in 2000. Despite the apparent decline in employer training expenditure since the mid-1990s, the majority of Australian workers seem to be receiving some form of training from their employers and many are undertaking formal, off-the-job training in their firms.

Further support for a more optimistic view of the incidence of industry training in Australia is provided by the Business Longitudinal Survey (BLS) (ABS, 1999). This survey comprises a composite of data gathered from a sample of business on the ABS business register. The BLS gathers data primary on business and financial performance of enterprises, but also includes some simple questions on the provision of training to employees. In 1997/98, the BLS data indicated that 54% of enterprises provided training to their employees and 23% provided structured training. While these figures fall between the data provided by the TES and TPS, it is important to note that the BLS collects data from enterprises with less than 200 employees. Thus, large enterprises are under-represented in the sample. This suggests that a higher rather than a lower estimate of industry training is warranted by the ABS data overall. Estimates of the number of employees receiving training from their employers in the period of the survey suggest that 68% received on-the-job training whilst 46% received structured training.

In summary, it appears from the information provided by different sets of data that a significant amount of training is being provided by Australian employers, and it may be higher than the current orthodoxy suggests. Some 80% of Australian workers report receiving some form of training from their employers. Over 80% of Australian employers claim to be providing some form of training for their employees. Between one third and one half of Australian workers are taking part in formal, structured training in the workplace with 70% of workers taking part in on-the-job training. Over 40% of Australian employers claim to provide structured training.

New Systems of Learning and Development

Research carried out in Australia since the mid-1990s has shown that the nature of training has changed rapidly in response to both the new competitive environment and to changes in vocational education and training policy.

Australian research in the mid-1990s developed a model of employer training developed to explain the interaction of firm level factors that influenced the decisions that enterprises took to train their employees (Smith & Hayton, 1999). The model is illustrated in Figure 1. The researchers made three key observations that relate to the development of employer training in Australian enterprises at that time. First, workplace change was a key driver for employer training. Thus the research confirmed the growing strength of the link between training and organisation development. Second, the research found that individuals played an increasingly important role in their access to training from their employers. Enterprises reported that training needs were increasingly fragmented to the individual level and that they were progressively abandoning the traditional approach to training programs that saw large groups of employees receive the same training, regardless of individual need.

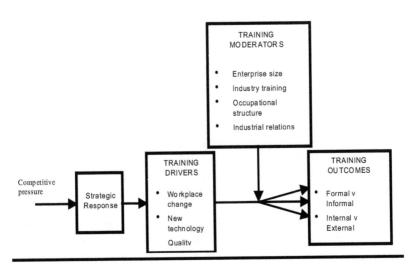

Figure 1

Model of enterprise training.

Source: Australian Bureau of Statistics (1990a, 1991, 1994a, 1997a).

Finally, based on Hendry's (1991) model which posited a strong link between training and corporate strategy for large UK firms, the research examined the relationship between training and business strategy. The results were mixed. Among senior managers in larger enterprises, there was a clear awareness of the importance of linking their investments in training to the strategy of the business. However, in small- and medium-sized enterprises and among middle and junior level managers, this perception was missing. Apart from the very large enterprises, few Australian enterprises that time appeared to possess a well-documented business strategy, which meant that much of the training observed and recorded in the research was operational in character and designed to meet the short-term needs of the enterprises.

In the late 1990s, a team of researchers from Charles Sturt University built on the model of employer training and investigated in more depth the relationship between employer training and organisational change in Australian enterprises (Smith, Oczkowski, Noble, & Macklin, 2003). In terms of the development of employer training, this research produced a number of useful findings suggesting that the emergence of new approaches to training first observed in the model of employer training earlier. First, the link between training and business strategy was far more pronounced in this research than had been the case previously. In modelling the strength of the impact of various enterprise level factors on the implementation of training, the research clearly showed that the link to business strategy was the most influential factor. Where enterprises made a strong link between their training and their business strategies, the result was a substantial increase in all forms of training and greater embedding of training into the management of the enterprise through the creation of training departments, use of formal training planning process and use of workplace trainers. The qualitative research suggested that many more enterprises were conscious of the importance of linking training to business strategy in order to capitalise more effectively on their training investments. The impact of business strategy on training was far greater than other factors that were tested in the research including the size of the enterprise, the competitive intensity of the market and the presence of a union in the workplace.

Second, the research underscored the individualisation of training that had been recorded in the model of employer training research. The results from the research showed that enterprises had largely abandoned the uniform, internal training approach in favour of training linked more clearly too individual performance management. Individuals were expected to increasingly take responsibility for their own training and secure their own employability in a contingent labour market. Thus, enterprises were shaping their training towards the fulfilment of individualised needs in order to enhance performance. Thirdly, training had become more decentralised in line with predictions from international research into the impact of the learning organisation on training provision

(Raper, Ashton, Felstead, & Storey, 1997). Large, centralised training departments were disappearing and the role of the trainer was changing from one of delivery to one of brokering training within the organisation and from external providers. Responsibility for training and the development of the skills of employees was increasingly viewed as the realm of the line manager and often appeared as a performance target for managers in larger enterprises.

The research confirmed the increasing strength of the link between the three classic elements of human resource development — individual career development, organisational development and training (McLagan, 1989). Enterprises appeared to have become more conscious of the need to get significant returns on their investments in training and were linking their training more closely to the business strategies of their enterprises. Thus, the strategic dimension that had been missing in the mid-1990s appeared to be gaining strength a few years later. Enterprises were also looking in-house for their training requirements. Nevertheless, the vocational education training (VET) system was not seen to be an effective partner in the search for better training.

Integrating With the VET System

Recent research has focused on the impact of nationally recognised training on larger Australian enterprises (Smith, E. Pickersgill, Smith, A, & Rushbrook, 2005). This research built on the changes to the VET system in Australia that have occurred in recent years. In particular, it is couched in the development of Training Packages. The research showed that the introduction of training packages has led to a massive increase in the uptake of nationally-recognised training amongst Australian enterprises. Many groups of workers in areas such as retail, hospitality and process manufacturing which have hitherto received very little employer sponsored training are now being offered not only training but also national, recognised qualifications by their employers. The research shows that among enterprises offering nationally-recognised training, the training effort is now more evenly distributed across the workforce with larger numbers of operational employees receiving training. This development is thus changing the chronic skewing of training distribution in enterprises to professional and managerial employees.

In some enterprises, the introduction of nationally recognised training has had a major impact on the development of employer training. The survey evidence in the research shows that nearly half of Enterprise Registered Training Organisations (Enterprise RTOs) are using the competency standards in the training packages to revise their recruitment, selection, and job classification and performance management systems. The use of competency standards in performance management is borne out in the case study component of the research, which shows that some enterprise RTOs have redesigned their performance management system to tie in tightly with the sequence of qualifications that they offer.

Thus, the qualifications become steps on promotional pathways for all levels of workers. Other enterprise RTOs have redesigned their training functions to become brokers, rather than deliverers, of training with the emphasis on the skill of the training co-coordinators to navigate their way through the national VET system rather than devise and deliver in-house programs of training.

The research demonstrates that the rapid adoption of training packages by Australian enterprises and the extension of nationally-recognised training are reshaping the training function in some Australian enterprises. The use of the competency standards embodied in training packages, together with the development of suites of qualifications for a large numbers of formerly untrained occupations, is pulling together the three elements of human resource development (HRD) — training, career development and organisation development — into a single learning and development function within larger enterprises in Australia. The development of this function has led to emergence of a new form of learning and development practitioner. This practitioner is very familiar with the national VET system and how to navigate it for the benefit of the enterprise. They have often been practitioners within the VET system — as senior managers in training providers or in intermediary bodies such as Industry Training Advisory Bodies — before taking up training management positions within business. With the changing nature of employer training in these enterprises, a new title has emerged for this field of practice — learning and development. This is quite consciously differentiated from the old training and development functions that used to dominate the training scene in Australian enterprises. The emergence of the learning and development function, with its internal emphasis on the integration of training with career and organisation development and business strategy, on the one hand and with the external VET system on the other constitutes a new learning and development system, perhaps unique to Australian enterprises.

As enterprises have increased their use of nationally-recognised training and their involvement with the VET system, they have also learned how this form of training can be integrated more effectively with career progression and organisational change processes leading to the development of a new approach to training in Australian enterprises. Whereas the United States model of human resource development is focused very firmly on the enterprise and the development of programs that meet the unique needs of each enterprise, the Australian approach of learning and development has emerged in relation to the national training system and the adaptation of national training systems to the needs of the enterprise. It is this integration of employer training with the national training system that is the unique feature of the new systems of learning and development in Australia.

Towards a New Approach

The results of these research projects track the development of employer training in Australian enterprises over a 10-year period from 1994 to 2003. The projects show the gradual development of a more integrated and strategic approach to training in Australian enterprises over this time. The model of enterprise training research in the mid-1990s established the strong link between the provision of training at the enterprise level with the major processes of organisational change that were common at that time, especially improvements to quality assurance. The project on enterprise training and new management practices showed that by the late 1990s, organisational change had become the major driver of the provision of training at the enterprise level. This research also suggested that the development of a more integrated approach to training in Australian enterprises had gone further with the individualisation of training demonstrating a link between training and individual career development and, perhaps more importantly, the apparent development of a stronger link between training and business strategy.

Thus, by the late 1990s, it appears that an integrated approach to employer training was emerging in Australian enterprises which brought together training, career development and organisation development with a growing relationship to the business strategy of the enterprise. The recent research into enterprises' use of nationally-recognised training suggests that this more integrated approach has now progressed in many Australian enterprises with the roll out of training packages to industry since 1997. Enterprises that provide nationally-recognised training either as RTOs in their own right or in partnership with training providers are not only providing more training for their employees, they are distributing that training to the most under-trained groups in the workforce at the operational level in their organisations. These enterprises are also increasingly integrating nationally recognised training with other human resource management systems such as performance management and selection/recruitment.

Why have these developments taken place? The industrial relations and VET policy context of Australia in the 1990s may provide some answers to this question. The early to mid-1990s was also a period of change to the Australian industrial relations system. Starting in 1987, the Australian Industrial Relations Commission led the way to the reform of the traditional system of industrial awards which have governed working conditions since the early 20th century. Under the process of award restructuring, industrial awards were simplified with job classification system reduced to shorter, clearer career paths for workers in most industries and occupations.

At the same time, the Australian VET system was beginning the decade-long process of reforms commonly referred to as the National Training Reform Agenda (NTRA). Launched by the federal Labor government in the early 1990s, the NTRA was concerned with creating a standards-based and national system of VET from the eight state-based training systems that had existed in Australian since federation (Smith & Keating, 2003). Then reforms centred on the development of national industry competency standards developed by tripartite bodies which became the basis for the universal introduction of competency-based training into the VET system. The process was overseen by a new national strategic training authority, the Australian National Training Authority (ANTA) which controlled the funding of VET through the states and territories. Of particular interest in the area of enterprise training was the introduction of a levy-like system to encourage employers to invest in training, the Training Guarantee Scheme in 1990. Under the Training Guarantee employers had to spend 1.5% of their payroll costs of eligible structured training or forfeit an equivalent amount to the Australian Taxation Office.

Together, these processes of award restructuring and training reform provided an unprecedented boost to the level of training activity in Australian enterprises. The more recent research confirms this picture of a policy-led expansion of training in Australian enterprises. There have been a few key developments, particularly in VET policy, that have prompted this evaluation. First, the creation of a significant private training market with access to government funds for training has considerably expanded employer choice of training provider. Enterprises are no longer locked into working with the public training providers (TAFE institutes) and the success of private training providers has put considerable pressure on public providers to become far more responsive to industry training requirements. Second, the expansion of the apprenticeship and traineeship system since the mid-1990s supported by government employment and training incentives has encouraged many more employers to buy into the national training system by employing trainees or putting their existing workers through traineeships (Robinson, 2001). Third, the ability of enterprises to become RTOs and to provide nationally-recognised training in their own right has encouraged the spread of structured training in those enterprises where external providers did not have the resources or the credibility to operate. Finally, the introduction of training packages, as discussed above, has helped to spread nationally recognised training into industries and occupations that have not traditionally provided their employees with much training.

Taken together, these policy developments have led to the development of a cadre of enterprise training staff who are very familiar with the VET system and know how to use it to benefit their organisations (Chappell & Johnston, 2003). As enterprises have increased their use of nationally recognised training and their involvement with the VET system, they have also learned how this form of training can be integrated more effectively with career progression and organisation change processes leading to the development of a new approach to training in Australian enterprises. Whereas the US model of HRD is focused very firmly on the enterprise and the development of programs that meet the unique needs of each enterprise, the Australian approach of learning and development has emerged in relation to the national training system and the adaptation of national training systems to the needs of the enterprise. It is this integration of enterprise level training with the national training system that is the unique feature of learning and development in Australia.

References

Australian Bureau of Statistics. (1990a). *Employer training expenditure Australia, July to September 1989.* Canberra, Australia: AGPS.

Australian Bureau of Statistics. (1990b). *How workers get their training, Australia.* Canberra, Australia: AGPS.

Australian Bureau of Statistics. (1991). *Employer training expenditure Australia, July to September 1990.* Canberra, Australia: AGPS.

Australian Bureau of Statistics. (1994a). *Employer training expenditure Australia, July to September 1993.* Canberra, Australia: AGPS.

Australian Bureau of Statistics. (1994b). *Employer training practices, Australia 1993.* Canberra, Australia: AGPS.

Australian Bureau of Statistics. (1994c). *Training and education experience Australia, 1993.* Canberra, Australia: AGPS.

Australian Bureau of Statistics. (1997a). *Employer training expenditure Australia, July to September 1996.* Canberra, Australia: AGPS.

Australian Bureau of Statistics. (1997b). *Employer training practices, Australia 1996.* Canberra, Australia: AGPS.

Australian Bureau of Statistics. (1998). *Training and Education Experience Australia, 1997.* Canberra, Australia: AGPS.

Australian Bureau of Statistics. (1999). *Business longitudinal survey* [confidentialised unit record file]. Canberra, Australia: AGPS.

Australian Bureau of Statistics. (2002). *Training and education experience Australia, 2001.* Canberra, Australia: AGPS.

Australian Bureau of Statistics. (2003). *Employer training expenditure and practices, Australia.* Canberra, Australia: AGPS.

Chappell, C., & Johnston, R. (2003). *Changing work: Changing roles for vocational education and training teachers and trainers.* Adelaide, Australia: NCVER.

Finegold, D., & Soskice, D. (1988). The failure of British training: Analysis and prescription. *Oxford Review of Economic Policy, 4,* 21–53.

Hall, R., Buchanan, J., & Considine, G. (2002). *'You value what you pay for'. Enhancing employers' contributions to skill formation and use: A discussion paper for the Dusseldorp Skills Forum.* Sydney, Australia: Dusseldorp Skills Forum.

Hendry, C. (1991). Training and corporate strategy. In J. Stevens & R. MacKay (Eds.), *Training and competitiveness* (pp.79–110). London: Kogan Page.

McLagan, P. (1989). *Models for HRD practice.* St Paul, MN: ASTD Press.

Raper, P., Ashton, D., Felstead, A., & Storey, J. (1997). Toward the learning organisation? Explaining current trends in training practice in the UK. *International Journal of Training and Development, 1*(1), 9–21.

Robinson, C. (2001). *Australian apprenticeships: Facts, fiction and future.* Adelaide, Australia: NCVER.

Smith, E., Pickersgill, R., Smith, A., & Rushbrook, P. (2005). *Enterprises' commitment to nationally recognised training.* Adelaide, Australia: NCVER.

Smith, A. (1998). *Training and development in Australia* (2nd ed.). Sydney, Australia: Butterworths.

Smith, A., Oczkowski, E., Noble, C., & Macklin, R. (2003). New management practices and enterprise training in Australia. *International Journal of Manpower, 24*(1), 31–47.

Smith, A., & Hayton, G. (1999). What drives enterprise training? Evidence from Australia. *International Journal of Human Resource Management, 10*(2), 251–272.

Smith, E., & Keating, J. (2003). *From training reform to training packages.* Wentworth Falls, Australia: Social Science Press.

Teicher, J. (1995). The training guarantee: A good idea gone wrong? In F. Ferrier & C. Selby Smith (Eds.), *The economics of education and training.* Canberra, Australia: AGPS.

Working Under AWAs: Perceptions From the Top

Val Siemionow

This chapter reports on perceptions of Senior Executive Service (SES) officers of the Australian Public Service (APS) on their transition to individual contracts under Australian Workplace Agreements (AWAs). It is based on the first part of a doctoral study on the impact of contract employment under Australian Workplace Agreements on performance management and accountability at the senior executive level of the Australian Public Service.

The data was gathered prior to the government's *Workplace Relations Amendment (Work Choices) Act 2005*. The 2005 Act reinforced AWAs, first introduced in the *Workplace Relations Act 1996*, as the government's preferred instrument for setting remuneration and employment conditions (Sappey et al., 2006, p. 2). As such, the findings remain relevant.

Background to Australian Workplace Agreements

When the Coalition took office following the 1996 election they brought with them a new industrial relations agenda based on individualised and market-driven workplace relations. This was formalised through the *Workplace Relations Act 1996 (WR Act)*, which introduced AWAs as the centrepiece of the government's workplace relations policy.

Much of the literature of the late 1990s (including the Australian Centre for Industrial Relations Research and Training [ACIRRT], 1999; Birmingham & Fox, 1997; Buchanan et al., 1998; Davis, Yeatman, & Sullivan, 1997; Deery, Plowman, & Walsh, 1997; Frazer, McCallum, & Ronfeldt, 1997; Gardner & Palmer, 1997; Hamberger, 1996; Heiler, 1998; O'Donnell, Allan, & Peetz, 1999; O'Donnell & O'Brien, 2000; Schroeder, 1997) approached the WR Act from its historical, political, ideological, legal, institutional, procedural and/or representational perspectives.

Gardner and Palmer (1997) saw the changes as shifts in the balance of power. The WR Act moved Australian workplace relations away from the arbitral model towards a framework based on 'private interest contractualism' (Gardner & Palmer, 1997, p. 37). They argued that bargaining now rested on assumptions that employers and employees were individual agents 'engaged in setting conditions of employment ... with only minimal recognition of the effects of the asymmetry of power between the employer and the individual employee' (Gardner & Palmer, 1997, p. 37).

ACIRRT (1999) found that people who traded off their conditions in the bargaining process were working longer and harder for less reward with less job security. The quality of jobs and people's relations at work was deteriorating, with greater earnings inequities and higher dispersion in income distribution.

This was at odds with the government's statements on the benefits of the new system. ACIRRT noted that 'growing numbers of Australians are being adversely affected by the rut within which policy is now stuck. Clearly we must move on to a more positive policy trajectory which simultaneously promotes fairness and efficiency at work' (ACIRRT, 1999, p. 176).

The 'official' view of the functioning of the WR Act, as put by the Department of Employment and Workplace Relations (DEWR) to a 2000 Senate committee, was that:

> The Workplace Relations Act 1996 (WR Act) is the Government's main vehicle for modernising workplace relations in Australia ... based on the principles of labour market flexibility; less regulated workplaces; a shift to employment arrangements being decided at individual enterprises and workplaces between employers and employees; and opportunities for better pay for higher productivity (and competitiveness). Agreement making at the workplace level is now at the core of the workplace relations system. Decentralised agreement making is aimed at allowing employers and employees to take direct responsibility for developing appropriate working arrangements that are tailored to the specific needs of the workplace. (Department of Employment, Workplace Relations and Small Business [DEWRSB], 2000, pp. 1–2)

Background to employment relations in the APS and to the SES
For most of the 20th century, the APS operated under tight central agency controls. The former Public Service Board was the central employing authority for determining all APS pay, job classification, and employment matters (Deery, Plowman, & Walsh, 1997; DEWRSB, 2000; Department of Industrial Relations [DIR], 1995, 1997; Gardner, 1993; Gardner & Palmer, 1997).

Agreements negotiated between central agencies and unions between 1992 and 1997 allowed agencies to develop their own agreements on a limited range of conditions; but were inhibited by centrally determined approaches and prescriptive, complex budgetary controls over gain-sharing arrangements (DEWRSB, 2000, p. 1).

Devolution of workplace relations accelerated after the 1996 election as the government pursued integrated public sector reforms in financial management, workplace relations and public sector employment (Schroeder, 1997). Their key policy features were promotion of greater labour market flexibility and less regulated workplaces.

Decision-making on employment arrangements at individual agency levels provided for workplace-based agreements between public sector employers and employees. This was seen as enabling employers and employees to take direct responsibility for working arrangements that could be tailored to specific workplace needs. The government argued this would provide opportunities for better pay, higher productivity and improved competitiveness.

According to DEWRSB (2000):

> The Government's APS workplace relations reforms have aimed to mainstream employment arrangements applying in the APS to those in the community more generally ...the APS has moved away from the excessive prescription and inflexibility of the traditional centralised system. Under current arrangements, terms and conditions of employment are decided at the agency level by agreement with employees through Australian Workplace Agreements (AWAs) and certified agreements (CAs). There is no longer a 'one size fits all' culture in the APS. Agencies are now delivering terms and conditions of service that are appropriate for their own employees and agencies' operating needs. This is particularly important as APS agencies are operating in an increasingly competitive environment where contestability, value for money, and efficient and effective services are essential. (DEWRSB, 2000, p. 2)

The 1997 policy parameters for agreement-making in the APS retained the SES as a three-tiered classification structure but determined that there be no maximum salary set for the three SES bands. The rationale was based on enabling agencies to attract and retain high quality personnel into the SES and pay appropriate rewards for high performance (DEWRSB, 1997, 1999a, 1999b; Taylor, 1997). There was a strong ideological perception of money as a prime attractor and performance motivator of high calibre people. Responsibility for SES employment and conditions was devolved to individual agency and departmental heads.

O'Donnell, Allan and Peetz (1999, p. 1) found that public sector employees 'were working more intensively, under greater stress and with less job security than private sector workers' with lower job satisfaction and a worse work/life balance than their private sector equivalents. They concluded that 'the reform agenda has imposed more discipline on the public sector than market forces have imposed on the private sector' (O'Donnell, Allan, & Peetz, 1999, p. 18) and that the:

> ... agenda to introduce market-based solutions, increase the prerogatives of managers, measure performance and cut costs, in particular labour costs, has tended to promote distrust, stress and dissatisfaction at the workplace and has been retarding the growth of high trust and non-authoritarian approaches to labour management. (O'Donnell, Allan, & Peetz 1999, p. 18)

AWAs were promoted as a tool for facilitating direct individual employer/ employee negotiations that would lead to greater flexibility resulting in more choice of outcomes and enabling improved performance management and accountability. The introduction of AWAs, combined with changes to the PS Act, changed basis of the SES employment relationship. What was unclear was the precise nature of that change.

Methodology

The theoretical framework for this study comes from the discipline areas of management (including human resource management, organisation development and organisational behaviour); employment relations; and public sector management.

The doctoral study on which this chapter is based explores SES perceptions of AWAs implementation, outcomes achieved under AWAs, relationships between AWAs and performance, and relationships between AWAs and accountability.

This chapter addresses the first two of these. It looks at SES perceptions on how their AWAs were implemented, outcomes achieved and some consequences for the APS (intended and unintended) of moving the SES onto AWAs.

The research commenced with a literature review on the WR Act, AWAs, contract employment, related Human Resources (HR) practices, performance and performance management, accountability, APS reforms and the SES. This was supported by archival searches on APS employment practices covering the introduction and use of AWAs, the SES, performance management and accountability in the APS. The review identified significant gaps in our knowledge on the way in which contract employment under AWAs impacted on people in organisations.

Data gathering commenced with an informal experience survey of SES officers who had moved onto AWAs and Human Resource Management (HRM) practitioners involved in introducing AWAs within their agencies.

This exploration reinforced the preliminary findings, helped narrow the topic, confirmed the practicality of the study, identified a number of data and information sensitivities, and enabled the development of survey and interview instruments.

The survey included both quantitative (Likert scale) and open-ended qualitative questions. The interviews targeted SES insights into contract employment under AWAs.

The instruments went through several iterations and were tested on some SES officers and academic staff at Charles Sturt University. Their feedback enabled the instruments to be finalised and data gathering proceeded.

Four APS agencies participated in this study: the Australian Taxation Office; the Department of Immigration Multicultural and Indigenous Affairs; the Department of Foreign Affairs and Trade; and the Department of Defence. There were 411 Australian-based SES officers employed in these agencies. A total of 77 (18.7%) of them responded to the survey and 15 participated in the interviews.

Table 1

SES Perceptions of Working Under AWAS (Based on Likert Scale Data)

Question	Disagree	Undecided	Agree
My AWA contract was individually negotiated between my employer and myself.	77.1%	6.5%	15.6%
I felt in control of the situation when negotiating my AWA.	80.5%	10.4%	9.1%
I entered into my AWA negotiations with a good understanding of the process.	32.5%	18.2%	49.4%
My expectations of the AWA process were fully met.	50.6%	19.5%	29.9%
I am satisfied with my AWA contract.	40.3%	13.0%	46.8%
I prefer working under an individual contract than under an enterprise agreement.	28.6%	37.7%	33.8%
I believe that under AWAs, everyone can win.	29.9%	31.2%	39.0%
I would like to see AWAs used more extensively throughout the APS.	39.0%	24.7%	36.4%
I would like to put all of my staff on AWAs.	64.9%	13.0%	22.1%
Working under an AWA is no different to working under an enterprise agreement.	42.9%	10.4%	46.8%

SES Perceptions of Working Under AWAs

When the survey was undertaken the SES had already been employed under AWAs for up to 6 years. Many were on contracts that had expired and they had either negotiated new AWAs or were in the process of doing so. The respondents therefore had considerable experience of working under AWAs and strong personal interests in the process. Tables 1 and 2 present SES officer perceptions of working under AWAs.

The majority of these perceptions are quite negative. Only 15.6% considered their AWA had been individually negotiated between themselves and their employer. The majority did not accept their AWA as an individually negotiated contract. This finding was strongly reinforced by the interviews. Fourteen of the fifteen interviewees responded very negatively on the AWA 'negotiation' process. Typical interviewee responses included:

> I don't think negotiation is an appropriate word. I'm not aware that there was negotiation … to me it was a subtle form of coercion … This is a very one-sided power structure … people aren't prepared to make too much noise about their AWA. (Interviewee 2)

> It wasn't. It was delivered. That simple … I rang and asked some questions because there were elements I didn't understand … told that was no matter of concern. (Interviewee 9)

> there's actually no negotiations on the AWA … You're given a template … a certain amount of time to sign up to it, and if you don't sign up to it you don't get a pay rise. I wouldn't call that negotiation. (Interviewee 15)

Only one of the fifteen expressed a positive attitude towards negotiation process, although what he described was restricted to a narrow range of issues and put limits on the 'individual' nature of the agreement.

> Our department uses a basic template approach for setting remuneration levels and conditions ... the outcomes tend to be at a similar level ... When we negotiate ... the officer is taken through the generic 'template' details for the common ingredients of the AWA. (Interviewee 1)

It appears that the APS's AWA implementation process adopted a 'one-size-fits-all' template-based approach with very limited individual variability. Based on the results above it is argued that the AWA is not an individual contract per se but an employer-initiated collective agreement that is signed individually.

Given this perception, it was unsurprising to find a significant majority (80.5%) reporting that they did not feel in control of the situation when 'negotiating' their AWAs.

Again, interviewee data supports this result. The key reasons given for the felt lack of control focused on the perceived compulsory nature of the process and the template based one-size-fits-all approach of the employing agencies. Many considered they had been coerced into their AWA, as illustrated in the following responses:

> I was not comfortable about the government pretending in Parliament that this was an open process and that all AWAs would be voluntary sign in ... the actual coercion that was underlying the whole deal was that if you didn't (sign) an AWA then you would stay on very old pay rates ... no mechanism to bring the old pay rates up in any way that anybody could see ... economically suicidal not to sign an AWA. To me that's dishonest at the Government level. (Interviewee 2)

> It was just something that I knew was going to happen. I mean it wasn't something you could resist in the organisation. (Interviewee 3)

> Even as a senior officer it's a given ... basically told 'this is the expectation, these are the terms and conditions, this is the salary'. It was a take it or leave it type thing. There's always the door. (Interviewee 9)

> Some people, perhaps a little naively, felt this was a chance for them to negotiate something specific. And of course in reality they couldn't. (Interviewee 14)

> I didn't feel comfortable with it 'cause it's inconsistent with the spirit of the AWA. (Interviewee 15)

Employees were not given a choice between AWAs and collective agreements. Several stated that the only options they had were to sign the AWA as presented to them, or to vacate their SES job through resignation, redundancy or transfer with a demotion. This indicated a level of coercion that severely restricted the freedom of choice provisions in the legislation and thus contravened it.

Another interesting result from Table 1 is that while just over a third of the SES would like to see AWAs used more extensively throughout the APS, only a fifth of them would like to move their own staff onto AWAs.

The data in Table 2 also presents a very negative set of perceptions on working under AWAs. The majority found nothing they liked about working under AWAs; nothing they gained by moving to AWAs; and no scope for negotiating different outcomes.

Table 2

SES Perceptions of Working Under AWAS (Based on Content Analysis)

Question	Most frequent response	Next most frequent response	Third most frequent response
What do you like most about working under an Australian Workplace Agreement?	Nothing (33.3%)	The potential to negotiate a tailored package (15.6%)	More Flexibility (9.1%)
What do you like least about working under an Australian Workplace Agreement?	No scope for negotiation (28.1%)	Nothing (11.7%)	Lack of transparency (10.4%)
What (if any) trade-offs did you make when negotiating your AWA remuneration package.	There was no negotiation and therefore no scope for trade-offs (40.3%)	Nothing was traded in the process (37.7%)	I don't know what was traded off (3.9%)
What is the single most important thing that you have gained from moving to an AWA?	Nothing (50.6%)	More money (16.9%)	Broader-based remuneration package (5.2%)
What is the single most important thing that you have lost from moving to an AWA?	Nothing (36.4%)	Tenure and security of employment (7.8%)	Ability to negotiate (5.2%)

SES Perceptions of AWA Outcomes

Respondents reported a range of AWA outcomes. Total remuneration ranged from $108,853 to $201,000 per annum (covering SES band 1 and 2). The majority, 75.7%, knew the components of their remuneration package while 24.3% did not. Those who knew the make-up of their package reported annual salary components from $90,000 to $140,000. Most reported access to annual bonuses/productivity payments ranging from $4,000 to $20,000. Their remuneration included a restricted mix of motor vehicles, spouse travel, home and mobile telephones, car parking, superannuation, additional leave, airline lounge membership, newspaper/magazine subscriptions and home computers/laptops — which they valued between $15,000 and $57,640.

These outcomes reflected differences in AWAs between agencies, rather than within them. Interviewees cited these variations as barriers to SES mobility. They reported that a transfer at an SES officer's substantive level from one agency to another could be seen as a straight transfer, a promotion, or a demotion depending on the remuneration relativities between those agencies. Many saw this as reducing their promotional/career opportunities and promoting an inward agency focus. Some described it as the death of the career service.

These outcomes need to be tempered with interviewee observations and criticisms that although significant pay rises were achieved by the SES when they first went onto AWAs, the value of those rises were eroded over time because their agreements did not provide for ongoing pay rises over the life of the AWA. As a result, they failed to maintain prior relativities with subordinate staff whose pay and conditions continued to be set through the Enterprise Bargaining Awards (EBA) process. They argued that despite receiving notionally more under their AWAs than under their former EBAs, they were falling behind in real terms. Some reported that their subordinates on EBAs were earning more than they were.

Despite the strict confidentiality requirements on AWA outcomes, respondents made direct comparisons between their remuneration and other SES officers within their agencies. Interviewees stated this transparency was facilitated by the template-based approach, the restrictions on the nature and extent of permissible negotiation, and because they talked to each other about it despite the prohibitions.

Thus transparency in remuneration and conditions within agencies persists, while transparency between agencies appears to have been lost with the advent of AWAs.

Respondents were asked to make value judgments on other AWA outcomes. Their responses are summarised in Table 3 below.

The majority perceived their AWAs as a win for their agency and a loss for themselves. They saw SES officers within agencies achieving similar outcomes; an initial increase in remuneration, but a decrease in the range of rewards available.

They saw their working hours increase, demands placed on them increase, overall working conditions diminish, and the balance between their work and

Table 3

SES Perceptions of Their AWA Outcomes (Based on Collapsed Likert Scale Data)

Question	Disagree	Undecided	Agree
My AWA outcome was a win for me.	37.7%	31.2%	31.2%
My AWA outcome was a win for my agency.	9.1%	33.8%	57.1%
All SES officers in my agency achieved similar outcomes in their AWAs.	10.7%	38.7%	50.7%
AWA outcomes achieved in my agency are generally better than those achieved in other agencies.	29.7%	55.4%	14.9%
Since moving to an AWA: The range of rewards available to me has increased.	53.3%	14.7%	32.0%
Since moving to an AWA: My overall working hours have increased.	18.4%	18.4%	63.2%
Since moving to an AWA: Demands placed on me have increased.	15.8%	15.8%	68.4%
Since moving to an AWA: My overall conditions of service have improved.	36.8%	35.5%	27.6%
Since moving to an AWA: I have achieved a better balance between my work and private life.	71.1%	19.7%	9.2%
Since moving to an AWA: I have more responsibility.	15.6%	19.5%	64.5%
Since moving to an AWA: I feel a greater commitment to my work.	32.9%	42.1%	25.0%
Since moving to an AWA: I feel more stressed at work.	17.1%	36.8%	46.1%
Since moving to an AWA: my career opportunities have been enhanced.	40.8%	36.2%	22.4%
Since moving to an AWA: I get more satisfaction out of my job.	31.6%	44.7%	23.7%
Since moving to an AWA: my total remuneration has increased.	13.2%	15.8%	71.1%
Since moving to an AWA: I feel more focused on my job.	25.3%	46.7%	28.0%
On balance, I gained more than I lost through moving to an AWA.	27.6%	38.2%	34.2%

private lives deteriorate. In addition, they saw themselves taking on more responsibility and feeling more stressed at work.

Having a third of the SES reporting reduced commitment to their work as a consequence of their AWA suggests a high degree of workforce alienation. Respondents stated that since moving to AWAs their career opportunities reduced and they got less satisfaction from their jobs.

These outcomes do not support claims that AWAs lead to greater flexibility and choice. Nor do they support arguments that AWAs provide opportunities to tailor remuneration and conditions packages to suit individual needs.

Although the majority linked reduced career opportunities to AWAs, the reduction might also be seen as an unintended consequence of cross agency pay differentials. Given that differential outcomes between agencies are also being achieved under individual agency-based enterprise agreements at lower levels of the APS, it is not possible to fully attribute the reduced SES career opportunities to AWAs, unless it can be argued that differentials under AWAs are considerably greater than they would have been under EBAs at the SES level, in which case this would be an unintended flexibility reducing outcome of the greater flexibility given to agencies for setting their own remuneration and conditions. This becomes a hypothetical argument beyond the scope of this study.

Conclusion

These findings are summarised in Table 4 through twenty-five 'negative' and five 'positive' conclusions about SES perceptions of AWAs.

Table 4

Summary of SES Perceptions of Working Under AWAs

A: Negative perceptions

- did not regard their AWA as an individually negotiated contract
- felt they had no control over the negotiating process
- found their expectations of the AWA process were not fully met
- did not know whether they preferred working under AWAs or EBAs
- would not like to see AWAs used more widely in the APS
- would not like to put their own staff on AWAs
- concluded that working under an AWA was no different to working under an EBA
- did not like anything about their own AWA
- disliked the fact that there was no scope for negotiation and tradeoffs
- gained nothing by moving to an AWA
- did not think their AWA outcome was a win for themselves
- thought their AWA outcome was a win for their agency
- thought the outcomes they achieved were worse that those achieved by SES officers in other agencies
- found the range of rewards available to them had decreased
- thought their overall working hours had increased
- considered that the demands placed on them had increased
- felt that their overall employment conditions had deteriorated
- felt they ended up with a poorer balance between their work and private lives
- thought they gained more responsibility
- felt a reduced commitment to their work
- felt more stressed at work
- suffered reduced career opportunities
- got less satisfaction out of their jobs
- were unsure whether they are more or less focused on their jobs
- were unsure on whether they gained more than they lost through moving to an AWA.

B: Positive perceptions

- thought they entered into their AWA negotiations with a good understanding of the process
- are satisfied with their contract
- believed that under AWAs there is potential for everyone can win
- considered that everyone within their agency achieved similar outcomes
- found their total remuneration had increased (initially).

These conclusions suggest significant intended and unintended consequences for the APS as a result of moving the SES onto AWAs. The coercive way in which SES AWAs were introduced alienated the majority of the SES and contributed to very negative perceptions of AWAs and AWA processes. They reported perceptions of disempowerment and a loss of control which, in some cases, led to reduced loyalty and commitment to the organisation.

Most perceived the AWA process as a management-initiated collective agreement, signed individually, with no scope for any negotiation on pay, benefits or conditions. They felt that the 'spirit' of the legislation put forward in the WR Act had been abandoned as choice and espoused flexibility were missing.

While the SES achieved initial pay increases they suffered significant erosion of their remuneration packages over the life of the agreements relative to other APS staff on EBAs. Many reported a loss of the collective 'SES' identity and their sense of public duty. They reported that they were seen as costs, rather than as valued officers and this contributed to heightened levels of distrust of agency Chief Executive Officers (CEOs) and further alienation.

Differential outcomes between agencies for work at the same level contributed to perceived losses of cross-agency mobility and reduced APS wide promotional/career opportunities. This caused many to conclude that the APS-wide concept of an SES career service has been abandoned, resulting in their being locked into an inward agency focus.

References

Australian Centre for Industrial Relations Research and Training. (1999). *Australia at work — Just managing.* Sydney, Australia: Prentice Hall.

Birmingham, A., & Fox, P. (1997). A guide to the *Workplace Relations Act 1996. Australian Bulletin of Labour, 23,* 33–47.

Buchanan, J., Woodman, M., O'Keefe, S., & Arsovska, B. (1998). Wages policy and wage determination in 1997. *The Journal of Industrial Relations, 40*(1), 88–118.

Davis, G., Yeatman, A., & Sullivan, B.A. (1997). *The new contractualism.* Melbourne, Australia: MacMillan.

Deery, S., Plowman, D., & Walsh, J. (1997). *Industrial relations: A contemporary analysis.* Sydney, Australia: McGraw-Hill.

Department of Employment, Workplace Relations and Small Business. (1997). *Workplace relations and agreement making in APS agencies.* Canberra, Australia: Author.

Department of Employment, Workplace Relations and Small Business. (1999a). *Agreement making and the New Public Service Act* (Advice No. 1999/17). Canberra, Australia: Author.

Department of Employment, Workplace Relations and Small Business. (1999b). *Review of agreement making in the APS: an interim report by the DEWRSB on a survey conducted by Twyford Consulting.* Retrieved September 14, 2000, from http://www.aph.gov.au/senate/committee/submissions/fapa_aps_docs.htm

Department of Employment, Workplace Relations and Small Business. (2000). *Submission from the Department of Employment, Workplace Relations and Small Business (Parts A & B) to the Finance and Public Administration References Committee Inquiry into Australian Public Service Employment Matters.* Canberra, Australia: Author.

Department of Industrial Relations. (1995). *Industrial relations reform in Australia: Fact sheet.* Canberra, Australia: Author.

Department of Industrial Relations. (1997). *Workplace Agreements demystified.* Canberra, Australia: Author.

Frazer, A.D., McCallum, R.C., & Ronfeldt, P. (Eds). (1997). *Individual contracts and workplace relations* (ACIRRT Working Paper No. 50). Sydney, Australia: University of Sydney.

Gardner, M. (1993). The Final Step? The devolution of Public Service industrial relations. In M. Gardner (Ed.), *Human resource management and industrial relations in the public sector* (pp. 136–149). Melbourne, Australia: MacMillan.

Gardner, M., & Palmer, G. (1997). *Employment relations: Industrial relations and human resource management in Australia* (2nd ed.). Melbourne, Australia: MacMillan.

Hamberger, J. (1996). *Individual contracts: Beyond enterprise bargaining?* (ACIRRT Working Paper No. 39). Sydney, Australia: University of Sydney.

Heiler, K. (1998). *The 12 hour workday: Emerging issues.* (ACIRRT Working Paper No. 51). Sydney, Australia: Australian Centre for Industrial Relations Research and Training.

O'Donnell, M., Allan, C., & Peetz, D. (1999). *The new public management and workplace change in Australia* (Working Paper Series, No. 126). Sydney, Australia: University of New South Wales School of Industrial Relations and Organisational Behaviour.

O'Donnell, M., & O'Brien, M. (2000). Performance-based pay in the Australian Public Service. *Review of Public Personnel Administration, 20*(2), 20–34.

Sappey, R., Burgess, J., Lyons, M., & Buultjens, J. (2006). *The new federal workplace relations system.* Sydney, Australia: Pearson.

Schroeder, P. (1997). An untitled overview of the Howard government's policy changes and how they impact on the APS. *Australian Journal of Public Administration, 56*(2), 12–17.

Taylor, M. (1997, December 9). Coalition wants PS seniors signed to job deals. *The Canberra Times.*

Capturing the 'Value-Addedness' of the Business Management Graduate

Zelma Bone

Identifying the graduate outcomes is the easy part. The challenge for universities lies in designing the educational programs that will concurrently and explicitly develop generic attributes, as well as discipline-based knowledge. A holistic approach is required. Few universities in Australia have actually developed a process for determining whether their graduates have achieved those attributes to confirm that the institutional rhetoric has practical outcomes. This chapter outlines the role of a graduation portfolio in higher education to meet the growing needs of industry, as well as the operational pros and cons of implementing such a system in higher education.

The University of Sydney's Faculty of Rural Management (FRM) believed that a graduate's university experience added up to more than the sum of the parts (subjects studied) and that the transcript did not tell the whole story of a student's development in the attributes or capabilities that employers wanted. Graduates have reflected on their experiences, both within the formal learning arena and outside of university, to develop a Portfolio of Capability Development that goes some way to representing their holistic experience to potential employers and to encourage lifelong learning. An important component of the quality assurance program, which is embedded in the capability education approach (Cairns 1997a, 1997b; Stephenson. 1995; Stephenson & Weil, 1992), was for employers to assess the portfolio at an end of (final) year interview, and for students to pass the portfolio as a prerequisite for graduation. At the end of each year the academics, students and participating employers complete a survey or participate in a focus group so the faculty can gain feedback on the process.

The Graduate Capabilities

In order to meet employers' needs, FRM identified nine capabilities initially and then reduced these to seven (see below) which it considered essential to the graduate in the 21st century. The faculty consulted widely with employers of graduates to identify what attributes they wanted in their employees. While the development of these capabilities was already largely *implicit* in the curriculum, the purpose of the more focused curriculum (which included a Portfolio of Capability Development) was to take this work forward and make these features *explicit*. Briefly, the seven capabilities are built around the concepts of:

Scholarship
- critical and creative thinking
- communication

Global Citizenship
- leadership and teamwork
- ethical, social and professional understanding

Lifelong Learning
- management skills
- personal and intellectual autonomy
- information literacy.

The Portfolio

The United Kingdom National Committee of Inquiry in Higher Education (NCIHE, 1997), otherwise known as the Dearing Report, recommended that all graduates have a progress file or portfolio which would consist of two elements:

- a transcript recording student achievement which should follow a common format devised by institutions collectively through their representative bodies
- a means by which students can monitor, build and reflect upon their personal development.

The first element of the portfolio, the transcript, is self-explanatory: a list of subjects and the level of achievement gained in each subject. The development of a 'vehicle' for the second element was more problematic, and after much consultation and discussion the faculty approved the use of a portfolio. The

Portfolio of Capability Development is a graduation requirement of FRM's undergraduate on-campus programs and its role is twofold:

- As a personal reflection document where the student could monitor and record their development in the seven capabilities over the period of enrolment in their degree. This could include statements, situational evidence and illustrations of their development within the formal learning experience as well as outside. The document could be as creative as they liked as long as they were comfortable that the document was a reasonably true reflection of their capability development.

- As a source of evidence to assist in the preparation of job applications and job interviews. Part of the portfolio is a job application letter and curriculum vitae that includes some reference to their capability development.

The portfolio is presented to an academic adviser for assessment and students participate in an interview with staff and employers.

How the Portfolio was Supported and Managed

The main objectives of the process was to improve the capacity of individuals to understand what and how they are learning, and to review, plan and take responsibility for their own learning. The ideas that underpin the process of producing a portfolio of capability development include that it is a structured process integral to higher level learning and concerned with learning in a holistic sense (both academic and nonacademic). The portfolio is something that a student does with guidance and support: the latter perhaps decreasing as personal capability is developed so that it becomes self-sustaining. The process involves self-reflection, the creation of personal records and is intended to improve the capacity of individuals to communicate their learning to others who are interested (e.g., academic staff and employers). The faculty recognised that an infrastructure was needed to support and manage the process and this involved:

1. A range of recording processes in order to create and maintain these records. The umbrella document was the portfolio, which outlined the evidence of development in each of the capabilities, as well as a career plan and current curriculum vitae.

2. Structured processes to develop the capacity of individuals to reflect upon their own learning and achievement and to plan their own personal, educational and career development. Curriculum mapping of subjects identified where the capabilities were taught, practised or assessed through a variety of teaching practices, assessment and a variety of learning environments with an emphasis on praxis (a balance of theory and practice) (Mezirow, 1991). Examples included formal classroom tuition, long and short tours, cooperator visits, guest speakers, practical classes (ranging

from the sheep yards to communication workshops). The reflective and planning skills on which the portfolio is based are integral to knowing how to learn in different contexts and to the ability to transfer learning.

3. Guidance materials and support structures to enable and encourage the learner to participate and benefit from this active learning process. Academic advisers were assigned to each graduating student with the aim of guiding the students through the process of developing their portfolio and preparing them for interview. Subject outlines and learning guides for each subject clearly summarised which capability was being developed and usually if it was to be practised, taught or assessed. The capabilities would sit beside the learning outcomes for the subject.

4. Opportunities within and outside the higher education curriculum to acquire, develop and practise the skills to engage in personal development planning. Students were encouraged to document capability development from participating in extracurricula activities as well as paid and unpaid work. Real world experience also provides students with opportunities to develop 'justified confidence' (Stephenson, 1995, p. 25). Stephenson maintains that a distinction exists between the mere possession of skills and knowledge, and the confidence in one's ability to use them (Cochrane et al., 2002).

Embedding the capabilities within the mainstream curriculum has the advantage of ensuring the process is built into core teaching and learning activities. It is preferable to imposing capability development as a compulsory additional requirement upon students, that is, as an extra subject. In some instances, it may present challenges to approaches to teaching and learning primarily associated with the transmission of content. If the subject assessment covers capability development as well as content then the assumption is that by passing the assessment the student has also achieved the stated capability. Reducing capabilities to a 'list' could result in a checklist approach. This can be dangerous as it 'inevitably encourages a fragmented curriculum and mechanistic approaches to teaching and learning' (Clanchy & Ballard, 1995, p. 159).

Benefits of the Graduation Portfolio

Students

The benefits of the process are in helping the students to:

•   become more effective, independent and confident self-directed learners
•   understand how they are learning and relate their learning to a wider context

- improve their general skills for study and career management
- articulate their personal goals and evaluate progress towards their achievement
- encourage a positive attitude to learning throughout life
- gain the specialist knowledge of their chosen field and also the skills, abilities and values sought by employers.

The last point was a significant objective of the capability program. In 2001, 67% of respondents indicated that the capability program gave them a way to present to potential employers a clearer and fuller description of themselves than the usual academic transcript. The average over the 4 years, from 2002 to 2005, was 74%, thus indicating a growing acceptance and understanding of the purpose of the program. Only 52% indicated that the program enabled them to demonstrate a degree of proficiency in those qualities that industry expects of its employees and the average over the 4 years only increased to 61%. A total of 30% neither agreed nor disagreed, but despite these results, their free response comments were particularly revealing:

> It made me more aware of the things industry employers are seeking in candidates and so I can work them into an interview and develop them in the future.

> I have been able to compile a set of readily identified and proven capabilities that will prove useful in interviews and the actual workplace.

> I can confidently display an understanding of my own capability.

> It has helped me to identify weaknesses and develop them to make me more 'industry ready'.

The students indicated that the portfolio effectively documented their growth and development as a learner (initially 71% to an average of 80% over the 4 years) and assisted them to become more reflective learners (62% to an average of 70%). The Capabilities Program also provided them with adequate opportunities to reflect upon and record the ways in which their personal learning developed (71% in 2001 to an average of 80% from 2002 to 2005). Their added comments in the free response section reinforced the strong message to emerge regarding their learning:

> It has allowed me to look at what I really have learned in the faculty.

> Makes you think about what you have done rather than just leave with a certificate.

> It has helped me to conceptualise and visualise how I have developed and grown at uni.

Furthermore, with students changing jobs and careers more frequently than past generations, the development of more transferable skills was seen to be 'very important': 'Many technical skills are relevant only for the current job but the people skills are both transferable and lifelong' (McCrindle, 2006, p. 23).

Academic Staff and Universities

The benefits for the academic staff are:

- helping students to be more independent/autonomous learners
- improving the quality of experience for tutors and tutees when it is linked to the academic advisers system
- making more effective use of off-campus opportunities for learning, such as work placements and study abroad
- creating a mechanism through which career-related skills and capabilities can be recorded
- improving their understanding of the development of individual students and their ability to provide more meaningful employment references on their behalf.

In 2001, 62% of students indicated that the program had effectively integrated their learning across course subjects and this increased to 68% (2002–2005). In response to capturing 'out-of-subject' experiences, 81% of students indicated that the capability program enabled them to 'reflect upon and record knowledge, skills and learning experiences gained outside the academic curriculum'. The average results remained high with three quarters of the students in agreement. Student comments in the free response section included:

> It has emphasised the need for critical and creative thinking in the workplace.
>
> Given me a positive outlook on my skills and abilities.
>
> Provided a link between study and the real world learning experiences.
>
> I have 'pulled together' different strands of my achievements in all areas (work, paid employment, university, community, sporting) to portray a picture of myself which is more rounded than just an academic transcript.

The benefits for the universities include:

- facilitating more effective monitoring of student progress
- resulting in more effective academic support and guidance systems
- enhancing their capacity to demonstrate the quality of support they are giving to students in external review processes.

Hager, Holland and Beckett (2002) identified that it is in the university's best interests to develop transferable skills or capabilities, as this aids the process of course development, improves teaching and learning, and assists in quality assurance measures that are suitable for use in higher education. The easy part is for the university to identify a list of graduate attributes. But if this is imposed from the top with little encouragement to link it to course development then it becomes a façade, with the assumption it will happen if students complete courses. At FRM the development of the seven capabilities was embedded within each subject and course taught at the undergraduate level and culminated in the compilation of the portfolio.

Employers

For the employers of graduates the highlights are:

- improving the capacity of individuals to explain and relate what they know and can do to their particular needs (application forms or employment interviews)
- developing the 'complete' graduate with a combination of specialist skills, generalist skills, connectedness and self-reliance.

A study conducted by the University of Leeds in the United Kingdom (Jackson, Conway & Millar, 1997) identified that from the employers' view employability and the concept of the complete graduate was someone who has the following attributes:

- Specialist skills — it helps to be an expert in something such as accounting, marine biology, aeronautical engineering or marketing
- Generalist skills — graduates must have general skills relevant to a broad range of vocational areas such as business skills, communication skills, use of IT systems
- Connectedness — graduates must be team players with, for example, skills in negotiation, networking, presentation, cultural sensitivity
- Self-reliance — graduates must be able to manage their own career and personal development (e.g., confidence, self-awareness, action planning and positioning).

At a debriefing session after the interviews with students the employers expressed strong support for the program, its achievements and its potential. One employer spoke of the power of the capabilities to support students' transitions, particularly in helping them to move their focus from a primary concern with learning towards an appreciation of things happening 'outside'. More than one employer spoke of the need for students to see their portfolio as a reference — a tool to be used in preparing for an interview or job, as a means rather than an end. This employer urged faculty staff to ensure that the task did not become too prescriptive. It was argued that while students might feel more secure in a system that enabled them to identify and supply the 'right' answer, the capabilities approach should be about students articulating their own 'self'. The employers commended the values and philosophies implicit in the capabilities because of the way in which they highlighted ethical considerations that were becoming increasingly important to industry.

There was general agreement amongst the employers that the experience had been 'good' and 'worthwhile' and that they were pleased to be involved with it (Squires, 2001).

Concerns With the Graduation Portfolio

For the program to succeed there needed to be considerable time and effort on the part of various stakeholders. Not just in time, but it also demanded a clear vision of the nature and purpose of the undergraduate curriculum, more skilful teaching, more complex curriculum pathways, improved student support arrangements and a determination to experiment with new methods. It was always going to be a challenge for staff, but also for students who were expected to take more responsibility for their learning and to decrease their dependence on the consumption of pre-packaged information.

Since 2001, the number of staff volunteering to be academic advisers (AAs) has increased significantly as a broader understanding of the value of the program has developed through a series of staff seminars and feedback from students. The numbers of AAs has almost doubled but the number still falls well short of full staff involvement. All staff who have volunteered to be an AA do so over and above other commitments. This is an issue and may ultimately impact negatively on the capacity of the program to continue in its current form.

During the last 5 years the faculty has seen a change in senior management and a push from the university for the faculty to increase its research performance. The focus on quality teaching and learning is being challenged as academics are required to fulfil research targets and teach 'more efficiently'. Where there are competing demands, such as teaching versus research, 'staff will invariably put time and effort into what they perceive gets the most reward' (de la Harpe & Radloff, as cited in Fallows & Steven, 2000, p. 173). Some academics have chosen to focus on their research rather than devote time to being an AA.

Many students still see the portfolio as an 'extra burden' when nearing graduation. Feedback postcompletion indicated that many students finally see the value, particularly after participating in the interview process. This reinforced the research findings of Bone and Downie (2003) that while skills are embedded in the curriculum, unless teachers are explicit when introducing them the students concentrate on the content and are often oblivious to the 'other' skills they are developing.

Conclusion

Increased accountability through quality assurance processes has shifted the role of a graduation portfolio from the periphery to the mainstream of higher education policy in the United Kingdom and similar moves are being echoed in Australian universities.

The plan for universities in the United Kingdom was for this process, or a similar process, to be operationalised across the whole higher education sector by 2005/2006. The higher educational system in Australia has not seen such a systemic approach to personal development planning. In contrast, the process has been ad hoc with some universities addressing the development of key attributes in their graduates in a variety of ways. Most universities have identified a list of graduate attributes, but many have not developed a process that monitors the development of these attributes. Within the University of Sydney, FRM within the was one example of implementing a process to address this need.

Students are expected to grow in their achievements during their time of study. This growth in knowledge, skills and attitudes is represented in the work in their portfolios. Through the synthesis and reflection process students have come to appreciate that each of the capabilities does not represent end points as such, but continuums which need lifelong attention. The combination of a discipline-based, content-driven curriculum with a holistic capability portfolio approach presented in this chapter offers the student a rich and multitextured learning experience.

References

Bone, Z., & Downie, N. (2003). Transferable skills in the curriculum: UK and Australian academic and student perspectives. *International Journal of Learning, 10*.

Cairns, L. (1997a). *Capability briefing notes*. Lismore, Australia: Australia Capability Network, Southern Cross University.

Cairns, L. (1997b). *Defining capability for education, training and industry* (Discussion paper prepared for Capable Organisations Research Project, third draft). Australian National Training Authority Research Advisory Council.

Clanchy, J., & Ballard, B. (1995). Generic skills in the context of higher education. *Higher Education Research and Development, 14*(2), 155–166.

Cochrane, K., Mahony, M.J., Bone, Z., & Squires, D. (2002, June). An assessment of generic outcomes as a graduate requirement in an undergraduate management education degree at the University of Sydney. *Proceedings of Lifelong Learning Conference*, Rockhampton, Australia.

Fallows, S., & Steven, C. (2000). *Integrating key skills in higher education*. London: Kogan Page.

Hager, P., Holland, S., & Beckett, D. (2002). *Enhancing the Learning and Employability of Graduates: The Role of Generic Skills* (A position paper prepared for the Business/Higher Education Round Table by a taskforce of its members). Melbourne, Australia: Business/Higher Education Round Table.

Jackson, P., Conway, J., & Millar, D. (1997). *Are students making links? Interim report of the DfEE Career Management Skills Project*. University of Leeds.

Mezirow, J. (1991). *Transformative dimensions of adult learning*. Oxford: Jossey-Bass.

McCrindle, M. (2006). *New generations at work: Attracting, recruiting, retraining and training Generation Y*. Sydney, Australia: McCrindle Research. Retrieved August 5, 2006, from www.mccrindle.com.au

National Commission of Inquiry into Higher Education. (1997). *Higher education in the learning society*. London: NCIHE..

Squires, D. (2001, November). *Evaluation of the Capability Education Program at the University of Sydney's Faculty of Rural Management, Orange* (Third and final report).

Stephenson, J. (1995, November). Developing the autonomous learner: A capability approach. *Proceedings from 2nd National Information Literacy Conference*, Adelaide.

Stephenson, J., & Weil, S. (1992). *Quality in learning: A capability approach in higher education*. London: Kogan Page.

The Development and Effects of Psychological Contracts: An Exploration of the Contracts Established by Academics Within an Australian University Business School

Branka Krivokapic-Skoko

Grant O'Neill

Marcelle Droulers

The past two decades have seen enormous change in the number, funding, and focus of Australian universities, and this has altered the context and conditions of academic work in Australasia (Curtis & Matthewman, 2005). University managers and academic staff have been compelled to respond to forces and pressures such as the rise of managerialism, increased external and internal accountability, commercialisation of higher education and tighter government funding. The following discussion provides insight into the emotional and behavioural effects of, and responses to, the changing workplace environment of the Faculty of Commerce at Charles Sturt University. It does so through an exploration of the perceived exchange relationship that exists between employee and employer that constitutes the psychological contract.

Psychological Contracts: A Brief Overview

Numerous definitions of the psychological contract have been conceived since the term was first used by Chris Argyris in 1960 (Conway & Briner, 2005), and much debate has been devoted to whether a psychological contract should be understood as a legal contract implying mutual agreement between two parties

(Herriot et al., 1997) or whether it is more usefully understood as a subjective construct reflecting an individual employee's perceptions of an agreement (Robinson & Rousseau, 1994). This research follows Robinson and Rousseau's (1994) conceptualisation and consequently focuses only on employees in analysing the content and effects of the psychological contract. We explore the psychological contract as it is perceived by employees.

Various typologies have been developed in order to categorise the vast range of contract elements listed and measured in the literature (Guest & Conway, 2002; Kickul & Lester, 2001; Thomas & Anderson, 1998; Thompson & Bunderson, 2003). One such typology that has dominated the literature on the psychological contract is the transactional–relational distinction. Transactional contracts involve highly specific exchanges and relate to employment obligations are more short-term, work content-based and less relational (Rousseau, 1990, 1995). Relational contracts, on the other hand, are concerned with ongoing relationship, and so lead to the creation of less well defined socioemotional obligations, which may be characterised by attributes such as trust and commitment (Shore & Tetrick, 1994).

Another typology, discussed by Bunderson (2001), is particularly pertinent to this research. Bunderson suggested that the psychological contract between a professional and his/her employing organisation is shaped by professional and administrative work ideologies. In these ideologically pluralistic work settings, the obligations of the administrative psychological contract confront the ideologies of professional work. The administrative role of the organisation is to be a coordinated and efficient bureaucratic system that may aim to achieve common goals, market success and legitimacy. The role of the organisation as a professional body is to be a collegial society aimed at furthering the profession and the application of professional expertise for the benefit of the community and wider society (Bunderson, 2001).

While there has been limited research into psychological contracts in academia, this study does draw upon earlier research conducted at Lincoln University in New Zealand (Tipples & Krivokapic-Skoko, 1996) and compares responses by academics at the two universities. At Lincoln, the academics were generally dissatisfied with the extent to which the university had met what were perceived as its promised obligations. That dissatisfaction was associated with a low level of job satisfaction. They also identified career development, payment, long-term job security and promotion as common areas for violation of the psychological contract.

This chapter offers a preliminary empirical discussion of the formation, content, and workplace effects of the psychological contracts[1] established by academics within the Faculty of Commerce at Charles Sturt University (CSU). Drawing upon data gathered through three focus group discussions with the academics, it is argued that, in an environment that is exhibiting increasing change and uncertainty, the formation and content of the psychological contracts that exist are of growing importance in terms of the effects upon levels of employee trust, satisfaction, commitment, motivation and teaching and research outcomes.

Research Approach

The literature suggests (see, e.g., Freese & Schalk, 1996; Guzzo & Noonan, 1994; Turnley & Feldman, 1999) that greater use of idiographic methods to assess individuals' psychological contracts would be appropriate in order to access and understand the diverse individual experience of the psychological contract. The focus group technique is a method through which dense subjective experience and interpretations can be addressed and discussed. The group interaction provides safety (McCracken, 1988) and generates synergistic effects (Morgan, 1997), so that responses can be far more revealing than those obtained from individual interviews. As elaborated in a number of the method texts addressing focus groups (e.g., Bloor et al., 2001; Morgan, 1997), this method typically assumes bringing together a small number of participants from a well-defined target population to discuss a set of presented topics under the guidance of a facilitator. Focus group methodology with a semi-structured format was chosen as it is known to be useful in the identification of issues and themes that can subsequently be drawn upon to assist with development of relevant survey questions (O'Brien, 1993; Saunders, Lewis, & Thornhill, 2003; Wolff, Knodel, & Sittitrai, 1993) in future research.

The empirical data presented in this chapter was generated through three focus groups with academics employed by the Faculty of Commerce, Charles Sturt University, in May 2006. It constitutes one of the few empirical studies which used a focus group approach to understand how academics interpret the psychological contract. Twenty-six academics (excluding the researchers) participated across the three focus groups. The focus group discussions were moderated by a research assistant experienced with group facilitation, so as to allow for an informal atmosphere and to minimise the power imbalance (Owen, 2001) between the facilitator and other participants. While a limitation of focus groups can be the tendency for participants to deviate from their usual thinking and behaviour in order to 'fit in' with group norms (Kenyon, 2004), the researchers were fortunate to be working with a relatively homogenous group of participants who regularly work with each other, thereby minimising the effects of this tendency. The focus groups were of the ideal size, being comprised of six to ten academics (Fern, 1982). To minimise the risk of loss of privacy, and perceptions of fear associated with focus group participation (Bloor et al., 2001), first names or pseudonyms were used during the discussion as, with the signed consent of the participants, each of the focus group sessions was audiotaped and transcribed verbatim.

Empirical Findings

Given that reciprocal exchanges form the basis of many definitions of the psychological contract (Conway & Briner, 2005; Guest & Conway, 2002; Robinson & Rousseau, 1994), we commenced the focus group discussions with an introductory listing exercise[2] designed to engage participants and assist them in identifying what they contribute to this exchange relationship.

The academics cited a range of personal qualities as a key aspect of what they bring to the university, consistently commenting that their work involves their 'whole person', their creativity, integrity, values and experience. Some of the categories of contractual elements presented in earlier studies (Guest & Conway, 2002; Kickul & Lester, 2001;Thomas & Anderson, 1998) failed to encompass the breadth of elements the academics named, which may be a result of the fact that the academics view their work responsibilities in a much wider context than their immediate institutional environment.

The academics spoke to a strong work ethic and this was evidenced in many comments relating to a willingness to work outside 'normal' working hours, being flexible in taking on various roles and tasks, and having an emotional engagement with their work. Commitment to the faculty and university, and its operations, was commonly named, and a number of academics also made reference to the importance of the university as a social institution. Further, it was consistently stated that disciplinary knowledge, teaching and industry knowledge and experience, and industry contacts and networks, are highly valuable. Several spoke of a deep commitment, even passion, for their discipline area.

Many of the responses (as shown in Table 1) reflected deeply felt social obligations associated with their professional status. Commitment and concerns were frequently linked to care for students and society through the institution of the university as a force for good and the service of 'higher goals'. For example, one academic noted, 'one of the reasons why I left the industry, is a sense of social justice and the notion that part of the role of being an academic is protecting and developing social justice in the community'. Interestingly, as Bunderson (2001) found in research among professionals, the tension between serving the institution as a bureaucratic entity and as a professional body was a theme that ran throughout our focus group discussions of the content of the psychological contracts the academics formed, as well as the promises and violations they perceived.

These elements can be meaningfully categorised into four main areas of responsibility. These are, responsibility to: the University; their discipline; society; and, students (see Figure 1).

Building upon perceived promises of reciprocal exchange (Conway & Briner 2005; Robinson & Rousseau, 1994), the academics spoke at length regarding what they were expecting from the university in return for what they bring to their job (Table 2). Their stated expectations lend support to Bunderson's (2001) observa-

Table 1

Academics' Beliefs About What They Bring to the University

- context for teaching
- networks/industry links
- practical experience
- personal experience
- stories
- active links to professions through professional organisations
- broad knowledge base
- creativity
- access to resources
- desire to convey importance of social justice/ethics issues
- desire to make a difference
- desire to make society a better place
- motivation to share experience/teach/work
- openness willingness to discuss ideas
- commitment to teaching/students/ the university and its success

- loyalty
- work ethic
- enthusiasm
- integrity
- creativity
- thirst for learning/passion for discipline area
- timidity/compliance
- challenge to the status quo
- wisdom
- salesmanship
- relationship building
- patience
- sacrifice
- assertiveness
- civility

tion that the relational nature of the psychological contract has greater influence on those who identify themselves as representing a profession.

Consistent with Bunderson (2001), the academics claimed to be offering loyalty and a willingness to fulfil role obligations that cannot be formally specified, such as excellent client service and productive effort. Their comments indi-

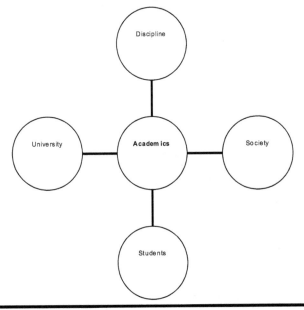

Figure 1

Categorisation of academics' responsibilities.

Table 2

Academics' Beliefs About What the University Owes Them

• academic freedom	• recognition of skill
• autonomy	• recognition of professionalism
• honesty	• consistency
• empowerment	• reciprocity
• job security	• recognition of family/outside commitments
• keeping a positive external image	• recognition for going beyond normal duties
• care in times of want	• fairness in promotion
• trust	• impartiality
• clear communication	• nondiscrimination for union involvement
• involvement in decision-making	• opportunities for development and promotion
• advocacy	• promotion
• transparency	• study leave
• respect	• flexibility
• competency of management	• work–life balance
• equitable pay, fair pay	• access to supervisors
• support (for ideas, initiatives, resource availability, career development, crises, personal issues)	• pleasant social/physical/emotional work environment

cated that, in return, they expect the organisation to provide a collegial work setting, defend professional autonomy and standards and for it to help the academic to fulfil his/her ethical obligations to the larger community. Figure 2 shows key themes that were drawn from discussion of what the academics expect from the university.

The desire for professional autonomy was often expressed as a strong expectation of job discretion, an expectation of academic freedom and inclusion in decision-making regarding issues that affect their professional activities. Flexibility and trust were noted as highly valued features of working at the University. As one of the academics commented:

> ... as long as ... [the head of school] knows that he can contact me ... there seems to be a real sense of trust there that he knows that if I'm not physically there in my office, that doesn't necessarily mean that I'm not getting the work done.

Another noted:

> I think everybody does [appreciate the low levels of surveillance], I think there is a degree of trust and obviously there are limits and boundaries and having set those the university is very relaxed about it.

Much of the discussion centred on the expectations of university leaders and managers, fairness and transparency in promotion, and recognition of one's personal commitment to the profession, discipline, the university and students. The most emotive responses were to do with leadership and management; with issues such as trust, clear and honest communication, transparency, advocacy, individual consideration and respect being prominent throughout the discussions. Even when managerial prerogatives were accepted, academics expressed considerable emotion when discussing perceived failures by the university to address such situations in an honest manner and communicate outcomes effec-

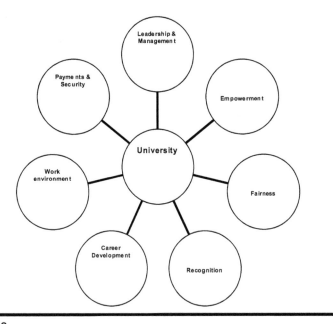

Figure 2

Academics' beliefs about what the university owes them.

tively. For example, in expressing frustration with the promotion process, it was stated that:

> ... the final thing is the question of transparency. I find it almost obscene that the deliberations of the promotion committee are not open to scrutiny by anybody outside that inner circle. If they are truly doing the job they are supposed to be doing, and objectively evaluating the applications against the criteria, what is the need for secrecy? I see none. Feedback is given to the applicants, but it is Clayton's feedback.[3]

Although many examples were given of instances where the university had fulfilled or exceeded expectations, numerous perceived violations were named.[4] Morrison and Robinson (1997) draw the distinction between a breach (defined as a cognitive comparison between what has been received and what has been promised) and a violation (defined as the emotional reactions that may accompany breaches). Our interest was in the more emotional reactions to psychological contract breach, that is, with perceived violations. While different issues and emphases emerged across the groups, there was a striking consistency in the unprompted use of the phrase 'changing the goalposts' in discussions of promotion in each of the focus groups. Perceived unpredictability in career advancement within the university has caused much disappointment and anger amongst the academics. This anger and disappointment was compounded by a perceived double standard. It is believed that

Table 3

Violations of the Psychological Contract as Perceived by the Academics

Violations of psychological contracts (ranked in order of the number of times they were cited)

1. Lack of fairness in promotion
2. Lack of communication/openness/transparency
3. Inconsistency in applying rules ('changing the goalposts')
4. Bureaucratic administrative system
5. Lack of respect for professional status
6. Poor management/university losing direction
7. Greater workload demands on staff
8. Lack of job security
9. Pay-related issues

while the university espouses the importance of quality teaching, it is the quantity and type of research that is recognised and rewarded. These findings are consistent with other case studies that found that employees perceive a psychological contract breach when there is a mismatch between management communication about human resource management practices and what they actually experience (for example Grant, 1999; Greene et al., 2001). It was often perceptions of a lack of honest communication around breaches that had turned them into perceived violations and even feelings of betrayal.

Another frequently cited area of psychological contract violation was when the expectation of being treated as a professional was met with the seemingly inflexible and bureaucratic requirements of the university's administrative system. 'You're expecting that you bring in a certain amount of professionalism but it's shoved in your face to a certain extent because of the bureaucracy', commented an academic with considerable experience outside the education sector.

While some in the focus groups were frustrated with the daily disruption to their work that resulted from the need to conform to bureaucratic rules and regulations, others were more deeply concerned with the long-term direction of the institution. Indeed, administrative rules and regulations constituted one of the two key issues that were at the heart of most of the reports of psychological contract violation. Many perceived an encroachment of administrative systems that emphasised compliance, conformity, rationality and efficiency upon their practice as academic professionals who require flexibility, personal discretion and autonomy. Some deemed a bureaucratic juggernaut to be a threat to the core competence of the university in teaching excellence and customer focus. An example that was given of the push for compliance was following rigid performance targets instead of professional development. It was commented,

> ... it's very important that ... [staff development] is done in a very open way rather than this performance review approach where you're told 'meet these things' instead of asking 'what are you trying to do, what do you see as important for you to develop your abilities and career?' rather than say 'attend this teaching course'.

The second key issue was the imperative to increase research output. While it was recognised that research output was an essential priority for the university in order to obtain government funding and remain a viable entity, the research imperative was almost unanimously named as a source of psychological contract violation. Perceived mismanagement of a tension between teaching and research goals was deemed to have caused inconsistency in expectations and behaviour, and this was thought to have had a major impact on staffing, promotion, performance management and workloads. It was noted, for example, that:

> ... there's this real inconsistency that one of the pillars of the university is our commitment and excellence in teaching but ... it's all about track record in research and in fact teaching doesn't seem to be highly valued at all ....

This tension, and the alleged greater reward given to high-output researchers, was associated with changing goalposts regarding promotion. This was reported as leading to feelings of disappointment, discouragement, anger, bitterness and betrayal. It was also linked to distrust amongst academics towards the university.

The focus group discussions also addressed what happens when there is a violation of the psychological contract. Following previous studies (Cavanaugh & Noe, 1999; Dabos & Rousseau, 2004; Freese & Schalk, 1996), the aim was to explore the impact of psychological contract violation on work outcomes such as job satisfaction (Sutton & Griffin, 2004), organisational citizenship behaviour (Othman et al., 2005), and intention to remain with the current employer (Sturges et al., 2005). Dabos and Rousseau (2004) argued that unrealised expectations can result in increased turnover, demotivation, loss of trust in the organisation and decreased commitment.

Utilising Turnley and Feldman's (1998) EVLN (Exit, Voice, Loyalty, Neglect) framework as a means of analysing the focus group transcripts, it was found that the most frequently cited responses to psychological contract violation could be categorised as a loss of loyalty or neglect behaviours. Some academics said that the decreased 'loyalty' was resulting in their feeling helpless and giving up. In what was a very informed comment, a management discipline academic noted, '... it goes back to equity theory of motivation ... you'll do one of two things, you'll either withdraw your labour totally ... or you will slow down'. Others referred to behaviour that saw them less likely to engage in extra-role behaviour. Increased neglect, particularly decreased attention to teaching quality, was a major issue of concern.

An important finding was that the academics possessed strong continuance commitment,[5] and this cannot be explained solely by the costs of resigning. This continuance commitment means that some of the ill-effects of poor psychological contracts could, at least in the short-term, be masked because the exit response to psychological contract violation is not strongly evident. More broadly, the negative effects of psychological contract violation were shown to be mediated by an approach to academic work that involved a commitment to the students even when frustration with the institution was high. Collective organisation and speaking out publicly were mentioned as responses, however, in the current environment they were considered to be rather futile activities. When an individual or group felt violated, 'corridor talk' was named as a common response.

Surprisingly, the reactions to violation were not altogether negative over time. Some academics have adapted to perceived violations and sought new opportunities for self-development. The adaptation response appears to be strongly related to the professionalism of the academic, for when loyalty to the institution declines, loyalty to the discipline and the commitment to students has powerful effects. Indeed, one of the academics went so far as to comment 'very few academics slacken off because of their commitment to the students and because of their professionalism' [several other focus group participants verbally expressed agreement with this point and none disagreed] 'so it doesn't matter how badly they're treated, they will still perform close to their optimal level and if they can't do this they then leave'.

Some scholars have argued that the psychological contract is likely to become more transactional after violation (Herriot & Pemberton, 1996; Rousseau & McLean Parks, 1993) and we certainly found evidence of this as a short-term response as is indicated in the following comment:

> I almost pull my head in and retreat and then just think and say 'all right I am just going to become a contract worker, so if they are going to treat me like this, they're not going to get the extras and I will just do my honest day's work, collect my pay every two weeks'.

In the long-term, however, responses consistently indicated a level of resistance to breaches and we posit that this may be related to the academics' wider professional, social and ideological commitments (Thompson & Bunderson, 2003). Emphasising the importance of their role as professionals, it was commented:

> ... you pull back a little bit for while but then the professional nature of what you do starts to take over again and you say 'oh bugger it' and you get back to your job. So there's a short-term down and then you level off and back up again.

Whatever the reaction to contract breach, there is no doubt that the emotional experience of violation can be extreme. Many academics gave considerable emphasis to their deep regret and pain over violations that are often masked by the variety responses taken by employees:

> ... there has been, on the part of the university, some fairly egregious departures from equity in the promotion process ... It has wreaked havoc with the morale of a lot people here, some of whom I know have moved on as a result and those who have stayed on and coped with it because of their professionalism or had no where else to go.

In summary, the focus groups revealed a number of issues and concerns that were common among academics in the earlier studies of the psychological contract at Lincoln University. These commonalities were most notable in the areas of job satisfaction and career development (Tipples & Krivokapic-Skoko, 1997). Our focus group research has provided deeper insights into the processes involved in psychological contract development and violation. Stated commitments to the profession, and the university as an important social institution, highlight important possible points of tension between bureaucratic and professional objectives. However, the high levels of personal commitment to the profession and social goals can have a moderating effect upon the experience and impact of breaches and violations of the psychological contract, thereby masking, at least in the short term, their often seriously damaging outcomes on staff and the institution.

Conclusions and Implications

From empirical evidence gathered through the focus groups, we have identified key elements of the psychological contracts formed by academics within the Faculty of Commerce at CSU. Our research suggests that situational factors such as procedural justice (Turnley & Feldman, 1998) and personal ideology (Bunderson, 2001) can moderate employees' reactions to psychological contract violation. More specifically, the research shows that commitment to society and the social good, one's discipline, student learning and development, and the institution of the university, frequently play a prominent part in the development, and moderation of the effects, of the academics' psychological contracts.

The focus group participants deemed their psychological contracts to be in a poor state and revealed many issues and concerns that were previously identified by Tipples and Krivokapic-Skoko (1997) in a study of psychological contracts among academics at Lincoln University, New Zealand. Many of the CSU academics expressed concern at being caught out by change and the unexpected, and noted that the university could do much better in terms of maintaining appropriate, clearly articulated, and consistently applied, strategy and expectations.

Perceived violations to the psychological contract, most notably in the areas of promotion and appointment, were identified as having generated considerable anger, disappointment and loss of trust in the university. The university's commitment to, and rewarding of, quality teaching was frequently criticised by academics who spoke of their considerable emotional, psychological and personal effort to achieve excellent teaching outcomes. That noted, as Anderson has argued (2006), the lived reality within universities is that the teaching performance record as a means of gaining promotion will always play a secondary role to research.

As found by Dabos and Rousseau (2004), our focus group discussions indicate that many of the potentially detrimental effects of psychological contract violation can be ameliorated, and even avoided, by ensuring that employer and employee perceptions of 'obligations' are congruent. To this end, greater understanding of the academic employment relationship could be gained by university managers through achievement of an awareness of academics' professional and administrative work ideologies, and awareness of how these ideologies influence academics' perceptions as to whether the university is 'living up to its end of the bargain' (Bunderson, 2001).

Irrespective of the existence of moderating factors, we hold that it is critical for all managers to be sensitive to possible differences in expectations, since perceived unrealised expectations commonly result in demotivation, decreased commitment, increased turnover and loss of trust in the organisation. Further, the empirical evidence gathered has revealed that damage to motivation, commitment and performance associated with psychological contract violation is compounded when the imperatives of pervasive 'managerialist' processes are not clearly and openly articulated, nor consistently applied.

Endnotes

1   An extended conceptual discussion of the psychological contract is available in an earlier Working Paper in this series: Krivokapic-Skoko, B., Ivers, J. & O'Neill, G. (2006). Psychological contracts: Conceptual and Empirical Considerations. *Faculty of Commerce Working Paper Series*, Charles Sturt University, No. 01/06.

2   See Table 1: Academic's beliefs about what they bring to the university.

3   Claytons is a nonalcoholic beverage that tastes like alcohol, but here the academic is speaking colloquially and uses the word Claytons to refer to something that is fake.

4   Table 3 outlines the key areas of perceived violation of the employment contract.

5   Following Allen and Meyer (1990), we understand continuance commitment to be based on an awareness of the costs associated with leaving or abandoning the respective entity.

References

Allen, N.J., & Meyer, J.P. (1990). The measurement and antecedents of affective, continuance and normative commitment to the organization. *Journal of Occupational Psychology, 63*, 1–18.

Anderson, G. (2006). Carving out time and space in the managerial university. *Journal of Organizational Change Management, 19*, 578–592.

Bloor, M., Frankland, J., Thomas, M., & Robson, K. (2001). *Focus groups in social research*. London: Sage.

Bunderson, J.S. (2001). How work ideologies shape the psychological contracts of professional employees: Doctors' responses to perceived breach. *Journal of Organizational Behavior, 22*(7), 717–741.

Cavanaugh, M., & Noe, R. (1999). Antecedents and consequences of relational components of the new psychological contract. *Journal of Organisational Behaviour, 20*(3), 328–351.

Conway, N., & Briner, R.B. (2005). *Understanding psychological contracts at work: A critical evaluation of theory and research*. Oxford, England: Oxford University Press.

Curtis, B., & Matthewman, S. (2005). The managed university: The PBRF, its impacts and staff attitudes. *New Zealand Journal of Employment Relations, 30*(2), 1–17.

Dabos, G.E., & Rousseau, D.M. (2004). Mutuality and reciprocity in the psychological contracts of employees and employers. *Journal of Applied Psychology, 89*(1), 52–72.

Fern, E.F. (1982). The use of focus groups for idea generation: The effects of group size, acquaintanceship, and moderator on response quantity and quality. *Journal of Marketing Research (JMR), 19*(1), 1–13.

Freese, C., & Scalk, R. (1996). Implications and differences in psychological contracts for human resource management. *European Journal of Work and Organizational Psychology, 5*(4), 501–509.

Grant, D. (1999). HRM, rhetoric and the psychological contract: a case of "easier said than done". *International Journal of Human Resource Management, 10*(2), 327–350.

Greene, A.-M., Ackers, P., & Black, J. (2001). Lost narratives? From paternalism to team-working in a lock manufacturing firm. *Economic & Industrial Democracy, 22*(2), 211–237.

Guest, D.E., & Conway, N. (2002). Communicating the psychological contract: An employer per-spective. *Human Resource Management Journal, 12*(2), 22–38.

Guzzo, R.A., & Noonan, K.A. (1994). Human resource practices as communications and the psy-chological contract. *Human Resource Management, 33*(3), 447–462.

Herriot, P., Manning, W.E.G., & Kidd, J.M. (1997). The content of the psychological contract. *British Journal of Management, 8,* 151–162.

Kenyon, A.J. (2004). Exploring phenomenological research. *International Journal of Market Research, 46*(4), 427–441.

Kickul, J., & Lester, S.W. (2001). Broken promises: Equity sensitivity as a moderator between psy-chological contract breach and employee attitudes and behaviour. *Journal of Business and Psychology, 16*(2), 191–216.

McCracken, D.G. (1988). *The long interview: Qualitative research methods* (Vol. 13). Newbury Park, CA: Sage.

Morgan, D.L. (1997). *Focus groups as qualitative research: Qualitative research methods series* (Vol. 16). Thousand Oaks, CA: Sage.

Morrison, E.W., & Robinson, S.L. (1997). When employees feel betrayed: A model of how psy-chological contract violation develops. *Academy of Management Review, 22*(1), 226–256.

O'Brien, K. (1993). Improving survey questionnaires through focus groups. In D.L. Morgan (Ed.), *Successful focus groups* (pp. 105–117), Newbury Park, CA: Sage.

Othman, R., Arshad, R., Hashim, N.A., & Isa, R.M. (2005). Psychological contract violation and organizational citizenship behavior. *Gadjah Mada International Journal of Business, 7*(3), 325–349.

Owen, S. (2001). The practical, methodological and ethical dilemmas of conducting focus groups with vulnerable clients. *Journal of Advanced Nursing, 36*(5), 652–658.

Robinson, S.L., & Rousseau, D. (1994). Violating the psychological contract: Not the exception but the norm. *Journal of Organizational Behavior, 15*(3), 245–259.

Rousseau, D. (1990). New hire perceptions of their own and their employer's obligations: A study of psychological contracts. *Journal of Organizational Behavior, 11*(5), 389–400.

Rousseau, D.M., & McLean Parks, J. (1993). The contracts of individuals and organizations. In L. L. Cummings & N.M. Staw, (Eds.), *Research in organizational behavior* (pp. 1–43). Greenwich, CT: JAI Press.

Rousseau, D. (1995). *Psychological contracts in organizations: Understanding written and unwrit-ten agreements.* Thousand Oaks, CA: Sage.

Saunders, M., Lewis, P., & Thornhill, A. (2003). *Research methods for business students* (3rd ed.). Harlow, England: Pearson Education.

Shore, L.M., & Tetrick, L.E. (1994). The psychological contract as an explanatory framework in the employment relationship. In C.L. Cooper & D.M. Rousseau (Eds.), *Trends in organiza-tional behaviour* (pp. 91–103). New York: Wiley.

Sturges, J., Conway, N., Guest, D., & Liefooghe, A. (2005). Managing the career deal: The psy-chological contract as a framework for understanding career management, organizational commitment and work behavior. *Journal of Organizational Behavior, 26*(7), 821–838.

Sutton, G., & Griffin, M.A. (2004). Integrating expectations, experiences, and psychological contract violations: A longitudinal study of new professionals. *Journal of Occupational & Organizational Psychology, 77*(4), 493–514.

Thomas, H.D.C., & Anderson, N. (1998). Changes in newcomers' psychological contracts during organizational socialization: A study of recruits entering the British Army. *Journal of Organizational Behaviour, 19*(S1),745–767.

Thompson, J.A., & Bunderson, J.S. (2003). Violations of principle: Ideological currency in the psychological contract. *Academy of Management Review, 28*(4), 571–586.

Tipples, R., & Krivokapic-Skoko, B. (1997). New Zealand academics and performance management. *International Journal of Employment Studies,5*, 103–117.

Turnley, W.H., & Feldman, D. (1998). Psychological contract violations during corporate restructuring. *Human Resource Management, 37*, 71–83.

Wolff, B., Knodel, J., & Sittitrai, W. (1993). Focus groups and surveys as complementary research methods. In D.L. Morgan (Ed.), *Successful focus groups* (pp. 118–136). Newbury Park, CA: Sage.

How to Manage University Staff With Individual Contracts: Some Experiences With Academic Psychological Contracts in New Zealand

Rupert Tipples

John Verry

Lorsch wrote of the psychological contract in the *Harvard Business Review* (1979, p. 180): 'Academics need to develop more theories that managers can use' and advocated situational tools, such as the psychological contract, for the more effective management of staff. After nearly twenty years of growing psychological contract research, Lorsch's advocacy still does not seem to have yielded its full benefit. Recently Conway and Briner have reviewed the evidence on how to manage the psychological contracts of staff and concluded that there is no really good evidence about how to do it, nor as to how successful such 'management' was (2005, pp. 157–178). However, that does not explain the relative popularity of the construct among United Kingdom (UK) managers (Chartered Institute of Personnel and Development [CIPD], 2006; Guest & Conway, 2002). Cullinane and Dundon have offered a more critical review, highlighting the unitary management rhetoric that the construct seems to have been used to promote (2006, p. 123–125). The authors of this chapter believe that useful guidance is offered by some of the earlier research on the subject. Consequently, this chapter reviews the evolving history of the psychological contract construct and how that may be useful in managing staff in the likely individualised employment relationships of Australian universities (Peetz, 2006, p. 196).

Origins

The origin of the term 'psychological contract' is unclear. Argyris and Levinson played key roles, and Schein developed the use of the construct (Roehling, 1997). Aspects of social contract and social exchange theories, and reciprocity, were central to these debates and the evolving definitions (Appendix A). Schein argued that when individuals joined an organisation they tacitly accepted the authority system of the organisation, which implied a willingness to obey because the individual consented to directions received. He suggested an approach to organisational effectiveness based upon 'good communication, flexibility, creativity, and genuine psychological commitment', obtained through '... a more realistic psychological contract'. This was the consistent pattern of his teaching (Schein, 1965, 1970, 1978, 1980).

First Phase Research 1965–1989

Kotter (1973) was one of the first to develop the construct in more operational terms (Appendix A). The expectations, matches and mismatches between employer and employee made up the psychological contract. In extent, the psychological contract might include thousands of elements in contrast to a legal contract of employment. A further complication was added by the extent to which those expectations were clear or unclear. New recruits might have a deep, clear understanding of some, all, or none of the employer's expectations and vice versa, and the contract might change as the mutual expectations of the parties changed over time. From his research, Kotter determined that good psychological contracts were related to greater job satisfaction, productivity and reduced staff turnover. The concept which showed a measurable relationship to productivity, satisfaction and turnover was 'matching', not to get more or less than was expected. Mismatches about a specific element which gave more than expected, caused as many problems as those which gave less. Matches were more likely to eventuate when the individual's or organisation's understanding about an element was clearer , and that understanding was likely to be greater when more thinking and open discussion had taken place concerning it. Mismatches could often occur by accident, out of neglect, rather than as the result of conscious decisions. The key to contract formulation was the extent of the match or fit between the parties' expectations, not getting more (Kotter, 1973, pp. 93–97), a finding endorsed by Schein (1980, p. 22).

The publication of Kotter's research coincided with that of the 'met expectations' hypothesis, explained as:

> ... the discrepancy between what a person encounters on the job in the way of positive and negative experiences and what he expected to encounter ... when an individual's expectations — whatever they are — are not substantially met, his propensity to withdraw would increase. (Porter & Steers, 1973, p. 152)

Job satisfaction was:

> ... the sum total of an individual's expectations on the job. The more an individual's expectations are met on the job, the greater his satisfaction (Porter & Steers, 1973, p. 169). Job satisfaction was negatively related to the decision to withdraw from a job. Role clarity and the receipt of recognition and feedback were also inversely related to turnover. Met expectations were central to the withdrawal decision, and 'each individual is seen as bringing to the employment situation his own unique set of expectations for his job (p. 170).

Staff turnover would be reduced if expectations of new recruits were clarified so as to align them with available rewards and thus meet expectations. The accuracy and realism of employees' expectations could also be increased through improved communications about the nature of the job and the probable rewards of effective performance. The probability of forming unrealistic expectations should be decreased where the employee fully understood what was expected of them and what the organisation provided in return. Clarification of expectations and potential rewards would increase the likelihood of expectations being met and there should also be a major focus on differential expectations at the time of entry to organisations — how much they were met and how they changed over time, with as much attention to expectations as to differential work circumstances (Porter & Steers, 1973, p. 173). Thus, met expectations achieved a matched psychological contract, much as Kotter had suggested.

Wanous, Poland, Premack and Davis (1992, pp. 292–294) carried out a meta-analysis on met expectations as they affected newcomer attitudes and behaviours and concluded that met expectations were most highly correlated with job satisfaction, and then in declining strength with organisational commitment, intent to remain and job survival. In terms of the degree of clarity/ambiguity in the work environment they concluded that environments which sent clear messages to newcomers, where the insiders sending the messages were in agreement, had the power to disconfirm the most strongly-held expectations of newcomers. Where the messages were ambiguous or conflicting, newcomers could maintain their initial expectations.

Second Phase Research 1989–1995: United States

Direct research on psychological contracts in the United States increased through Rousseau and her team in the late 1980s (e.g., Rousseau, 1989, 1990). They differentiated between mutual expectations and psychological contracts by focusing on the beliefs of the individual employees in the promissory aspects of their psychological contracts. The latter only arose where there were perceived mutual obligations. In practice, this distinction seems to be a matter of degree rather than substance. Robinson, Kraatz and Rousseau (1994) reported much stronger relationships between the violation of psychological contracts (their definition, Appendix A) and unmet expectations (Wanous et al., 1992), and respectively job satisfaction or dissatisfaction, intentions to stay or leave, and job turnover. In effect, they identify a much stronger form of the concept earlier described by Levinson, Price, Munden, and Solley (1963), Schein (1965) and Kotter (1973).

Second Phase Research 1989–1995: United Kingdom

In contrast, Herriot's team's approach in the United Kingdom viewed psychological contracts as the invisible glue which attached individuals to employing organisations over time, and focused their definition on mutual obligations (see Figure 1), which were not necessarily made explicit and were subject to continuous change in the realities of individual and organisational life. Herriot helped popularise psychological contracts and their role in understanding recruitment, current managerial employment relationships and careers (Herriot, 1989a, 1992; Herriot & Pemberton, 1995).

Paucity of Empirical Research

Recent research indicates that elaboration of the psychological contract construct has undergone minimal development (Conway & Briner, 2005; Cullinane & Dundon, 2006). There was little empirical research in earlier years (1960–1988), for which reasons are not difficult to suggest. The psychological contract is dynamic — it is continuously changing, as Herriot put it:

> At any one point in time we can take a snapshot of the contract, but that's merely a fix on a moving target. Organisations' expectations change and so do individuals' — which is why a contract that meets some of both today may meet few of either in a year or two's time. (Herriot, 1992, p. 7)

An individual may also have a number of psychological contracts at the same time, perhaps as many as the social roles he/she occupies. Consequently, researchers had not often focused on empirical investigation.

In spite of the lack of empirical research, especially before 1996, integrating the research on the two constructs — psychological contracts and met expectations — has been mutually reinforcing. It has suggested some practical ways that mutually matching expectations and psychological contracts can be established and maintained. This 'Contracting' strategy was developed by Tipples (1996). It was subsequently used to investigate employment relations at Lincoln University and to assist in resolving dairy farming employment problems in New Zealand (Tipples, Hoogeveen, & Gould, 2000).

Psychological Contract Research at Lincoln

In the mid-1990s, Lincoln University was undergoing the ravages of the 'New Public Management' policies (Boston, Martin, Pallot, & Walsh ,1996, pp. 25–28) and academics were frustrated. A realisation that management had unilaterally reduced the 'career' grade to which most academics could rise led to investigation of their psychological contracts — had they been violated? Initial investigations borrowed heavily from Rousseau et al.'s research (Tipples & Krivokapic-Skoko, 1996), and later from Herriot, Hirsh and Reilly (1998; Tipples & Jones, 1998). With the alternative research method based on critical incidents, provided by Herriot et al., we were then in a position to examine the content of academics' psychological contracts in a new and totally fresh way, with none of Rousseau et al.'s preconceptions whatsoever. The tantalising question: 'Would the answers provided by the two different techniques be consistent or variant, and would that have practical implications for academic management?' drove the research. In 1997, we were not aware of any previous attempt to link the results of Rousseau et al.'s American research team and Herriot et al.'s UK-based team. Nor were we aware of these methods being applied to the same base population, albeit at marginally different time periods. Consequently, our objective was to explore the content of academics' psychological contracts de novo using Herriot et al.'s critical incident method, and compare the results with those obtained formerly in 1996 with Rousseau et al.'s methods.

If we compare Tipples and Jones's (1998) results from Herriot et al.'s critical incident technique with Tipples and Krivokapic-Skoko (1996) using questions derived from Rousseau et al.'s research, we find that there is a degree of consistency between the results. In 1996, academic employees believed that the university owed them, above all else, 'job satisfaction'. In 1997, the major component of the psychological contract was imputed as being concerned with the work environment. The Rousseau measure did not differentiate between the components of job satisfaction, but data were also collected from each respondent for the Job Descriptive Index (JDI:(Smith, Kendall, & Hulin, 1969). One of those elements related to 'satisfaction with work', which was significantly lower than the satisfaction with work of an equivalent group of US academics. Further, 94% of the incidents cited, which were classified in the work environment class, were concerned with the university treating its employees in a way that was below that expected. So the two sets of results seem consistent in that respect.

'Loyalty' and 'work outside ordinary office hours' were the most important factors academics believed they owed to the university. Hours and loyalty were the second and third major components of individual's psychological contracts most cited by the employee group studied, and first and third of those cited by employers. The weakness of Rousseau et al.'s research appears to be its failure to identify the quality and quantity of employees' work as one of the major components of individuals' psychological contracts. Consequently, the original speculation that Rousseau et al. might have omitted important components of psychological contracts appeared to be correct. Rousseau et al. developed their questions from talking to a group of Human Resource and Personnel managers. Apparently, they did not consult real employees and have appeared to leave out the obvious. Therefore, there must be some doubt as to whether Rousseau et al.'s questions for elucidating the content of individuals' psychological contracts were really as adequate as they were thought to be.

Conclusions from New Zealand Research

Herriot, Manning and Kidd's critical incident approach provided a way to assess the content of psychological contracts de novo. Utilisation of Rousseau's questions was not appropriate without substantial pretesting to discover if they were applicable to the New Zealand academic situation, and then only after appropriate modification. In terms of the obligations facing employees, the content of psychological contracts appeared to be concerned with the traditional issues of quantity and quality of work done, time applied to that work and loyalty to the employer. Obligations of the employer centred around providing a suitable work environment, supportive management, appropriate recognition for special achievements, adequate consultation, fairness and job security. Employer/managers and employees had different views on the most salient features of their psychological contracts, but there was no consistency to these differences.

Implications

In 1998, Tipples and Jones concluded that Herriot et al.'s 'critical incident' approach could be used to investigate de novo the content of psychological contracts for other groups of workers. The differences between the employer/manager group and the employee group in terms of their perceptions of the mutual obligations, promises, and expectations forming the reciprocal exchanges of psychological contracts were a continued cause for concern for both groups, with a lack of match causing unstable psychological contracts and employment relationships. For both parties this was undesirable. It was also highlighted in a study of the New Zealand dairy farming industry, which had experienced acute difficulties in recruiting and retaining staff. An industry strategy through matching expectations and perceived obligations for improving employment relationships was suggested as a remedy (Tipples, 1996; Tipples, Hoogeveen,& Gould, 2000). Exactly the same principles could be adopted in individualised academic management.

While such a strategy has appeared to help the dairy farming industry with its labour recruitment and retention concerns, Conway and Briner (2005, pp. 40–3, 96) have highlighted the limitations of this 'critical incident' approach. They suggested the technique told more about violations and exceeded expectations than about the content of the psychological contract, but had to admit that the results were consistent with some reported by Guest and Conway (1998) for UK employees. It did suffer from the weakness of not assessing the exchange aspects of the deal, and being dependent on the accurate memory of the interview subjects. They also believed it might overlook the more mundane aspects of work if there were no 'incidents'. That was not a problem with dairy farming or academia at Lincoln! Why should it be a problem for any Australian universities?

Failure to combat dysfunctional psychological contracts can lead to damaging the mutual trust between the parties. Prior trust has been shown to have an impact on the recognition and interpretation of breaches of contract. If prior trust moderates the impact of a breach, it may be suggested that actively establishing and maintaining trusting relationships with employees within universities inoculates the employees from the effects of potential contractual transgressions, which Fox had previously suggested (Fox, 1974). Where employers can earn the trust of employees early on, employees will be less likely to perceive a contract breach in the first place and more likely to retain their trust despite possible changes or breaches (perceived or actual) in the employment agreement (Robinson, 1996, p. 596). A vicious circle of mistrust, interpreting a breach of trust as a violation rather than a breach, and further loss of trust, may incapacitate any organisation, even a university. A trust-building strategy would be more facilitating, a conclusion also reached by Herriot, Hirsh and Reilly (1998), which would also apply to university management. Sharkie has reinforced this point with his argument that trust is essential for the sharing of knowledge in organisations such as universities (2005, p. 43).

Recent Research — Post 2000

Since 2000, the literature on psychological contracts has increased exponentially,[1] but a unifying theoretical position has yet to be established. A recent critical review reported that the 'theoretical assumptions that seem to pervade the psychological contract literature are not without major deficiencies, which in turn pose serious questions around the continued sustainability of the construct as presently constituted' (Cullinane & Dundon, 2006, p. 113).

In part, the deficiency is with the term psychological contract, which is drawn from two different disciplines — psychology and law. Legally, a contract arises from a meeting of two minds; there has to be an offer and acceptance of the offer by another. While a contract can be verbal, the issue then arises as to what the two parties agreed. This is less likely to be an issue where the contract is written, as the terms of the agreement will be recorded. This is the approach that has been followed by Herriot et al. (1997) and better reflects the reality of the psychological contract in the employment relationship. The limitation, from a legal perspective, is that while the core contractual obligations of the employment relationship, namely the terms and conditions of employment, can be clearly stated and agreed, it is the relational aspects that provide the challenge as there is reliance on the personal performance of the individual employee and the individual employer.

The psychological perspective has tended to takes a more unilateral approach. The emphasis is on the individual's perception. Krivokapic-Skoko, Ivers, and O'Neill (2006), following Rousseau et al., see this conceptualisation as emphasising that the psychological contract is formulated only in the mind of the employee and is therefore about

> ... individual beliefs, shaped by the organization, regarding the terms of an exchange between individuals and their organization ... A key feature of the psychological contract is that the individual voluntarily assents to make and accept certain promises as he or she understands them. (Rousseau, 1995, p. 9–10)

It is from this disjunctive position that the psychological contract has developed into an important construct which has focused on understanding the employment relationship. The early research was undertaken in a period where jobs did provide security. Before the restructuring and downsizing of the 1990s, employee expectations were different from the current employment market which has changed from providing certainty to one where change is the norm. The arguments for employee flexibility have tended to have strongly managerialist overtones and have taken a firmly unitary rather than pluralist position (Cullinane & Dundon, 2006). It must be remembered that in an undersupplied labour market, as is the prospect in many developed economies (Deloitte, 2005), employees have the freedom to move around whereas employers need to keep them to sustain levels of labour productivity. With future academic labour supplies likely to be constrained, university managers need to bear this in mind when negotiating future jobs to ensure good psychological contracts contribute to good productivity.

Conway and Briner see the psychological contract as helping in the understanding of human behaviour at work.

> Put simply, the psychological contract is about the exchange relationship between employer and employee ... The assumption is that the relationship is based on an exchange in which each party will exchange something they can provide for something the other party can provide. (2005, p. 1).

The reality of the employment relationship is that it encompasses both transactional and relational aspects. The former can be governed by the employment contract, which identifies agreement in regard to the basic terms and conditions between the employee and employer. However, it is the relational components of the employment relationship that provide a challenge, as these are usually specific to the person and are where the psychological contract construct is able to advance our knowledge. Sharkie argues that:

> the lifetime employment model has largely been disbanded and replaced with a new psychological contract with the potential for employment insecurity, income insecurity and working time insecurity, all of which may be exacerbated by a lack of effective representation. (2005, p. 43).

Sharkie considers that trust will be central to the psychological contract in the new precarious employment environment. This is supported by Pate's model which provides a 'holistic view of causes and potential reactions to psychological contract breach and as such provides a useful overview of complex reactions' (2006, p. 43).

For a better understanding of employee behaviour, motivation and productivity, particularly in the university workplace, the time is ripe for further studies to draw on the input from recent research (Conway & Briner, 2005; Cullinane & Dundon, 2006; Krivokapic-Skoko et al., 2006; Pate, 2006) and use a range of qualitative methodologies to explore the relational aspects, such as the interpersonal and restorative. A good point to start may be David Guest's diagrammatic formulation of the psychological contract (Guest, 2004) informed by Pate's amended model of psychological contract development. Such further studies clearly need to be based on a triangulation of research methods (Denzin, 1989) to provide more convincing and reliable results.

Endnote

1   Google Scholar's Advanced searching facility for Business, Administration, Finance and Economics, and Social Sciences, Arts and Humanities on March 27, 2007, recorded 80 mentions in articles of 'Psychological Contracts' between 1960–1988, 189 from 1989 to 1995, 805 from 1996–2000, and 1990 from 2001–2006 (July). These dates represent particular periods of the primary author's research activity on psychological contracts. While this has to be recognised as an imprecise measure, it does indicate the growing level of awareness of the psychological contract construct and the increase in scholarly activity in relation to it since it first appeared around 1960.

References

Boston, J., Martin, J., Pallot, J., & Walsh, P. (1996). *Public management: The New Zealand model.* Auckland: Oxford University Press.

Chartered Institute of Personnel and Development (CIPD). (2006, January). *Managing the psychological contract.* .Retrieved July 10 , 2006, from http://cipd.co.uk/subjects/empreltns/psycntrct/psycontr.htm?IsSrchRes=1

Conway, N., & Briner, R.B. (2005). *Understanding psychological contracts at work: A critical evaluation of theory and research.* New York: Oxford University Press.

Cullinane, N., & Dundon, T. (2006). The psychological contract: A critical review. *International Journal of Management Reviews, 8*(2), 113–129.

Deloitte. (2005, December). *University staff remuneration and resourcing: A comparison of New Zealand and selected international (Australia, Canada, England, USA) Data.* Prepared for the New Zealand Vice Chancellors Committee and the Association of University Staff of New Zealand.

Denzin, N.K. (1989). *The research act* (3rd ed.). New Jersey: Prentice-Hall.

Fox, A. (1974). *Beyond contract: Work, power and trust relations.* London: Faber and Faber.

Guest, D.E. (2004). The psychology of the employment relationship: An analysis based on the psychological contract. *Applied Psychology: An International Review, 53*(4), 541–555.

Guest, D.E., & Conway, N. (1998). *Fairness and the psychological contract.* London: IPD Research Report.

Guest, D.E., & Conway, N. (2002). Communicating the psychological contract: A employer perspective. *Human Resource Management Journal, 12*(2), 22–38.

Herriot, P. (1989a). *Recruitment in the 90s.* London: Institute of Personnel Management.

Herriot, P. (1992). *The career management challenge.* London: Sage Books Ltd.

Herriot, P., & Pemberton, C. (1995). *New deals: The revolution in managerial careers*. Chichester, England: John Wiley and Sons.

Herriot, P., Manning, W.E.G., & Kidd, J.M. (1997). The content of the psychological contract. *British Journal of Management*, 8, 151–162.

Herriot, P., Hirsh, W., & Reilly, P. (1998). *Trust and transition: Managing today's employment relationship.*, Chichester, England: Wiley.

Kotter, J. (1973). The psychological contract: Managing the joining-up process. *California Management Review*, 15(3), 91–99.

Krivokapic-Skoko, B., Ivers, J., & O'Neill, G. (2006, January). *Psychological contracts: Conceptual and empirical considerations* (Working Paper No. 01/06). Bathurst, Australia: Faculty of Commerce, Charles Sturt University.

Levinson, H., Price, C.R., Munden, K.J., & Solley, C.M. (1963). *Men, management and mental health*. Cambridge, MA: Harvard University Press.

Lorsch, J. (1979, March–April). Making behavioral science more useful. *Harvard Business Review*, 57(2) , 171–180.

Pate, J. (2006). The changing contours of the psychological contract: Unpacking context and circumstances of breach. *Journal of European Industrial Training*, 30(1), 32–47.

Peetz, D. (2006). *Brave new work place: How Individual contracts are changing our jobs*. Sydney, NSW: Allen and Unwin.

Porter, L.W., & Steers, R.M. (1973). Organisational, work and personal factors in employee turnover and absenteeism. *Psychological Bulletin*, 80(2), 151–176.

Robinson, S.L. (1996). Trust and breach of the psychological contract. *Administrative Science Quarterly*, 41, 574–599.

Robinson, S.L., Kraatz, M.S., & Rousseau, D.M. (1994). Changing obligations and the psychological contract: A longitudinal study. *Academy of Management Journal*, 37(1), 137–152.

Robinson, S.L., & Rousseau, D. (1994). Violating the psychological contract: Not the exception but the norm. *Journal of Organizational Behavior*, 15(3), 245–259.

Roehling, M.V. (1997). The origins and early development of the psychological contract construct. *Journal of Management History*, 3(2), 204–303.

Rousseau, D. (1989). Psychological and implied contracts in organisations. *Employee Responsibilities and Rights Journal*, 2(2), 121–139.

Rousseau, D.M. (1990). New hire perceptions of their own and their employer's obligations: A study of psychological contracts. *Journal of Organisational Behavior*, 11(5), 389–400.

Rousseau, D.M. (1995). *Psychological contracts in organizations: Understanding written and unwritten agreements*. Thousand Oaks, CA: Sage Publications, Inc.

Rousseau, D.M., & Tijoriwala, S.A. (1998). Assessing psychological contracts: Issues, alternatives and measures. *Journal of Organizational Behavior*, 19, 679–695.

Schein, E. (1965). *Organisational Psychology* (1st ed.). Englewood Cliffs, NJ: Prentice-Hall Inc

Schein, E. (1970). *Organisational Psychology* (2nd ed.). Englewood Cliffs, NJ: Prentice-Hall Inc

Schein, E. (1978). *Career dynamics: Matching individual and organizational needs*, Reading, MS: Addison-Wesley Publishing Co.

Schein, E. (1980). *Organisational Psychology* (3rd ed.). Englewood Cliffs, NJ: Prentice-Hall Inc

Sharkie, R. (2005). Precariousness under the new psychological contract: The effect on trust and the willingness to converse and share knowledge. *Knowledge Management Research & Practice*, 3, 37–44.

Smith, P.C., Kendall, L., & Hulin, C.L. (1969). *The measurement of satisfaction in work and retirement*. Chicago: Rand McNally.

Tipples, R.(1996, December). Contracting: The key to employment relations. *International Employment Relations Review, 2*(2), 19–41.

Tipples, R.S., & Krivokapic-Skoko, B. (1996, October). New Zealand academics and performance management: Changing academic careers, legal and psychological contracts at Lincoln University since 1990. *International Journal of Employment Studies, 5*(2), 103–116.

Tipples, R.S., & Jones, P. (1998). Extra contractual relations: The substance of academics' psychological contracts in New Zealand. In R. Harbridge, C. Gadd, & A. Crawford (Eds.), *Current Research in Industrial Relations: Proceedings of the 12th. AIRRANZ Conference* (pp. 377–385). Wellington, New Zealand: Victoria University of Wellington.

Tipples, R.S., Hoogeveen, M., & Gould, E. (2000, June). Getting employment relations right. *Primary Industry Management, 3*(2), 23–26.

Wanous, J.P., Poland, T.D., Premack, S.L., & Davis, K. (1992). The effects of met expectations on newcomer attitudes and behaviors: A review and meta-analysis. *Journal of Applied Psychology, 77*(3), 288–297.

Appendix A

Evolving Definitions of the Psychological contract

The expectations of both employees and company were … conceived as components of a psychological contract. Such a contract is rarely made formal. It is a much broader conception than the traditional use of the word in industrial relations where it has come to mean the specifics of a written legal agreement between management and labor. The psychological contract is a series of mutual expectations of which the parties to the relationship may not themselves be even dimly aware but which nonetheless govern their relationship to each other. (Levinson et al., 1963, p. 21)

The notion of a psychological contract implies that the individual has a variety of expectations of the organization and the organization has a variety of expectations of him. These expectations not only cover how much work is to be performed for how much pay, but also involves the whole pattern of rights, privileges, and obligations between worker and organization … Expectations such as these are not written into any formal agreement between employee and organization, yet they operate powerfully as determinants of behavior. (Schein, 1965, p. 11)

… the psychological contract is an implicit contract between an individual and his organization which specifies what each expects to give and receive from each other in their relationship. (Kotter, 1973, p. 93)

The psychological contract, unlike expectations, entails a belief in what the employer is obliged to provide, based on perceived promises of mutual exchange. (Robinson & Rousseau, 1994, p. 240)

… individual beliefs, shaped by the organization, regarding the terms of an exchange between individuals and their organization … A key feature of the psychological contract is that the individual voluntary assents to make and accept certain promises as he or she understands them. (Rousseau, 1995, pp. 9–10)

The perceptions of mutual obligations to each other held by the two parties in an employment relationship, the organisation and the employee. (Herriot et al., 1997, p. 151)

An individual's belief in mutual obligations between that person and another party such as an employer. (Rousseau & Tijoriwala, 1998, p. 679)

The perception of both parties to the employment relationship, organization and individual, of the reciprocal promises and obligations implied in that relationship. (Guest & Conway, 2002, p. 22)

... the psychological contract is considered to be an employee's subjective understanding of promissory-based reciprocal exchanges between him or herself and the organization. (Conway & Briner, 2005, p. 35)

... the perceptions of the two parties, employee and employer, of what their mutual obligations are towards each other". These obligations will often be informal and imprecise: they may be inferred from actions or from what happened in the past, as well as from statements made by the employer, for example during the recruitment process or in performance appraisals. Some obligations may be seen as 'promises' and others as 'expectations'. The important thing is that they are viewed by the employee to be part of the relationship with the employer. (CIPD, 2006, p. 1)

Happy High-Performing Managers

Peter Hosie

Peter Sevastos

Antonio Travaglione

There has long been an adherence to the intuitively appealing notion that happy employees perform better. But decades of research have been unable to establish a strong link between job satisfaction and performance. In large part, this has resulted from researchers erroneously conceiving and operationalising job satisfaction as being identical to affective wellbeing. Belief in the 'happy-productive worker' thesis has its roots in the human behaviour school of the 1950s. Similarly, the 1970s human relations movement had a significant influence on job redesign and quality-of-life initiatives and was credited with specifying the original satisfaction–performance relationship (Strauss, 1968). Despite mixed empirical evidence, there is support in the literature to suggest that a relationship exists between managers' affective wellbeing, intrinsic job satisfaction and their performance.

This study investigated the relationship between managers' job-related affective wellbeing ('affective wellbeing'), intrinsic job satisfaction and their contextual and task job performance ('managers' performance'). Specifically, the main goal was to establish which indicators of managers' affective wellbeing and intrinsic job satisfaction might predict dimensions of their' contextual and task performance.

Justification for the Research

A strong causal link has been established between people management and business performance by Patterson, West, Lawthom and Nickell (1998). Compared to other management practices (e.g., strategy, quality focus, investment in research and development), human resource practices explained 18% of the variation in productivity and 19% in profitability of companies in the United Kingdom. Two clusters of skills — acquisition and development of employee skills (including the use of appraisals), and job design — were shown to be particularly important. Patterson and colleagues have provided an empirically compelling argument supporting the relationship between people management practices and commercial performance.

Managers are pivotal to an organisation's productivity and effectiveness, as they have ultimate responsibility for maximising the resources available for organisations to create value (Jones, 1995). The resource-based view of the firm recognised the value added by human capital (Hamel & Prahalad, 1994; Wernefelt, 1984). Regardless of the industry or country concerned, managers represent the human capital that is critical to an organisation's success (Williams, 1991). Any decline in managers' performance inevitably results in revenue foregone, opportunities lost and increased costs. In turn, this hampers the capacity of organisations and, ultimately, national economies to create wealth.

Organisations are under increasing pressure to improve productivity, while simultaneously reducing costs, resulting in an epidemic of 'corporate anorexia' (Hamel, 1996). A new enterprise formula is emerging — '$1/2 \times 2 \times 3$' — whereby half as many people are being paid twice as much, to produce three times more (Handy, 1996). This trend to 'squeezing the pips' is particularly evident for managers, where the incidence of stress and burnout is increasingly common (Quinn, Faerman, Thompson, & McGrath 1996; Reinhold, 1997). Affective wellbeing is treated in this study as a first-order concept that underpins stress. Thus, affective reactions are conceived of as a precursor to 'stress' in the workplace. Emotional reactions, resulting from intrinsic and extrinsic stimuli, determine a person's reactions to stressful situations.

Organisational dynamics experienced by Australian managers are indicative of those facing most nation-states and economies. Australian managers are under increasing pressure to produce superior results in shorter timeframes, with fewer resources (Coles, 1999; Forster & Still, 2001). Handy (1996) considered the $1/2 \times 2 \times 3$ formula 'about right' for Australia, New Zealand, the United Kingdom and North America. To reach and sustain heightened levels of performance, and to avoid burnout in this environment, it is desirable that organisations develop strategies for maintaining managers' affective wellbeing and intrinsic job satisfaction. Of the three psychological aspects of burnout (emotional exhaustion, depersonalisation, diminished sense of personal accomplishment), emotional exhaustion is increasingly prevalent in western workplaces (Lee & Ashforth, 1996).

By establishing how affective wellbeing and intrinsic job satisfaction influences performance, it will be possible to predict how deterioration, or an improvement, in affective wellbeing and intrinsic job satisfaction impacts on managers' performance. Similarly, management practices that increase managers' affective wellbeing and intrinsic job satisfaction may result in corresponding reductions in workplace tension and improved efficiency. Such information may be used to develop recommendations about changes that are likely to promote a healthier and more supportive work environment for managers.

Happy–Productive Workers

Decades of research have found inadequate evidence to support the 'happy–productive worker thesis' (Staw, 1986) or the proposition that 'a happy worker is a good worker' (Katzell & Thompson, 1995, p. 111). Research has also been unable to establish a close link between job satisfaction and performance (see Brayfield & Crockett, 1955; Iaffaldano & Muchinsky, 1985; Locke, 1976; Vroom, 1964). This may be a result of researchers erroneously conceiving and operationalising job satisfaction as being synonymous with affective wellbeing (Cropanzano & Wright, 2001; Cropanzano, James & Konovsky 1993; Wright & Cropanzano, 2000). Later meta-analyses have indicated that there is a stronger relationship between job satisfaction and job performance than was previously evident (Harter, Schmitt, & Hays, 2002; Judge, Thoresen, Bono, & Patton 2001).

Researchers have mostly ceased investigating whether satisfied employees are more productive, possibly as a consequence of using job satisfaction as the predictor variable, instead of more appropriate measures such as 'happiness' (Wright & Staw, 1999a, 1999b), or affective wellbeing (Sevastos, 1996). The construct 'managers' job performance' has also not been robustly measured, making associations between these constructs problematic. These results seem partly due to conceptual misspecification and inadequate research methodologies. Rather than being an aberrant stream of investigation, these findings are argued to result from poorly specified and measured constructs. Despite the lack of empirical evidence, the notion that satisfied or happy workers are more productive is firmly entrenched in management ideology (Ledford 1999; Wright & Staw, 1999a, 1999b). Studies from the 1930s onwards found only modest support for the link between worker satisfaction and improved job performance (Organ & Paine, 1999).

Apart from a study by George and Bettenhausen (1990), affective wellbeing has seldom been investigated as a predictor of favourable work outcomes for managers. Wright and Staw (1999a, 1999b) rekindled the general debate about whether happy workers are more productive. They also found a 'plausible link' between employees' affective states and work behaviour that justified 're-opening the question of whether happy workers are also more productive' (1991, p. 2). Reasoning and research into the construct of happiness preceded research into affective wellbeing. Emotions and happiness form the conceptual bases of affective wellbeing. There is a case for extending the happy–productive worker thesis into an examination of the extent to which managers' affective wellbeing influences performance, using a more robust methodology to measure these constructs. Reinvigorating this debate may also inform the more general, but unproven proposition that happy employees perform more effectively.

A Partial Model of Managers' Affective WellBeing, Intrinsic Job Satisfaction and Performance ('Model')

Warr has suggested that researchers should explore 'what is known about the relationship between rated work performance and the components of mental health' (1987, p. 293). A range of organisational variables have been found to predict 20% of the unique variance in job satisfaction, and an additional 5% of unique variance in affective wellbeing (Sevastos, 1996). Research has mainly focused on job satisfaction when, as has been suggested, affective wellbeing and intrinsic job satisfaction may provide an improved explanation of performance in the workplace. From the literature and information collected for this study, a model was developed and tested that may have predictive power, as illustrated in Figure 1.

Methodology

A cross-sectional questionnaire of 19 Western Australian organisations was undertaken during 1998–1999 to collect data to test the hypotheses underpinning the model. Data were collected using self-report measures of affective wellbeing and intrinsic job satisfaction, and downward appraisal of managers' performance using the evaluations of the person to whom managers then reported. A composite selection of private, public and 'third sector' organisations was surveyed, representing managers from a range of occupational groups. A total of 400 usable questionnaires were returned from the 1552 distributed, representing a 26% usable response rate.

Self-report data from the sample was used to measure managers' affective wellbeing and intrinsic job satisfaction. Published scales of job-related affective wellbeing (Sevastos, 1996) and intrinsic job satisfaction (Cook, Hepworth, Wall, & Warr, 1981; Sevastos, 1996;) items were used. The properties of the instruments

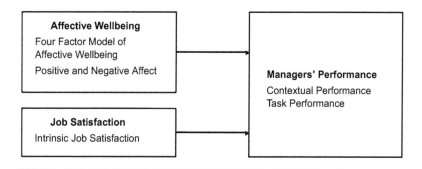

Figure 1

A partial model of managers' affective well-being, intrinsic job satisfaction and performance.

used were acceptable for measuring state and trait affective wellbeing and managers' performance. Self and superior appraisals were used to gauge managers' performance. No suitable validated measures of managers' performance were identified in the literature. Managers' contextual and task performance items were devised by the researcher from Borman and Brush's (1993) and Borman and Motowidlo's (1997) taxonomies of managers' performance. Generic behaviour dimensions were also included from the literature (Borman & Brush, 1993; Konovsky & Organ, 1996; Organ & Lingl, 1995; Podsakoff, MacKenzie, Mormon, & Fetter, 1990; Quinn et al., 1996).

Methods

Measures used in this study are consistent with the established theory base in this stream of research and were closely aligned to the constructs being investigated. From the literature review it became apparent that there were a considerable number of well-validated instruments for measuring affective wellbeing and intrinsic job satisfaction, but few that were suitable for collecting data on variables identified as determining behavioural outcomes of managers' performance. Affective wellbeing items were drawn from published and validated scales used to measure managers' affective wellbeing and intrinsic job satisfaction:

- 20-item Positive And Negative Affect Schedule (PANAS; Watson & Clark, 1984)
- 12-item Four Factor Congeneric Model of Job-related Affective Well-being (Sevastos, 1996)
- 7-item intrinsic job satisfaction subscale (Cook et al., 1982; Sevastos, 1996).

This study extends upon Wright and Staw's (1999a, 1999b) research by more reliably measuring state affect (mood) and managers' performance. Ledford also determined that the 'most important problem to address in research on the happiness–productivity connection is the operationalization of the two key constructs' (1999, p. 30). Wright and Staw conceded that their 'data might have been stronger had there been better calibration in the measurement of mood and rated performance' (1999a, p. 11).

Statistical Attributes of Affective WellBeing and Intrinsic Job Satisfaction Scales

Two affective wellbeing and intrinsic job satisfaction scales were compared and evaluated before selecting those suitable for multivariate analysis. Both of these scales were suitable for measuring managers' affective wellbeing in relation to their contextual and task performance. In particular, the scales were theoretically congruent with the notion of 'happiness' (Sevastos, 1996; Warr, 1990b).

Table 1
Alpha Coefficients and Items for Wellbeing Scales and Subscales*

Construct	Scales/Subscales	Items	α
Trait affectivity	Positive affect	10	.89
	Negative affect	10	.87
Job-related	Enthusiasm	3	.90
Affective wellbeing	Depression	3	.83
	Anxiety	3	.80
	Relaxation	3	.84
Job satisfaction	Intrinsic Job Satisfaction	7	.85

Note: * (n = 200)

The four (independent variable) scales (affective wellbeing and intrinsic job satisfaction) used were robust as they have been developed and replicated with large samples and are widely published. The affective wellbeing scales were not altered because the properties of these scales had already been established. Nevertheless, the psychometric properties of the scales were still pertinent. As with the pilot data, the scale properties are reported to ensure that the measures are within statistically acceptable parameters. Table 1 provides a summary of the alpha coefficients for affective wellbeing and intrinsic job satisfaction data.

All alpha coefficients for affective wellbeing and intrinsic job satisfaction were well above the recommended threshold of .70 (Nunnally, 1978), ranging from .80 to .90.

Exploratory Factor Analysis of Affective Wellbeing Indicators and Variables

Maximum Likelihood Estimation (MLE) is a more effective factor analysis for using only eigenvalues ≥ 1. Maximum Likelihood (ML) assumes that the data being analysed are multivariate normal. ML represents and separately estimates the unique portion of each variable measured. ML has more restricted assumptions and only analyses shared variance (latent dimensions). The ML begins with the input of Pearson product-moment correlation using squared multiple correlations to make initial estimates of communality. Theoretically based solutions, uncontaminated by unique and error variance, are produced by ML (Hair, Anderson, Tatham, & Black, 1995).

Positive And Negative Affect Schedule (PANAS) was used as a dispositional (personality) control of affect. Consistent with Watson, Clark and Tellegen's (1988) intention, all the PANAS variables had strong primary loadings on the appropriate factor with acceptable loadings on secondary factors, indicating relatively pure markers of PA and NA. PANAS has two factors that contained positive and negatively worded items. Schmitt and Stutts (1995) warned that factor analysis on scales with polar opposites (e.g.,

Table 2

PANAS Pattern Matrix[a*]

	Factor	
	1 PA	2 NA
1. Interested	.78	
3. Excited	.59	
5. Strong	.61	
9. Enthusiastic	.81	
10. Proud	.63	
12. Alert	.62	
14. Inspired	.77	
16. Determined	.76	
17. Attentive	.67	
19. Active	.54	
2. Distressed		.54
4. Upset		.57
6. Guilty		.46
7. Scared		.82
8. Hostile		.42
11. Irritable		.44
13. Ashamed		.52
15. Nervous		.71
18. Jittery		.72
20. Afraid		.91

Note: [a] Rotation converged in 7 iterations
* (n = 200)

happy–sad) that are intended to represent a trait or descriptor, may result in spurious negative factors being identified. Variable loadings have been found to be lower when positively worded variables are loaded on the same factor (Raghunathan, 1995). Alphas for the scales in Table 2 indicated that the NA factor was authentic. Table 2 gives the item loadings for the pattern matrix loadings for PANAS. Total variance explained for PANAS was 50.6%.

The Four Factor Model of Job-Related Affective Wellbeing scale taps the entire state affect space. Table 3 gives the ML with oblimin pattern matrix loadings for this model.

The amount of variance for the Four-Factor Model of Job-Related Affective Wellbeing explained was 77.9%. All items exhibited substantial loadings > .5, except 'Gloomy' (.389). Six of the 12 items loaded > .80, indicating the presence of a large number of marker variables. This pattern matrix supports the four-factor unipolar model rather than the bipolar model. Item 1.098 loaded 1.026 on the item and factor 'Enthusiasm'. When structure matrix values are very high, pattern matrix values slightly > 1.00 may be obtained. This happens occasionally with empirical data since loadings are not correlations and consequently are not limited to values of < 1.00 (Child, 1990).

Table 3
Four Factor Model of Job-Related Affective Wellbeing*

	1 Enthusiasm	2 Anxiety	3 Depression	4 Relaxation
24. Enthusiastic	1.026			
25. Motivated	.873			
30. Optimistic	.598			
26. Worried		.772		
23. Anxious		.764		
28. Tense		.628		
29. Depressed			.905	
32. Miserable			.849	
21. Gloomy			.389	
31. Relaxed				.882
27. Restful				.811
22. Calm				.612

Note: ᵃ Rotation converged in 9 iterations
* (n = 200)

Exploratory Factor Analysis of Intrinsic Job Satisfaction Indicators and Variables

Intrinsic job satisfaction variables were predicted to be closely aligned with affective wellbeing. As anticipated, the intrinsic job satisfaction indicators exhibited a very high internal reliability (α =.85), and loaded strongly on the predicted factor (see Table 4). Total variance accounted for was 54.4%.

Exploratory Factor Analysis of Managers' Performance Indicators and Variables

Answering the research questions required the development of an instrument to measure the structure of managers' contextual and task performance. An eight-dimensional measurement model of managers' performance, derived from the survey data, was tested by exploratory and confirmatory factor

Table 4
Intrinsic Job Satisfaction*

Factor Matrixa	Factor IntJS
33. The amount of variety in your job?	.535
34. The recognition you get for good work?	.702
35. Your chances of promotion?	.566
36. The opportunity to use your abilities?	.793
37. The attention paid to suggestions you make?	.797
38. The amount of responsibility you are given?	.757
39. The freedom to choose your own method of working?	.624

Note: ᵃ 1 factor extracted, 5 iterations required
* (n = 200)

Table 5

Ranked Factor Loading for Indicators on Managers' Self-Ratings Contextual Performance*

Factor matrix[a]	Factor			
	1 Endorsing	2 Helping	3 Persisting	4 Following
58. Exhibiting a concern for organisational objectives	.859			
57. Showing loyalty to the organisation	.838			
60. Representing the organisation favourably to outsiders	.755			
61. Demonstrating concern about the image of the organisation	.698			
59. Working within the organisation to effect change	.537			
49. Helping others who have been absent		−.968		
48. Helping with heavy workloads		−.794		
50. Maintaining effective working relationships with co-workers		−.481		
40. Demonstrating perseverance and conscientiousness			.889	
41. Persisting with effort to complete work successfully despite difficult conditions and setbacks			.868	
42. Putting extra effort into your job			.588	
43. Trying to make the best of the situation, even when there are problems		.534		
54. Obeying the rules and regulations of the organisation				.942
53. Adhering to organisational values and policies				.888
55. Treating organisational property with care				.489
56. Paying attention to announcements, messages, or printed material about the organisation				.384

Note: [a] Rotation converged in 11 iterations
* ($n = 200$)

analyses to differentiate the structure of managers' contextual and task performance. Table 5 shows the ranked factor loading for indicators on contextual performance using subsample 1 ($n = 200$) on managers' self-ratings. Four distinct factors were evident. Table 6 gives the alpha coefficients for the contextual performance variables.

Table 7 shows the ranked factor loading for indicators on task performance using subsample 1 ($n = 200$) on managers' self-ratings.

As with the contextual performance factor loadings, four distinct factors were evident. Task performance indicators and alpha coefficients are presented in Table 8. Several high loading indicators were evident in both the contextual and task performance subsamples.

Table 6

Managers' Self-Report Contextual Performance: EFA Data Reduction by Variables

Construct	N	ξ	α
Persisting	199	4	.84
Helping	179	3	.79
Following	199	4	.83
Endorsing	199	5	.88
Total contextual performance		16	

Note: $n = 200$ matched pairs; ξ = number of constructs

Table 7

Ranked Factor Loading for Indicators on Managers' Self-Ratings on Task Performance*

Factor matrix[a]				
	Factor			
	1 Monitoring	2 Technical	3 Influencing	4 Delegating
118. Monitoring and overseeing appropriate use of funds within existing constraints and guidelines	.994			
119. Monitoring and overseeing utilisation of funds	.961			
117. Controlling budgets by allocating funds internally	.910			
120. Controlling personnnel resources	.557			
84. Solving technical problems		.975		
85. Applying technical expertise		.898		
83. Providing technical advice to others in organisation		.882		
82. Keeping technically up-to-date		.678		
126. Persuading others in the organisation to accept your ideas and position			.985	
127. Convincing those holding opposing or neutral opinions and promoting own positions or ideas			.891	
125. Influencing others inside and outside of the organisation			.803	
128. Presenting own position clearly and decisively			.672	
122. Effectively delegating responisibility and authority				.942
124. Delegating authority and responsibility to assist staff's professional development				.811
121. Assigning staff duties and responsibilities consistent with their abilities as well as the organisation's needs				.666
123. Avoiding interfering with areas of responsibility delegated to others				.644

Note: [a] Rotation converged in 8 iterations
        * (n = 200)

There were seven high loading 'marker' variables (> .80) for contextual performance (see Table 6), and 11 task performance factors representing 18 high-loading indicators. This indicated that the limits to parsimony for this matrix had been reached.

Table 6

Managers' Self-Report Contextual Performance: EFA Data Reduction by Variables

Construct	N	ξ	α
Technical	179	4	.91
Monitoring	162	4	.93
Delegating	187	4	.84
Influencing	196	4	.90
Task performance		16	

Note: n = 200 matched pairs; ξ = number of constructs

Measurement Model of Managers' Performance

Answering the hypotheses required the development of an instrument to measure the structure of managers' contextual and task performance. Managers' performance items, developed for the measurement instrument used, were closely tied to the literature (Borman & Brush, 1993; Borman & Motowidlo, 1997). Separate scales were designed and piloted to measure contextual and task performance dimensions. A measurement model of managers' performance was developed to differentiate the structure of managers' contextual and task performance.

The measurement model was tested by exploratory and confirmatory factor analysis using supervisory ratings and found to be multivariate and consist of an 8-dimensional construct of performance. Managers' performance and was found to be composed of mutual and distinct measures that are generalisable across group. The performance construct was operationalised in terms of four contextual dimensions (Endorsing, Helping, Persisting, Following) and four task dimensions (Monitoring, Technical, Influencing, Delegating). These dimensions were confirmed through multisample analysis and crossvalidation techniques of managers' and superiors' ratings (see Hosie, Sevastos, & Cooper, 2006, for details).

Canonical correlation and standard multiple regression were used to analyse the linear combination of managers' affective wellbeing and job satisfaction with contextual and task performance. Indicators of affective wellbeing and intrinsic job satisfaction were found to predict dimensions of managers' performance, irrespective of whether the performance scores were from self-ratings or supervisory ratings.

Linking Managers' Affective Wellbeing and Job Satisfaction With Contextual and Task Performance

A number of gaps arise from the literature about affective wellbeing, intrinsic job satisfaction and managers' performance that are worthy of investigation. These are summarised as follows:

- Does the construct of managers' performance consist of the two dimensions, contextual and task performance?
- Is there an association between affective wellbeing, intrinsic job satisfaction and managers' contextual and task performance?
- To what extent does affective wellbeing and intrinsic job satisfaction predict different dimensions of managers' contextual and task performance?
- Does positive affective wellbeing result in enhanced managers' performance, and is poor affective wellbeing detrimental to managers' performance?

These research questions were developed into a series of hypotheses. An empirical methodology was used to test these hypotheses to enable the research questions to be answered and to develop a partial model of managers' affective wellbeing, intrinsic job satisfaction and performance as shown in Figure 2.

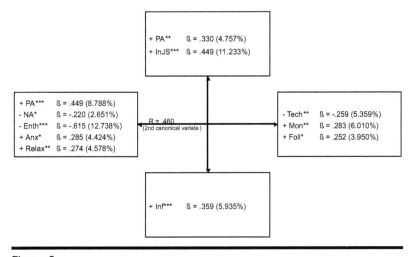

Figure 2

A partial model of managers' affective well-being, intrinsic job satisfaction and performance.

Note: (n = 125)

As predicted, positive affective wellbeing was related to enhanced managerial performance, whereas poor affective wellbeing indicated diminished performance, since the relationship between wellbeing and performance is positive linear, high performance is expected to be associated with high wellbeing, and low performance with low wellbeing. Thus, hypothesis 1 was confirmed.

- **Hypothesis 1.** Affective wellbeing is associated with managers' contextual and task performance (as rated by their superiors), so that high levels of affective wellbeing are strongly associated with higher rated performance, while low levels of affective wellbeing will lead to lower rated performance.

Hypothesis 2 was also confirmed. Self-report of affective wellbeing variables and Intrinsic Job Satisfaction was found to predict dimensions of superiors' report on task performance. Affective wellbeing (PA = .330**, 4.757%; Anxiety = .285*, 4.424%; Relaxation = .274**, 4.578%) were positively associated with managers' task performance (Monitoring = .283**, 6.010%) and contextual performance (Following = .252*, 3.950%) that was negatively associated with task performance (Technical = −.259**, 5.359%). However, NA (−.220*, 2.651%) and Enthusiasm (−.615***, 12.738%), were negatively associated with (Monitoring = .283**, 6.010%; Following = .252*, 3.950%) that was negatively associated with (Technical = −.259**, 5.359%).

- **Hypothesis 2.** Components of affective wellbeing are differentially associated with contextual performance and task performance.

Hypothesis 3 was not confirmed. Enthusiasm (−.615***, 12.738%) accounted for a large amount of unique variance and was highly significantly ($p =$ < .001) negatively associated with the contextual performance variable Following (.252*, 3.950%).

- **Hypothesis 3.** There is a positive association between managers' enthusiasm and contextual performance.

Hypothesis 4 was not confirmed. Anxiety (.285*) accounted for 4.424% of unique variance and was positively associated with the task performance variables Technical (−.259**, 5.359%) and Monitoring (.283**, 6.010%).

- **Hypothesis 4.** There is a negative association between managers' anxiety and task performance.

Hypothesis 5 was not confirmed. Enthusiasm (−.615***, 12.738%) had a highly significant ($p =$ <.001) negative association with the contextual performance variable Following (.252*, 3.950%). Relaxation (.274**, 4.578%) was positively associated with Following but was less significant ($p =$ <.01) and accounted for less variance (8.16%). Anxiety (.285*, 4.424%), an 'activation-based' affect, was positively associated with Following (.252*, 3.950%). Depression was not a significant variable because it may be categorised as 'disengagement' rather than an 'activation-based affect'.

- **Hypothesis 5.** Enthusiasm and relaxation (pleasantness-based affect) are stronger predictors of rated contextual performance than anxiety and depression (activation-based affect).

Hypothesis 6 was partly confirmed. Intrinsic Job Satisfaction (.449***, 11.233%) had a highly significant ($p =$ < .001) positive association task performance variable (Influencing = .359***, 5.935%) but not with any contextual performance variables. Endorsing, a contextual performance variable, contributed 1.507% of the unique variance for the superiors' ratings of performance but the β (.180) determined that this variable was not statistically significant.

- **Hypothesis 6.** There is a positive association between managers' overall intrinsic job satisfaction and their rated contextual and task performance.

Hypothesis 7 was partly confirmed. Affective wellbeing (PA = .449***; 8.788%) had a highly significant ($p =$ < .001) positive association with managers' task performance dimension (Influencing = .359***, 5.935%). Affective wellbeing (PA = .330**, 4.757%; Anxiety = .285*, 4.424%; Relaxation = .274**, 4.578%) was positively associated with managers' contextual performance variable (Following = .252*, 3.950%) and task performance variables (Technical = −.259**, 5.359%; Monitoring = .283**, 6.010%). However, the affective wellbeing variables NA (−.220*, 2.651%) and Enthusiasm (−.615***, 12.738%), were negatively associated with task performance variables (Technical = −.259**, 5.359%; Monitoring = .283**, 6.010%) and the contextual variable Following (.252*, 3.950%). An ambiguous association between affective wellbeing and intrinsic job satisfaction variables was evident, specifically related to contextual and task performance variables. In other words, affective wellbeing and intrinsic job satisfaction variables were not supported in relation to contextual and task performance variables.

- **Hypothesis 7.** Managers' affective wellbeing is positively associated with contextual performance, while managers' cognitions are positively associated with task performance.

Hypothesis 8 was confirmed. Positive values were predicted for Intrinsic Job Satisfaction, Enthusiasm, Relaxation, Anxiety and negative values for Depression for attitudinal and affective outcomes of complexity on work pressure model. The Partial Model predicted that enriched job characteristics were associated with intrinsic job satisfaction and low depression, while impoverished jobs will be associated with job dissatisfaction and depression. High work pressure will be associated with high anxiety, while low pressure will be associated with low anxiety. For 'low strain' jobs the outcomes are satisfaction, enthusiasm, relaxation, and low depression and anxiety; and for 'active jobs' the outcomes are satisfaction, enthusiasm, relaxation, anxiety and low depression.

In the first canonical variate, Intrinsic Job Satisfaction (.449***, 11.233) was highly significantly positively associated with Influencing ($p = < .001$) and contributed substantial unique variance to the performance variable Influencing and could thus be considered 'elevated'. Enthusiasm (−.615***, 12.738) was highly *negatively* elevated and Relaxation (.274**, 4.578) and Anxiety (.285*, 4.424) were moderately *positively* elevated. All variables, except Depression, were significant and contributed considerable unique variance in the second canonical variate that was associated with the task performance variables Technical, Monitoring and the contextual performance variable Following and Depression which indicates low activation.

- **Hypothesis 8.** Managers who report intrinsic job satisfaction and enthusiasm will have elevated relaxation, anxiety and low depression.

Hypothesis 9 was partly confirmed. Intrinsic Job Satisfaction and Enthusiasm were found to be in different uncorrelated canonical variates, in relation to managers' performance, making it difficult to confirm or disconfirm hypothesis 9. In the first canonical variate, Intrinsic Job Satisfaction (.449***, 11.233) was highly significantly positively associated ($p = < .001$) and contributed substantial unique variance to the task performance variable Influencing. In the second canonical variate, Anxiety (.285*, 4.424) was significantly associated ($p = < .05$) and contributed more unique variance than with the task performance variables Technical, Monitoring and the contextual performance variable Following.

- **Hypothesis 9.** High performing managers will report positive intrinsic job satisfaction and high anxiety but low depression.

Hypothesis 10 was partly confirmed. Since the relationship between affective wellbeing and performance was positive linear, high performance was expected to be associated with high wellbeing, and low performance with low wellbeing. As predicted, positive affective wellbeing (Intrinsic Job Satisfaction = .449***, 11.233), a cognitive variable, was related to managerial performance, whereas poor performance indicated decrements in affective wellbeing (Anxiety = .285*, 4.424). Depression and Enthusiasm were not significantly associated with the task performance variables Technical, Monitoring and the contextual performance variable Following and could therefore be considered low but not to have increased activation.

- **Hypothesis 10.** Low performing managers will report low levels of intrinsic job satisfaction and low anxiety but increased depression.

Analysis of the Model

A Partial Model of Managers' Affective Wellbeing, Intrinsic Job Satisfaction and Performance ('model') was developed from the literature for testing. This model was refined into two orthogonal dimensions of affective wellbeing, intrinsic job satisfaction and performance as illustrated in Figure 2.

Unless otherwise stated, it is assumed, as reported in the literature, that the direction of the relationship between the variables is from affective wellbeing, intrinsic job satisfaction to performance (Warr, 1999a). However, this should not be taken to infer causality between the dimensions of affective wellbeing, intrinsic job satisfaction and managers' performance.

The model shows that for the first canonical variate, PA and Intrinsic Job Satisfaction are strongly associated with Influencing. PA is a trait personality characteristic associated with extroversion, and is central to managerial jobs in dealing with peers, superiors, subordinates and external constituents. Possibly, an engaging personality is the reason that individuals are promoted, or self-select into managerial positions. PA may enable managers to influence decisions, from which they derive considerable intrinsic job satisfaction, which has a substantial cognitive component. Alternatively, the opportunity to influence decisions within an organisation may result in enhanced intrinsic job satisfaction and heightened PA.

The second canonical variate or dimension showed a complex set of relationships between aspects of affective wellbeing, intrinsic job satisfaction and performance. PA, Anxiety and Relaxation were positively associated with the contextual performance variable, 'Following', and the task performance variables 'Monitoring' and 'Technical', while 'NA' and 'Enthusiasm' were negatively associated with performance variables (Technical, Monitoring and Following). This indicated that high arousal (positive PA with negative NA) was present, but job dimensions were not particularly motivating (as indicated by negative Enthusiasm but positive Relaxation). This finding indicates that managers will experience arousal but low distress when undertaking transactional roles.

Another explanation for the second canonical canonical variate may be that aspects of managers' job requiring essentially transactional or administrative roles (negative Technical, with positive Monitoring and Following) may lead to high arousal with positive PA and Anxiety, but provide opportunities for Relaxation in conjunction with negative Enthusiasm and NA. A positive association with Monitoring and Following indicated that these performance characteristics require vigilance and consequently high arousal (Anxiety and PA with the attendant NA), but do not lead to a motivating environment (negative Enthusiasm).

However, Monitoring and Following provide opportunities for Relaxation, due to their prescriptive content that leads to acceptable levels of affective wellbeing. Managers also reported PA, a personality trait, to be the only variable common to both dimensions of contextual and task performance, indicating that it may be a prerequisite for managerial jobs. From this finding it could be inferred that managers will have a positive disposition to work. This has implications for the recruitment, selection and development of managers.

Conclusions on Research Hypotheses and Model

Development and testing of the hypotheses and the model contributed to gaining an understanding of how affective wellbeing and intrinsic job satisfaction impact on managers' performance variables. A number of research questions were investigated that were derived from the literature of affective wellbeing, intrinsic job satisfaction and managers' performance.

Contextual and task performance was found to be a significant predictor for PA. As anticipated by Judge et al. (2001), intrinsic job satisfaction was found to be associated with performance. Affective wellbeing self-report (PA, Intrinsic Job Satisfaction) was positively associated with a dimension of superiors' report on task performance (Influencing). Positive associations for dimensions of affective wellbeing self-report (PA, Anxiety and Relaxation) were negatively associated with dimensions of superiors' report on task performance (Monitoring) and contextual performance (Following). PA, Anxiety and Relaxation were also negatively associated with a task performance dimension (Technical). As predicted, positive affective wellbeing was related to enhanced managerial performance, whereas diminished affective wellbeing indicated poorer performance. Certain aspects of managers' affective wellbeing and intrinsic job satisfaction (Enthusiasm, PA, Intrinsic Job Satisfaction and, to a lesser extent, Anxiety) were found to be most important for managers' contextual performance (Following) and task performance (Monitoring, Influencing, Technical).

A large amount of this variance of performance was explained by affective wellbeing and intrinsic job satisfaction that enhanced the predictive power of the model. The first canonical variate explained 31.25% of the variance of performance and the second canonical variate explained 21.16% of the variance of performance. Thus, each of the canonical variates separately accounted for substantial amounts of managers' performance in relation to affective wellbeing and intrinsic job satisfaction.

Consistent with Warr's Vitamin Model, a link between managers' affective wellbeing, intrinsic job satisfaction and performance was evident. Also consistent with Warr's (1992) findings, those in higher-level jobs (e.g., managers) reported less job-related depression, but significantly more job-related anxiety. Positive affective wellbeing was related to enhanced managerial performance, whereas poor affective wellbeing indicated reduced performance. PA was found to be a significant predictor of task and contextual performance, supporting George and Brief's (1996) argument that positive affect (one of the indicators of extraversion) is related to distal and proximal measures of motivation.

PA, Anxiety and Relaxation were positively associated with the task performance variable Monitoring, and the contextual performance variable Following, but negatively associated with the task performance variable Technical. This result is consistent with the Hay Group (1999) finding that less than 10% of FORTUNE 500 companies attributed technical ability to result in high potential managers' and leaders' careers becoming 'derailed'. NA and Enthusiasm were negatively associated with Technical, Monitoring and Following, indicating a level of 'disengagement'. PA is an 'activation-based' affect that was positively associated with the task performance variable, Influencing. Thus, managers' who have high PA and intrinsic job satisfaction are more likely to influence decisions.

Feelings of intrinsic job satisfaction are more important than money for persuading people to increase productivity (Herzberg, 1966). Remuneration only motivates people to a certain threshold of performance, beyond which affective wellbeing and job satisfaction are likely assist in achieving goals. Organisations providing pleasant work environments that are challenging and supportive are likely to have managers who are more creative, energised and productive. Climate has been shown to have a direct impact on productivity and efficiency, accounting for up to 25% of performance (Hay Group, 1999). Thus, organisations could increase the efficacy of managers by initiating and sustaining built and emotional work environments that are in sympathy with their psyche.

Managerial and Practitioner Implications

This study investigated affective wellbeing, an important aspect of emotions and was intended to contribute to the broader debate over what underpins human performance at work. A more sophisticated understanding of how affective wellbeing and intrinsic job satisfaction interacts with managers' performance, contributes to a better comprehension of aspects of the relationships underlying these constructs. Evidence of how affective wellbeing and intrinsic job satisfaction interacts with managers' performance will be valuable in determining job designs and organisational level interventions. Such an understanding has the potential to translate into improved managerial practices. These findings are also intended to progress the debate about how work might be structured to improve employees' performance.

Factors that indicate how managers sustain heightened levels of performance are identified in the model. In turn, this helps to explain the process of upward and downward spirals of managerial effectiveness, whereby positive or negative affective wellbeing and intrinsic job satisfaction leads to increased or reduced performance, which in turn either enhances positive, or exacerbates negative affective wellbeing and intrinsic job satisfaction. These issues need to be addressed if organisations are to operate effectively, in an integrative manner. Uncoordinated and inappropriate initiatives may result in costly and ineffectual outcomes for organisations.

Successful initiatives to improve managers' affective wellbeing and intrinsic job satisfaction depend on individual and situational contingencies. Contingency theory indicates that one general intervention is unlikely to be effective for all managers in all situations; combinations of approaches are likely to be result in longer-term benefits. Mitchell reports that 'people who are high in achievement needs or growth needs respond more favourably (are more satisfied, perform better) when faced with enhanced, challenging jobs than do people low in these needs' (1979, p. 246). In isolation, job enrichment may only enhance motivation for those managers who desire autonomy and challenge at work and in an organisation where executives support participative decision-making.

Assessments of affective wellbeing and intrinsic job satisfaction need to closely match the work environment in which a manager is located, a general consideration frequently overlooked, according to Warr (1987). Managers who spend long periods in jobs that lack opportunities for control and skill use are likely to have a negative affect on job-related competence. However, in some cases job-related anxiety, when linked to aspirations, is not necessarily linked to diminished affective wellbeing and intrinsic job satisfaction. For example, highly motivated managers who desire challenges may react to risks in a way that raises their anxiety level, but does not negatively impact their affective wellbeing and intrinsic job satisfaction.

Conclusion

This study aimed to establish which components of managers' affective wellbeing and intrinsic job satisfaction predicted dimensions of their performance. A model was proposed for linking indicators of affective wellbeing and intrinsic job satisfaction to a number of the dimensions of managers' performance. In the process, a new instrument was developed and refined to establish the structure of the dimensions of managers' performance.

This study was based on the popular notion that affective wellbeing and intrinsic job satisfaction predict performance. The 'happy–productive' worker thesis is yet to receive unequivocal empirical support. This seminal management issue was revisited using robust measures of the constructs of affective wellbeing, intrinsic job satisfaction and managers' performance. Rated performance of managers was previously conceived as a unidimensional construct. Multi cross-validation of self- and superiors' ratings found managers' performance to be a multivariate construct consisting of both contextual and task performance.

As predicted, positive affective wellbeing and intrinsic job satisfaction was related to enhanced managerial performance and poor affective wellbeing indicated reduced performance. Affective wellbeing self-report (Positive Affect, Intrinsic Job Satisfaction) was found to be positively associated with a dimension of superiors' report on task performance (Influencing). Positive associations for dimensions of affective wellbeing self-report (Positive Affect, Anxiety and Relaxation) were found to be negatively associated with dimensions of superiors' report on task performance (Monitoring) and contextual performance (Following) which was also negatively associated with the task performance dimension (Technical).

As predicted, performance was posited to account for some of the remaining 75% of affective wellbeing and intrinsic job satisfaction. This study found that a considerable amount of the variance of performance was caused by affective wellbeing and intrinsic job satisfaction, and vice versa. Explaining a large amount of this variance made it possible to develop a model with enhanced predictive power. Using two independent DVs (supervisors' one-to-one ratings) of IVs (affective wellbeing and intrinsic job satisfaction) eliminated unnecessary noise in the data caused by common method variance.

As previously noted, the analysis described does not provide evidence of causation. As Ashkanasy, Hartel, Fischer and Ashforth stated, '[p]erformance is another likely concomitant of affect at work, though whether it is a cause or a consequence is unclear' (1998, p. 4). The analysis does provide for certain inferences to be made about the relationships between aspects of managers' affective wellbeing, intrinsic job satisfaction and performance. However, it is difficult to conclude from this study that happiness contributes to self-motivation, and that this facilitates organisational effectiveness, or that performance is a barometric of the feeling that managers are effective. Well-performing managers could also be happy as a consequence of their effective performance and the resulting rewards.

Replication of the model and managers' contextual and task performance scales is recommended. This study extended upon the existing theoretical base of managers' affective wellbeing, intrinsic job satisfaction and performance, by devising a model that included performance constructs that have not been comprehensively dealt with in previous theoretical and empirical work. Specifically, measurements of contextual and task performance constructs were identified as deserving of further development. In the process of refining these scales, consideration should be given to devising a crosscultural version of the instrument suitable for use in a range of organisations and countries.

References

Ashkanasy, N.M., Hartel, C.E., Fischer, C., & Ashforth, B. (1998, April). *A research program to investigate the causes and consequences of emotional experience at work.* Paper presented at the Annual Meeting of the Australasian Society Psychologists, Christchurch, New Zealand.

Borman, W.C., & Brush, D.H. (1993). More progress toward taxonomy of managerial performance requirements. *Human Performance, 6*(1), 1–21.

Borman, W.C., & Motowidlo, S.J. (1997). Task performance and contextual performance: The meaning for personnel selection research. *Human Performance, 10*(2), 99–109.

Brayfield, A.H., & Crockett, W.H. (1955). Employee attitudes and employee performance. *Psychological Bulletin, 52,* 396–424.

Child, D. (1990). *The essentials of factor analysis* (2nd ed.). London: Cassell.

Cook, J., Hepworth, S.J., Wall, T.D., & Warr, P.B. (1981). *A compendium and review of 249 work review measures and their use.* London: Academic Press.

Cropanzano, R., & Wright, T.A. (2001). When A 'happy' worker is really a 'productive' worker: A review and further refinements of the happy–productive worker thesis. *Consulting Psychology Journal, 53,* 182–199.

Cropanzano, R., James, K., & Konovsky, M.A. (1993). Dispositional affectivity as a predictor of work attitudes and job performance. *Journal of Organizational Behavior, 14,* 595–606.

Forster, N., & Still, L. (2001). *A report on the effects of occupational stress on managers and professionals in Western Australia.* Perth, Australia: Centre for Women and Business, Graduate School of Management, The University of Western Australia and the Australian Institute of Management.

George, J.M., & Bettenhausen, K. (1990). Understanding prosocial behavior, sales performance, and turnover: A group level analysis in a service context. *Journal of Applied Psychology, 75,* 798–709.

George, J.M., & Brief, A.P. (1996). Feeling good — doing good: A conceptual analysis of the mood at work-organizational spontaneity relationship. *Psychological Bulletin, 112*(2), 310–329.

Hair, J.F., Anderson, R.E., Tatham, R.L., & Black, W.C. (1995). *Multivariate data analysis with readings.* New York: Maxwell Macmillan International.

Hamel, G., & Prahalad, C. (1994). Competing for the future. *Harvard Business Review,* July–August, 122–128.

Hamel, G. (1996). Strategy as revolution. *Harvard Business Review,* July–Aug, 69–82.

Handy, C.B. (1996). *Beyond certainty: The changing worlds of organizations.* Boston: Harvard Business School Press.

Harter, J.K., Schmidt, F.L., & Hays, T.L. (2002). Business-unit-level relationship between employee satisfaction, employee engagement, and business outcomes: A meta-analysis. *Journal of Applied Psychology, 87*(2), 268–279.

Hay Group (1999). *What makes great leaders: Rethinking the route to effective leadership: Findings from Fortune Magazine/Hay Group 1999 Executive Survey of Leadership Effectiveness.* Retrieved December 1, 2004, from http://ei.haygroup.com/downloads/pdf/Leadership%20White%20Paper.pdf

Herzberg, F. (1966). *The work and the nature of man.* Cleveland, OH: The World Publishing Company.

Hosie, P.J., Sevastos, P.P., & Cooper, C.L. (2006), Happy-performing managers: The impact of affective wellbeing and intrinsic job satisfaction in the workplace. In C.L. Cooper (Ed.) *New horizons in management.* Northhampton, MA: Edgar Elgar.

Iaffaldano, M.T., & Muchinsky, P.M. (1985). Job satisfaction and job performance: A meta-analysis. *Psychological Bulletin, 97,* 251–273.

Jones, G.R. (1995). *Organizational theory: Text and cases.* Reading, MA: Addison-Wesley.

Judge, T.A., Thoresen, C.J., Bono, J.E., & Patton, G.K. (2001). The job satisfaction–job performance relationship: A qualitative and quantitative review. *Psychological Bulletin, 127:* 376–407.

Konovsky, M.A., & Organ, D.W. (1996). Dispositional and contextual determinants of organisational citizenship behaviour. *Journal of Organizational Behavior, 17*(3), 253–266.

Katzell, R.A., & Thompson, D.E. (1995). Work motivation: Theory and practice. In D.A. Kolb, J.S. Osland, & I.M. Rubin (Eds.), *The organizational behaviour reader* (6th ed. pp. 110–124). Englewood Cliffs, NJ: Prentice-Hall.

Ledford, G.E. Jr (1999). Happiness and productivity revisited. *Journal of Organizational Behavior, 20*(1), 31–34.

Lee, T., & Ashforth, B.E. (1996). A meta-analytic examination of the correlates of the three dimensions of job burnout. *Journal of Applied Psychology, 81,* 123–133.

Locke, E.A. (1976). The nature and causes of job satisfaction. In M.D. Dunnette (Ed.), *Handbook of industrial and organizational psychology* (pp. 1297–1349). Chicago: Rand McNally.

Mitchell, T. (1979). Organizational behaviour. *Annual Review of Psychology, 8,* 44.

Nunnally, J.C. (1978). *Psychometric theory* (2nd ed.). New York: McGraw-Hill.

Organ, D.W., & Lingl, A. (1995). Personality, satisfaction, and organisational citizenship behaviour. *Journal of Social Psychology, 135*(3), 339–350.

Organ, D.W., & Paine, B.P. (1999). A new kind of performance for industrial and organisational psychology: Recent contributions to the study of organisational citizenship behaviour. In C.L. Cooper & I.T. Robertson (Eds.), *International Review of Industrial and Organisational Psychology* (pp. 338–368). Chichester, NY: John Wiley & Sons.

Patterson, M., West, M.A., Lawthom, R., & Nickell, S. (1998). Impact of people management practices on business performance. *Issues in People Management* (No. 22.). Institute of Personnel and Development.

Podsakoff, P.M., MacKenzie, S.B., Morman, R.H., & Fetter, R. (1990), Transformational leader behaviors and their effects on followers trust in leader, satisfaction, and organizational citizenship behavior. *The Leadership Quarterly, 1*(2), 107–142.

Quinn, R.E., Faerman, S.R., Thompson, M.P., & McGrath, M.R. (1996). *Becoming a master manager: A competency framework* (2nd ed.). New York: Wiley.

Raghunathan, T.R. (1995). A review of scale development practices in the study of organizations. *Journal of Management, 21*(5), 967–988.

Reinhold, B.R. (1997). *Toxic work: How to overcome stress, overload and burnout and revitalize your career.* New York: Plume Publishers.

Schmitt, N., & Stults, D.M. (1986). Methodology review: Analysis of multitrait–multimethod matrices. *Applied Psychological Measurement, 10,* 1–22.

Sevastos, P.P. (1996). *Job-related affective well-being and its relation to intrinsic job satisfaction.* Unpublished doctoral dissertation, Curtin University, Perth, Australia.

Staw, B.M. (1986). Organisational psychology and the pursuit of the happy/productive worker. *California Management Review, 28,* 40–53.

Strauss, G. (1968). Relations — 1968 style. *Industrial Relations, 7,* 262–276.

Vroom, V.H. (1964). *Work and motivation.* New York: Wiley.

Warr, P. (1987). *Work, Unemployment and mental health.* Oxford University Press.

Warr, P.B. (1992). Age and occupational well-being. *Psychology and Aging, 7*(1), 37–45.

Warr, P. (1999a). Well-being and the workplace. In D. Kahneman, E.Diener & N. Schwarz (Eds.), *Well-being: The foundations of hedonic psychology* (pp. 392–412). New York: Russell Sage Foundation.

Warr, P. (1999b). The measurement of well-being and other aspects of mental health. *Journal of Occupational Psychology, 63*(3), 193–210.

Watson, D., & Clark, L.A. (1984). Negative affectivity: The disposition to experience aversive emotional states. *Psychological Bulletin, 96*(3), 465–490.

Watson, D., Clark, L.A., & Tellegen, A. (1988), Development and validation of brief measures of positive and negative affect: The Panas Scales, *Journal of Personality and Social Psychology, 54*, 1063–1070.

Wernefelt, B. (1984). Resource-based view of the firm. *Strategic Management Journal, 5*, 171–180.

Williams, R. (1991). Transformation or chaos? Human resources in the 1990s. *HRMonthly*, November, 1–10.

Wright, T. A., & Cropanzano, R. (2000). Psychological well-being and job satisfaction as predictors of job performance. *Journal of Occupational Health Psychology, 5*, 84–94.

Wright, T.A., & Staw, B.M. (1999a). Affect and favorable work outcomes: Two longitudinal tests of the happy–productive worker thesis. *Journal of Organizational Behavior, 20*, 1–23.

Wright, T.A., & Staw, B.M. (1999b). Further thoughts on the happy–productive worker. *Journal of Organizational Behavior, 20*, 31–34.

Intellectual Property Protection and the WTO TRIPS Agreement: Finding a Global Balance for Development as Part of the Doha Round

Anne Ardagh

Intellectual property — including copyright, trademarks, designs and patents — has become progressively more important as the trade in goods and services, as well as foreign direct investment, increases in the global environment. PricewaterhouseCoopers reports the global intellectual property (IP) licensing market doubled from 1990 to 1999, when it reached more than $100 billion (Idris, 2003). A PricewaterhouseCoopers' study (2006) notes a rapidly growing marketplace for US technology licensing because of the continued explosion of technological innovation and increasing protections for intellectual property. Large companies dominate this market, with more than 500 licensing agreements in areas such as technology, biotechnology, entertainment and media.

Legislative Protection of Intellectual Property

National laws to protect some forms of intellectual property preceded international treaties by several centuries. It is thought that the first law to protect inventions by a form of patent was in Venice in 1474, with modern laws being established in many countries towards the end of the 19th century during a period of rapid growth in industrialisation (Idris, 2003).

International Protection

There are numerous international treaties and agreements relating to intellectual property, some having been in existence since the late 19th century. Treaty regimes include the Paris Convention for the Protection of Industrial Property (Paris Convention, 1883), which largely covers patents, and the Berne Convention for the Protection of Literary and Artistic Works (Berne, 1889), covering copyright law. They have been amended several times. These treaties give international protection by providing foreigners equal treatment to nationals of signatory countries. The Paris Convention also gives priority rights to applicants of trademarks, designs and patents in other member countries. These treaties are administered by the World Intellectual Property Organisation (WIPO), which is a UN specialised agency located in Switzerland. There are also a number of newer international treaties, for example, the Patent Cooperation Treaty (PCT; 1970), which streamlines and reduces the cost of obtaining international patent protection, as well as providing protection for a new invention in member states throughout the world. There are also related international agreements, for example, Convention on Biological Diversity and Convention for the Protection of New Varieties of Plants (1968). An increasing number of bilateral and regional treaties governing intellectual property have also developed — so-called 'TRIPS-plus' agreements.

The Need for Further International Property Protection

Although the Paris and Berne Conventions provided international intellectual property protection during most of the 20th century, these conventions were, in more recent decades, deemed unsatisfactory by developed nations. This was due in part to increasing globalisation and new discovery areas, for example, in biotechnology and inventions such as integrated circuits and computer software. Additionally, there has been the reality of growing technological capabilities of some developing countries that may not have joined the international agreements and/or did not enforce the IP laws on a national level (Revesz, 1999, p. 51). Furthermore, because dispute resolution in general between countries at the International Court of Justice is not compulsory — with countries having to agree to jurisdiction, this added to problems of enforcement in the IP area. Many countries were able to acquire IP-protected goods at cheaper prices through copying, with 'piracy' of books, videos and computer software, as well as counterfeiting of fashion and other goods, being simple and readily saleable. The loss of revenue to US corporations was the motivation for the United States' (US) push in the Uruguay Round of negotiations to have an agreement on intellectual property included in the World Trade Organization (WTO). The sectors that were mainly affected were pharmaceuticals, entertainment, publications, speciality chemicals and information technologies.[1] The aim was to have a stricter international system of protection providing a minimum baseline of standards for all members, backed by a mandatory enforcement mechanism (Islam, 2006).

The Agreement on Trade Related Aspects of Intellectual Property Rights

The Agreement on Trade Related Aspects of Intellectual Property Rights (TRIPS) was finalised at the end of the Uruguay Round of world trade negotiations in 1993[2] and entered into force on January 1, 1995. Blakeney (1996) describes TRIPS as being probably the most significant development in intellectual property in the 20th century. It supplemented and modified existing conventions and resulted in the most wide-ranging international agreement for the protection of intellectual property (Yusuf, 1998, p. 20).

Breadth of TRIPS Protection

What is significant about the TRIPS Agreement is that it links intellectual property rights to trade under the WTO and incorporates the Berne and Paris Conventions, as well as the more recent International Convention for the Protection of Performers, Producers of Phonograms and Broadcasting Organisations (Rome Convention, 1961). This means that a country cannot become a member of the WTO, and thereby part of the world trading system, without acceding to TRIPS. It also involves enacting legislation in home countries to give effect to TRIPS and its enforcement mechanisms, which include seizure of counterfeit and pirated goods at the border. This has raised concerns regarding the capacity of developing countries to comply with enforcement standards, as well as the financial burden of doing so.

Intellectual property has become an increasingly broad concept in the new knowledge era, as well as a most important element of trade advantage. The TRIPS Agreement does not define intellectual property. It simply states in Article 1.2 that intellectual property includes the seven categories dealt with in the Agreement (Part II, sections 1–2). However, the TRIPS Agreement has greatly extended IP protection to new areas, for example geographical indications, trade secrets, layout designs of integrated circuits and rights of performers, producers of sound recordings and broadcasting organisations. There are also new areas of patent protection not required under the Paris Convention, such as pharmaceuticals, agricultural chemicals and food and new plant varieties.

The TRIPS Agreement means a shift from what were minimum standards of protection under WIPO to global harmonisation of IP protection laws administered by a WTO Council. The result is a set of worldwide rules with stronger enforcement, protecting a vast range of intellectual property, which is largely owned by industrialised countries.[3]

Different Implications of TRIPS for Developed and Poor Countries

The consequence of TRIPS is that for rich and developed countries, whose transnational corporations develop and export technology, there is a huge advantage. Intellectual property protection is now mandatory; the scope of protection is extended under TRIPS, tied to trade and enforceable by the WTO, which may impose trade sanctions. Moreover, the owners of IP may impose other retaliatory measures on those who fail to provide adequate protection, including blacklisting and trade sanctions.

For importing, developing, and least-developed countries there is severe disadvantage. Lacking bargaining power, needing technology and wishing to become part of the world trading system, they had little choice but to accept the TRIPS Agreement. They have been denied the 'soft' protection of WIPO and have been placed on a level playing field with the most advanced countries (Islam, 1999, p. 191). Additionally, TRIPS further disadvantages developing countries in those areas of great need in terms of health and development; for example, pharmaceuticals, agricultural chemicals, food and new plant varieties, where patent protection was not required under the Paris Convention.

According to a report of the Commission on Global Governance (1995), TRIPS is another manifestation of the globalisation process being in danger of widening the gap between the rich and poor. A sophisticated, globalised, increasingly affluent world coexists with a marginalised global underclass, and TRIPS further contributes to the disparity. In the era of UN Millennium Development goals and focus on the Doha Development Round of trade, policy choices need to be made with more debate on the role played by intellectual property and international business regulation generally.

Redressing the Balance

The TRIPS Agreement has elevated the IP rights policy formulation to the international trade level. TRIPS is one of the so called 'three pillars' of the WTO, the other two being trade in goods and trade in services. It means a huge increase of IP profits in the rich countries of the north. Because of the increasing need in the poor countries of the south for technology as well as for essential medicines and foodstuffs, it is seen as a transfer payment from the poor to the rich in the form of royalty payments and income losses (Revesz, 1999, p. 52–53). It is also a direct challenge to developing countries' ability to play a significant role in the world economy. 'While IPR protection is in large part an economic issue, moral arguments couched in terms of "equity" and "fairness" still play an important role in IPR policy formulation and the judicial process', according to the author of an Australian Productivity Commission paper on

TRIPS (Revesz, 1999). Developed nations argue that weak protection means unfair competition. Developing countries argue that strong regulation means unfair burdens.

Needed Reforms

The first review of the new intellectual property regime by the TRIPS Council was scheduled to begin in 2000; the original agreement being seen by developed countries as providing only minimum protection. Negotiations are continuing, but have stalled, with industrialised countries wanting tighter controls to protect and expand intellectual property rights and developing countries wanting more recognition of national sovereignty and the right to address to health, safety and development needs. Although transition periods for developing nations for compliance with TRIPS were built into the agreement and some of these have been extended, more fundamental reforms are needed to redress the balance.

TRIPS-plus Agreements

The need for agreement on amendments to TRIPS is exacerbated by the development whereby those countries wanting tighter protection of intellectual property are bypassing the TRIPS Agreement altogether in what have been labelled 'TRIPS-plus' Agreements. These agreements, which are concluded through bilateral and regional agreements, establish much stronger protection for intellectual property than does TRIPS. They are making so much headway that it is feared by some that TRIPS is being bypassed to the extent that it may become 'obsolete' (Genetic Resources Action International, 2003). Burnett (2004, p. 403) cites the example of the 2003 Free Trade Agreement between the US and Singapore as 'an example of how far the "TRIPS plus" agenda has been pushed in the area of intellectual property'. As well as affording national treatment to members, TRIPS also affords most favoured nation treatment (MFN) to signatory nations. This is likely to bring about uniformity and also increasingly high levels of IP protection as a result of technology exporting countries bringing pressure to bear on countries to increase the level of IP protection (Islam, 2006). The increased level may then have to be afforded to other nations under the MFN doctrine. Drahos and Braithwaite (2002, p. 208) call for a unified veto coalition of developing countries against further ratcheting up of intellectual property standards to avoid being 'picked off one by one by the growing wave of US bilaterals on both intellectual property and investment more broadly'. A number of suggested areas for reform of TRIPS are now addressed.

Patent Protection Under TRIPS

One of the most problematic areas of global intellectual property protection under TRIPS is the patent. Patents are a valuable source of technical knowledge encompassing 'state of the art' inventions (Van Houtte, 1995). However, today patents extend far beyond technical knowledge and inventions. The Paris Convention (1883) applies to 'industrial property', which includes inventions, marks, industrial designs, utility models and trade names. Patent protection was traditionally provided for inventions, not discoveries. This distinction has been eroded. The TRIPS Agreement goes much further in what may be patented. Article 27 provides that all parties of the WTO must allow patents on products and processes in all fields of technology. This includes 'micro-organisms' and 'nonbiological processes', genetic materials (animal and human), as well as pharmaceuticals. These are life-creating and life-sustaining substances. There is a qualitative difference between life-sustaining substances, many of which are 'discovered', and technical innovations. Article 27(2) does allow exclusions from patentability; for example, the European Union (EU) and the United Kingdom (UK) exclude methods of treatment and diagnosis of the human or animal body. Additionally, under Article 27(3) (b), countries must provide protection for plant varieties, either by patents, *sui generis* protection or a combination of both. A concern of developing countries is that Article 27 allows bio-engineering and patenting of genetically modified seeds, which may mean the inability to reuse seeds where new genetic varieties are non–self-perpetuating. Additionally, genetically modified seeds need product specific fertilisers and other chemicals manufactured by the same owners of the seeds (e.g., Monsanto Corporation). Blakeney (2002) examines agricultural research and Article 27(3)(b) and the conflicts between the rights embodied in TRIPS and international human rights law.

Prohibition of Certain Patents

Instead of allowing exclusions from patentability, as noted above, the contentious issue that remains is whether patents over certain products should be granted at all. Patents on life forms and life saving remedies are controversial, as already noted. For example, Primo Braga (1989) contends that the less-developed countries tend to assign a higher weight to social welfare interests than to private interests. Therefore, he maintains that arguments against IP protection for pharmaceuticals and food products are based on social considerations, such as the objective of avoiding price increases in health and nutrition. According to Long (1997), this unique role as an instrument of public health and safety supports the desirability of providing unrestricted access to intellectual property in scientific development in medicine and agriculture. Watkins and Fowler (2002) argues that one of the basic requirements for reform is that

Article 27 of the TRIPS agreement should forbid patents on plant-based products obtained from national and international germplasm banks. The African group has tabled a proposal to amend TRIPS so that it prohibits patents on all living organisms in all the WTO member states. This has been described by Genetic Resources Action International (2003) as 'the most logical solution to bio-piracy'.

According to the UNDP *Human Development Report* (1999) there is a social responsibility to share scientific advancement and wealth, given that it is the developing countries that account for 90% of the world's biological resources on which many of the patents depend. Petersen (1997) has pointed to the developed world's pharmaceutical industry as being a prominent source of the heightened interest in the rainforest, as pharmaceutical companies explore the forest more intensively for medicinal plants and information on their possible uses. This has been accompanied by a growing interest in the traditional knowledge of indigenous peoples. Likewise, Peterson says the international seed industry depends on plant materials derived from crop varieties selected and improved by farmers in developing countries. In this regard, more international attention needs to be given to the Convention on Biological Diversity (www.biodiv.org/ convention) and the World Intellectual Property Organisation's efforts to protect traditional knowledge (TK), genetic resources and traditional cultural expressions against misappropriation and misuse (www.wipo.int.tk/en).

The extended scope of patents under TRIPS means that importing poor countries have to pay large sums of money, which they may not be able to afford, to sustain life itself in the form of certain foodstuffs and pharmaceuticals. This expense is quite apart from outlays for the technology required for development needs. The example often given is of the need in developing nations of antiviral medicines to combat such illnesses as HIV/AIDS, tuberculosis, malaria and yellow fever. These are fatal illnesses, with HIV/AIDS having reached pandemic proportions in Africa, Asia and South America. Prior to TRIPS, countries could make or import cheaper generic drugs because patents on pharmaceuticals were not part of the world IP protection regime.

Article 31 of the TRIPS Agreement does allow 'compulsory licensing' of patents (including pharmaceuticals) in areas essential to human wellbeing or national emergencies or other circumstances of extreme urgency. However, a strict procedure must be followed and adequate remuneration must be paid to the patent holder. The TRIPS Agreement has figured in high profile disputes. For example, in South Africa, 39 drug companies began a court action to prevent the South African government from importing cheap generic copies of HIV/AIDs drugs and the US-threatened trade sanctions. Subsequent to this, the US took Brazil to a WTO dispute panel to prevent Brazil from producing generic copies of vital drugs (Oxfam Community Aid Abroad, 2003) and it has exerted diplomatic pressure or threatened trade sanctions against a number of countries. Worldwide attention to the health crisis in developing countries resulted in the declaration at the Doha Ministerial Conference in 2001 affirming the right of members to make full use of the TRIPS compulsory licensing provision. This left the problem of some countries, without manufacturing capacity, being prohibited because of Article 31(f) from importing generic drugs made elsewhere. In 2003, the TRIPS General Council, against the wishes of the US, issued a waiver permitting members who could demonstrate a lack of manufacturing capacity to import generic drugs made under compulsory licence (Anton, Mathew, & Morgan, 2005).

Length of Patents

Patents create a monopoly which, under TRIPS, is for a universal period of not less than 20 years. In some areas it is longer than 20 years. This is a longer duration than may have been provided by existing domestic legislation. For example, Australia had to increase its patent protection term from 16 to 20 years to comply with TRIPS.

For those traditional areas where patent protection has traditionally been granted the patent term should be reduced. Twenty years is an unnecessarily long period to grant a monopoly to major transnationals for any invention, let alone over such items such as drugs, medicines, plant varieties and seeds. Additionally, time and effort that may be expended in obtaining some patents may be minimal recognising that small changes are constantly being made, while the global reward over 20 years may be astronomical. For example, IBM is being granted ten new patents every working day, with revenues from licensing increased by a factor of three to $1.5 billion, or one-fifth of total profits in the second half of the 1990s, according to *The Economist* (Watkins & Fowler, 2002, p. 212). Even for a country like Australia that is a net technology importer, the increased patent term (from 16 to 20 years) under TRIPS costs outweigh gains, according to an Australian Productivity Commission Report on TRIPS (Revesz, 1999).

Extensions of IP Terms

Long patent terms under TRIPS may delay the introduction of spin-off inventions by others, which could impose a 'serious threat' to world technological progress (Revesz, 1999). The Australian Productivity Report on TRIPS concludes that there is no certainty that extending patent lives beyond 16 years is a cost-effective approach to foster global technological development. Accordingly, *extensions* of patent terms under TRIPS should be prohibited.

Exhaustion of Intellectual Property Rights

Islam (2006) notes that technology-exporting countries are able to dictate when their IP rights are to be exhausted through trade-offs in other areas. For example, they may lengthen IP rights in exchange for greater market access for developing countries' agricultural products, or the promise thereof. Matthews (2002, pp. 48–49) explains that in the US, the European Communities (EC) and Japan it is possible for a contract of sale for patented goods to specify limitations on the buyer's right to export or re-sell the goods. Elsewhere it is often the case that no such restriction is possible. Article 6 currently provides that the TRIPS Agreement is not meant to 'address the issue of exhaustion of intellectual property rights'. The issue of whether the first sale of a patented good can exhaust the rights of a patentee is still subject to debate; the ability to extend intellectual property rights in this way being viewed as anticompetitive conduct.

International Competition Laws

Strong international competition laws are needed. Gurry (1997) points to the growing number of interfirm alliances and collaborative arrangements engaged in the international exploitation of intellectual property, with competition policy remaining largely on the national level. The TRIPS Agreement, Article 40, acknowledges that 'some licensing practices or conditions pertaining to intellectual property rights which restrain competition may have adverse effects on trade and may impede the transfer and dissemination of technology', but largely leaves open what to do about it.

Gerber (1997) explains that competition is harmed where coercion is used to exclude a competitor or potential competitor; the combination of increased technological and economic integration with expanded intellectual property rights poses a threat to competition because it increases the likelihood of exclusionary conduct. Gerber maintains that we can expect the capacity to engage in such conduct to increase, as more firms possess extended monopoly rights which in turn protect technological networks that are larger, tighter and more important for competitive survival. With tens of thousands of transnational corporations worldwide, foreign investment is growing faster than trade. The Commission on Global Justice (1995) says the challenge is to provide a framework of rules and order for global competition in the widest sense. It argues that the WTO should adopt a strong set of competition rules, with a global competition office set up to provide oversight of national enforcement efforts and resolve inconsistencies between them. Drahos and Braithwaite (2002) chronicle the history of global knowledge cartels and the use of intellectual property to structure and enforce them.

Recognition of National Sovereignty and National Diversity

The TRIPS agreement provides in its preamble that it is committed to take into account differences in national legal systems. Rather than giving credence to this provision, TRIPS has been viewed as an imposition on the majority world of a western-style protection regime and western values of creative expression and innovation, where development needs take priority over corporate profits (Islam, 1999). Developing countries need to be free to respond to their own development and public health needs. This entails the right to be able to use traditional remedies, technologies, plant varieties, seeds and generic drugs and to import the latter from other generic producing countries. Long and D'Amato (1997, p. 26) note that one of the challenges of the 21st century is to encourage the enforcement of intellectual property laws while avoiding unwarranted interference in the domestic politics and policies of foreign countries. For example, the US asserted the right to compulsory licensing of an anthrax vaccine during a public health/terrorist threat post September 11, 2001. It is paradoxical that, 2 years later, the US failed to recognise the public health need in developing countries for generic drugs when it voted against the waiver allowing the developing countries without manufacturing capacity to import generic drugs to combat HIV/AIDS.

Commitment to Development

Continuing negotiations concerning TRIPS need to keep in mind the global commitment to development as embodied in the WTO Ministerial Declaration adopted in Doha, Qatar on November 14, 2001. Variations in the levels of development need to be considered rather than the 'level playing field' view that has prevailed. There are numerous 'country levels' that can be distinguished from major industrialised countries that have the great bulk of IP to be protected. These include newly industrialised countries, emerging economies of the former Soviet Union, developing countries, and those that are classified as least-developed countries. Most of these groups are in a losing position as net importers of technology. Whereas some developing countries may benefit from TRIPS through protecting their own intellectual property, overall they are 'consumers', not 'producers' of intellectual property (Matthews, 2002). The equal treatment of such unequal countries raises severe problems of equity. Islam (1999) argues that substantive differences must be treated differently and this requires the TRIPS Agreement to be amended by introducing a well-defined 'tiers system' as opposed to a uniform system for all.

International Code of Conduct on the Transfer of Technology

The Commission on Global Governance (1995, pp. 203–204) points to the concern in developing countries that the transfer of technology is becoming more difficult. This is partly because research and development (R&D) on the most advanced technologies — information, biotechnology and new materials — are overwhelmingly concentrated in rich countries that have an estimated 97% of the R&D. As the transfer of technology is largely unregulated, renewed attention needs to be given to the implementation of an international Code of Conduct. The International Code on the Transfer of Technology (TOT Code) prepared by UNCTAD in the 1970s and 1980s has not been adopted by the UN, although a more recent EU Regulation on Technology Transfer Agreements came into effect in 1996. According to Mo (2003), it is the only formal regulation of technology at the international level. As it covers only EU firms it is an incomplete solution to the problem.

Conclusion

The divide between rich and poor has not improved since the Commission of Global Governance 1995 Report. The position worsened after the introduction of the TRIPS Agreement. In 2000, the World Bank reported the 'progress in poverty reduction appears to have stalled ... with a resulting increase in the total number of poor people in many regions'.[5] The collapse of the Doha Development Round of trade talks in July 2006 is a further setback.[6] In continuing reviews of TRIPS, global social, health and development requirements need to be the focus in order to redress the balance between competing private and public interests, which manifest themselves in the north–south divide. A fairer system, taking into account some of the reforms mentioned above, would increase the effectiveness of intellectual property regimes by gaining international cooperation and more certain protection and enforcement. While it can be argued that fair compensation to the corporations of developed countries for intellectual property 'privileges'[7] needs to be guaranteed, the commitment to development must be renewed, including an assurance concerning the transfer of technology on an equitable basis. The commitment to development is further worsened by 'TRIPS-plus' agreements which disadvantage developing countries in their individual negotiations with the countries of the developed world and which insist on even tighter protection of intellectual property than the more open and uniform rules that the multilateral TRIPS Agreement provides.

Whereas TRIPS was part of the Uruguay Round dominated by the 20th century economic concerns of the developed nations, the 21st century Doha round must remain focused on enhancing sustainable development and food and health security for developing nations. Reform of the TRIPS Agreement would assist with this endeavour and with helping to achieve the Millennium goals. According to Drahos and Braithwaite (2002), instead of being a platform for increasing intellectual property protection, TRIPS needs to remain a ceiling and be rolled back. Maskus and Reichman (2005, pp. 368–370) call for a moratorium on stronger intellectual property standards to 'evaluate growing fears that overprotection of research results in developed countries will produce anti-commons effects and lost competitive opportunities likely to retard the pace of innovation over time'. They contend that the 'turmoil generated by the TRIPS Agreement and its aftermath suggests that we stand at the threshold of an era in which unanswered questions about the role of intellectual property in a networked information economy demand a lengthy period of trial and error experimentation, as occurred after the adoption of the Paris and Berne Conventions in the 1890s'.

Global alliances of developing countries, nongovernment organisations, academics, health professionals, businesses, world governance organisations, consumers and other representatives of civil society are needed in order to devise a coherent and reasoned argument for improved access to knowledge and lower royalty payments for technology for the benefit of all society (Drahos & Braithwaite, 2002; Matthews, 2002; Mayne, 2002).

Endnotes

1   Revesz (1999, p. 53) cites a survey of the US International Trade Commission which estimated US companies losses at between US$10 billion and US$25 billion in sales and royalty income in 1986. It is acknowledged that these figures are based on speculation and are not verifiable.

2   It was signed at Marrakesh, Morocco in April 1994 as an annex (Annex 1C) to the Agreement establishing the World Trade Organisation (WTO).

3   Some of the rationales for protecting intellectual property and countervailing arguments, addressing the global dimension, were addressed in Ardagh, A. (2003), *Globalisation, intellectual properties and the transfer of technology: Finding the right balance under the TRIPS Agreement* (Proceedings of the Hawaii International Conference on Business, 18–21 June).

4   Cited in Marin, P.L.C. (2002), *Providing protection for plant genetic resources: Patents, sui generis systems, and biopartnerships* (Kluwer Law International), referring to a paper submitted by the World Bank to the World Summit for Social Development Five Year Review in Geneva, June 2000.

5   Director General Pascal Lamy has made several 2007 announcements concerning completing the round in 2007. See http://www.wto.org/english/news_e/sppl_e/sppl_e.htm

6   Drahos, P. (1996) in *A Philosophy of Intellectual Property* (Dartmouth) argues that the language of 'rights' be changed to privileges.

References

Agreement on Trade Related Aspects of Intellectual Rights (TRIPS Agreement). (2004.) *Butterworth's intellectual property collection.* Sydney, Australia: LexisNexis Butterworths.

Anton, D., Mathew, P., & Morgan, W. (2005). *International law; Cases and materials.* Melbourne, Australia: Oxford University Press.

Ardagh, A. (2003, June). Globalisation, intellectual properties and the transfer of technology: Finding the right balance under the TRIPS Agreement. *Proceedings of the Hawaii International Conference on Business,* 18–21 June, Honolulu.

Blakeney, M. (2002). Agricultural research: Intellectual property and the CGIAR System. In P. Drahos & R. Mayne (Eds.), *Global intellectual property rights; knowledge, access and development* (pp. 108–24). Basingstoke, England: Palgrave Macmillan.

Blakeney, M. (1996). *Trade-related aspects of intellectual property rights: A concise guide to the TRIPS Agreement.* Basingstoke, England: Palgrave-Macmillan.

Burnett, R. (2004). *Law of international business transactions* (3rd ed.). Sydney, Australia: The Federation Press.

Commission on Global Governance. (1995). *Our global neighbourhood: The report of the commission on global governance.* New York: Oxford University Press.

Drahos, P. (1996). *A philosophy of intellectual property.* Brookfield, VT: Dartmouth.

Drahos, P., & Braithwaite, J. (2002). *Information feudalism: Who owns the knowledge economy?* London: Earthscan.

Genetic Resources Action International (GRAIN). (2003). *Open letter to Pascal Lamy, Directorate-General for Trade, European Commission,* February 26, 2003. Retrieved March 25, 2003 from http://www.grain.org/publications/lamyopenletter-en.cfm

Gerber, D (1997). Intellectual property rights, economic power and global technological integration. In F. Abbot, & D. Gerber (Eds.), *Public policy and global technological integration* (pp. 127–39). London: Kluwer Law International.

Gurry, F. (1997). The evolution of technology and markets and the management of intellectual property rights. In F. Abbot, & D. Gerber (Eds.), *Public policy and global technological integration* (pp. 25–28). London: Kluwer Law International.

Idris, K. (2003). *Intellectual property: A power tool for economic growth* (2nd ed.). Geneva: World International Property Organization.

Islam, M.R. (2006). *International trade law of the World Trade Organisation.* Melbourne, Australia: Oxford University Press.

Islam, M.R. (1999). *International trade law.* Sydney, Australia: Law Book Co.

Long, D.E., & D'Amato, A. (1997). Introduction. In A. D'Amato & D.E. Long (Eds.), *International intellectual property law* (pp. 1–26). London: Kluwer Law International.

Long, D.E. (1997). The role of intellectual property in developing nations. In A. D'Amato & D.E. Long (Eds.), *International intellectual property law* (p. 61). London: Kluwer Law International.

Marin, P.L.C. (2002). *Providing protection for plant genetic resources: Patents, sui generis systems, and biopartnerships.* London: Kluwer Law International,

Maskus, K.E., & Reichman, J.H. (2005). The globalization of private knowledge goods and the privatization of global public goods. In A. George (Ed.), *Globalization and intellectual property* (pp. 335–377). Ashgate Publishing.

Matthews, D. (2002). *Globalising intellectual property rights: The TRIPS agreement.* London and New York: Routledge.

Mayne, R. (2002). The global campaign on patents and access to medicines: An Oxfam perspective. In P. Drahos, & R. Mayne (Eds.), *Global intellectual property right: Knowledge, access and development* (pp. 244–58). Basingstoke, England: Palgrave Macmillan.

Mo, J. (2003). *International commercial law.* Sydney, Australia: LexisNexis Butterworths.

Oxfam Community Aid Abroad. (2003). *Global patent rules that safeguard public health in poor countries: Promise 6.* Retrieved March 4, 2003, from http://www.caa.org.au/campaigns/trade/wto/patents.html

Petersen, K. (1997). Recent intellectual property trends in developing countries. In A. D'Amato, & E. Long (Eds.), *International intellectual property law* (pp. 62–63). London: Kluwer Law International.

PricewaterhouseCoopers. (2006). *2006 Licensing Competitiveness Study.* Retrieved September 2, 2006, from http://www.pwc.com/extweb/pwcpublications.nsf/docid/D9EAAF72D8548530852571BE0061F491

Primo Braga, C.A. (1997). The economics of intellectual property rights and the GATT. In A. D'Amato & D. Long (Eds.), *International intellectual property law* (pp. 48–52). London: Kluwer Law International.

Revesz, J. (1999). *Trade-related aspects of intellectual property rights.* Canberra, Australia: Productivity Commission Staff Research Paper, AGPS.

United Nations Development Programme. (1999). *Human development report.* New Yorka nd Oxford:Oxford University Press.

Van Houtte, H. (1995). *The law of international trade.* London: Sweet & Maxwell.

Watkins, K., & Fowler, P. (2002). *Rigged rules and double standards: Trade, globalisation, and the fight against poverty.* Oxford: Oxfam.

Yusuf, A.A. (1998). TRIPS: Background, principles and general provisions. In C. Correa, & A. Yusuf (Eds.), *Intellectual property and international trade: The TRIPS agreement* (pp. 3–20). London: Kluwer Law International.

Part 3

Financial and Accounting Issues in a
Globalised World

Contextualising and Profiling Contemporary Financial Management

Estian Calitz

A Brief Economic Perspective on the Function of Finance (Money) in the Economy

Financial markets as institutions have acquired new dimensions under globalisation.[1] But the financial sector still functions as an intermediary between surplus and deficit savers, between lenders and borrowers. The financial manager of an organisation could at different times be on any side of the financial market.

The financial manager is a competitive participant in the determination of the price of *money* (i.e., interest rates) — mostly a price taker rather than price maker, except maybe if you are a George Soros or a Warren Buffett. In the determination of the prices of *goods and services* in the economy, the financial manager sometimes participates as a price maker, especially if you have a say in Microsoft, Anglo American or OPEC, or if your company is in the business of developing new products. Ironically, the idea of 'price-makers' defies the efficient market hypothesis advanced by Paul Samuelson, which boils down to the following: the more efficient the market, the more random the sequence of price changes generated by such a market must be, and the most efficient market of all is one in which price changes are completely random and unpredictable (Farmer & Lo, 1999, p. 9991).

The financial manager is a key role-player in the generation and allocation of resources in the economy. The financial manager's role in generating economic value therefore goes far beyond the contribution to the GDP of the economic sector 'finance and insurance, real estate and business services'. The major value is the financial manager's role in leading or underpinning a successful value-adding operation in whatever economic sector he or she finds himself or herself. The challenge is to successfully link the business to the financial markets in the economy and to co-manage the allocation of resources in pursuing organisational goals. At the national level, successful financial management has to do with prioritising and pursuing fiscal and monetary policy goals, and with legislating or regulating the rules of the (financial markets) game (i.e., with setting the policy framework within which the goals of individual organisations are pursued in the different economic sectors).

Because financial markets are subject to market failure, governments have a role to play. Government intervention has to do with stability, efficiency and equity — and the associated risks. I will now look at these issues and in the process highlight external influences that shape the world of financial management.

Stability, Efficiency and Equity

International financial stability is linked to the role of the International Monetary Fund (IMF) in facilitating balance-of-payments stability and in facilitating monetary cooperation,[2] a role that came under serious scrutiny in recent years when the global financial architecture appeared to be incapable of containing contagion.

Within most countries, exchange rate flexibility (as shock absorber),[3] inflation targeting and conservative fiscal policies are the main contemporary stabilisation instruments. Temporary controls are also used to protect the capital account of the balance of payments.[4] They are accepted by the market, albeit sometimes with retaliation, provided they do not stealthily substitute for structural reforms. The Malaysian experience towards the end of the 1990s is a case in point.

The advance of market-based policies has strengthened the view, however, that inefficiencies in markets (and therefore in financial markets as well) are not necessarily reflections of market failure that warrant government intervention. The accrual of high profits to an investment professional, for example, need not reflect market inefficiency but simply the fair reward for unusual skill, extraordinary effort, or breakthroughs in financial technology (Farmer & Lo, 1999, p. 9992). Besides, inefficiency may well be the result of distortions caused by governments on account of inappropriate interventions or government failure in general.[5] The judicious reduction of, rather than more, government intervention may then well be the indicated way forward.

Be that as it may, financial managers operate in markets exhibiting huge volatility, especially the foreign exchange market and this happens in industrial countries and developing countries alike. Developing countries are, however, more exposed to the adverse consequences of financial contagion, which they sometimes experience despite having sound financial policies. The impact on wealth can be devastating — as Malaysia experienced in 1997.[6] IMF managing director De Rato's (2006) indication that they are to develop a new instrument to provide financing to emerging market countries that have strong fundamentals, but which remain vulnerable to shocks, may introduce a welcome measure of differentiation within this group of countries.

De Rato's proposal is yet another attempt at improving the functioning of financial markets in an international monetary dispensation of (predominantly) floating exchange rates. We need to remind ourselves that financial markets are characterised by problems of limited and unequal information, making them inherently imperfect and prone to failure — hence international and national attempts at improving financial regulations and supervision. Prominent in this regard is the Basel Committee on Banking Supervision (2006). The aim is for international convergence on regulations that govern the capital adequacy of internationally active banks (known as Basel II).

Proper disclosure (code word for full and reliable information) remains a cornerstone of efficient markets. In this regard, the development and implementation of International Financial Reporting Standards (IFRS), which gained momentum in the aftermath of Enron[7] and other subsequent confidence-shaking financial scandals, represent another important step towards restoring financial confidence and integrity internationally.

All these (and other similar) measures are — or, at least should be — reinforcing, rather than reversing the major financial market liberalisation which many countries undertook during the past two to three decades.[8] It is indeed folly to think that liberalisation and regulation are in conflict. On the contrary, we all know that a successful, competitive market economy cannot function without strong and transparent regulation of the right kind (just note the strict rules laid down by the Security Exchange Commission in the United States, a country widely regarded as a role model of a free enterprise economy).

Recent financial regulations in many ways reflect the major rethink on the role of goverment(s) in the high degree of financial market integration in the globalisation era. What we have seen is a major shift away from direct controls (including price controls) to indirect (market-based) controls and self-regulating systems.[9] Monitoring by regulatory bodies runs the risk of closing the door after the horse has bolted. One of the most important benefits that financial institutions could derive from the prescribed reporting to regulating authorities, therefore, is the early-warning signals that are created and which enable preemptive risk-reducing action by the monitored organisation itself. Regulatory measures of the supervisory kind should be seen as supplements to, and not substitutes for, other measures to protect the interests of shareholders, depositors, consumers and other stakeholders.

So far most of our discussion has pertained to the stability and efficiency of financial markets. Another important issue capturing the attention of authorities and business organisations all over the world is financial market access:[10] access of developing countries to international capital, access of small and medium enterprises to loan and venture capital and access of low-income people to credit. Access is a matter on which considerations of efficiency and equity go hand in hand.

Sometimes the pursuance of efficiency has high opportunity cost in the form of inequity. But sometimes efficiency and equity are *complementary*: when better market information improves access to financial sources of hitherto excluded groups, organisations and individuals, efficiency *and* equity are served. By addressing poor and biased information and reducing the transaction cost of obtaining information, efficiency *and* equity (improved market access) are served.

Of course, one cannot deny that inadequate governance in many developing countries is an important factor inhibiting access (World Bank, 2006, pp 123–138). With regard to international capital flows, for example, the financial systems and many individual banks are still weak in some countries in sub-Saharan Africa. Many banks fail to meet tests of basic capital adequacy, a sign of persistent problems in banking supervision. In 2004, average nonperforming loans stood at 15%, which will be much higher if South Africa and other middle-income countries are excluded (see Gulde & Pattillo, 2006).

At the same time, however, country differentiation is warranted. With reference to criteria[11] of good governance, 70 to 80% of low-income countries are now rated as having good policies in the areas of monetary policy and exchange rate regimes. The same is true of macroeconomic policy consistency and financial sector governance: less than one-fifth of countries are rated as unsatisfactory. By contrast, fiscal policy and especially the composition of public spending are viewed with concern (World Bank, 2006, p. 23).

The problem of 'adverse' selection in respect of countries due to built-in biases, historical comfort zones, poor or inadequate information and risk assessments based on the performance of the weakest member in the club, manifests within countries as well. Financial sources do not flow easily towards regions of low economic activity and to new, small or medium companies with potential, especially when the banking sector is exceptionally risk averse and the venture capital sector or futures market is not well developed. Is it incumbent on the individual business to fight the battle for market access all by itself? Some would say it is, and often they may be right; after all, people's savings are at stake. But if market inaccessibility has to do with market imperfections and not with the inherent worth of the company or the project, then clearly market development and/or government intervention is indicated.

It is the existing or prospective small and medium business enterprises (SME) that often bear most of the brunt of market imperfections and, quite often, of government inefficiencies. Ours is a world in which new businesses are a vital source of economic growth and job creation in any country. Yet, the World Bank's (2006, p. 32) *Doing Business* surveys show that it is poor countries that place the highest burdens on entrepreneurs, loading them down with administrative requirements that divert energy from running the business. Poor countries also reform their business regulations the least.[12] Given the high expectation of SMEs to create jobs, their failure to gain access to finance due to market imperfections or to get going on account of an overregulated and unfriendly investment policy climate may thwart the realisation at grass roots level of any set of development goals. This also applies to the realisation of the United Nation's (2005) millennium development goals, notably the eradication of extreme poverty and hunger, and the promotion of gender equality and the empowerment of women.[13]

Unbiased access to finance on sound business grounds also serves to position SMEs as suppliers of the type of products that are likely to be associated with the changing pattern of economic development implied by the pursuance of national and global development goals. To name but a few possible fields of increased importance: investment in health-related business, education, agricultural production, transport and communications, energy supply, international trade, development of environmentally-friendly consumer goods and business processes, government purchases that reflect the authorities' changing priorities and ecotourism.

One of the hardest nuts to crack in the developing world is to commercially extend access to finance for SMEs and the lower income side of the market. Financial institutions give the same well-known reasons why they cannot extend commercial business to the low income side of the market: high cost and excessive risk. So they ask for government guarantees, in one form or another.

A recent South African example indicates that the solution need not always depend on government intervention. Business Partners is a specialist private company that invests in formal SMEs in most sectors of the economy and offers a wide range of services to small and medium start-up companies. During the 2004/2005 financial year, Business Partners invested R660 million[14] into 538 entrepreneurial businesses, 40% of which was made in businesses owned and run by black entrepreneurs. Of the total number of businesses invested in, 30% were owned and run by women.[15]

Dynamics Shaping Financial Management Within the Organisation

The single-purpose business organisation of the profit bottom line has made way for the multipurpose organisation of the triple bottom line. In addition to profit or wealth (and the related secondary goals), environmental impact and corporate citizenship (CC)[16] are today included (or expected to be included) in the objective function of the firm. The focus in financial management can no longer be on internal financial results only; it needs to be externally aligned as well.

Today, there are many questions which the financial manager cannot ignore.
- There are questions about the *production process*. How was the wealth accumulated? Whence and how are resources procured? Is there a policy to switch from the use of nonrenewable to renewable resources?
- What about the *operational systems* (finance, human resources, sales, procurement, inventory control, and so on)? Are they sufficiently safeguarded

against fraud and bribery? Is the integrity of the systems of information technology and (financial) management information above suspicion?

- Questions are asked about *investments*. Where are corporate funds invested? How reputable are the companies whose stocks are purchased?

- The organisation's *orientation to society* is scrutinised. What are the contributions to society? To shrug it off as 'that is what my tax payment is for' is not a convincing answer.

- The *process of decision-making* is under the magnifying glass. How are decisions made? Is the company honest in the disclosure of information to shareholders, clients and staff? Do directors understand their responsibilities and their obligations as trustees in the generic sense of the word? Is there a proper system of risk management in operation?

But it is also the nature of management of the government organisation that has changed over the past 20 to 30 years. The perceived low-risk environment of the public official has made way for fixed-term appointments and performance contracts for top management in the public sector, increasingly cascading through the hierarchy. Many countries have emulated the businesslike approach to public management that countries like Canada and (especially) New Zealand[17] introduced in the 1980s and 1990s. In South Africa, the 1999 Public Finance Management Act (PFMA; RSA, 1999) heralded the introduction of similar reforms. University business schools are nowadays approached to offer training to middle, senior and top management in government or to enrol them in MBA programs. This seems to demonstrate the spreading view that even if an organisation is not a pure business (in the corporate sense of the word), there is no reason why it cannot be managed like a business.

An important development in South Africa has been the release of the King Report on Corporate Governance for South Africa (Institute of Directors of Southern Africa, 2002). The requirements have been passed into law in respect of companies listed on the Johannesburg Stock Exchange; for other organisations (including government agencies and state enterprises) they serve as compelling guidelines. The report serves as an important yardstick for debates and reforms regarding proper accountability and financial integrity and to ensure role clarification of boards and management in government and business. Countries the world over have been adopting similar principles of good governance into laws and regulations.[18]

How do all of the above factors interact with the dynamics internal to the organisation, and what then about financial management? What follows are a few selective observations about the *dynamics* of organisations undergoing change (transformation) in a changing world.

The global spread of market-based economic systems has been complemented by increasing scrutiny of the way in which companies conduct their affairs (the *nature of business*). Issues like the rights of workers, the relative remuneration of labour, capital and entrepreneurship within the firm, the environmental impact[19] of production processes, the role that the organisation plays in the local (or international) community and with reference to national (or international) social issues, have multiplied organisational goals and made their pursuance more complex.

Various factors have changed the *business form and the form of business*. Globalisation[20] has increased international partnerships, mergers and takeovers, sometimes (but not always) enhancing competition[21] and creating global companies. Internet business has changed the nature of transactions, contracts and payments. New information technology is eroding the distinction between different parts of finance, such as banking and insurance (Li, 2003, p. 119). Globalisation has made tax issues and the appropriate business structure more complicated, irrespective of where one stands on tax-driven businesses. Public–private partnerships have become fashionable, as an attempt to properly organise government and business responsibilities in respect of activities producing goods and services with characteristics of public and private goods (e.g., certain infrastructure facilities).

The *competitiveness* of firms has been challenged by many of the issues just mentioned. In general, globalisation underpinned by trade and financial liberalisation has contributed to a more competitive business environment. This also applies to government agencies and semigovernment organisations, which are monitored and peer evaluated with reference to criteria of international best practice of some sort, or of competitive standards designed for the particular purpose. Financial management is challenged to help design cost-effectiveness criteria with a view to the self-evaluation of divisions and activities and the facilitation of enhanced efficiency.

More volatile financial markets and the digital age have made *risk management* more important and complex. Decision-makers can now use sophisticated algorithms programmed into computers to carry out real-time calculations that were not possible before; the ability to carry out such calculations creates a whole new range of risk measurement and risk management possibilities (Li, 2003, p. 115). At the same time, the derivative industry continues to develop risk management instruments — some available in the market,[22] some structured uniquely for a particular need. Companies always have the choice of setting up their own treasury function so as to actively engage with financial markets, or outsource it (like many do with their internal audit function). Back in 1989 Lessard (1989, p. 213) already pointed out that 'nonfinancial firms increasingly performed many of the analytical and trading functions for which they previously relied on outside specialists'. An in-house treasury function, of course, complicates the financial management function substantially and can be rather expensive and even risk-enhancing in the hands of inexperienced or adventurous employees, or if the operation is too small to generate economies of scale. Outsourcing, on the other hand, often exposes the business to the risk profile of the contractor. Whatever the choice, a sensible guideline is to clearly separate the treasury or financial risk management function and its guiding goals from that of the financial management of the business per se.[23]

In the above context, I suggest that there are a number of things that the financial manager should guard against; simultaneously, a number of things on which to focus strongly.

Financial management is *not* about *massaging or manipulating financial data.* It is about knowing and understanding (which are two different things) the nature of the business in all its dimensions, about understanding how the financial data came about. (Sometimes I think every financial manager should have served a spell in the production and marketing divisions.) It is about ensuring that data measure the results with integrity so as to do justice to the performance of divisions and individuals, especially if and when rewards and remuneration are dependent on these measurements.

Financial management is *not* about *draconian controls* that eliminate any chances of intelligent judgment when faced with questions that do not fit some rule in a thick regulations manual. Of course, financial principles and rules are necessary, especially if you are surrounded by creative people that would rather (even though reluctantly) apologise afterwards than ask permission upfront. But having said all this, financial management should first and foremost be an enabling service: helping others to do better — and with integrity.

The financial manager has a wonderful opportunity of participating in *seeking solutions,* which in any case is much more exciting career-wise than having to be the symbol of the closed door. A key to successful financial management is that the financial manager should be able to design and present the correct options in as unbiased a manner as possible — disclosed to and understood by everyone (even if they disagree on the eventual choice) — and to articulate the risks, trade-offs and opportunity costs.

Financial management is *not* about *financial judgment alone.* It is about understanding the many factors that impact on the organisation and the aspirations of co-decision makers who have other perspectives and mindsets. As managers, they are financial managers too! It is about the ability to understand the multidisciplined nature of life (of the business) and how to interact with different mindsets. It is about understanding the thinking in the human resources department, of the legal adviser, of the person in charge of management information and of the tax, information technology and marketing expert. That is why management training at university business schools has become increasingly multidisciplinary in its approach.

Financial management is *not just* about *record financial results* and financial sustainability. It is not just about presenting financial statements with huge headline earnings and high dividends, and convincing the market of the company's liquidity and solvency. It is about putting the financial resources in service of the organisation's strategic goals, allocating funds in a way that glues the multipurpose organisation together and motivates people. It is about integrating normative, strategic and operational management (Bleicher, 1994: Lessard, 1989).

There is likely to be more than one management model which could ensure integrative strategic and financial management in a multipurpose organisation. My vote goes to the age-old management-by-objectives (MBO) model,[24] a management tool associated with big corporations like General Electric and General Motors as many as 50 years ago (Bromwich & Lapsley, 1999, pp. 185–189) and with various governments.

Requirements of the Contemporary Financial Manager

The skills required of the financial manager of the 21st century are much more demanding than those required 100, 60 or even 20 years ago. If you want to functionally integrate financial management with the main line of business of your organisation, financial expertise in all its standard dimensions is obviously the first requirement. But it is not sufficient. You need a good understanding of the nature of the financial sector in your country and of the government policies and regulations that impact on financial markets. You need to be computer software proficient; have a good knowledge of the legal system — including contract and labour law, the tax system and its impact on your business, industrial relations and good interpersonal relations. If you are in international business or face international competition, knowledge of international financial, legal and tax matters is also indispensable. You need to be on top of the latest product developments in the primary and secondary capital market and an expert at risk management.

The financial director therefore needs the support of a much wider range of skills than accounting. It is not for nothing that financial businesses have people highly skilled in mathematics, actuarial science, statistics and even engineering heading up or working in the risk management division and involved in developing new financial products! As Lessard (1989, p. 210) put it:

> The financial function must simultaneously be differentiated and yet integrated into a variety of other specialist domains, which in turn calls for an expert manager — neither an isolated technical specialist or a 'thin veneer' generalist, but one who can operate in both domains.

Not only are all organisations challenged to rethink the task description and performance contract of the financial manager. Continuous reflection, by all institutions concerned, on the appropriateness of education and training of people likely to end up as financial managers, is also indicated. The financial manager, like all professionals, also needs to continuously keep abreast of the latest relevant developments — which go far beyond the 'pure financial'.

Author Note

This is an edited version of his keynote address delivered at the Third International Conference on Contemporary Business, Leura, Blue Mountains, Australia, September 21, 2006. The author is grateful to various colleagues for useful comments. The usual disclaimer applies.

Endnotes

1   Volcker (2000, p. 201) describes globalisation as 'the world in which finance theory, statistical analysis, and mathematics have combined with electronic technology to produce new techniques for bringing lenders and borrowers together, for reallocating risk, and for enhancing leverage'.

2   For a list of IMF functions, see De Rato (2006).

3   A large stock of foreign reserves is part of the equation, of course. Arguably, its value lies more in its availability than in its use. Various countries have experienced counterproductive results when using foreign exchange reserves to protect the external values of their currencies.

4   For example, Chilean-type restrictions on capital inflows or Malaysian-type controls on capital outflows.

5   For example, in a fairly recent OECD survey (2005) in which the Italian economy was found to perform relatively poorly in terms of competitiveness and product market performance, the service sector in particular was found to lack competitive pressure to resist cost increases and to innovate, in part because of remaining *direct public-sector involvement* in some subsectors, especially transport and energy.

6   For example, the value of the Malaysian ringgit fell by 40% and the capitalisation of the Kuala Lumpur Stock Exchange fell by more than 50% during 1997 (Calitz, 2002, p. 48).

7   Baker and Hayes (2005) concluded that, had there been an appropriate level of transparency in the financial statements of Enron, investors and creditors would have been provided with a more realistic view of the company's financial position and its results of operations, thereby facilitating their ability to assess the viability of the company and avoid their bankruptcy losses.

8   For an outline of the process and nature of financial liberalisation, see Kirkpatrick (2002). For two examples of the nature of financial market liberalisation in different parts of the world, see Akinboade and Makina (2005), on South Africa, and India and 'India and the global economy' (July 6, 2006), on India.

9   See for example the experience regarding prudential regulation in Kirkpatrick (2002).

10 With reference to developing countries, the World Bank (2006, p. 29) points out that, in finance, a concern for equity may mean balancing the focus on financial stability and performance of well-served clients with approaches to expand financial access to underserved clients.

11 Measured as elements of the World Bank's Country Policy and Institutional Assessments (CPIAs; World Bank, 2006, pp. 128–129).

12 The 2004 *Doing Business* survey showed that Serbia, Montenegro and Georgia topped the global country rankings for enacting the most reforms to make things easier for business. At the other end of the scale, sub-Saharan Africa reformed the least as a region. But again, differentiation is necessary. Mauritius and South Africa both rank in the top 30 economies globally on the ease of doing business. (World Bank, 2006, p. 33).

13 Women, who make up three-quarters of the workforce in some developing economies, are big beneficiaries of regulatory reform; so are young people looking for their first job (World Bank, 2006, p. 34).

14 Converted at the rand-dollar exchange of March 12, 2007, this amounts to about US$90 million.

15 See the website of Business Partners at http://www.businesspartners.co.za/

16 Godfrey (2002, n.p.) actually links corporate governance to, in his words, 'the wider concept of corporate citizenship. Any successful modern company has to take responsibility, in co-operation with government, in developing sustainable business and commercial activities that serve communities'.

17 For an account of some of the financial aspects of the New Zealand experience, see Pallot (2001).

18 A prominent example is the OECD principles (Mallin, 2006, p. 1), revised in 2004 to take account of developments in the corporate governance arena. Another example is the principles set out by the Commonwealth Association for Corporate Governance, which are a well-recognised benchmark within the British Commonwealth (see Godfrey, 2002).

19 See World Bank (2006, p. 29) for a few examples of current environmental risks.

20 In the academic literature issues of globalisation and the implications for financial management have understandably received much attention. See, for example, many articles in this respect in the *Journal of Financial Management and Analysis*, the *Journal of Multinational Financial Management* and the *Journal of International Financial Management and Accounting*.

21 Kaufman (2002, p. 179) argues that, in the long run, the massive consolidation that is taking place in business and finance and in nonfinancial sectors and that extends beyond national borders, will drastically reduce competition and turn us completely away from any tendencies toward economic democracy. Volcker (2000, p. 211), by contrast, maintains that 'the risks to small financial institutions in economically small countries, sailing in a turbulent sea of global finance, are reduced if not eliminated by becoming a part of a large international organization'. He sees parallel trends in nonfinancial companies.

22 Li (2003, p. 118) refers to the nascent markets in weather-linked contracts, telecom bandwidth and corporate-earnings insurance, for example. He mentions that since September 1999, the Chicago Mercantile Exchange has traded weather-linked derivatives whose value varies with the temperature measured by an index of warmth in four large American cities.

23 Lessard (1989, p. 213) observed that, as nonfinancial firms develop an in-house capability in financial transactions, many of them began to treat the finance function as a business in its own right. For example, British Petroleum organised BP Finance as a separate entity with the objective not only of providing financial services for BP at large, but also of functioning *as a transactional treasury*, seeking to profit from its trading activities.

24 Bransson (2002, p. 190) dates this particular management technique back to the 1920s, or even to the time of Moses.

References

Akinboade, O.A., & Makina, D. (2005). Financial sector development in South Africa, 1970–2002. *Studies in Economics and Econometrics, 30*(1), 101–127.

Baker, C.R., & Hayes, R. (2005). The Enron fall out: Was Enron an accounting failure? *Managerial Finance, 31*(9), 5–28.

Basel Committee on Banking Supervision. (2006). *International convergence of capital measurement and capital standards*. Basel, CH: Bank for International Settlements.

Bleicher, K. (1994). Integrative management in a time of transformation. *Long Range Planning, 27*(5), 136–144.

Bransson, K.H. (2002). Management or politics — or both? How management by objectives may be managed: a Swedish example. *Financial Accountability and Management, 18*(2), 189–209.

Bromwich, M., & Lapsley, I. (1999). Decentralisation and management accounting in central government: Recycling old ideas? *Financial Accounting and Management, 13*(2), 181–201.

Calitz, E. (2002). Structural economic reform in South Africa: lessons from international experience. *Bureau for Market Research: Research Report 2002/1*. Pretoria, RSA: Bureau for Market Research, University of South Africa.

De Rato, R. (2006, June 13). *The changing role of the IMF in Asia and the global Economy.* Speech delivered at the National Press Club. Canberra, Australia. Washington, DC: International Monetary Fund. Retrieved July 21, 2006, from http://www.imf.org/external/np/speeches/2006/061306.htm

Farmer, J.D., & Lo, A.W. (1999). Frontiers of finance: Evolution and efficient markets. *The Proceedings of the National Academy of Sciences USA* 96 (August), 9991–9992.

Godfrey, S. (2002). Benchmarks and indicators for corporate governance: A private sector perspective. *African Security Review, 11*(4), 25–29.

Gulde, A.M., & Pattillo, C. (2006). Adding depth. *Finance and Development,* 43(2), 44–47.

India and the global economy, Economywatch.com, 7 July 2006. Retrieved July 15, 2006, from http://www.economywatch.com/index1.jsp.

Institute of Directors of Southern Africa. (2002). *King Report on Corporate Governance for South Africa 2002*, Executive Summary. Retrieved July 17, 2006, from http://www.iodsa.co.za.

Kaufman, H. (2002). If Adam Smith were alive today. *Journal of International Financial Management and Accounting,* 13(2), 175–182.

Kirkpatrick, C. (2002, March). Finance matters—Financial liberalization: Too much too soon?' *Insights, 40.* Retrieved July 15, 2006, from http://www.id21.0rg/insights/insights40/insights-iss40-art00.html

Lessard, D. (1989). Corporate finance in the 1990s: Implications of a changing competitive and financial context. *Journal of International Financial Management and Accounting, 1*(3), 209–231.

Li, S. (2003). Future trends and challenges of financial risk management in the digital economy. *Managerial Finance, 29*(5/6), 111–125.

Mallin, C. (Ed.). (2006). *International corporate governance.* Northampton, England: Edward Elgar.

Organisation for Economic Cooperation and Development (OECD). (2005). *Economic survey of Italy 2005: Corporate governance and market liberalisation: the scope for improvement.* Retrieved July 21, 2006, from http://www.oecd.org/document/37/0,2340.en_2649_201185_34752381_1_1_1_1,00.html

Pallot, J. (2001). A decade in review: New Zealand's experience with resource accounting and budgeting. *Financial Accountability and Management,* 17(4), 383–400.

RSA. (1999). *Public Finance Management Act (PFMA),* 1999 (Act No. 1 of 1999) (as amended by Act No. 29 of 1999). Retrieved July 18, 2006, from http://www.treasury.gov.za/showpfma.htm

United Nations. (2005). *The millennium development goals report.* Retrieved July 18, 2006, from http://unstats.un.org/unsd/mi/pdf/MDG%20Book.pdf

Volcker, P.A. (2000). The implication of globalisation is globalisation. *Journal of International Financial Management and Accounting,* 11(3), 207–214.

World Bank. (2006). *Global monitor report 2006. Millennium development goals: Strengthening mutual accountability, aid, trade, and governance.* Washington, DC: The International Bank for Reconstruction and Development/The World Bank. Retrieved October 6, 2007, from http://siteresources.worldbank.org/DEVCOMMINT/Documentation/20898106/DC2006-0004(E)-GMR2006Add1.pdf

Chapter

13

Capital Flows to Emerging Markets From Australia: Facts

Rakesh Gupta

Over the past 3 decades equity markets over the world have experienced exceptional growth and expansion. Total market capitalisation of the world equity markets have increased from a modest US$1 trillion in 1974 to in excess of US$16 trillion by the end of 1997.[1] The process of growth in the world markets could be because of improved macroeconomic and financial fundamentals or because of investors' enthusiasm, which may have distorted the relationship between market fundamentals and equity valuations. Net private capital inflows into Asia during the mid-1990s were exceptional in terms of the total dollar amounts and also in terms of the size of these economies (Grenville, 1998). During 1998, when these countries ran into financial crisis, this inflow of US$100 billion reversed into an outflow of US$55 billion. There have been numerous studies after the crisis providing a general overview of the crisis and to identify reasons of crisis to provide possible measures to prevent future crisis.

The Asian crisis was different from other crises in the world (Gupta & Basu, 2005). With the passage of time now we have a clearer picture on the crisis and what happened to capital flows in East Asia during the crisis period. This chapter briefly describes the Australian financial sector and summarises the available data, drawing primarily from the Australian Bureau of Statistics (ABS) and Axiss Australia. It focuses on size and volatility of capital flows to emerging markets from Australia, especially into Asia and particularly equity flows. The chapter concludes with the evidence that the equity flows from Australia to Asian countries is picking up and the future prospects for equity flows to these countries look brighter.

Australian Financial System

Changes in the international capital markets and deregulation of 1980s in Australia opened new possibilities for raising capital, investing and hedging risk. Australia has a highly developed financial sector. Historically, Australia was viewed as a commodity-based economy but has become a services-based economy during the past decade. Currently, the Australian financial sector (including insurance industry) ranks as the third largest industry sector.[2] The financial sector's contribution to economy during 2001–02 was around 7.4% of Australia's gross domestic product (GDP) for the year.

The Australian financial market comprises banks, investment bankers, insurance industry, capital markets, foreign exchange market, equities market, debt securities market and the derivatives market.

Banks. Australia has a competitive and technologically advanced banking infrastructure. Australian banks have sound capital backing, low levels of impaired assets and high levels of provisioning. There are 50 authorised banks in Australia, 36 foreign owned, 14 domestic and 83 money market companies or merchant banks.[3] The Australian banking sector has an established base in Australia after the deregulation of 1980s. As at June 2002, Australian banks had total assets of A$958.1 billion, which was 18.7% more than the assets in 2001.

Investment management. Government-backed retirement income policy helped the growth of the managed funds industry and the total funds pool at the end of 2002 is quoted as A$645 billion and is estimated to be A$2.3 trillion by the end 2015. The funds management market in Australia grew owing to the government's compulsory superannuation policy and this growth has attracted foreign asset management companies to Australia. This growth in the size of the funds has given rise to the increased use of specialist investment managers. Increase in

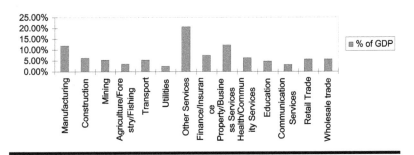

Figure 1

Percentage of GDP.

Source: Australian Bureau of Statistics, 2003.

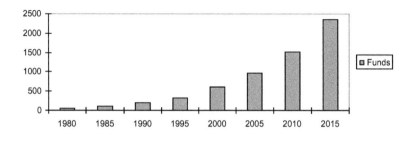

Figure 2
Australia's assets of managed funds.

the funds placed with the professional investment managers is faster than the growth in the underlying investment funds pool itself, funds with the professional managers has increased from A$154 billion in June 1990 to A$628 billion in June 2002. Figure 2 shows the growth in Australia's pool of managed funds, including the projections up to 2015 by Reserve Bank of Australia (RBA, 2004).

Insurance. Australia has a well-developed insurance industry, comprising of 200 firms including general, life and reinsurance businesses. As at December 2001, insurers held approximately A$265 billion in financial assets. The insurance industry is the second largest employer group after banks in Australia. Export of insurance services earned A$680 million in 2001 (Axiss Australia, 2005).

Financial markets. Australia is a key centre in the Asia–Pacific region for capital market activity. Australian markets have deep liquidity in foreign exchange, equities, debt and derivatives markets. Australian markets have benefited from the timely deregulation and high quality of institutional and operational infrastructure, supported by a highly skilled workforce.

Foreign exchange. Australia has a large, liquid and open foreign exchange market. In a survey by the Bank for International Settlements (BIS), Australia was ranked eighth largest centre for foreign exchange trading. During the period 1998 to 2001, Australia's daily turnover on foreign exchange grew by 11%, over the same period the world market declined by 19% (Axiss Australia, 2005).

Debt securities. The Australian debt market accounts for less than 1% of the global outstanding debt. During the period, 1997–98 to 2001–02 the Australian debt market has experienced a growth of 27%. With the decrease in budget deficit in Australia during the period and resulting decline in the government debt, there has been a rise in the issuance of nongovernment debt securities. In 1996, nongovernment debt issuance accounted for 12% of total debt issuance, which rose to 46.2% in 2002 (Axiss Australia, 2005).

Derivatives. The Sydney futures exchange (SFE) along with Australian stock exchange (ASX) provides markets for traders to trade in the derivatives. A wide variety of derivative products is available at these markets and these products provide significant risk management benefits to the participants. In 2001, 35.8 million contracts were traded on SFE; this represents a notional value of US$5.8 trillion, (Axiss Australia, 2005). An active over-the-counter derivative market also exists in Australia, mainly trading in swaps and repos.

Equities. In terms of market capitalisation, the Australian Stock Exchange (ASX) is currently the twelfth largest stock exchange in the world and third largest in Asia–Pacific region after Japan and Hong Kong. In 2001, Australia had a weighting of 1.5% in the Morgan Stanley Capital Index (MSCI), (Axiss Australia, 2005). In terms of MSCI Asia–Pacific ex-Japan index, Australia has a weighting of approximately 35%. During the same period, market capitalisation of domestic securities was approximately A$732.8 billion and of overseas based equities A$376.8 billion (Axiss Australia, 2005).

A Reserve Bank of Australia bulletin (2004) documented the inflow and outflow of capital between 1952 and 2002. The comparisons show that up to about 1980, the current account deficit was around 2% of GDP and there was a similar inflow of capital. After 1980, the current account deficit jumped to approximately 4% and the capital inflow to a similar level. During the same periods, the report document indicated there was a negligible outflow of capital due to the capital controls, these controls were specifically designed to restrict these flows. After the removal of the controls in 1983, the outflow of capital from Australia has averaged around 3% of GDP and the capital inflows increased to 7%.

The reserve bank report shows that, as a percentage of the GDP, the outflow of portfolio capital from Australia has, on average, stayed constant over the last 10 years (approximately 2%). An important point, which the Reserve Bank report highlights, is the increase in investment by the superannuation funds into overseas equities (currently 25% of the total of superannuation funds are invested in the overseas equities).

The level of Australian investment reached $649.7 billion at 31 December 2004, an increase of $ 110.2 billion on the previous year, an increase of 16.96%. Equity has been the main form of Australian investment abroad, as at December 31, 2004, total equity investment abroad was $403.6 billion out of which portfolio investment was $147.7 billion, with the balance in foreign direct investment (Australian Bureau of Statistics, 2004). Figure 3 shows the growth of Australian investments abroad during the period.

Flow of equity from Australia into overseas markets has grown consistently over the period from 1993 to 2004 (except during the year 2002). Table 1 shows the break-up of these equity investments into different emerging markets, despite the missing data for some of the emerging market countries, sufficient data is

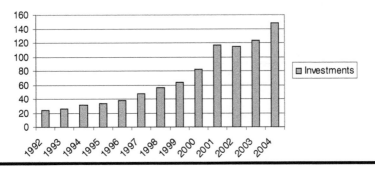

Figure 3

Australian equity investments.

Source: Australian Bureau of Statistics; International Investment Position (2005).

available to infer that emerging markets are an important destination for the equity investments for Australian investors.

Around the Asian crisis of mid-1990s, Asian emerging markets were out of favour and international investors were withdrawing from the emerging markets in general, more importantly from Asian markets. The data show that around the year 2000 this reversed and equity investments again started to flow into emerging markets.

When dealing with the emerging market data, there is a problem of missing values and incomplete data. Even the incomplete dataset is sufficient to show that the equity investments to emerging market economies have risen and more countries are being added to the dataset, which suggests that emerging markets are in favour. Table 2 shows the proportion of Australian equity investments into emerging markets as a percentage of total investments abroad. Australian equity investments into emerging markets were at their highest around the Asian crisis. The Asian crisis may have caused the withdrawal of these investments and now the flow of investments into emerging markets has started to rise from 2000, with a slight fall in the year 2002.

Table 1

Equity Investments Into Emerging Markets 1999–2004 (millions of AUD)

Year	Chile	Greece	India	Malaysia	Philippines	Thailand	EM total
1999	6	55	n.a.	139	n.a.	n.a.	200
2000	2	n.a.	n.a.	152	n.a.	81	235
2001	6	39	n.a.	109	13	41	208
2002	7	n.a.	n.a.	65	36	45	153
2003	5	n.a.	539	100	19	139	802
2004	5	n.a.	787	173	26	188	1179

Source: Australian Bureau of Statistics; International Investment Position (2005); all figures in million Australian dollars.[4]

Table 2

Australian Equity Markets Into Emerging Markets 1999–2004

Year	EM total	% of total	Year	EM total	% of total
1992	115	0.48	1999	354	0.56
1993	547	2.09	2000	240	0.29
1994	440	1.40	2001	214	0.18
1995	47	0.14	2002	153	0.13
1996	58	0.15	2003	802	0.65
1997	144	0.30	2004	1179	0.80
1998	545	0.97			

Note: (EM figures are Australian investments into emerging markets (millions Australian dollars) and % shows the emerging markets investments as a percentage of total equity portfolio investments from Australia during the period.)

[Figure 4 shows Australian equity investments into emerging markets and Australian investments into emerging markets as a percentage of total equity portfolio outflows from Australia during the years.

Figure 5 shows equity portfolio investment into emerging markets from rest of world. Investments into emerging markets from rest of the world are consistently rising with a small decline in 2006 estimated figures.

Conclusion

This review shows emerging markets have been, and are becoming, more important for equity portfolio investments from the rest of the world. As the heat from the Asian crisis settles, the flow of portfolio investments is returning to the emerging markets. In Australia, since the removal of exchange controls and other financial deregulation the flow of equity capital has been consistently rising to the emerging markets. This is except for the period surrounding the Asian crisis, which caused a reversal in the flow of equity investments to the emerging markets.

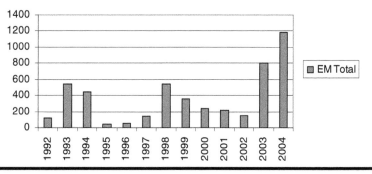

Figure 4

Estimated markets investments.

Source: Australian Bureau of Statistics, 2005.

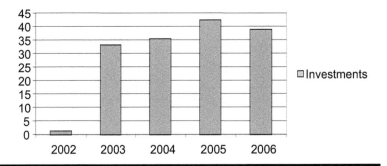

Figure 5
Estimated Investments (billions of US dollars).
Source: Institute of International Finance, September 2005.

Further, despite the reservations expressed by some researchers and practitioners the flow of equity to the emerging markets is in the interest of Australia. The growth in equity investments into emerging markets and improved sentiment towards the investments into emerging markets will reflect in portfolio strategies pursued by the portfolio managers seeking international diversification.

Acknowledgment

I would like to thank Garry Hobbes for his helpful comments.

Endnotes

1 Li (2002).
2 Axiss Australia, *Executive Briefing, 2005, Financial Services in Australia.*
3 Axiss Australia, *Executive Briefing, 2005, Financial Services in Australia.*
4 EM market total is the total of the data available from ABS. Actual figures may vary as figures for some of the emerging markets is not available with the ABS.

References

Australian Bureau of Statistics. (2001–2002). *International investment position, Australia: Supplementary country statistics 2001–02* (Cat. no. 5352.0). Canberra, Australia: Author.

Australian Bureau of Statistics. (2003). *International investment position, Australia: Supplementary country statistics 2003* (Cat. no. 5352.0). Canberra, Australia: Author.

Australian Bureau of Statistics. (2004). *International investment position, Australia: Supplementary country statistics 2004* (Cat. no. 5352.0). Canberra, Australia: Author.

Australian Bureau of Statistics. (2005). *International investment position, Australia: Supplementary country statistics 2005* (Cat. no. 5352.0). Canberra, Australia: Author.

Axiss Australia. (2005). *Financial Services in Australia.* Retrieved July 3, 2006, from http://www.axiss.com.au/index.cfm?event=object.showContent&objectID=60CF03DE-65BF-4956-BD235DB1B9CF5690

Grenville, S.A. (1998). Capital flows and crises. *Reserve Bank of Australia bulletin,* December, *99,* 16–31.

Gupta, R., & Basu, P.K. (2005). *Is India vulnerable to a financial crisis? Lessons from the Asian experience.* Paper presented at Australian Banking and Finance Conference, Sydney, Australia.

Li, K. (2002, Fall). What explains the growth of global equity markets? *Canadian Investment Review,* 23–30.

Corporate Debt Default and Developmental Role of Development Banks: A Theoretical Approach

Mohammad Ziaul Hoque

Persistent industrial loan defaults and massive loan losses have become a regular feature in developing countries. According to Hoque (2004) and the World Bank (1993) 150 development banks in 33 developing countries have been haunted by massive debt default and loan loss. Industrial Development Finance Institutions (IDFIs) are expected to stimulate industrial investment in both private and public sectors in developing countries. It is their role not only to inject capital, but also to blend capital with entrepreneurial skills to support industrial advancement in an underdeveloped economy.

A great variety of IDFIs has been established in the developing countries since 1945, 'many following independence in the late 1950s and 1960s of former British and French colonies' (Kitchen, 1986, p. 123), to provide both medium- and long-term loans to industrial and agricultural projects (Perera, 1968, p. 152; Ramirez, 1986, p. 22). There is hardly any developing country where there is not at least one development bank. Regardless of their variations in the set and functional roles, a large number of development banks in Asia, Africa and Latin America are now jaundiced by persistent debt defaults. In fact, there are few IDFIs in developing countries which have not been adversely affected by persistent debt defaults. The default-prone IDFIs in Bangladesh are such examples.

This chapter is an attempt to construct a theory of the causes of corporate debt default experienced by the IDFIs in developing countries. The theoretical aspect of the developmental role of IDFIs in developing countries is discussed, followed by the presentation of a theoretical model for reducing corporate debt.

Developmental Role of IDFIs: A Theoretical Approach

Several authors (Hoque, 2004; Kane, 1975) found that debt default occurs due to borrower's inability or unwillingness to repay debt. It may be that there are borrowers who are willing, but not able to repay debt. Again, there are borrowers who are able, but not willing to repay debt — debt default arises in both cases. However, this chapter concentrates on the borrowers' ability to repay industrial debt, rather than willingness to repay industrial debt. The ability to repay industrial debt is influenced by a number of factors relating to industrial financing. In particular, what industrial project is financed; how it is financed; how its management from the set up stage to loan liquidation stage is helped by an IDFI are very important. As regards what type of industrial project is to be financed, Kane (1975) advocated that the development bank must, of necessity, restrict itself to financing only those development projects which are bankable. He defined a bankable project as

> ... that investment which will generate enough income within a specific period of time to: (1) cover the cost of operation once the plant begins operations; (2) repay the principal of the bank's loan; (3) pay the interest charge of the loan; and (4) have residual profit large enough to induce the entrepreneur(s) to undertake and remain with the operation. (Kane, 1975, pp. 17–18)

At the same time, such a project should have the largest catalytic impact on economic development of developing countries. The choice of a project lies within the developmental role of an IDFI. As a development institution, an IDFI should deal with 'those projects with the highest ranking on the development-impact scale and as a banking institution, it should finance those projects with the highest ranking on the interest-rate scale' (Kane, 1975, p. 20). It means that a bankable project should satisfy both developmental and financial criteria, unlike a commercial bank which stress the financial role rather than the developmental role.

It appears from the above that debt default may arise if the development bank finances nonbankable projects that are not capable of generating enough income within a reasonable time to cover the costs of operation, repay the principal debt, meet costs of borrowing and earn enough profit to motivate its promoters to remain in operations.

The role of a development bank, particularly a public industrial development bank, is not solely confined to the supply of medium- and long-term loans and/or equity. Unlike other financial institutions such as trading or commercial banks, development banks are expected to direct and guide the use of loans, to nurse an enterprise (Basu, 1965), and to play a developmental or promotional role in addition to their financial role.

The developmental or promotional role of an industrial development bank means getting involved in the formulation, initiation and organisation of industrial development; behaving like an entrepreneur who, perceiving or seeking out profitable investment opportunities, actually takes the initiative and leadership to conceive, fashion proposals and organise finance for new enterprises and actually execute them. Briefly put, it involves the entrepreneurial activity of taking the initiative of shaping up a business and getting it started.

There are two extreme sides of this promotional or developmental role. At one extreme spectrum, a development bank originates an idea, translates it into a financeable project (using consultants and other experts as necessary in the process), arranges financing, organises the company and, if only for a time, manages the new enterprise.

The other spectrum of the developmental role is the involvement of the industrial bank in the assessment of the viability of an industrial project submitted by the entrepreneurs and giving decisions whether to accept or reject the investment proposal. Between these extremes developmental or promotional role include the following:

- organising general industrial surveys and carrying out feasibility studies for specific projects
- evolving proposals for new enterprises
- helping to find technical and entrepreneurial partners for local clients or investors
- taking equity shares and underwriting securities in order to attract other investors
- organising mergers in order to evolve more efficient industrial/production units
- nurturing a capital market by broadening ownership and by other methods
- encouraging the adoption of innovations in the economic sectors
- providing management and consultancy services to both client and non-client enterprises
- training and development of manpower to meet the needs for highly skilled staff with a broad professional orientation
- taking the initiative to identify and develop projects of critical importance to the economy or sector of involvement.

Along with these promotional roles, development banks are expected to provide guidance to budding or new generation entrepreneurs in respect of selecting viable projects consistent with country's industrial development objectives. While selecting industrial projects, a development bank should examine the 'ability and integrity of the top management of the enterprise' (Bhatt, 1993, p. 50).

Supervision of an enterprise, both at the initial developmental stage and at the operational stage, constitutes part of the developmental role. The commercial or economic environment within which an enterprise operates changes from time to time and inexperienced management of the enterprise may not be able to withstand such changes, which may affect the profitable operations of the enterprise. Bhatt (1993, p. 50) believes that it is

... essential to have vigilant supervision of the project or enterprise even during its operational stages so that timely adaptive action can be taken to ensure its profitability and success. Such supervision requires a fairly close connection between a development bank and the enterprise. It is easier to have such supervision if a development bank also provides short-term finance and is represented at the board of directors of the enterprise as in India, Botswana, Iran and Germany.

Enterprise supervision places a development bank in a position by which it can sense imminent or emerging problems of an enterprise. In changing circumstances, it can provide timely and appropriate suggestions to the entrepreneurs so they can overcome them successfully. The necessity for entrepreneurial guidance from the industrial development bank emanated from the fact that developing countries lack 'a substantial nucleus of entrepreneurs' (Ramirez, 1986, p. 34) 'capable of identifying, assembling, and financing sound industrial projects' (Perera, 1968, p. 200). Though the supply of entrepreneurial talent is abundant in these countries (Nienhaus, 1993), there is acute shortage of experienced entrepreneurs to set up and operate firms there.

However, a new 'entrepreneurial class' can emerge only if talented people get a chance for access to financial resources which exceed their present capacity by far. Bhatt (1993, p. 48) argued that the 'available talents should be harnessed in a development bank'. In Japan, the industrial banking system was the locus of much of the early promotional and entrepreneurial talent which initiated the industrial spurt. Similarly, the Credit Mobilier implicitly contributed to the economic development of France during the 19th century by embodying the spirit of enterprise.

Perera (1968, p. 200) argues that 'by locating and channelling missing elements — such as know-how and capital — to local businessmen, development banks which are de facto agents of the government can play invaluable roles'. At the same time, he believes that

> ... to justify its title as well as its institutional existence, the (development) bank should be a strong supplier of both know-how and capital to local entrepreneurial endeavour; otherwise, it would only serve in the same capacity as a commercial or investment bank ... Only advanced industrialized nations can afford to de-emphasise the promotional role of the development bank. (p. 201)

Kane (1975) identified capital, entrepreneurship, technical and managerial capabilities, promotional activities and availability of foreign exchange as missing ingredients for industrialisation in developing countries. By supplying catalytic increments of these missing factors on its own initiative (Kane 1975), a development bank can further industrialisation efforts in developing countries.

From the opinions of these authors it may be asserted that an industrial development bank cannot remain passive in a developing country where latent entrepreneurial talents have to be activated through technical, managerial and entrepreneurial guidance. Such a role was undertaken by the most successful development banks in developing countries; for example, the Development Bank of Singapore, ICICI of India, Industrial and Mining Development Bank of Iran

(IMDBI), Long Term Credit Bank of South Korea and the Botswana Development Corporation (BDC) (as cited by Bhatt [1993]). The developmental role was also played by the development bank in the industrialisation of the relatively backward countries of Europe during the nineteenth century. The Credit Mobilier and Universal Bank played a momentous role in the industrialisation of France and Germany, respectively (Bhatt, 1993).

In describing the role of German investment banks, Gerschenkron (1966, p. 137) stated:

> in Germany, the various incompetencies of the individual entrepreneurs were offset by the device of splitting the entrepreneurial function: the German investment bank — a powerful invention, comparable in economic effect to that of the steam engine — were in capital supplying function. ... Banks participated actively in shaping the major — and sometimes even minor — decisions of individual enterprises. It is they who very often mapped out a firm's path of growth, conceived far-sighted plans, decided on major technical innovation, and arranged for mergers and capital increases.

Japan adopted the German model in its industrialisation process — a leading example being the formation of the state-owned Industrial Bank of Japan (IBJ) which initiated the industrial spurt through promoting entrepreneurial talent (Patrick, 1966). France also adopted this functional dualism of an industrial bank in her own way (Hu, 1981).

The public development banks have also played a vital role in adopting and absorbing technological change in the country where they are located. They 'goaded the enterprises to adapt, diffuse and improve upon the technology borrowed from the advanced countries' (Bhatt, 1993, p. 50) like England and, in many cases, emphasised the latest technology that was not even adopted elsewhere. All these indicate that IDFIs 'do not simply finance development projects', (Kane, 1975, p. 14) but accompany an enterprise 'from cradle to grave, from establishment to liquidation through all vicissitudes of its existence' (Gerschenkron, 1966, p. 14).

Thus, the developmental role of an IDFI constitutes entrepreneurial and managerial guidance, supervision and direction; and technical assistance to new enterprises. At least the success of the Universal Banks in Germany, IBJ in Japan, IMBDI in Iran, BDC in Botswana, Industrial Development Bank of India in India and Korea Development Finance Corporation in South Korea bear ample testimony to the importance of the developmental role of the an IDFI in initiating and sustaining industrial development in a developing country.

The Model

Based on the arguments provided previously an attempt has been made to construct the following model. The model assumes that if the developmental role is flawed, the entrepreneurs will be unable to choose viable projects, be unable to implement and run the firm as efficiently as it ought to be, and be unable to generate sufficient cash

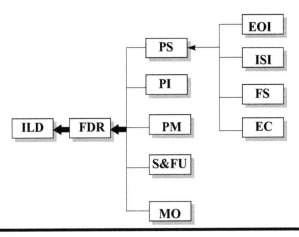

Figure 1
Model of industrial loan default and flawed developmental role.

flow to service the debt. Ultimately, they may end up with loan default. If the development role is plagued by inadequacies and inconsistencies, inhibitions may be created to make the financial role of the IDFI ineffective, which may lead to debt default. These flaws in the developmental role may be the outcomes of the flaws in a number of developmental variables as shown in the model (Figure 1).

Project Selection
The model deals with the relationship between industrial loan default (ILD) and project selection (PS). It is assumed that PS happens in terms of types of firms, size of firms and capacity of firms. As regards types of firms, it is assumed in the model that the earning prospect of the firm belonging to the export-orientated industries (EOI) and import-substituting industries (ISI) is better than all other types of firms and hence, they are expected to repay more loans than other firms. The size of the firm (FS) is also an important variable. Since the big firms are better managed than small firms, their loan repayment performance should be better than small firms. However, firms belonging to an industry having excess capacity (EC) may suffer from idle capacity, which is responsible for low level of income. The low level of income may cause them to default in making repayment to the bank. This suggests that debt defaults are associated with firms other than EOIs and ISIs and firms having no excess capacity. In other words, corporate debt default is related to flawed PS.

Project Implementation (PI)
The loan default risks of a project can be reduced or eliminated if it is implemented in schedule time. If excessive time is taken to acquire land, construct buildings, procure and assemble machinery, the interest burden will continue to grow. The IDFI is required to provide assistance to the entrepreneurs at the time

of project implementation, given that they lack adequate experience in aspects such as factory building construction, machinery selection, erection of plant and assembling of machinery. Unless they are given assistance and guidance by the IDFI, they may end up with long construction periods, improper assembly or installation of machinery, cost overruns and inordinate delay in commercial operation. The model shows that delayed PI contributes to debt default.

Project Management (PM)

The model assumes that ILD is positively related to inadequate participation by the IDFI in the management of the project it financed. Given the shortage of managerial skills and people in the developing countries, it is expected that IDFIs should provide effective guidance and assistance for efficient management of the various affairs of the project. These affairs may be related to production, marketing, sales, finance, human resources and response to competition. Moreover, it can organise and conduct training programs for entrepreneurs to impart the skills required for PM. It is to be pointed out here that the quality of the enterprise management is of paramount importance in assessing the prospect of repayment. This suggests that if the enterprise is ravaged by persistent mismanagement due to the IDFI's inadequate attention to such problems, it is highly likely that the enterprise will not be able to generate sufficient income to service the debt. That is, debt default may be an outcome of inadequate engagement of the IDFIs in the management of the client enterprise.

Supervision and Follow-Up

Supervision and follow-up (S&FU) of loans and investment are an essential part of the work of development banks. The objective of S&FU is to keep the bank informed of programs, to provide an opportunity for advice in anticipation of difficulties and for assistance if trouble nevertheless arises. The model assumes that if an IDFI fails to supervise and follow up at the various stages of the implementation and operations of the industrial firms, inexperienced entrepreneurs may commit costly mistakes, such as cost-overruns and delayed commencement of production, which may contribute to debt defaults. The model suggests that loan default is related to the flawed S&FU.

Monitoring (MO)

An effective monitoring of the firm's overall performance is helpful to detect difficulties as early as possible so that advice and assistance, if accepted, may not come too late. An IDFI should treat monitoring as an important conduit for technical advice and financial accommodation. If there is insufficient monitoring of the activities of the firms, it is highly likely that credit will not be used for the purpose for which it was granted, main risks for the firms will remain undetected and the poor operational and financial position of the firm will go unnoticed. This model suggests that poor monitoring may lead to debt defaults.

Conclusion

Though a great variety of industrial development banks was established in developing countries with a view to stimulating industrial investment in both public and private sectors, many of them have been experiencing financial distress due to persistent loan defaults. Theoretically, loan default arises when borrowers are unable or unwilling to repay loans. There are a number of factors which influence borrowers' ability and willingness to repay loans. Among these, flaw-free developmental roles of the development banks, particularly, IDFIs are very prominent.

For having a flaw-free financial role, entrepreneurs should be nursed from the set-up stage of the firm to the liquidation of the loans. Especially at the stage of selecting, implementing, supervising and monitoring and managing industrial firms, the IDFI should provide guidance and play a paternalistic role. Again, the efficiency and effectiveness of the financial and developmental roles of the IDFI are influenced by government policy regimes. If the public policy regimes suffer from inconsistencies and inefficiencies, it may trigger flaws in the developmental role of IDFIs. If entrepreneurs are deprived of the benefits associated with developmental role of IDFIs, they will not be able to implement and run the firm efficiently to generate sufficient income to repay loans. As such, the flawed developmental role of the IDFI can contribute to corporate debt defaults in developing countries.

References

Basu, S.K. (1965). *Theory and practice of development banking*. Delhi, India: Asia Publishing House.

Bhatt, V.V. (1993). Development banks as catalysts for industrial development. *International Journal of Development Banking, 11*(1), 47–61.

Gerschenkron, A. (1966). *Economic backwardness in historical perspective: A book of essays*. Cambridge, MA: Belknap Press.

Hoque, M.Z. (2004). Flawed working capital loan policy and loan default: Evidences from Bangladesh. *Journal of Accounting, Business and Management, 11*(2), 202–213.

Hu, Y. (1981). The World Bank and Development Finance Companies. *Journal of General Management, 7*(1), 47–57.

Kane, J.A. (1975). *Development banking*. London: Lexinton Books.

Kitchen, R.L. (1986). *Finance for developing economies*. New York: John Wiley and Sons.

Nienhaus, V. (1993). The political economy of development finance. *Managerial Finance, 19*(7), 8–20.

Ramirez, M.D. (1986). *Development banking in Mexico: The Case of the Nacional Financiera*. New York: S.A. Praeger.

Patrick, H.T. (1966). Financial development and economic growth in underdeveloped countries. *Economic Development and Cultural Change, 14*(2), 174–189.

Perera, P. (1968). *Development finance: Institutions, problems, and prospects*. London: Praeger Publishers.

World Bank. (1993). *World development report*. New York: Oxford University Press.

On Foxes Becoming Gamekeepers: The Capture of Professional Regulation by the Australian Accounting Profession

Graham Bowrey

Brian Murphy

Ciorstan Smark

Ted Watts

> There are such persons as liars, damned liars and experts, and there are accountants, bad accountants, and worse accountants. (Debate on the introduction of the *Public Accountants Registration Act*, New South Wales Parliament, 1944, p. 856)

Both the state and the professions have an important interest in safeguarding the quality of service and the protection of the public with respect to the provision of professional services. In the main, the states focus on professional performance and accountability, and the professions emphasise the maintenance of quality and improvement in the skills of members.

With respect to the accounting profession the state has taken two basic approaches to improving professional performance and accountability. The first approach, through imposed competencies embedded in various state registration Acts, regulates a minimum level of performance. The second approach addresses the issue of accountability through the imposition of specific standards of conduct, sanctions and reporting requirements. A recent example of this approach is the decision, in April 2004 by the Singapore government to introduce the Accounting and Corporate Regulatory Authority, through the amalgamation of the Register of Companies and Businesses and the Public Accountants Board. This authority is responsible for administering the *Accounting and Corporate Regulatory Act (2004)* and represents a proactive move by government away from professional self-regulation following the many accounting scandals of recent times, such as Enron and WorldCom. However, the perceived need for government regulation is not new. State regulating authorities exist in most (if not all) the states in the United States (for example, the Accountants Board of Ohio, Nevada State Board of Accountancy, the Board of Public Accountancy in Massachusetts), and central regulating authorities also exist, for example in the Republic of South Africa (the Public Accountants, and Auditors Board). In countries where a regulating authority does not exist (for example, in the United Kingdom, New Zealand and Australia) the professional accounting bodies have been lobbying (to date without success) for regulation.

To protect the public the professions require members to undertake continuing professional development programs, and impose a system of certification on members engaged in public practice. These programs generally require skills be demonstrated at levels higher than the competency requirements necessary for registration. Most professional bodies also enforce strict self-regulation requirements to discipline delinquent members.

Thus one might expect that in Australia an 'accountant' is a person of integrity, professional competence and has adequate indemnity cover. Unfortunately this is not the case, because currently there is no legal impediment in Australia preventing any person, of whatever qualifications and experience, from presenting themselves to the public as an accountant.

This chapter considers the paradoxical case of the Australian accounting profession in New South Wales, which was once government regulated, but lobbied successfully to remove this regulation and more recently attempted, without success, to reinstate it. The chapter focuses on this regulatory vacuum and the impact, in terms of protection of, and redresses by, the general public, whose accounting requirements are undertaken by accountants in public practice.

Theoretical Background

Three general theories explain regulation that limits professional licensing of accountants: capture theory, public interest theory and, at a general level, political economy theory. While these theories are well known in the professional regulation literature, a brief overview is provided for background.

Capture theory, in its simplest form is a straightforward application of self-interest. Accounting professionals 'capture' the regulations, or the regulator, governing licensing and structure them to limit the supply of accountants and thereby increase their incomes.

Public interest theory, by contrast, suggests that professional licensing occurs due to some market 'failure', and that its intent is to increase the welfare to society. Public interest theory presumes that, due to the complex nature of the service and uncertainty about the efficacy of competent service, consumers of professional services lack complete information about the quality of such services. Public interest theory asserts that the professional licensing corrects this market deficiency by ensuring that accounting professionals are of a sufficiently high and standard quality.

Political economy theory, in contrast to both capture theory and public interest theory, entertains the possibility that both the public and accounting professionals affect the existence and form of accounting professional licensing regulations. Political economy theory is basically a theory of checks and balances.

Government Regulation and General Public Protection

This study asks why the accounting profession in Australia is the only group of professionals offering services to the public which is not regulated by either state or Commonwealth legislation.

The *Public Accountants Registration Act 1945* received assent in the New South Wales (NSW) Parliament on April 5, 1945. It had two major purposes: to provide for the audit of certain accounts by registered public accountants, and to regulate the qualifications for registration as a registered public accountant. Under the Act, a 'public accountant' was defined as:

> an accountant who maintains an office as a principal either alone or with others for the business of General Accountancy and the auditing of accounts and in that office places his services in any such regard at the disposal of the public generally for remuneration and whose services are not either entirely or mainly at the disposal of any individual firm, trust or association. (*Public Accountants Registration Act 1945*, p. 107) [emphasis added]

The Act was quite clear that its purpose included protecting the public interest, specifically the offering of accounting services to the general public, in addition to the wider arena of auditing. To achieve this protection, the Act clearly set out the qualifications necessary for registration, which included: being over 21 years of age, being of good fame and character, having passed prescribed examinations and acquired practical experience in accountancy, or be the holder of a certificate of membership issued by an approved institute of accountants, or having passed the final examinations of any approved institute of accountants. To ensure compliance with the requirements and the spirit of the Act, specific disciplinary provisions were included. These required that a complaint or charge against any registered public accountant of infamous misconduct as a public accountant be referred to the Public Accountants Registration Board for investigation. The board was empowered to conduct any inquiry, investigation or hearing, and hold any such inquiry, investigation or hearing in open court. Where the public accountant was judged guilty, the board could choose to reprimand or caution him, suspend his registration, or direct that his name be removed from the register (*Public Accountants Registration Act 1945*, pp. 117–118).

So intent was the Act on protecting the specialist title of 'public accountant' and the public interest and enforcing the educational and practical requirements of registration, that it prescribed penalties for persons posing as a registered public accountant without registration:

> ... either alone or having regard to the circumstances in which it is taken or used indicates or is capable of being understood to indicate or is calculated to lead persons to infer that he is a registered public accountant *shall be guilty of an offence* .... (*Public Accountants Registration Act 1945*, p. 120). [emphasis added]

This provision meant that only accountants registered under the Act could undertake accounting work on behalf of the general public, and the specialist title was protected by legislation.

Creation of the *Public Accountants Registration (PAR) Act*

Three theories underpin the conceptual framework used in this chapter to examine the creation and implementation (in 1945) and dissolution (in 1989) of the PAR Act: public interest theory, political economy theory, and capture theory. The conceptual framework of this change is depicted in Figure 1.

The desire of the NSW government to regulate is supported by Mitnick's (1980, p. 20) definition of regulation as 'the intentional restriction of a subject's choice of activity, by an entity not directly party to or involved in that activity'. Merino and Mayper (2001) provide a more theoretical description of regulation

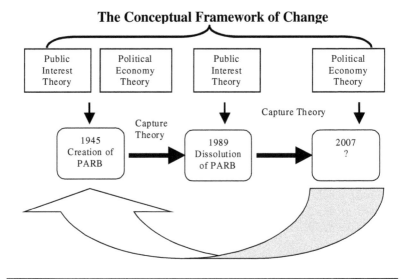

The Conceptual Framework of Change

| Public Interest Theory | Political Economy Theory | Public Interest Theory | Political Economy Theory |

1945 Creation of PARB → Capture Theory → 1989 Dissolution of PARB → Capture Theory → 2007 ?

Figure 1
The conceptual framework of change.

as that which results in the redistribution of economic resources among various competing interest groups through the use of state power.

The key objective of the theories of economic regulation is to explain who will be positively, and who negatively, impacted by the regulation (Stigler, 1971). Roberts and Kurtenbach (1998) contend that the public interest theory, political economy theory, and capture theory of regulation explain state intervention in the economy.

Roberts and Kurtenbach (1998) provide the example of the *Model Accountancy Act* developed by the American Institute of Certified Public Accountants in 1981. They argue that regulation of the public accounting profession is desirable because the public makes critical decisions based on the financial statements examined by public accountants, the public relies on their competence, and the public cannot be reasonably expected to investigate the underlying qualifications of each accountant.

Public Interest Theory

Public interest theory proposes that regulation maintains and protects the public. Regulation of industry and organisations protects and benefits all of society (Deegan, 2005; Stigler, 1971). The public needs protection through regulation because when economic markets are left alone they are unlikely to operate efficiently (Posner, 1974). While Roberts and Kurtenbach (1998, p. 211) conclude that the 'existence of a market imperfection is sufficient rationale for government intervention'.

The debate and discussion in 1944 and 1945 reveals that the NSW Government believed that the PAR Act was based primarily on the protection of the public. For example, the Assistant Minister who introduced the Bill, Mr Evatt, declared '(T)he chief merit of the measure is that the public will be protected' (NSW Parliament, 1944, p. 855). His view was supported, but described somewhat disrespectfully by Mr Sheahan MLA, as 'a bill for the purpose of protecting the public against quackery and dishonesty in accountancy' (NSW Parliament, 1944, p. 858)

This theme is repeated throughout the various readings and debates: however, over time, other 'reasons' for the Bill were also put forward. For example, 'the first consideration is the protection of the public and the second is the protection of the practitioner or the would-be practitioner' (NSW Parliament, 1944, p. 857), a view first introduced by Mr Williams MLA, who also happened to be an accountant. Later in the debate Mr Evatt explained that 'the Government desires to place a measure on the statute book, not only to protect the public, which is its primary purpose, but also to give to the accountancy profession the prestige and importance that it now lacks' (NSW Parliament, 1945, p. 1764)

Political Economy Theory

Political economy theory postulates that economic regulation protects the private interests of politically effective groups, in this instance, the professional accounting bodies (Deegan, 2005; Posner, 1974). This theory explains the majority of the debate and discussion that the Opposition used during the introduction, and up to the adoption of the Bill. For example Lieutenant-Colonel Bruxner of the Country Party argued that 'the profession itself should have majority representation on the [PAR] board' (NSW Parliament, 1945, p. 1756). This view was supported by his colleague Mr Brain, who suggested 'most emphatically that the accountancy profession, which has done an excellent job over the years, should have a preponderance of representation on the board' (NSW Parliament, 1945, p. 1806).

One of the main roles of the Public Accountants Registration Board (PARB) was to set the standard of qualifications necessary for registration as a Public Accountant. Mr Brain and Lieutenant-Colonel Bruxner, among others, constantly argued that the majority of members on the board should come from the profession. Their position is consistent with Stigler's (1971) assertion that every occupation that has the enough political strength will seek to control the regulator.

Capture Theory

This theory contends that regulated parties will capture the regulatory mechanism, in this case the accounting profession and the PARB (Mitnick, 1980). Both Mr Brain and Lieutenant-Colonel Bruxner argue that such an event 'capture' is preferable. This confirms Deegan's (2005, p. 115) view that 'regulated parties seek to take charge of (capture) the regulator so that the rules that are subsequently released (post-capture) will be advantageous to the parties subject to the requirements of the rules'. The Opposition's discussion is an example of the theory defined by Laffont and Tirole (1991, p. 1089) whereby regulation 'is acquired by the industry and is designed and operated primarily for its benefit'.

Mitnick (1980) identifies two events which show that an organisation has 'captured' its regulatory mechanisms. The capture events relevant to the PARB are where the regulated organisation, the accountancy profession, has control over the regulation and the regulatory body. The second relevant event is where the activities of the organisations coordinate the regulatory body's activities. The debate and discussion of the Bill shows that the accounting profession had the potential to capture the regulator in due course. Even though the Opposition amendment to change the structure of the board (from two to three members from the profession) failed, two of the remaining three members were the Auditor General and the Under Secretary of the Treasury, both generally trained and qualified accountants. The only possible non-accountant on the PARB would have been the chairman. Even though the Bill had passed with only two members of the PARB to be from the profession, the Board would likely have contained predominantly accountants. Regulatory capture was probably expected in the drafting and development of the Bill. This conclusion dovetails with Walker's (1987, p. 281) finding that 'the general literature on "regulation" is replete with allusions to the tendency for regulatory agencies to be "captured" by the interest groups and thereafter to operate in the interest of those elements of the community that the agencies were established to regulate'.

The Removal of General Public Protection

From 1945 to 1989 the general public of New South Wales was protected by the provisions of the *Public Accountants Registration Act*, and through this had a mechanism that ensured an acceptable level of competency. While the profession did capture the regulatory body, the regulator could still protect the public interest. It also provided some reassurance that every accountant offering an accounting service to the public was so registered, and that this registration (and therefore the ability to practice) could be removed for infamous misconduct. However, from 1989 onwards, this protection of the general public was removed with the adoption of the *Public Accountants Registration (Repeal and Amendment) Act, 1989*.

Deficiency was well known in the accounting profession, as evidenced by a statement made by a senior advisor of the Institute of Chartered Accountants in Australia when addressing the Joint Committee on Corporations and Securities in 2001. In response to a question on licensing from a member of the Committee, the ICAA representative responded:

> Senator Cooney, *you could be, and call yourself, an accountant if you wanted to.* If you were going to charge to prepare a tax return you would have to be licensed and registered. If you wanted to audit companies you would have to be registered, but *if you wanted to provide very sophisticated financial advice, very sophisticated taxation advice, there is no licensing requirement.* (Commonwealth of Australia Parliamentary Papers, 2001) [emphasis added]

The purpose of the repeal Act, it was claimed, was to remove the parallel system of registration of auditors in New South Wales, specifically, the registration of company auditors under the then *Companies Act* and registration under the *Public Accountants Registration Act*. It was stated in the parliamentary debate that the dual system was 'an unnecessary burden and a costly duplication of effort' (NSW Parliament, 1989a, p. 6318). It was also argued that the need to obtain registration in New South Wales as a registered public accountant stemmed solely from the requirements of various state Acts, which required audits to be carried out by a registered public accountant. Further, the then Minister for Business and Consumer Affairs, claimed that the repeal legislation was consistent with the government's policy of removing unnecessary regulation and duplication where it was in the public interest to do so. This completely overlooked that the public interest extended to the general public and was not limited to public companies, large private companies or statutory authorities.

The parliamentary debate also referred to the fact that both the professional bodies associated with accounting (the then Australian Society of Accountants and the Institute of Chartered Accountants in Australia) supported the repeal Bill. For example, Mr Dowd NSW Attorney General stated 'the proposal to repeal the Act is supported by the Australian Society of Accountants, the Institute of Chartered Accountants and the Public Accountants Registration Board' (NSW Parliament, 1989c, p. 5785). While the exact reason for this is not clear from the debate, the professional accounting bodies may have considered that this step would enhance their professional standing through increased professional self-regulation. At the time of the repeal of the *Public Accountants Registration Act*, changes were also being made to the *Corporate Affairs Commission (Auditors and Liquidators) Amendment Act*, which became the sole registration required for company auditors in New South Wales.

During the discussion of the repeal of the *Public Accountants Registration Act* and the establishment of the Companies Auditors and Liquidators Board (CALDB), it was recorded in Hansard that 'under the Bill, the Institute of Chartered Accountants and the Society of Accountants will supervise such registration and virtually set the requirements for registration' (NSW Parliament, 1989b, p. 6322). This was never the case however, and registration with the CALDB is controlled under Section 128 of the Corporations Law. Membership of a professional accounting body was not a prerequisite (P. Oakes, personal communication, November 23, 1994).

While the professional accounting bodies may have been misled, their action in supporting the repeal legislation is consistent with professional organisations' striving for the attainment of self-regulation and claims to autonomy, together with the balancing of private and public interest (Gyarmati, 1975; Macdonald, 1985; Parker, 1994).

The Reality of Nonregulation

The following cases are representative of the problems facing the accounting profession and the general public when unqualified persons, in terms of the former public accountant registration requirements, are allowed to provide accounting services to the general public or are allowed to continue in public practice following blatant exhibitions of improper conduct and complete disregard of acceptable standards of professional behaviour. They are not cases relating to public companies or statutory authorities, which would have been protected by the CALDB, but represent issues relating to the general public.

The first case concerns a member of the then Australian Society of Certified Practising Accountants (ASCPA) who had been registered under the Public Accountants Registration Act and held a practising certificate from the ASCPA. This member was found guilty of fraud involving $1,500,000 relating to the unauthorised use of clients' monies and improper investments. Despite his conviction and forfeiture of his society membership he still continued to act as an accountant in public practice. The second case involved an ASCPA member, a young woman who, after graduating from university and obtaining associate status with the ASCPA, established an accounting practice and defrauded the Commonwealth Government of an estimated $800,000. She was sentenced to six years' imprisonment and also forfeited her society membership. In a third case, a society member who held himself out to be in public practice, without the experience and public practice certificate required by the ASCPA, was found guilty of obtaining a financial advantage by deception when he misappropriated a client company's cheque directly into his personal bank account.

In the first case nothing stops the former accountant from starting in business again. This compares to the prohibition that would have been placed on him under the Public Accountants Registration Act, specifically the requirement to be of good fame and character. In the other two cases, under the old legislation neither of the former accountants would have been allowed to commence business because they did not have the experience required under the Act. While legislation would not necessarily have prevented these occurrences (particularly the first case), the old legislation would have prevented the accountant in the first case from returning to public practice, and would have made it difficult for the accountants in the other two cases from commencing public practice.

It is questionable whether the disciplinary action, which can be initiated against a member by their particular professional organisation, offers any protection to the public. Greater protection would be gained by an attempt to prevent the problems outlined above from occurring, rather than exact ineffective disciplinary action after the event. Such protection was provided to the public through the *Public Accountants Registration Act*, specifically in the minimum experience requirements and the prohibition that, once disqualified, it was no longer possible to provide accounting services to the general public.

Conclusion

The chapter argues that the establishment and the repeal of the *Public Accountants Registration Act* was an example of regulatory capture theory and demonstrated by Mitnick's (1980) identifiable events. It also provides empirical data to support the argument that the removal of the universal protection left a gap in the protection provided to the general public.

The repeal of the *Public Accountants Registration Act*, with the focus on company auditors, completely overlooked the impact this would have on the general public, who were left without any legislative protection from those offering their accounting services and not members of the professional bodies. It also created a loophole which allowed unqualified and professionally disbarred individuals to operate with apparent impunity.

Taken together, these events to purportedly achieve government efficiency and competition have debased the image of accounting in the minds of the general public and possibly destroyed years of professional upgrading by the professional accounting bodies.

While governments are unlikely to protect the generic title 'accountant', restriction of the title 'public accountant' previously afforded the general public the protection, to some extent, they expect from their elected representatives. Such a direction would be consistent with the legal profession, where the generic title 'lawyer' indicates a person who has graduated in law, while 'solicitor' and/or 'barrister' are protected titles. Similarly the term 'doctor' is a generic description with public protection given to the protected title 'registered medical practitioner'.

References

Commonwealth of Australia Parliamentary Papers. (2001, June 14). *Joint committee on corporations and securities.* Canberra, Australia: Commonwealth Printing Office.

Deegan, C. (2005). *Australian financial accounting* (4th ed.). Sydney, Australia: McGraw-Hill Australia.

Gyarmati K.G. (1975). The doctrine of the professions: Basis of a power structure. *International Social Science Journal, 27*(4) 629–654.

Laffont, J.J., & Tirole, J. (1991). The politics of government decision making: A theory of regulatory capture. *The Quarterly Journal of Economics, 106*(4), 1089–1127.

Macdonald, K.M. (1985). Social closure and occupational registration. *Sociology, 19*(4), 541–556.

Merino, B.D., & Mayper, A.G. (2001). Securities legislation and the accounting profession in the 1930s: The rhetoric and reality of the American Dream. *Critical Perspectives on Accounting, 12*(4), 501–526

Mitnick, B.M. (1980). *The political economy of regulation.* New York: Columbia University Press.

New South Wales Parliament. (1944). *New South Wales parliamentary debates/Legislative Council and Legislative Assembly,* 175. Sydney, Australia: NSW Government Printer.

New South Wales Parliament. (1945). *New South Wales parliamentary debates/Legislative Council and Legislative Assembly,* 176. Sydney, Australia: NSW Government Printer.

New South Wales Parliament. (1989a). *New South Wales parliamentary debates/Legislative Council and Legislative Assembly,* 206. Sydney, Australia: Government Printer.

New South Wales Parliament. (1989b). *New South Wales parliamentary debates/Legislative Council and Legislative Assembly,* 207. Sydney, Australia: Government Printer.

New South Wales Parliament. (1989c). *New South Wales parliamentary debates/Legislative Council and Legislative Assembly,* 208. Sydney, Australia: Government Printer.

Parker, L.D. (1994). Professional accounting body ethics: In search of the private interest. *Accounting Organisations and Society, 19*(6), 507–525.

Posner, R. (1974). Theories of economic regulation. *Bell Journal of Economics and Management Sciences, 5*(2), 335–358.

Roberts, R.W., & Kurtenbach, J.M. (1998). State regulation and professional accounting educational reforms: An empirical test of regulatory capture theory. *Journal of Accounting and Public Policy, 17,* 209–226.

Stigler, G. (1971). The economic theory of regulation. *Bell Journal of Economics, 2,* 3–21.

Walker, R.G. (1987). Australia's ASRB: A case study of political activity and regulatory 'capture'. *Accounting and Business Research, 17*(67), 269–286.

Regulatory Cycles:
Or Why Does the Tax Code
Get Bigger Every Year?

Roderick Duncan

In their 1978 series *Foreign Trade Regimes and Economic Development* Bhagwati (1978) and Krueger (1978), drawing on examples of changing tariff structures in developing countries and in a simple narrative, identified several phases that regulatory structures go through. Over time the complexity of a regulatory structure changed as it went through these phases. By an increase in complexity, Bhagwati (1978) and Krueger (1978) meant an increase in the number of different categories, distinct rules, exemptions or processes contained within the regulations.

The phases were described as:

- Phase I — initial implementation of a simple set of rules
- Phase II — the regulatory structure becomes increasingly complex as changes are made incrementally
- Phase III — a sudden episode of reform in reaction to the complexity of the structure.

At this point Krueger (1978) and Bhagwati (1978) set out two possible futures — either a return to a simple set of rules and a continuation of rising complexity in a following Phase II, or an end to change and a stationary structure in Phase IV (or an abolition of the structure altogether which they labelled Phase V).

- Phase IV — liberalisation of the structure — no further changes.

As Krueger (1978) and Bhagwati (1978) saw it, regulatory structures have two possible sets of structures of time. Structures either alternate between Phase II and Phase III or end at Phase IV or V.

The first type of history is what I call 'regulatory cycles'; the second type, either Phase IV/V or Phase I, I will call 'stationary' regulatory structures. It is an

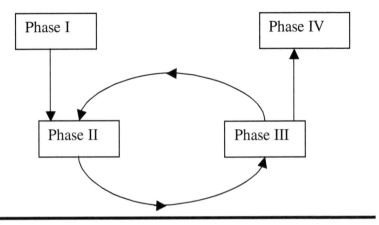

Figure 1
Bhagwati (1978) and Krueger (1978) phases of regulatory structures.

open question currently why some structures have regulatory cycles while other structures do not. These phases are shown in Figure 1.

Data-Stylised Facts

There is some support for the descriptive narrative of the evolution of some regulatory structures as described by Bhagwati (1978) and Krueger (1978). There does seem to be a built-in tendency for gradually increasing complexity over time in these structures (Phase II). There are also the episodes of reform (Phase III).

Krueger and Duncan (1993), in an earlier work by one of the authors, set out a short history of the rising complexity of the United States (US) income tax code.

- Initially instructions for the 1040 US Income Tax Form consisted of half a sheet of paper.
- By 1948 these instructions had grown to 10 pages.
- By 1961 they had doubled to 20 pages.
- By 1975 they had doubled again to around 40 pages.
- By 1992 the instructions for the 1040 Form cover 81 pages.

The gradual rise in complexity of the tax code is evidenced by the rising number of pages of instructions. Over the history of the tax code, this slow increase in complexity is a normal feature. Yet there are also rare moments of reform, such as the 1976 and 1986 *Tax Reform Acts*, which flattened some of the tax scales and removed certain exemptions — reducing the complexity of the regulatory structure. The trend in complexity for the tax code was then a slow trend upwards, interrupted by sudden drops during periods of reform. The reform periods were again followed by periods of gradually increasing complexity.

Many regulatory structures do not exhibit this cyclical behaviour. Regulations, such as traffic laws or building codes, are relatively stationary. These structures display neither a tendency to increase in complexity over time nor to undergo periodic episodes of reform.

What Does the Existing Theory Explain or not Explain?

There are two features of regulatory structures that stand out from this analysis:

1. Some structures grow more complicated over time, whereas other structures remain the same.

2. Some structures undergo regular episodes of reform, whereas other structures can remain the same for very long periods.

The dominant models of regulatory structures in economics do not have either of these features. The lobby group models grew out of the papers of Stigler (1971), Peltzman (1976) and Posner (1974). Regulations are assumed to be the equilibrium outcome of a competitive process between competing lobby groups. In these papers, the decision-makers are the lobby groups, while the government takes only a passive role. The outcome will be a set of taxes and subsidies — the size of which depends on the relative political power of the different groups.

The political contestability approach is an alternative formulation of this problem where the state takes on a maximising role. This literature is well set out in Hillman (1989). The more recent versions of this framework are based on Grossman and Helpman (1994) where a maximising state balances off the political gains from the contributions of lobby groups to the political losses from the economic inefficiencies of higher tariffs. Mitra (1999) used the Grossman–Helpman framework, but instead of assuming a fixed number of lobby groups, assumed that there were potential lobby groups that would be formed if the net benefit of this formation was positive. The outcome again will be a set of taxes and subsidies that depend on the relative weighting in the government's utility of social welfare versus political contributions.

A very different and only partial analysis was used in Krueger and Duncan (1993). The analysis explained incremental addition of complexity to a regulatory structure by the pressures brought to bear by three different groups:

- regulatees — parties subject to the regulations
- regulators — parties who administer the regulations
- intermediaries — parties who interpret the regulation and advise the regulatees.

It is in the interest of all three parties to make changes to the regulations that will result in an increase in the complexity of the regulatory structure.

- Regulatees seek to make changes which exempt or lessen the burden of the regulation on themselves by creating more and different categories of goods or behaviours to be regulated.

- Regulators seek to make changes to close loopholes used by regulatees.
- Intermediaries seek to increase the complexity of the regulation so as to make their services more valuable.

To the extent that regulators become future intermediaries, current regulators desire increased complexity since increased complexity will increase the value of their human capital when they become intermediaries. Regulators may also desire increased complexity with more discretion, as greater discretion increases the power of the regulators and the possibility and value of corruption of regulators.

There are several weaknesses of the Krueger and Duncan (1993) analysis. Firstly it is not placed in an equilibrium setting. Secondly there is no mechanism to explain why these groups would delay increasing complexity. If it is in a lobby group's interest to increase complexity, why would this not happen immediately? The cross-country case studies in Bhagwati (1978) and Krueger (1978) showed that regulatory complexity evolves slowly during Phase II, but we have no current model to explain this fact. The model developed in the next section is an attempt to solve some of the difficulties in the literature.

A Model of Endogenous Complexity

Of the three groups presented in the Krueger and Duncan (1993) paper, the weakest group is the intermediaries. The existing literature stresses the roles of the regulatees, or their lobby group representatives, and the regulators, the state. An explanation that turns on the power of a 'conspiracy of accountants' is a weak one, so we will follow the Hillman framework and consider only the regulatees and the state as actors.

There are M regulatees in the economy divided across N potential lobby groups. If all the regulatees in a lobby group are identical or the regulatory burden falls at a constant rate across all regulatees, we can ignore the regulatees and treat the lobby groups as the decision-making parties. The decision-making units are assumed to be the lobby groups, rather than the individuals within each lobby group.

Initially we assume that the regulatory structure is an income tax or business tax code. The application of this model to tariff structures and to pollution regulations is discussed later. Assume each lobby group has an income I_i for i over 1 to N and that this income is simply the sum of the incomes of all the regulatees in the lobby group. Taxable income is taxed at a constant marginal rate of τ.

Each lobby group is only a potential lobby group. We assume that each lobby group can control the free riding problem among its own members, so that the decision of the lobby group and of its individual members is identical. Each potential lobby group can form at a cost of c_i, where c_i will depend on the characteristics of the members of the lobby group. Once a lobby group forms, it organises the legislators to exempt 50% of the lobby group's incomes from taxation. Lobbying then is an example of a 'rent-seeking' activity from Krueger

(1974) or of a 'directly unproductive, profit-seeking activity' (DUP) in Bhagwati's (1982) terminology.

When a lobby group forms and creates a special exemption for its members, the lobby group increases the complexity of the regulatory structure, as additional regulations will have to be created to handle the new exemption. More complex regulatory structures are therefore ones with more formed lobby groups.

The state or government has a budget constraint which requires the state to raise the amount B in taxes. The state sets the tax rate after the lobby groups have formed. Let L denote the set of lobby groups that have formed. We can express the state's budget constraint as

$$B = \sum_{i \notin L} \tau I_i + \sum_{i \in L} \frac{\tau}{2} I_i$$

The tax rate then depends on the number and size of the lobby groups that have formed.

This model is a simplified version of the Mitra (1999) model but with the addition of a government budget constraint. The budget constraint changes the dynamics considerably. As we will see, the act of forming a lobby group imposes an externality on all other potential lobby groups — directly by raising the average tax rates for all and indirectly by making the formation of other lobby groups more likely.

The Case of Identical Potential Lobby Groups

The following analysis will hold for any number of identical groups, so for simplicity assume there are only two. There are two potential lobby groups with identical incomes I and costs of formation c. Each lobby group is assumed to make up 50% of the population. The average tax rate for the economy depends on how many lobby groups are formed:

- no lobby group forms — $\tau = B/2I$
- one lobby group forms — $\tau = 2B/3I$
- two lobby groups form — $\tau = B/I$

If we imagine a game where the strategies of the two groups are to form a lobby group 'Lobby' or not form a lobby group 'NL', then we have a pay-off matrix, as shown in Figure 2.

Both groups prefer the outcome (NL, NL) to (Lobby, Lobby). However, for $c < B/6$, forming a lobby group is the dominant strategy, so (Lobby, Lobby) is the Nash equilibrium. The cost of lobbying activities or the DUP activities could be as large as $B/3$ for society.

This is a standard Prisoner's Dilemma matrix. Intuitively, both groups are better off agreeing to not form lobby groups; however, neither group could

		Lobby group 2	
		Lobby	NL
Lobby group 1	Lobby	I—$B/2$—c, I—$B/2$—c	I—$B/3$—c, I—$2/3B$
	NL	I—$2/3B$, I—$B/3$—c	I—$B/2$, I—$B/2$

Figure 2
Lobby game with two identical players.

credibly commit to not forming a lobby group. Both groups are 'stuck' in the obviously inferior (Lobby, Lobby) outcome.

If we introduce this game into a setting of repeated interaction with discounting, we have the standard 'Folk Theorem' result that a cooperative (NL, NL) solution could arise if the future was not discounted too heavily by the lobby groups. In a repeated setting, both the cooperative (NL, NL) and noncooperative (Lobby, Lobby) outcomes can be supported, depending on the strategies of the lobby groups — see standard texts such as Fudenberg and Tirole (1991).

One interpretation of the Bhagwati (1978) and Krueger (1978) phases in this setting would be based on changing strategies or changing beliefs about the strategies of the lobby groups. Periods of rising complexity, the Phase IIs, are periods of noncooperative interaction between the potential lobby groups. The reform episodes, the Phase IIIs, are cooperative periods where the lobby groups agree to dissolve themselves and lose their exemptions.

Where the Potential Lobby Groups Differ in Lobbying Costs

Instead of identical potential lobby groups, we now allow for lobby group formation costs, c_i, to differ across the N potential lobby groups which are otherwise identical. Lobby groups will differ in lobby costs due to existing organisation within the groups, the costs of monitoring and communication within the groups and the degree with which individual interests are aligned within groups among other factors. Order the groups so that lobbying costs increase in the index variable i. As in the case for identical groups, there can again be multiple equilibria. The number of equilibrium will depend on the distribution of the lobbying costs.

Let m be a particular value of the index variable. At a given tax rate, if it is profitable for lobby group m to form, then it will also be profitable for all lobby groups i for 1 to m-1 to form. Likewise, if it is not profitable for lobby group m to form, then it will also not be profitable for any lobby group i for $m + 1$ to N to form. To specify an equilibrium, we only need to specify the index number of the highest cost lobby to form and the tax rate, τ, that satisfies the government budget constraint for that set of lobby groups.

If m lobby groups are formed and $N\text{-}m$ are potential lobby groups, the tax rate is

$$\tau = \frac{B}{(N - \frac{m}{2})I}$$

If $m\text{-}1$ lobby groups are already formed, then the m potential lobby group will form if the gain from a lower taxable income is larger than the loss due to a higher tax rate as well as the cost of forming the lobby group. This is true for lobby group m if

$$I - \frac{B}{(N - \frac{(m-1)}{2})} \le I - \frac{1}{2}\frac{B}{(N - \frac{m}{2})} - c_m$$

We can use this inequality to define a new function, $c^*(i)$, which is the highest value for c_i for which the lobby group i will form given that $i\text{-}1$ other lobby groups have already formed.

$$c*(i) = \frac{(2N - i - 1)B}{(2N - i)(2N - i + 1)}$$

where is $c^*(i)$ is increasing in i for i between 1 and N.

An equilibrium in this case is a τ and an m so that for all lobby groups i in $L = \{1 \ldots m\}$:

$$c_i \le c*(m) \, for \quad i \in L$$

and lobbying costs exceed $c^*(m)$ for all lobby groups not in L and

$$B = \sum_{i \in L} \tau I + \sum_{i \in L} \frac{\tau}{2} I$$

For a given budget constraint B and a distribution of lobbying costs, the equilibria can be derived by comparing lobbying costs to the maximum lobby formation cost, $c^*(i)$. This is illustrated graphically in Figure 3. In this example potential equilibria involve 2, 6 or 11 lobby groups forming.

As in the previous case, there can be gains from cooperation. Lobbying is a pure rent-seeking activity — simply redistributing resources at a positive cost to society. A sufficiently large coalition of lobby groups could agree to disband their lobbies and shift the regulatory structure from one equilibrium outcome, say 11 lobby groups, to another equilibrium outcome, say six lobby groups. It is not in the interest of any one lobby group to individually disband, but the externalities created by a sufficiently large coalition of lobby groups could create sufficient gains from cooperation.

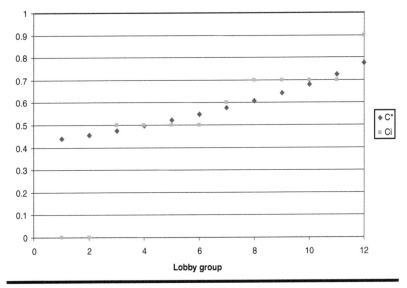

Figure 3
Multiple equilibria in the lobbying model.

It could be these episodes of cooperation that we observe in Phase IIIs. Only a large coalition of lobby groups can generate a sufficiently large drop in the average tax rate to warrant the individual lobby groups giving up their income exemptions. The difficulty of organising large coalitions of lobby groups might explain why Phase IIIs are observed to be rare events.

Over time, governments in developed and developing countries have generally been increasing the share of national income that is taken in income taxes. In this model we would represent this by an increase in the state budget constraint, B, relative to the lobby groups' income, I. An increase in B will shift up the $c^*(i)$ function. Examining Figure 3, there are three possible outcomes to a small shift in $c^*(i)$.

1. An equilibrium might remain an equilibrium. In this case, we simply have a small increase in τ with no response by the lobby groups.

2. The equilibrium might shift up by one lobby group. A higher tax rate has encouraged one more potential lobby group to form. A shift could induce the seventh lobby group to form if six were already formed in Figure 3.

3. The equilibrium might disappear and lead to a large increase in the number of lobby groups. A higher tax rate will encourage new lobby group to form, but the externalities from the formation of the new lobby groups magnifies this effect. A shift could lead to a jump from an equilibrium with two lobby groups formed to one with six lobby groups formed in Figure 3.

In an economy where the budgetary demands of the national government are rising over time, we would observe a corresponding shifting up of the number of lobby groups formed. This process would appear like the Phase II of the regulatory cycles that Bhagwati (1978) and Krueger (1978) observed.

A rising budget constraint in a lobby group model can replicate the dynamics that were reported about the US income tax code over time. Slowly rising budget demands result in an increase in complexity of the code over time as more lobby groups form. When coalitions of lobby groups can form, we can observe dramatic reductions in complexity, such as the reforms of 1976 and 1986.

However, as the B and $c^*(i)$ is rising over time, the minimum number of lobby groups that occurs at the lowest potential equilibrium in Figure 3 (or the minimum complexity of the code) is also rising over time. In this case, we would observe a regulatory cycle around a slow upward trend in complexity over time, with rising levels of political lobbying, greater use of intermediaries and rising costs of compliance for regulatees.

The driving force in the dynamics is the rising budget constraint over time. While the application here has been one of an income or company tax code, changing government budget constraints can occur in other applications, such as in tariff schemes or in pollution control regulations. Rising tariff revenue needs of a government lead to the same budget process for a tariff scheme. Lower total pollution emissions of a government lead to the same budget process for pollution control. Lobby groups for industries lobby for industry exemptions under income tax codes, just as the lobby groups do under tariffs and pollution regulations. We would expect to see regulatory cycles in tariff schemes, as Bhagwati (1978) and Krueger (1978) did, and in pollution control regulations.

Statements about comparative statics are difficult to make given that we have placed little structure on the distribution of the lobbying costs. Making some strong assumptions about the distribution of the c_i's in Figure 3 would enable us to derive some comparative statics results but at the cost of further loss of generality. Without a structure to the lobbying costs, we are left with the possibility of multiple equilibria and the result that small changes in parameters can lead to abrupt changes in the equilibria.

We can make statements about the lowest equilibrium — the equilibrium with the fewest number of lobby groups. There is not sufficient room to provide proofs for these statements. In the lowest equilibrium:

- The number of lobbies formed (and the complexity of a tax code) is positively related to the amount of revenue that needs to be raised and is negatively related to the costs of lobbying.
- The tax rate is positively related to the amount of revenue to be raised and the number of lobby groups formed.

What policy proscriptions can be drawn? Since lobbying is a rent-seeking activity, an increase in the number of lobby groups formed is a loss to social welfare. We can rank the equilibria according to social welfare, as social welfare is declining in the number of lobby groups formed. Higher government revenue requirements and lower lobbying costs lead to a fall in social welfare. Reform episodes in which complexity is reduced and lobby groups disbanded improve social welfare. Measures that improve communication and coordination between lobby groups may then improve social welfare.

Conclusion

The current economic literature in regulation develops equilibrium for regulatory structures which are constant over time. However, the observed dynamics of some regulatory structures such as tax codes are not static, but rather go through stages of slow increases in complexity and sudden bursts of reform, as evidenced by Bhagwati (1978) and Krueger (1978) and in Krueger and Duncan (1993).

The introduction of a rising government budget constraint in a lobby group model allowed us to replicate these observed dynamics. This simple model suggests that further research on endogenous regulatory structures should include budget constraints where these are empirically relevant.

References

Bhagwati, J.N. (1978). *Foreign trade regimes and economic development: Anatomy and consequences of exchange control regimes.* Cambridge, MA: Ballinger Press for the National Bureau of Economic Research.

Bhagwati, J.N. (1982). Directly unproductive, profit-seeking (DUP) activities. *Journal of Political Economy, 90*(5), 988–1002.

Fudenberg, D., & Tirole, J. (1991). *Game theory.* Cambridge, MA: MIT Press.

Grossman, G.M., & Helpman, E. (1994). Protection for sale. *American Economic Review, 84*(4), 833–50.

Hillman, A.L. (1989). *The political economy of trade protection.* London: Harwood Academic.

Krueger, A.O. (1974). The political economy of the rent-seeking society. *American Economic Review, 64*(4), 291–303.

Krueger, A.O. (1978). *Foreign trade regimes and economic development: Liberalization attempts and consequences.* Cambridge, MA: Ballinger Press for the National Bureau of Economic Research.

Krueger, A.O., & Duncan, R.G. (1993). The political economy of complexity. In L. Stetting, K.E. Svendsen & E. Yndgaard (Eds.), *Global change and transformation.* Copenhagen: Munksgaard International.

Mitra, D. (1999). Endogenous lobby formation and endogenous protection: A long-run model of trade policy determination. *American Economic Review, 89*(5), 1116–34.

Peltzman, S. (1976). Towards a more general theory of regulation. *Journal of Law and Economics, 19*, 211–40.

Posner, R.A. (1974). Theories of economic regulation. *Bell Journal of Economics and Management Science, 5*(2), 335–58.

Stigler, G.J. (1971). The theory of economic regulation. *Bell Journal of Economics and Management Science, 2*(1), 3–21.

Part 4

Cultural Change and Its Effects on Management and Workplace Performance

Leading the iGeneration With a More Social Approach to Intelligence

Linda MacGrain Herkenhoff

The references for this chapter include several newspaper and magazine articles, alongside more scholarly articles. These more public items allowed me to gain insights into the social and cultural aspects of the iGeneration that are too recent to be published in academic journals. The iGeneration experiences that are captured journalistically allow us to develop our understanding of these contemporary people, while we look forward to more rigorous analytical studies in the near future. Another source of information included my direct observation of people informally. As John Locke (1998, p. 15) suggests, 'Ordinary life if we treat it as such is an Institute for the Study of Human Communications. The labs are the street corners, university campuses, airplanes, dinner tables, commuter trains …'.

The current literature includes a variety of temporal definitions and qualitative labels for this group. One of the most common neologisms is 'Echo Boomers', in recognition that this group is the echo after the Baby Boomers. We also find labels such as Millennials (Howe & Strauss, 2000; MSNBC, 2006), Generation M (Suetens, 2002), MySpace Generation (Hempel, 2005), Net Generation (Tapscott, 1998) and Loli-boomers (Loliboom, 2006). Even the term iGeneration (Hermida, 2003) gets used in different ways: iPodGeneration, I-Generation (as in the pronoun I), and Individualistic Generation.

From a temporal perspective Wikipedia (2006) defines them quantitatively as being born between 1986 and 1999. Quinion (1999) defines them as anyone born between the late 1970s and early 1990s. They approximate 80 million in the United States, making them the largest group of young people since the 1960s. This chapter will use a combination of qualitative and quantitative information to define them as the group who has no nostalgia for a pre-Internet history; they have had no adaptation to this new technology because the Internet is taken for granted as a natural part of who they are. They are the first generation to claim the computer as their birthright (Quinion, 1999).

They are technophiles who have not only grown up with the Internet but also with mobile phones, instant messenger, e-mail, ATMs, DVDs, and blogs. But how ubiquitous are they on a global basis? Are we only describing digital Darwinism that exists in a few well-developed countries? Accordingly to the *Sydney Morning Herald* (Philipson, 2006) in 2000, there were a total of 426 million mobile phone connections existing globally and in 2005 there were 2.5 billion. That equates numerically to about 40% of the world population, with China currently being the largest mobile phone market on earth. Mr Ignacio Gonzalez Plana, Minister of Informatics and Communications of the Republic of Cuba, points out that only a little more than half of those using mobile phones and Internet servers are found in developed countries (WSIS, 2006). The future is unequivocally here, it is just not evenly distributed yet.

In Eastern Europe, the iGens are the generation without mature memories of communism or dictatorship. In South Korea, they are the generation who has grown up in developed world standards of living, while their grandparents had most likely grown up in developing world country standards.

In 2003, the World Summit on the Information Society (WSIS), organised by the United Nations, succeeded in having 170 countries endorse the first constitution for the information age. They set goals to ensure that more than 50% of the world will have access to some form of electronic media by 2015 (Hermida, 2003). The second summit was held in Tunisia in November 2005, with a continued focus on building a global information society that is fair, equitable and accessible to everyone (Twist, 2005). Archbishop Foley, in his Vatican address to the WSIS, recognised that providing better access to digital communications in developing countries is the responsibility of the entire international community (WSIS, 2006).

China is already setting up its own Chinese net addresses, allowing the Chinese authorities to have more control over a more regionalised Internet. Efforts by nongovernmental groups, charities, and the private sector are working in conjunction with local governments to ensure that both wired and wireless infrastructures are in place and sustainable in developing countries. Companies such as Microsoft and Intel are being encouraged to help developing nations leapfrog directly to the wireless world.

The iGens are destined to be the next global workforce, but they will be arriving in the workplace at different times. In some countries, such as Australia and the United States, they have already started arriving in the workplace. In other more developing nations it may still be a few years before we start feeling their presence. But they will arrive and with them will come their iGen characteristics.

One of those characteristics is that they do not prefer hard copy instruction manuals, but prefer to download instructions from online when needed. They tend to learn new video games almost by osmosis. Those thick binders filled with policies and procedures are now on the endangered species list. Fundamentally, the iGens worship the soft copy and despise the hard copy.

One of their most important characteristics is that they are master information sorters. When Baby Boomers studied for exams, typically anything outside of the primary task of reading the textbook was considered a distraction. Not so with the iGens. They seem to take in parallel flows of information and sort the input data by importance. A typical scenario includes: iPod in the ear, mobile phone turned on to receive both regular phones calls as well as text messages, instant messenger on their laptop, and a vodcast playing on their portable DVD player. Despite these multiple information inputs, these iGen students still manage to get As in their exams. So while Baby Boomers take information in one channel at a time, the iGens use multiple channels simultaneously. They are always plugged in with a world of information and communication tools at their fingertips (Irvine, 2004). Internet access feeds their insatiable appetite for information.

The iGen concept of time seems to be in the nanosecond world. Instant gratification is the name of the game. One of the best examples of an iGen real-time tool is instant messaging (IM). This is communication between two or more people based on typed text conveyed via computers connected over a network such as the Internet. Other developments by several small companies like MXIT Lifestyle (Pty) in South Africa include downloadable applications in an attempt to create their own version of IM that can run on most mobile phones worldwide.

The iGens are inherently multicultural with the Internet playing a pivotal role in their global cultural ecosystem, along with related CNN-type services and products. The iGens are among the most diverse generations. In the United States 35% are non-White and 27% are from one-parent households (Layman, 2004). Characteristically, iGens are generally more tolerant towards multiculturalism and internationalism. It has become more common for iGens to grow up dating people outside their own race or ethnic group. Many iGens themselves are multiracial in background, which is a considerable change from previous generations (All Experts, 2006). According to Howe and Strauss (2000, p. 3), 'In the Millennial world, race is less a cutting edge issue than a game of political nostalgia in which the language of oppression has become pop culture play'.

They are sophisticated social net-workers. They can efficiently build teams of people, whom they never meet, to play online games that may last for months. They negotiate sales of almost anything over the Internet. An online rebellion swept over university campuses in the United States during the week of September 18, 2006, and as the *San Francisco Chronicle* pointed out, if you were over the age of 25 you never knew it happened (Nevius, 2006). A social networking service called Facebook was designed in 2004 to allow members to get to know other students on a college campus and to make them aware of possible groups to join. The service required that members have a college campus e-mail account. On September 19 they decided to add a feature called 'Newsfeed' which automatically sent information to members about their registered friends whenever those friends changed anything on their personal profiles. This became a privacy train wreck as members quickly become incensed that their personal information was being distributed without their permission. Ironically, the Newsfeed feature helped encourage members to join groups that were bashing the new concept. By 2:15 pm on the Tuesday release date, the 'Students against Facebook Newsfeeds' numbered more than 100,000 and by Friday the members numbered over 700,000. The iGens have no problem in the art of technology-aided social networking. <MySpace.com> is one of the most popular iGen social-networking sites. This site has more than 100 million profiles with an estimated 230,000 new members joining daily (Andrews, 2006; Hempel, 2005).

So, will this group respond positively to the same type of leaders and managers who were successful with the Baby Boomers? Most likely, like their immediate predecessors, they will join companies but leave managers. How do you prevent your investment from walking out the door, or, more importantly, how do you prevent them from migrating through cyberspace to your competitors?

Research Methodology

To better understand the generational definition of 'Good Leadership', a survey was conducted that combined both a random sample and a convenience sample. The samples included 119 Baby Boomers and 56 iGens with 100% response rate. The data were collected globally via personal interviews by the author, over a 6-month period during the first half of 2006. The research question was 'What are the top three qualities of a leader who you were willing to follow or would be willing to follow?' The samples included a diverse representation from the three cultural subsets: national, organisational and professional. Detailed descriptions of the sample compositions are presented in Table 1.

Research Findings

The three most frequent responses from both samples are presented in Table 2.

Both of the generational data sets in Table 2 include representation from the cognitive and emotional sides of intelligence. In the Baby Boomer data the cognitive side is encompassed in 'High IQ and competent'. The iGen data includes the cognitive side under the 'Knowledgeable' characteristic.

The emotional perspective is represented in the Baby Boomer data 'Treating people with respect' and 'High level of integrity'. In the iGen sample the emotional side is represented by the 'Passionate' and 'High level of integrity' characteristics.

So although the top three leadership characteristics may have changed somewhat, both cognitive and emotional aspects are still represented in both generational samples.

Discussion

The cold tentacles of technology do not appear to have diminished the role of emotional intelligence (Goleman, 1995) for the iGens, but rather have made it

Table 1

Sample Descriptions

National	Organisational	Professional
United States, Australia Canada, Iraq, India, New Zealand, Spain	Government, academic, religious, biotech, energy security, military, supply chain, transportation, financial, research, sports, education, medicine, consulting, IT	Pilot, doctor, priest, geophysicist, chancellor deep-sea diver, taxi diver, football coach, gold medal Olympian, US Men's Olympic water polo team coach, nuclear submarine commander, former US Assistant Secretary of Defense, FBI agent, navy officers, army officers, marine officers, students, provost, CFO, CEO, airline attendant, secretary, trainer, power plant worker, tourist guide, mail courier, police officer, professor, nurse, fire fighter, financial investor, auditor, lawyer, dentist, geologist, nuclear physicist, human resources officer, probation officer, customs officer, consultant, salesperson, high school students, college students, waitress, lifeguard, reporter, healthcare worker, coffee shop worker, swim instructor, architect, journalist, professional musician, psychologist

even more visible as an important part of the formula for successful leadership. The iGen cues indicating the need for emotional intelligence (EI) are already there and just waiting to be seen. Perhaps EI, not IQ, will be the key differentiator in those who successfully manage and lead the iGens.

Starting with e-mail, we know this is a low context form of communication, but the iGens have found a way to remedy the problem. They have developed an intricate and creative system of emoticons derived from the smiley face. Two different systems of emoticons are displayed in Figure 1.

iGens often add these emoticons to both conventional e-mail and instant messenger communications.

In my own MBA classes, iGens want the flexibility of online learning, yet rank face-to-face (f2f) classes as the most effective learning format. So we have combined f2f classes with synchronous online learning tools. The students prefer vodcasts to podcasts, citing they feel more of a personal relationship with seeing the professor rather than just hearing a voice.

Current technology is linked with stress (Mueller, 2001; Palmer, 2006; Weil & Rosen, 1997). There is an inherent promise that technology will give you more

Table 2

Leadership Survey Results

Response frequency	Baby Boomers	Response frequency	iGens
76%	High IQ and competent	71%	Knowledgeable
60%	Treat people with respect	61%	High level of integrity
47%	High level of integrity	40%	Being passionate

Invision MSN Emoticons: -

Name:	Invision MSN Emoticons
Samples:	
No. of Emoticons:	20
Added by:	Athar Rasool

Old MSN Emoticons: -

Name:	Old MSN Emoticons
Samples:	
No. of Emoticons:	23
Added by:	Athar Rasool

Figure 1
Emoticons.

freedom and a higher quality of leisure time. But in reality we know voicemail, e-mail, and instant messenger make iGens more accessible, creating even less real leisure time for them. The iGens have to perform many of the day-to-day tasks that were once done by others, such as pumping petrol for their cars and checking tyre pressures. The advent of the ATM and online banking means they handle their own financial reconciliations and transactions, tasks which were once done for you by a bank teller. The friendly travel agent has been replaced with such online services as <Expedia.com> and <Kayak.com>. In many countries, grocery stores now allow shoppers to scan their own groceries, rather than waiting in line to have a checkout operator do this for you.

Technology loads more and more onto the iGens, potentially building a platform for stress. In Goleman's (2007) discussion of web rage, the cousin of road rage, he points out that 'thoughts expressed while sitting alone at the keyboard would be put more diplomatically or go unmentioned in a face-to-face environment'. So although iGens may be good social net-workers, their skills in building healthy, human relationships may be weaker.

We know that increased stress can lead to workplace violence. A recent workplace study of Scottish 16- to 24-year-olds, sanctioned by the Scottish Executive Campaign, revealed that 31% had been verbally or physically attacked, threatened, sworn or spat at by a member of the public in the last 12 months (*BBC News*, 2005). The iGens will need even more management of maladaptive emotions in the workplace than their predecessors.

More and more of the work will be done at home. For example, in one large IT firm in the Silicon Valley, 80% of their employees work some part of the time at home (personal communication, 2006). I interviewed an iGen at Sun Microsystems who explained to me his working model of flexing. He had an electronic pass that he wore around his neck that gave him access to workstations throughout the building. The computers were only portals which allowed him to access his files on the central server. He had no office, no cubicle, no chair, and no personal physical space. When I asked him where he kept his personal things like his family photos, he replied those could be found on his webpage. I tried to make my point about physical space by asking where he kept his coffee cup. His reply was that his Starbuck's coffee came in a disposable cup. Finally, I asked what he would put in his cardboard box if Sun laid him off and he was permanently leaving the office. After thinking about it for a nanosecond, he decided that he would have to hand in his electronic pass but would not have anything to put in the cardboard box.

So as work and personal time merge, leaders of the iGens may have to lead a workforce they rarely see. The personal connection will be more challenging, more taxing, but even more important.

Workplace Implications

When the workplace situation is congruent with employee values and beliefs, the outcome is neutral to positive (adaptive) employee emotions. However, when the situation is incongruent with employee values and beliefs, we create negative to destructive (maladaptive) emotional responses.

To determine congruency the following five dimensions will be used: power, time, gender, risk and individualism. These are derived from Hofstede/Bond national culture dimensions (Bond, 1988; Hofstede, 1980).

The power dimension recognises that varying degrees of power exist in groups. High power indices reflect a high degree of hierarchy and well-defined rules. The iGens perceive leadership as a behaviour rather than as a position. They are more into collaboration than authority. They are less reliant on hierarchical approvals for decision-making than their predecessors. Low power index workplace situations are most likely congruent with the iGen culture.

Time orientations can vary from short-term to long-term focused. Short-term, or a high-time index, focuses on the here and now, and long-term focuses on future outcomes. We know that iGens are very short-term focused and they live in a turbulent nanosecond world with instant gratification. They have access to 1-hour dry cleaning, 1-hour photo shops, 30-minute pizza delivery. High-time index workplace situations are most likely congruent with the iGen culture.

Tolerance for risk varies across groups. Control over outcomes and predictability are more important to some groups than others. High-risk indices indicate a high tolerance for risk and a comfort with uncertainty. In terms of risk, the iGens have been provided with a low risk, low accountability culture courtesy of the Internet. There is no punishment for bad behaviour online. However, we are now seeing potential employers visiting the blogs of candidates. One recruiter explained to me that his company frowns upon potential candidates who have included photos of themselves in an inebriated state on their blogs (M. Reid, personal communication, January, 2006). High-risk index workplace situations are most likely congruent with the iGen culture.

The gender index refers to the degree of role differentiation based on gender. Matriarchal groups place women in the key roles, while patriarchal cultures place men in the key roles. Both of these groups have a high degree of gender differentiation. High-gender indices indicate a high degree of differentiation by gender. In the gaming world of the Internet, gender roles are not well defined. In many online games, the real gender of your team-mates is irrelevant. Low-gender index workplace situations are most likely congruent with the iGen culture.

Individualism captures the degree to which the individual is put ahead of the group. Those groups that put the individual ahead of the group have a high degree of individualism, whereas those that value the collective ahead of the group have low-individualism indices. The collective becomes harder to find when more and more of the work is being done at home. The iGens seem to be more individualistic than their predecessors. High-individualism index workplace situations are most likely congruent with the iGen culture.

These indices are used in the Congruency model (Figure 2) to help predict when neutral, positive (adaptive), or negative (maladaptive) emotions (Goleman, 2004) will result from workplace situations involving iGens.

The simple act of being born during the Internet era does not replace other cultural influences such as your country of birth, profession or organisation. However, the generational filter may also be important and should be considered in conjunction with the other cultural filters. The Emotional Process model (Druskat & Wolff, 2001) has been modified to include the generational filter which may also influence emotional outcomes (Figure 3).

The iGens demonstrate a low-power index, short-term time orientation, a high-risk tolerance, low-gender role differentiation and a high-individualism index. This information, when used in conjunction with both models, may help leaders better predict emotional outcomes and interpret emotional responses that have already occurred within their iGen workforce. If iGens really are arriving at the workplace with diminished skills in anger and stress management, then perhaps EI is not only important, but critical for those who wish to lead this next generation successfully.

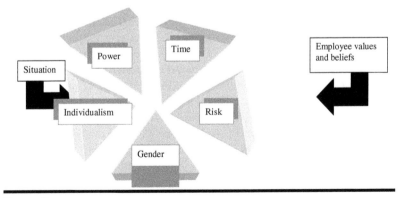

Figure 2
Congruency model.

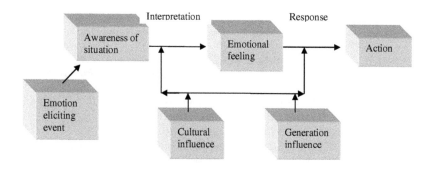

Figure 3
Influences in the Emotional Process model.

Conclusion

No one knows what the future will bring but some aspects are highly probable. According to Gandossey and Effron (2004), leaders will be faced with an environment in which:

1. speed and uncertainly will prevail
2. technology will continue to disrupt and enable
3. the iGens will dictate much of what happens in business.

A more social approach will be vital to successfully lead the iGens. In other words, being emotionally intelligent and intelligently emotional should be the mantra.

There is a huge difference between what is visible and what is actually seen. We need to have a good hard look now at the future workforce because they have started arriving. We need to leverage that knowledge to provide insightful research and workplace practices to build effective leaders for the iGeneration.

It took 35 years to get telephones into 25% of US homes, 26 years for television, 22 years for radio, 16 years for personal computers and only 7 years for the Internet to get into 25% of US homes (Gandossey & Effron, 2004, p. 163). We do not have much time to learn how to effectively manage these new workers who have been 'bathed in bits since birth' (Tapscott, 1998, p.1), so perhaps we should get started now …

References

All Experts. (2006). Retrieved August 23, 2006 from http://experts.about.com/e/g/ge/Generation_Y.htm

Andrews, M. (2006, September 10). Decoding MySpace. *US News.* Retrieved September 15, 2006, from http://www.usnews.com/usnews/news/articles/060910/18myspace.htm

BBC News. (2005, November 15). Concern over workplace violence. *BBC News*. Retrieved May 15, 2006, from http://news.bbc.co.uk/1/hi/scotland/4438798.stm

Bond, M.H. (1988). Finding unusual dimensions of individual variation in multi-cultural studies of values: The Rokeach and Chinese value survey. *Journal of Personality and Social Psychology, 55,* 1009–1015.

Druskat, V.U., & Wolff, S.B. (2001). *Group emotional competence and its influence on group effectiveness*. In C. Cherniss & D. Goleman (Eds.), *The emotionally intelligent workplace* (pp. 132–155). San Francisco: Jossey-Bass.

Gandossy, R., & Effron, M. (2004). *Leading the way*. New Jersey: Wiley & Sons.

Goleman, D. (1995). *Emotional intelligence*. New York: Bantam Books,.

Goleman, D 2004, *Destructive emotions*, Bantam Dell, New York.

Goleman, D. (2007, February 20). *Flame first, Think later: New clues to e- mail misbehaviors*. Retrieved February 28, 2007, from http://www.danielgoleman.info/blog

Hempel, J. (2005, December 12). The MySpace generation. *Business Week*. Retrieved August 8, 2006, from http://www.businessweek.com/magazine/content/05_50/b3963001.htm

Hermida, A. (2003, December 15). Nations wrestle with internet age. *BBC News*. Retrieved June 8, 2006, from http://newsbbc.co.uk/1/hi/technology/3318371.stm

Hofstede, G. (1980). *Culture's consequences: international differences in work-related values*. Beverley Hills, CA: Sage Publications.

Howe, N., & Strauss, W. (2000). *Millennials rising: the next generation*. New York: Vintage Books.

Irvine, M. (2004, December 5). The internet generation riding technological wave into the future. *Arizona Star*. Retrieved July 4, 2006, from http://www.azstarnet.com/sn/specialreports/51140.php

Layman, M. (2004, October 14). *Spectator Online*. Retrieved July 11, 2006, from http://www.spectator-online.com/vnews/display.v/ART/2004/10/14/416f5b374eab5

Locke, J.L. (1998). *The de-voicing of society*. New York: Simon and Schuster.

Loliboom. (2006). *Welcome to the loli-boom!* Retrieved July 15, 2006, from http://www.loliboom.co.uk

Mueller, J. (2001, July). Technology and stress. *Stress News, 13*(3). Retrieved August 8, 2006, from http://www.isma.org.uk/stressnw/techstress.htm

MSNBC. (2006, July 17). Watching the watchers. *Newsweek*. Retrieved August 9, 2006, from http://msnbc.com.id/13773301/site/newsweek/

Nevius, C.W. (2006, September 12). The revolt you didn't hear about. *The San Francisco Chronicle*. Retrieved 15 September 2006 from cwnevius@sfchronicle.com

Palmer, S. (2006, September 12). Is modern life ruining childhood? *BBC News*. Retrieved September 14, 2006, from http://news.bbc.co.uk/1/hi/uk/5338572.stm

Philipson, G. (2006, September 19). Your poor, your tired-your mobiles. *Sydney Morning Herald*. Retrieved September 19, 2006, from http://www.smh.com.au/news/perspectives/

Quinion, M. (1999, September 11). Echo Boomer. *Word Wide Words*. Retrieved September 15, 2006, from http://www.worldwidewords.org/turnsofphrase/tp-ech1.htm

Suetens, J. (2002, September 26). *The new needs of 'Generation M' hit the Belgian market*. Retrieved May 31, 2006, from http://strategis.ic.gc.ca/epic/internet/inimr-ri.nsf/en/gr108770 e.html

Tapscott, D. (1998). *Growing up digital*. New York: McGraw-Hill.

Twist, J. (2005, November 19). Essential test for the UN net summit. *BBC News*. Retrieved August 10. 2006. from http://news.bbc.co.uk/1/hi/technology/4451959

Weil, M.M., & Rosen, L.D. (1997). *Technostress*. New York: Wiley.

Wikipedia. (2006). *Internet generation*. Retrieved June 30, 2006, from http://en.wikipedia.org/wiki/IGeneration

WSIS. (2006). Retrieved September 18, 2006, from http://worldsummitoninformation society.org

Innovation Development
Early Assessment System

John (Jack) English

Australia's Industrial Performance

How does Australia's industrial performance compare with other nations and what are the implications for the role of innovation? Table 1 reflects Australia's rankings in four of the United Nations Industrial Development Organization's indicators for industrial performance in 1990 and again in 2002.

UNIDO's industrial performance indicators focus upon countries' competitive ability to produce and export manufactured goods. Australia ranked 25th in 2002 for manufacturing value added per capita, falling one place from 24th position in 1990. While Australia improved the dollar value of manufacturing value added per capita, so did many other countries resulting in a fall in the relative ranking.

Australia ranked 43rd in 2002 for manufactured exports per capita, falling eight places from 35th position in 1990. This indicator reflects the component of manufacturing value added that is exposed to international competition. Australia more than doubled the dollar value of manufactured exports per capita, but it did not match the increases in many other countries resulting in a significant drop in the relative ranking.

Table 1
Australia's Industrial Performance (World Ranking)

	1990	2002
Manufacturing Value Added	$2488 (24th)	$2797 (25th)
Manufactured Exports	$688 (35th)	$1390 (43rd)
Technological Structure of MVA	50.6% (27th)	49.5% (35th)
Technological Structure of ME	31.3% (43rd)	41.3% (52nd)

Source: United Nations Industrial Development Organization (UNIDO), Industrial Development Report 2005 (adapted).

Australia ranked 35th in 2002 for the share of medium- or high-technology production in manufacturing value added, falling eight places from 27th position in 1990. The higher a country ranks on this indicator, the more technologically complex is its industrial structure. This indicator reflects a disappointing setback in the agonisingly slow structural shift in Australia from lower technology to higher technology activities.

Australia ranked 52nd in 2002 for the share of medium- or high-technology production in manufactured exports, falling nine places from 43rd position in 1990, despite a significant improvement in the indicator. It reflects the slow evolution of Australia's industrial and export structure compared with a large number of other nations and further highlights the need to shift both manufacturing value added and exports up the technology scale.

It is clear that Australia's recent industrial performance does not compare favourably with the industrial performance in many other nations. Despite improvements in three out of the four performance indicators, Australia has slipped in all four relative rankings. If we want to entertain any notions about playing in the major league of exporting nations, then we need to refine our ability to identify new ideas with genuine commercial potential and bring them to market.

Purpose of Early Assessment

An innovation is a complex series of activities in which an idea is conceived, proceeds through a succession of developmental steps and culminates in a product, a process, or a service that is accepted in the marketplace. It starts with an idea, or initial discovery, that needs to be assessed, developed and tested. Everything, from the smallest incremental improvement to the most radical innovation, starts with an idea.

Prospective innovators generally believe that the leap from an idea to market entry is only a short distance and they often do not recognise how complex, costly, and time consuming the process can be. Consequently, it is important to be able to assess the commercial feasibility of new ideas very early in the innovation process, because it is the least costly stage in which to identify and eliminate likely failures (English & Udell, 2004). Inasmuch as many new ideas turn out not to be commercially feasible, indiscriminately investing time, money and effort in them only dilutes the resources available for projects with genuine potential. Innovation is not a democracy in which all ideas are created equal. It is a meritocracy in which those ideas with demonstrated commercial merit should be developed further.

There are scores of systems designed to evaluate business plans that have been compiled after market research and product development have taken place. The Innovation Development Early Assessment System, or IDEAS, however, is designed to make an *early* assessment of the commercial feasibility of a new idea.

An IDEAS assessment takes place long before there is enough tangible information to do a business plan, and its purpose is to decide if further development of the idea is warranted. Idea assessment does not need to be expensive or time-consuming, particularly in the early stages of the innovation process, but it does need to be systematic and comprehensive. There are three basic approaches to determining if an idea warrants further development.

The first approach is an informal and unstructured *yes* or *no* assessment that amounts to little more than a beauty contest. It is the least expensive approach, but it is also the least beneficial because it is not likely to provide much insight into, or information about, the idea. Moreover, there is no way to control for quality or to insure the use of uniform criteria.

The second approach is an in-depth analysis by a panel of specialists who have the requisite technical and marketing expertise. This approach usually provides the best possible assessment and the greatest amount of information about strategies for commercialisation. However, it is also the most expensive approach and beyond the capacity of most individuals to underwrite.

The third approach is the *IDEAS* approach. It consists of a standardised analysis designed by a cross-section of specialists representing a broad range of technical and commercial expertise. It is a low-cost, comprehensive and systematic analysis that can be undertaken by anyone trained in the *IDEAS* protocol. It provides a uniform, easily communicated and easily understood basis for assessment coupled with comprehensive and valuable feedback. It is intended to be an efficient and cost-effective way to provide an assessment of the commercial strengths and weaknesses of an idea.

Most assessment models require information that does not exist or is too costly to obtain in the very early stages of the innovation process. The result is that many prospective innovators skip assessment altogether and move directly into research and development. In other words, the day of reckoning for low potential ideas is postponed until the cost of abandonment is much higher. The rationale for making an informed decision early in the innovation process is two-fold. First, few prospective innovators have the resources to withstand failure and early assessment can be extremely valuable in order to avoid costly mistakes. Second, both individuals and organisations need to focus their resources on the most promising innovations, and early assessment is an important tool in identifying ideas with genuine commercial potential.

Origins of the IDEAS Program

IDEAS is based on the Preliminary Innovation Evaluation System (PIES) developed by Professor Gerald G. Udell and his colleagues at the Experimental Center for Invention and Innovation in the United States with financial support from the US National Science Foundation, the US National Bureau of Standards and the US Small Business Administration (Udell, 2004). Professor Udell formed the

Table 2
PIES Evaluation Results

Evaluation Categories	Successful firms (n = 93) mean score	Failed firms (n = 1130) mean score	Significance (p value)
Social impact	82.4%	81.4%	NS
Business risk	91.0%	84.0%	0.010
Demand analysis	64.6%	58.0%	0.001
Market acceptance	72.3%	66.4%	0.001
Competitive capability	60.4%	57.9%	0.010
Experience and strategy	66.7%	59.7%	0.001
Venture assessment	66.2%	59.1%	0.001
Overall mean	71.5%	66.8%	0.001

Innovation Institute in which his system has been used to evaluate an estimated 30,000 ideas and inventions — primarily in the United States and Canada. A European version of the system has also been launched at the University of Nottingham with a planned rollout throughout the European Union.

In the initial version of PIES, the criteria were selected after a considerable amount of research in the new-product literature and discussions with a number of experts involved in invention and innovation — including independent inventors, technologists, patent attorneys, consultants, licensing agents, corporate researchers, and new-product planning specialists. Since that time, new criteria have been added as experience, changes in market conditions and continued validating research have suggested they are warranted.

A study of the *PIES* protocol found that it was effective in discriminating between success and failure in 1223 cases in the United States (Knotts, Jones, & Udell, 2003). Table 2 contains the results.

For each evaluation category, the difference between the mean scores for failed firms and successful firms is significant, except for social impact. This exception might have been the result of a de-selection process in which firms with products that were illegal, unsafe or inappropriate for the mass market might have chosen to withdraw earlier from the program. Overall, failed firms had a lower mean rating than successful firms (66.8% to 71.5%, $p < .001$).

A license was granted by the Innovation Institute to adapt the *PIES* system for use in Australia and New Zealand. Now called *IDEAS*, the Australian adaptation takes a broader approach and expands the scope of assessment beyond products to include processes and services. It also incorporates an assessment of the strategic alternatives for commercialisation by applying a resource-based model of the firm that was originally designed to teach entrepreneurship at the University of Tasmania (Jones & English, 2004). In addition to changes made as a result of the experience gained from using the system, the Australian version also reflects research and study by Australian academics as well as input from Australian specialists.

IDEAS Assessment Framework

IDEAS is concerned with commercial feasibility. There are many ideas that are technically feasible, but not all of them are commercially feasible. If an idea is both technically and commercially feasible, then it is generally worthwhile to develop the idea further with a view to identifying a commercialisation strategy and compiling a business plan. IDEAS consists of a series of questions that do not require a great deal of information in order to make a preliminary judgment. In most cases, there is sufficient information inherent in the basic concept to arrive at an informed assessment about the commercial feasibility of an idea.

The first objective of IDEAS is to determine if a new idea ought to be developed further. There are two ways to approach this: identify ideas that have the potential to become successful innovations, or identify ideas that do not have the potential to become successful innovations. The second approach is much easier to operationalise because there are too many unknowns to be able to predict success accurately this early in the innovation process. Occasionally, an idea or invention will occur with such clarity of technical and commercial feasibility that its potential for success is obvious, but this is a rare event.

The second objective of IDEAS is to provide feedback. Without genuine feedback, aspiring innovators can be left confused and/or frustrated because they do not know what to do next. For example, if an assessment shows a short product life cycle, it does not necessarily mean the idea should be abandoned. However, it does mean that certain financial, production, and marketing strategies will be more appropriate than others. Feedback is important because it:

- reduces misunderstandings
- creates an environment that is conducive to creativity
- provides insight into the innovation process
- presents an opportunity to correct errors
- stimulates consideration of strategies for further development.

IDEAS consists of 35 questions. Each question contains five possible responses ranging from *very favourable* to *very unfavourable*. The question for stability of demand is an example.

Stability of Demand

Fluctuations in demand are likely to be:

- highly stable — not susceptible to fluctuations
- stable — modest variations can be accurately foreseen
- predictable — variations can be foreseen with reasonable accuracy
- unstable — susceptible to moderately unpredictable fluctuations
- highly unstable — subject to severely unpredictable fluctuations.

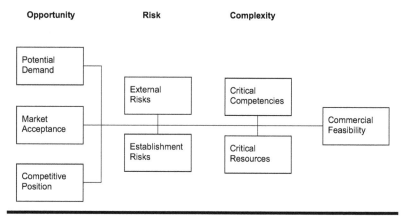

Figure 1
Assessing commercial feasibility.

During an IDEAS workshop, the information that each question is attempting to elicit and the meaning of each of the responses is carefully explained. The main activity of the workshop is for each participant to rate their idea across the 35 questions by selecting the most accurate responses. The responses are then combined into a series of diagnostic diagrams and a Commercial Feasibility Rating.

IDEAS is organised into three themes: the market *opportunity*, the associated *risk*, and the degree of *complexity* involved in putting the idea into operation. The assessment of commercial feasibility is divided into seven sections depicted in Figure 1.

Opportunity
The first theme is designed to assess the market opportunity. It is divided into three sections composed of potential demand, market acceptance and competitive position.

Potential Demand
One of the important determinants in evaluating commercial feasibility is potential demand. Demand is also difficult to assess because it requires some insight into the behaviour of the marketplace and a certain amount of guesswork about the firm that will eventually take the idea to market. Potential demand questions, although general at the early assessment stage, are designed to explore several key aspects about demand.

- What is the relative size and distribution of the potential market?
- Is the trend of demand increasing or decreasing?

- Is demand likely to be stable or unstable?
- How long is the life cycle likely to be?
- What potential is there for related products, processes or services?

Market Acceptance

Market acceptance is an important determinant in converting potential demand into sales. It affects both the rate of adoption and the extent to which the market can be penetrated. There are a variety of reasons why the market may accept or reject a new idea. These questions focus on five of the most important reasons.

- Is it compatible with existing attitudes and patterns of use?
- What degree of learning is required to consume or use it?
- What level of need is fulfilled or utility provided?
- How visible are the benefits and what degree of promotion is needed to create customer awareness?
- How difficult will it be to establish distribution channels?

Competitive Position

Competitive position questions assess how an idea for a new product, process, or service is likely to fare compared with the dominant competitive pressures already in the marketplace or likely to emerge after market entry.

- How is it different from similar products, processes or services?
- How will its perceived value compare with equivalent products, processes or services?
- Is it vulnerable to the bargaining power of customers?
- Is it vulnerable to the bargaining power of suppliers?
- Is it vulnerable to the bargaining power of competitors?

Risk

The second theme is designed to assess the risk associated with an idea by searching for its fatal flaws. Risk is divided into two sections composed of external risks and establishment risks.

External Risks

External risks are dangers that are generally beyond an innovator's control but nevertheless affect the commercial feasibility of their idea. They originate from a variety of sources such as government, advocates of various popular causes, existing and potential vested interests and the public. The questions in this section deal with the following types of external risks.

- Does it meet legal, safety and other regulatory requirements?
- Is it vulnerable to changes in technology?

- Does it have an effect on the environment?
- Is it vulnerable to any of the dominant forces in our society?
- To what extent could sales be limited by dependence on other external factors?

Establishment Risks

Establishment risks also represent obstacles that have the potential to affect the commercial development of an idea. The difference between these and external risks is the degree of control that an innovator may have over them. The innovator needs to recognise what they are, the extent to which they can be resolved or avoided and whether or not they want to take these risks. Establishment risk questions focus on the following five business-related uncertainties associated with commercialising an idea.

- Will this product, process or service actually perform the way you want it to?
- Are the start-up components available and reliable?
- What market research remains to be done?
- What research and development remains to be done?
- What sort of money will it take to get started?

Complexity

The third theme is designed to assess the degree of complexity associated with trying to put an idea into operation. Complexity is divided into two sections composed of critical competencies and critical resources.

Critical Competencies

For the most part, an innovation is the result of a successful marriage between commercial potential and the essential expertise and resources to make it happen. The relative importance of the critical competencies depends upon the sophistication of the idea and the nature of the market it faces. At times, very sophisticated ideas can be relatively easy to implement. It is also true that some very simple ideas can require a high degree of management, marketing or financial expertise. We are concerned with identifying the critical competencies needed to develop and successfully launch an idea and whether the innovator can realistically provide or acquire them. The critical competencies examined include:

- marketing expertise
- technical expertise
- financial expertise
- operational expertise
- managerial expertise.

Critical Resources

Successfully commercialising an idea not only depends on expertise, but also on key resources that, together, form the basis for creating and sustaining value. These questions are concerned with identifying critical resource intensity as well as what the innovator can realistically provide or acquire. Critical resource requirements form the basic dimensions for a business plan. The critical resources examined include:

* operating resources
* human resources
* financing resources
* knowledge resources
* reputational resources.

Commercial Feasibility Rating

The objective in an IDEAS workshop is to arrive at a judgment about the overall attractiveness of the opportunity, the risks associated with commercialisation and the degree of complexity involved in putting the idea into operation. The result is a Commercial Feasibility Rating, together with diagnostic diagrams for the underlying drivers. A Commercial Feasibility Rating is not merely a mechanical procedure. It is a method designed to assist an innovator to exercise their judgment. It depends upon an understanding of the IDEAS protocol and the extent to which the assessment has been objectively undertaken.

An integral part of the assessment process is to plot diagnostic diagrams of the responses. This can be done for each of the sections and each of the themes. The example in Figure 2 is a template for the diagnostic diagram for market opportunity. The diagrams help to visualise the way in which the responses have contributed to the overall assessment. Each diagram contains an Area of Concern. Responses that fall into the Area of Concern highlight potentially important issues that may affect an idea's commercial feasibility. Engaging in a visual evaluation for each component of the system reveals a great deal more insight into the strengths and weaknesses of an idea than the overall

The commercial feasibility rating consists of a standardised scoring system with a maximum score of 100. The purpose of the Commercial Feasibility Rating is to provide a prospective innovator with an overall estimate of the commercial potential of their idea. The estimate should not be taken too literally because it is basically a 'best guess' based on their own evaluation. The commercial outcome of a new idea is essentially a function of three variables: the idea, the enterprise that will take it to market and the marketplace itself. During the early stages of the innovation process there is typically very little information about the enterprise that will take the idea to market. In addition, information about the target market is often incomplete. Hence, there are inevitably a number of unknowns that

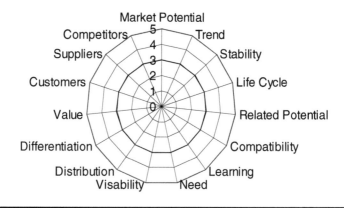

Figure 2
Market opportunity diagram.

remain unanswered at this very early stage. The Commercial Feasibility Rating falls into one of three bands that are described in terms of a traffic light.

Red Light

If an idea's Commercial Feasibility Rating is under 60, then its commercial potential is considered unacceptably low and further development is not recommended. A Commercial Feasibility Rating below 60 generally represents a poor opportunity, unacceptable risks, and/or impractical operational complexity. In this situation, abandonment may be the best course of action. Sometimes it is the idea itself that is flawed and sometimes the flaw is in the marketplace.

Yellow Light

If an idea's Commercial Feasibility Rating is between 60 and 79, then its commercial potential is considered marginal, but it may nevertheless warrant some degree of cautious development. A Commercial Feasibility Rating in the lower half of this range generally represents a modest opportunity, significant risks, and/or considerable operational complexity. It may have sufficient potential to warrant very limited and cautious development. A Commercial Feasibility Rating in the upper half of this range generally represents an appealing opportunity, but typically has some significant unknowns about risk and/or operational complexity that ought to be resolved before further development takes place. Development should be limited to those activities that are not costly and they should focus on resolving some of the unknowns that contributed to a low rating.

Green Light

If an idea's Commercial Feasibility Rating is between 80 and 100, then its commercial potential is good and further investment of time, energy and money is usually recommended. A Commercial Feasibility Rating in the lower half of this range generally represents a good opportunity, an acceptable level of risk and is operationally realistic — but it may still have one or two important unknowns that need to be resolved. A Commercial Feasibility Ratingin the upper half of this range generally represents an excellent opportunity, a low level of risk and is operationally practical.

This does not mean that an idea with a Commercial Feasibility Rating over 80 is automatically accepted. On the contrary, all new products, processes and services have some degree of risk and managing that risk is part of the key to long-term success. Ignoring even relatively minor risk factors can be serious, if not fatal, to the commercialisation process. Therefore, careful attention is paid to responses that fall into the area of concern even though the Commercial Feasibility Rating is high.

Reaching a Decision

It should be apparent that IDEAS does not make decisions. Its purpose is to provide a useful framework for assisting a prospective innovator to exercise their judgment about whether or not to move to the next stage in the innovation process. There are three more factors that are also likely to influence a decision to abandon, revise or go ahead with their idea.

The first factor is their willingness to accept the risk and how far they will go before saying 'No.' Some people can tolerate very high levels of risk and others have a very low tolerance for risk. Most successful innovators, however, do not fall into either group. Rather, they are willing to take some risks, but they also work hard to avoid or overcome them. There are always concerns with every new idea, so it is expected that some responses will fall into the Area of Concern. The questions in which a response falls into the Area of Concern need to be carefully reviewed. Many of these concerns can be resolved. What seems to get so many individuals into trouble is their failure to deal with these concerns early in the innovation process.

The second factor is the financial returns that that an idea is expected to generate. If an innovator can see the potential for a very high return, then they may be more likely to invest their time and money in a high-risk venture. If they expect a moderate return, then they will probably be more conservative.

The third factor is the relative size of the initial investment. The more money they need to invest, the lower will be the degree of risk they consider acceptable. However, this may be mitigated by the financial returns they expect to earn. In other words, ideas that offer big margins and appeal to large markets generally warrant a greater investment than specialty items with limited market appeal and modest prospects for profits.

Conclusion

Launching a new product, process or service is far more difficult than most people anticipate. This is, in part, due to the complicated nature of the innovation process and the unexpected obstacles that inevitably occur along the way. *IDEAS* is one method for evaluating the attractiveness of the market opportunity, the risks involved and the degree of complexity in attempting to commercialise a new idea. The objective is to help prospective innovators to come to a conclusion about the commercial feasibility of their idea and whether or not they want to develop it further. To the extent that Australian innovators become skilled at identifying and acting upon genuine commercial opportunities, the more likely Australia will see its rankings improve in UNIDO's indicators of industrial performance.

References

English, J. (2006). *IDEAS: Innovation Development Early Assessment System, workshop manual.* Canberra, Australia: Innovation Evaluation Systems.

English, J., & Udell, G.G. (2004). Preliminary evaluation system for economic development agencies. *Journal of New Business Ideas and Trends, 2*(1), 11–20.

Jones, C., & English, J. (2004). A contemporary approach to entrepreneurship education. *Education + training, 46*(8/9), 416–423.

Knotts, T.I., Jones, S.C., & Udell, G.G. (2003). Small business failure: The role of management practices and product characteristics. *Journal of Business and Entrepreneurship*, October, 8–16.

Udell, G.G. (2004). *Assessing the commercial potential of ideas, inventions and innovations: A balanced approach.* Southwest Missouri State University: Innovation Institute.

United Nations Industrial Development Organization. (2005). *Industrial development report 2005: Capability building for catching-up.* Retrieved July 15, 2006, from http://www.unido.org/doc/5156

Moral Judgment in Management: The Role of *Phronesis* and *Aporia*

Robert Macklin

Ethics

Ethics can be defined in many ways but in this chapter I take it to be a collective noun for what is seen in any social grouping as the norms[1] of right and wrong. These ethical norms will help people who wish to act decently (Mautner, 1997).

For example, in any organisation ethical behaviour is guided by formal norms, contained perhaps in codes of conduct, and informal norms guiding what constitutes 'right' and 'wrong' conduct. The ethics of an organisation is thus that collection of norms that inform decent managers and employees. However, these norms do not form a closed system. They reflect and reproduce other group, community and social norms and form part of a complex web of normative criteria guiding conduct. Moreover, they are social constructs. That is, ethical norms are not transcendent phenomena that stand outside human construction. They are part of the history and culture of groups and societies (Heller 1988).[2]

Thus, for example, Macklin (2003) has identified the importance to some human resource (HR) managers of the norms of justice, respect, valuing the individual and not using employees as mere means. In the global context, as another example, while there will be differences across different societies or cultures, there are transcultural norms that decent managers can use to guide decisions. Examples include international conventions such as the 1997 OECD Anti-Bribery Convention and the ILO's Fundamental Principles on Rights at Work, voluntary principles such as the Caux Round Table Principles for Business, and internal codes of practice developed by multinational corporations (Grace & Cohen, 2005; Mellahi & Wood, 2003; Trevino & Nelson, 2006).

Ethical Decision Making in Management Practice

I think normative criteria are essential aids for anyone who wishes to be decent, but using them in concrete everyday management practice is rarely straightforward.

Ethical dilemmas are frequent and, over a career, a manager will find him or herself having to deal with a great variety of them (Hosmer, 2002). This is particularly the case in international contexts, where globalisation and crosscultural and economic differences create ethical dilemmas that add to the difficulties faced by decent managers. For example, writers such as De George (2006) Fritzsche (2005) and Mellahi and Wood (2003) discuss issues such as whether one should comply with home or foreign country ethical norms, whether to buy goods made in sweatshops or by child labourers, and whether to trade in countries where human rights are abused. In these contexts, in the absence of any domestic or foreign corrupt practices legislation, managers must determine whether a proposed action is unethical and thus whether it puts their own and their organisation's decency at risk.

Given all this, much work has been put into trying to give guidance to managers. Writers point to 'codes of ethics' and other less formal ethical norms as a way forward (e.g., Coady & Bloch, 1996; Harrison, 2001; Hosmer, 2002; Shaw & Barry, 2004). Moreover, genuine attempts have been made to establish norms and principles to guide the actions of managers and corporations in international business activity. The Caux Round Principles, as a prime example, suggest that managers draw on seven principles as a base for discussion and socially responsible decision-making. The seven principles cover responsibilities to stakeholders, the economic, environmental and social impact of business, the importance of trust, respecting rules, supporting multinational trade, and avoiding illicit operations. The principles are detailed and underpinned by the assumptions that laws and the market cannot be solely relied upon as guides for conduct, that the interests and dignity of stakeholders are central to socially responsible actions, and that shared values are of importance to both the global community as well as smaller communities (Trevino & Nelson, 2006).

With norms and codes at hand, surely dilemmas should not present great difficulties. Surely managers just need to examine the problem, refer to existing codes and norms such as justice and care and the solution will be obvious? If justice is threatened, managers should to protect it. If care is at risk, managers should insist on its reinforcement. If innocent people will suffer, managers should just find another way to achieve their ends.

However, making the 'right' decisions is rarely straightforward. Most ethical dilemmas are very complex: discovering who is involved, why there is a problem and how to act are not simple processes. Further ethical dilemmas often involve clashes between ethical norms or between ethical norms and other imperatives. Sometimes, for example, care clashes with justice[3] or one or the other threatens organisational performance. Moreover, every individual dilemma will be singular and unique (Heller, 1990). It will derive from a time- and place- bound coincidence of very many influences including, inter alia, resources, skills, competing interpretations and divergent interests.

In the international context, managers using the Caux Round Principles might find that in a particular context and circumstances the needs of employees as stakeholders do not square with those of owners and investors. For example, one stakeholder subprinciple requires that business leaders have a responsibility to '(p)rovide jobs and compensation that improves workers' living conditions' (Trevino & Nelson, 2006, p 392). Another subprinciples requires business leaders to 'conserve, protect, and increase the owners/ investors' assets' (Trevino & Nelson, 2006, p. 393). Both are clearly important principles, which many people are likely to support, but clearly they may conflict in certain circumstances.

Given this, it has been pointed out (e.g., Coady, 1996; Write-St Clair & Steedhouse, 2005) that normative criteria such as codes cannot replace what is called 'moral reasoning' or 'good judgment'. That is, to quote Write-St Clair and Steedhouse (2005, p. 24):

> Being moral is about continuously considering how things ought to be. It is therefore suggested that the solution lies in practitioners holding a rich awareness of the moral dimensions of practice, a genuine mindfulness of the complexity in everyday environments and professional relating, a deep reflection on the intuitive ways of being and acting, an openness to receive alternative views and a commitment to thoughtful considered reasoning.

Making a good judgment, therefore, is not simple; it demands flexibility, insight and sensitivity. In addition, it can be argued that an overreliance on ethical norms or principles can itself be ethically problematic. For example, writers such as Bauman (1993, 1995) and Caputo (1993, 2003) argue that any attempt to use established ethical norms threaten individual discretion. To rely on ethical norms is to risk supplanting autonomous moral responsibility with heteronomous ethical duty. Moreover, Caputo (2003) suggests that principles may remove the individual's responsibility for choosing the way to act: 'A principle often amounts to a way to excuse ourselves or absolve ourselves of responsibility, to relieve ourselves of the responsibility to make a decision, even to an abdication of responsibility that passes itself off for high-mindedness (Caputo, 2003, p. 172).

Thus, for example, it is likely that most people would support a principle requiring managers to be just in all their dealings with employees. But it is possible that a norm requiring justice could be used by a manager to avoid his or her responsibility to look after a particular employee who faces some kind of highly distressing personal circumstance. One can imagine the manager saying something to the effect that he or she would love to help the employee but doing so would be unfair to others and thus, unfortunately, his or her hands are tied.

I agree up to a point with these observations and suggest that ethical norms should not be seen as laws or 'straightjackets'. However, perhaps counter to Bauman and Caputo, I suggest that we do not abandon normative criteria. They should not be seen as laws but, as Heller (1990) suggests, we can still use them as 'crutches'. Crutches do not take away our responsibility but they are aids we can reach for when we want support. Quoting Heller:

> No crutch (law, norm, orientative principle) eliminates contingency and the risk. But they can illuminate — up to a point — the way to show the character, if not the amount of risk. 'Crutches' do not determine action. For example, there are people who prefer a more risky course of action to a less risky one. And anyway, we leap with our legs not with our crutches. Moreover the use of crutches is not obligatory. But if there are crutches, one can use them, provided that one feels the need to use them. (1996, p. 5)

Nevertheless, one might argue that suggesting we rely on complex and rich moral reasoning still begs too many questions. How does one do this? Is there some kind of technique we can follow?

As one would expect, much effort has been put into this by writers who have devised a diversity of decision-making models. For example 'Manner's 12-stage ethical decision making model' (Harrison, 2001); the American Accounting Associations Seven Step Model for Ethical Decision Making (Harrison, 2001); and numerous others (see Grace & Cohen, 2005, for a useful list).

Avoiding the Tyranny of Guidelines and the Role of Phronesis

An obvious problem here is that we may simply replace the tyranny of norms with the tyranny of guidelines. We must be careful about models as they can become similar traps to those created by an obsession with norms, especially, I suggest, if they are portrayed as techniques. That is, it is possible to imagine a manager sticking to a particular model in a highly prescriptive manner. Once again, autonomy would be replaced with heteronomy and the individual becomes not so much an 'agent' as an unreflective transmitter of moral code.

I therefore suggest that managers do not use decision-making guidelines as tightly scripted lists of questions to follow verbatim. Rather, they should treat them as loose guides to deliberation. From situation to situation their use of norms and guidelines must vary depending on the circumstances. Moreover, over time as a manager's experience grows, their use of guidelines will change as they become more confident. Here, under pressure and time constraints, the guides may become habits of thought that are nevertheless finely tuned to the uniqueness of the situation. Further, in deliberations upon different ethical decisions the consideration of some points will be longer, deeper or more complex than it will be in others. Thus, ethical decision-making should not be seen as a standardised procedure; it is about being flexible and sensitive to the richness of a situation. This will especially be the case in global contexts, I suggest, where the impact of cultural, political, and economic diversity will complicate the situation faced by decent managers even further.[4]

Articulating all this in Aristotelian terms, in the realm of ethics we must not rely on theoretical and technical reasoning. Rather our emphasis should be on practical reasoning or *phronesis*.[5] *Phronesis* focuses on the variable and largely nonreproducible facets of the world. It is about knowledge of the contingent features of the world and its focus is on human conduct and how we act on our interpretation of contextual particulars. It is aimed not at developing universal rules or repeatable techniques, but about fitting knowledge to circumstances (Halverson, 2004).

Phronesis is about the ability to evaluate particular, nonreproducible and mutable circumstances in order to work out what should be done in a given situation. Moreover, it is about knowing how to act suitably in the face of ambiguity without any a priori valid formulae or detailed plans of action. It involves the capacity to combine knowledge, judgment, understanding and intuition in order to act 'fittingly' in a particular situation and in the face of contingency. It is thus case-based, customised to particular contexts and not easily susceptible to empirical generalisation (Dunne, 1993; Halverson, 2004).

With experience *phronesis* becomes a habit. But developing this habit is not about developing a capacity to unreflectively repeat techniques in order to reproduce some end. It is about developing the habit of applying knowledge and normative criteria to unique and nonrepetitive events. It thus, in part, involves learning how *not* to make a habit of acting routinely. In addition, it does not involve intellect alone, it requires sensitivity and intuition and hence a capacity to draw on emotions. In also involves what the Greeks called '*metis*' — cunning, cleverness, flexibility, quick wittedness, alertness, perspicuity and a 'good eye' but oriented by sensitivity and a commitment to decency (Halverson, 2004; Statler, Roos, & Victor, 2006).

Norms and guidelines, I suggest, are part of the knowledge and normative criteria that we may draw on in concrete situations to help us determine the right thing to do. But we must not overemphasise their status. In this respect, the following quote from Caputo resonates quite strongly for me: 'On their best day, principles are the faded copies of the singularity of concrete situations, the scores of a music still under composition, the map of a territory that has not yet been explored' (2003, p. 179).

Caputo's intent here is to decentre the role of norms and place them on the periphery. He prefers to place our responsibility for facing the challenge of concrete situations in the centre. While I agree in broad terms with his argument, I do not marginalise normative criteria to the same extent as he does. For me, the metaphor of the 'faded copy' alludes to the role of history in any of our deliberations. Norms and guidelines are historical constructs. They may be faded and imprecise, but the decent person always looks back at the lessons learnt and then, in conversation with others, designs crutches to help him or her make choices. Moreover, norms and guidelines are never complete — they are always being reinterpreted and thus forever being composed and rediscovered.

Aporia

My approach here, which draws on the work of Agnes Heller (1985, 1990, 1996) will undoubtedly antagonise some people. Some will say I have gone too far. Caputo (2003) for example, as I have already pointed out argues that principles 'are at best of provisional use' (p. 171); I suggest a crutch is more than this. But I will also frustrate those people who still beg an answer to the question of how precisely one reasons practically about ethical dilemmas. I cannot help them because I can go no further without destroying the complexity and subtlety of the situation facing the individual who must judge.

Worse still, I wish to add one more complexity. I do not think people should sit comfortably with the notion that while ethical judgment is difficult, we can rely on *phronesis* to mysteriously clear the mists and reveal *the* answer. Rather, I suggest that we must accept that in very many cases ethical judgment will ultimately remain perplexing. That is, I suggest, following Derrida (1990) and Caputo (1993), that all ethical deliberations are haunted by *aporia*; perplexities and inconsistencies that mean that judgments will never flow in readily calculable ways from evidence. Caputo in *Against Ethics* (1993) applying Derrida's idea to ethics writes of three 'aporias':

- the 'aporia of suspension' — the inability to simply apply a principle in a mechanical way because every decision requires a unique interpretation that no principle or code can cover absolutely;
- the 'ghost of undecidability' — the perplexity associated with the necessity to make a choice between 'respect for equity and universal right ... (and) ... for the always heterogeneous and unique singularity of the unsubsumable example' (Derrida, quoted in Caputo, 1993, p. 104); and,
- the 'aporia of urgency' — decisions must be made here and now and people rarely have the time, knowledge and mastery to think through a decision thoroughly and completely. Even if time is available 'still there comes a time — "a finite moment of urgency and precipitation" — when the leap must be made, the gap crossed, the decision taken' (Caputo, 1993, p. 105).

These aporias reinforce the idea that codes, principles and guides should never be applied inflexibly but must be adapted to circumstances and that we must accept that ethical judgment will often involve leaps of faith. We may seek out norms and guides such as 'Never treat another purely as a means to your ends' or 'Determine which acts (if any) breach which norms'. But these can only ever be 'rules of thumb' — every situation and every decision will require different orientations and approaches. We must also live with the responsibility that every norm and guideline will do violence to an individual's singularity and uniqueness, that justice and singularity will always clash and that we will also always face time limits. We must rely on *phronesis* to help make good judgments but it will always be the case that our judgments will be made in the face of uncertainty. *Phronesis* does not deliver definitive answers. We ultimately have to make a choice about what the right thing to do is without knowing for sure if we are actually making the right decision. We will always be judging gaps and making leaps across a void. Here, all we have left to help us is our courage.

Conclusion

This view of moral decision-making has implications for any effort to develop decent managers. Here I can only discuss these implications of development briefly and by way of a conclusion. It remains an area where more work could be very fruitful.

In terms of teaching students in undergraduate or postgraduate management courses, accepting the claim that *phronesis* and *aporia* are fundamental to ethical judgment means that ethics subjects or topics must not overemphasise the importance and efficacy of ethics theory or the role of ethical norms. I suggest that students be given the opportunity to discuss the norms and values that they think are important in their families, in the groups they interact with, the organisations they work for, and the societies they live in. I suggest they be introduced to, and given the opportunity to debate, the validity and efficacy of competing ethical theories. I also suggest that they be given a range of decision-making models to consider. However, none of this instruction should be done in a dogmatic way. The norms, values, theories and models should all be introduced as guides or crutches for their attempts to reason practically. Therefore, above all, they should be given the opportunity to develop their skills for *phronesis*.

According to Aristotle, excellence in practical wisdom only comes with experience and time (Dunne, 1993) thus we must not expect too much from students who are new to world of employment. But here case studies and discussion with experienced practitioners should at least provide them with direction and a base to build on. It will then be up to experience, helped by the processes of management development, to ensure that new managers move from novices to sensitive and wise ethical judges. A host of development approaches may help in this respect. For example coaches, mentors and opportunities for group discussions may all help a manager to consider what the right thing to do is in a particular circumstance and to learn how to use his or her crutches in a flexible manner.

Finally, managers must be helped to understand that they may never come up with an 'ideal' solution to ethical problems and that on some occasions their judgments will follow hunches, intuitions, or leaps of faith. They must come to terms with this and be helped to develop the courage to act without any support.

Endnotes

1   The word 'norms' here is used to collect all types of normative criteria including codes, principles, maxims and rules.

2   For examples of this approach to ethics see communitarian writers such as MacIntyre and Sandel. The work that underpins my approach is that by Agnes Heller (1990). For Heller principles, norms and rules are dialogically developed over time by decent people. That is, ethical principles are devised by people who have committed themselves to striving to be decent and who have engaged in discussions with each other in order to help them establish what the right thing to do is.

3   As Heller (1985) argues justice is a cold virtue: we must treat everyone consistently and continuously according to the norms that cover a group's conduct. However, care calls for us to do the best we can to meet the unique needs of the individual.

4   Here I do not wish to enter the debate about cultural relativism in any depth other than to claim that while cultural diversity is a significant issue there are enough common norms and common human conditions to enable translation. Diversity makes judgments even more problematic and aporias (see below) even more stark, but still we must leap and we can still talk about the crutches that will help us launch ourselves.

5   Aristotle contrasted *phronesis* with *techne* and *episteme*. *Episteme*, is wisdom concerning the eternal laws of the universe. That is knowledge that can be traced back ultimately to first principles or ultimate causes. Knowledge that is necessary and eternal such as mathematical entities, heavenly bodies, divine beings (Dunne, 1993). It is knowledge that is objective and representable apart from the knower and that can be reproduced under similar circumstances (Halverson, 2004; Statler, Roos, & Victor, 2005). In its highest form it is concerned with the pursuit of philosophical truths (Dunne, 1993). Technical wisdom or '*techne*' is concerned with know-how or craft. It is the knowledge or expertise associated with producing a state of affairs or an object (Dunne, 1993). That is, it is wisdom about how best to produce, make or fabricate things. It is thus, the knowledge that a craftsperson must have in order to be able to fabricate some kind of product such as a house, or clothing or a state of affairs such as a safe journey or a highly tuned motor cycle (Dunne, 1993). It is a concrete, variable, and context-dependent form of knowledge that focuses on the most instrumentally rational way to achieve ends (Halverson, 2004). For the technically wise, the end or purpose of the product or activity determines the form that the product or activity takes and it requires that the craftsperson deliberate and plan the steps he or she will take to complete his or her goal. It also requires the craftsperson to be able to give an account of the steps and procedures so that the fabrication of the product or activity can be traced back through its production to its original starting point. Technical wisdom is context-dependent in that the craftsperson's technique varies in line

with the desired end product. Different products require different techniques. Nevertheless, it is also about the reliable reproduction of things and activities.

References

Bauman, Z. (1993). *Postmodern ethics*. Oxford: Blackwell.

Bauman, Z. (1995). *Life in fragments: Essays in postmodern morality*. Oxford: Blackwell.

Caputo, J. (1993). *Against ethics: Contributions to a poetics of obligation with constant reference to deconstruction*. Bloomington, IN: Indiana University Press.

Caputo, J. (2003). *Against principles: A sketch of an ethics without ethics*. In E. Wyschogrod & G.P. McKenny (Eds.), *The ethical*. Oxford: Blackwell.

Coady, M., & Bloch, S. (Eds.) (1996). *Codes of ethics and the professions*. Melbourne, Australia: Melbourne University Press.

Coady, M. (1996). The moral domain of professionals. In M. Coady & S. Bloch (Eds.), *Codes of ethics and the professions*. Carlton, Victoria, Australia: Melbourne University Press.

De George, R.T. (2006). *Business ethics* (6th ed.). Upper Saddle River, New Jersey: Pearson.

Derrida, J. (1990). *Spectres of Marx: The state of the debt, the work of mourning, and the new international*. New York: Routledge.

Dunne, J. (1993). *Back to the rough ground: Practical judgement and the lure of technique*. Notre Dame, IN: University of Notre Dame Press.

Fritzsche, D.J. (2005). *Business ethics: A global and managerial perspective*. Boston: McGraw-Hill Irwin.

Grace, D., & Cohen, S. (2005). *Business ethics: Problems and cases* (3rd ed.). New York: Oxford University Press.

Halverson, R. (2004). Accessing, documenting and communicating practical wisdom: the phronesis of school leadership practice. *American Journal of Education, 111*(1). 90–121.

Harrison, J. (2001). *Ethics for Australian business*. Frenchs Forest, New South Wales: Pearson Education Australia.

Heller, A. (1985). *Beyond justice*. Oxford: Blackwell.

Heller, A. (1988). *General ethics*. Oxford: Blackwell.

Heller, A. (1990). *A philosophy of morals*. Oxford: Blackwell.

Heller, A. (1996). *An ethics of personality*. Oxford: Blackwell.

Heller, A. (1990). *A Philosophy of Morals*. Oxford: Blackwell.

Hosmer, L.T. (2002). *The ethics of management* (4th ed.). Boston: McGraw-Hill Irwin.

Macklin, R. (2003, March). Guidelines for dealing with moral conflicts in human resource management. In P. Rushbrook (Ed.), *Innovations in professional practice: Influences & perspectives — proceedings of the 2003 Continuing Professional Education (CPE) Conference.* Wagga Wagga, Australia: CSU.

Mautner, T. (1997). *Dictionary of philosophy*. Harmondsworth, England: Penguin Books.

Mellahi, K., & Wood, G. (2003). *The ethical business: Challenges and controversies*. Houndsmills, UK: Palgrave.

Shaw, W.H., & Barry, V. (2004). *Moral issues in business* (9th ed.). Belmont, CA: Thompson.

Statler, M., Roos, J., & Victor, B. (2006). Illustrating the need for practical wisdom. *International Journal of Management Concepts and Philosophy, 2*(1), 1–30.

Trevino, L.K., & Nelson, K.A. (2006). *Managing business ethics: Straight talk about how to do it right* (4th ed.). Hoboken, NJ: Wiley.

Write-St Clair, V., & Steedhouse, D. (2005). The moral context of practice and professional relationships. In G. Whiteford & V. Write-St Clair (Eds.), *Occupation & practice in context* (pp. 16–33). Sydney, Australia: Elsevier Churchill Livingstone.

The Importance of Perceived Organisational Support in Encouraging Positive Employee Discretionary Extra-Role Behaviour

Robert Sharkie

Organisations operate in all areas through people and it is their contribution that will ultimately determine the success or otherwise of the organisation. Whether employees will be predisposed to contribute to the organisation by engaging in discretionary extra-role behaviour is likely to depend on their perceptions about the supportiveness, or otherwise, of the organisational culture and the expected benefits that may flow to them from the organisation. Aselage and Eisenberger (2003) support this by their argument that employees increase their efforts to help the organisation, to the degree that the organisation is perceived to be willing, and able, to reciprocate.

The culture of the organisation will reflect the policies, practices and philosophies of management, and the tone and expression of these, and this chapter will argue that perceptions of these will influence the contributory actions of the employees. These perceptions are likely to encourage, or discourage, employees from sharing their knowledge and acting in a cooperative way.

The Importance of a Functional Employment Relationship

The foundations of functional employment relationships are that the exchanges between employees and employers are characterised by a shared understanding or mutuality of all obligations and commitments. Dabos and Rousseau (2004) suggest that the development of mutuality of understanding, between employees and employers produces not only better employment relationships, but may also improve career success on the one hand, and improved employee performance on the other.

Organisational membership encompasses both rights and protections for the individual and the organisation, according to Masterson and Stamper (2003). Organisations are owed obligations from their employees (e.g., performance and attendance) and in return employees are entitled to basic rights (e.g., safe workplaces, pay). But while these rights and protections will vary from organisation to organisation, all organisational members have some basic rights and the responsibility to deliver on their basic obligations.

Success for an organisation is therefore likely to depend on management's ability to foster the development of a culture which supports and encourages the accessing, developing and then the utilisation of the knowledge and skills of their employees to enable the organisation to build on its capabilities. Zwell (2000) argues that a successful culture in this context will be one which displays to employees that employee development is valued, and a culture that encourages highly competent employees to exercise their talents to impact positively on the organisation.

An organisation's culture will be seen as setting the conditions under which employees are expected to work and a positive culture would provide a working environment in which people are engaged, motivated and rewarded in a positive way for their contribution to the success of the organisation.

Deal and Kennedy (1982) support the argument that creating a strong organisational culture can be a significant factor in determining the extent to which employees will contribute to the organisation. Guest (1994) also supports this proposition by arguing that culture, by helping employees understand what their obligations to the organisation are, is a better motivator to perform in a cooperative way to support the organisation's interests, than would financial incentives or bureaucratic requirements.

According to Eisenberger, Huntington, Hutchison and Sowa (1986) employees will form perceptions about the organisation's policies and practices to determine the likely effect of these policies and practices on them. If the culture is perceived by the employee to be favourable to them, then the prospects for knowledge sharing and cooperation are likely to be maximised. On the other hand, if the perception is unfavourable then employees will be discouraged from participating in these activities, to the detriment of the organisation.

Axtell, Holman, Unsworth, Wall, Waterson and Harrington (2000) argued that the perception of a supportive, nonjudgmental climate would be conducive to encouraging positive cooperative actions by employees. Further, they found that employees were more likely to behave cooperatively if their ideas were positively received and not subject to ridicule.

The importance of this nonjudgmental culture was also supported by Oldham (2003), who argued that organisations need to develop a culture of sharing, but that they also needed to acknowledge both the ideas that were submitted and the person who submitted them, because this would encourage employees to share their creative ideas with others. Cabrera (2003) also argued that a nonjudgmental acceptance of an employee's contribution would be likely to encourage further contributions. In a similar way, Shalley and Perry-Smith (2001) also argued that if employees expected that their work would be critically judged, then their creative contributions were likely to be lower. Likewise Edmondson (1999) alleged that the anticipation of a critical judgment would constitute a threat to the employee's self-interest and self-esteem and result in lower contributions and in the sharing of fewer ideas.

Alternatively, treatment that greatly exceeded the organisation's obligation to an employee would have a much more favourable effect on perceived organisational support than if the obligation was just met, according to Aselage and Eisenberger (2003). In contrast, favourable treatment that an organisation was highly obliged to provide would not indicate any high level of regard for the employee, as it would be viewed as less discretionary.

The Reciprocity Norm

Employees' perceptions of perceived organisational support towards them, through the reciprocity norm, contribute to a sense of general obligation to care about the organisation and contribute to the organisation's objectives. Eisenberger, Armeli, Rexwinkel, Lynch and Rhoades (2001) found that the relationship between perceived organisational support and felt obligation towards the organisation was highest for employees with a strong exchange ideology, but also that most employees accept the reciprocity norm to some degree.

Bowen, Gilliland and Folger (1999) argue that the relationship between employer and the employee is through the psychological contract, which is an implicit agreement about what each party gives and gets from the relationship; it also embodies the implicit rules and regulations that determine the relationship. Rhoades and Eisenberger (2002) argue that it is the expectation of reciprocity that enables the employee to reconcile the differing contributions that are sought by them and by their employer.

It is important to view the psychological contract as a dynamic set of expectations (Vos, Buyens, & Schalk, 2003). The psychological contract being refined, in a sense-making process, during the socialisation period is a result of employees forming perceptions about promises made to them and their interpretations of experiences encountered in the work setting.

The key motivation for sharing knowledge and ideas and acting cooperatively was the expected reciprocity from their organisations, according to Cabrera (2003) while Wayne, Shore and Liden (1997, p. 83) state that '... employees seek a balance in their exchange relationship with the organisation, by having attitudes and behaviours commensurate with the degree of employer commitment to them as individuals'.

Employees are primarily concerned with the commitment by the organisation to them and their perception that the organisational support will potentially provide benefits to them. An assessment that the organisation values their contribution and shows an interest in their wellbeing, is likely to create an expectation of approval, monetary rewards, access to resources and respect for the employee.

Perceptions of the psychological contract will be influenced by expectations about the support likely to be given to the individual. Aselage and Eisenberger (2003) argue that individuals have distinct expectations about the level of treatment they can expect and that violations of these expectations will affect the assessment of perceived organisational support. Where expectations are that favourable treatment will be forthcoming, any violation of promises will have very detrimental effects on perceived organisational support. This is because a failure to fulfil the terms of the psychological contract conveys a low valuation of the employee's contributions and lack of concern for the employee's wellbeing (Aselage & Eisenberger, 2003). On the other hand, where expectations are lower, then the violation of these expectations will have a smaller detrimental effect on perceived organisational support.

Rousseau and Tijoriwala (1998) argue that it is an individual's perception of the psychological contract that will determine the reciprocal contribution by the employee, with repeated violations of this contract likely to result in withdrawal behaviours by the employee. Yet a build-up of confidence in this relational contract, over the longer term, is likely to lead to the continued satisfaction of the employee's wants and needs. This, in turn, is likely to increase the perception and trust that the organisation will meet its obligations and be supportive of the employee, according to Robinson and Wolfe Morrison (1995).

Guest (2002) argues that an employee's response, by way of an increased willingness to contribute, will be reflected through the psychological contract and its links to performance and hence output. The need for a worker-centred or worker-friendly approach is supported by Guest (2002) to encourage the development of trust and the consequent discretionary extra-role activities, by employees, which organisations need. This discretionary contribution will be encouraged, according to Ashforth and Saks (1996), by the reinforcement of a supportive environment, which in turn contributes to the self-worth of the employee. Grover and Crooker (1995) also found a strong connection between a worker's commitment and the demonstration by the organisation that it provided organisational support, care and concern and that the organisation was fair in its dealings with employees.

Perceived Organisational Support

Prior employment and organisational experiences help clarify an employee's perception of organisational support (Lester, Kickul, & Bergmann, 2007). These prior perceptions will be continually challenged by perceptions of current employer support for them. Perceptions that employer support is improving and obligations to them are fulfilled show to the employee that the employer values their relationship, which in turn will encourage employees to view the relationship as a continuing one.

Perceived organisational support is defined by Rhoades and Eisenberger (2002) as the view that employees form about the level of care and consideration that they see is being directed towards them by the organisation. This view is about how the organisation ' ... values their contribution and cares about their well being' (Eisenberger et al., 1986, p. 504).

Employees form a global view about the level of organisational support being offered to them, according to Rhoades and Eisenberger (2002). Eisenberger et al. (1986) argue that it is this perceived level of support which will determine the level of the employee's reciprocal contribution to the organisation. An individual's perception of this perceived support will be based on their anticipated satisfaction of their own emotional needs for approval, esteem and affiliation. This will be moderated by their assessment of the likelihood that the organisation will positively respond to greater effort by them, by adequately rewarding them for this extra effort.

Psychological contracts reside within individuals, but both firm- and societal-level factors help to frame them. Thomas, Au and Ravlin (2003) contend that although psychological contract theory is related to the willingness of employees to rely on employer promises and respond with a felt obligation in return, individual differences are likely to produce differing responses. These differences are likely to influence how concepts of the psychological contract are perceived, how violations are evaluated and what responses may occur.

Wayne, Shore and Liden (1997, p. 90) argue that '... employees who feel they have been well supported by their organisation, need to reciprocate by performing better and engaging more readily in citizenship behaviour than those who reported lower levels of perceived organisational support'. In this context, perceived organisational support therefore is a measure of the likelihood of reciprocal behaviour by an employee because, according to Goulder (1960), when one does a favour for another there is an expectation of some return in the future.

The perceived level of fair treatment was the most significant determinant of perceived organisational support according to Rhoades and Eisenberger (2002). Perceptions of fairness are closely associated with assessments of procedural justice and expectations that your opinions will be valued, your contributions recognised and your wellbeing cared for. An individual's assessment of the level of procedural justice is likely to take into account the type of controls exercised by management and the extent to which the allocation of resources and rewards are seen as discretionary and going to those whose contribution has been the greatest.

Eisenberger et al. (1990) argue that a positive assessment of perceived support from the organisation is likely to result in the following behaviours:

1. An increased conscientiousness in performing their in-role responsibility.
2. An increased desire to be involved with the organisation.

3. An increased desire to assist the organisation.

4. An increased commitment to innovative behaviour.

5. An increased contribution to spontaneous problem-solving.

6. An increased likelihood that the employee will interpret the organisation's gains and losses as their own.

7. An increased likelihood that the employee will internalise the values and norms expressed by the organisation.

Support for the above findings also comes from Shore and Tetrick (1991, p. 637) who argued that a positive assessment of perceived organisational support will have a direct influence on '... the employee's subsequent commitment to the organisation', because it engenders a perception that there is an equitable and fair relationship between the employee and the organisation. Support also comes from Eisenberger, Huntington, Hutchison and Sowa (1986) with their argument that positive assessments of perceived organisational support can increase an employee's level of obligation to engage in behaviour that supports the goals and objectives of the organisation. It is likely also that the Human Resource (HR) policies and practices of the organisation that have positively affected an employee's history of rewards, such as early job assignments and promotion, would be positive for the growing perception of perceived organisational support and on how employees feel they have been cared for and valued by the organisation.

Developing an Environment of Trust

McAllister (1995) argued that trust could be affective, as represented by a special reciprocal relationship between employees and the organisation, or cognitive trust, which is based on a judgment about management's reliability and integrity. A similar distinction was made by Dirks and Ferrin (2002) between affective/relational trust between two parties, and character/cognitive-based trust. This paper is based on a discussion of the affective/relational perceptions and its effect on an employee's predisposition to share their knowledge with others, for the benefit of the organisation, and their willingness to engage in discretionary extra-role activities.

'Trust' is defined by Cook and Wall (1980, p. 39) as '... the extent to which one is willing to ascribe good intentions and have confidence in the words and actions of other people' and is about the perceptions of the future behaviour of another person and the potential for positive benefits that may result. Tyler (2003) argues that this social capital or attitudinal approach to trust is important because of its effect on the internal motivation of the employee in positively responding to an expectation of returns or rewards from positive behaviour towards the organisation.

This social capital view of trust is important, according to Barney and Hansen (1994), because it can result in positive social outcomes as a result of improved individual or group contributions to the organisation and potential competitive advantage. Nahapiet and Ghoshal (1998) also support this view that the development of social capital can provide a basis for trust, and the dependent cooperation and collective input which can assist the organisation to achieve its objectives.

A failure to develop an environment of trust between employees and the organisation is likely to involve the organisation in high transaction costs, according to Beccerra and Gupta (1999). This is likely because, in the absence of a high trust relationship, management is likely to be faced with considerable costs, time and energy in seeking the compliance of employees. The importance of obtaining support from employees, rather than trying to shape their behaviour via incentives or sanctions, received strong support from Tyler (2003, p. 563) who claims that 'Attitudes, commitment and intrinsic motivation are the most important predictors of extra-role behaviour'.

Lester, Kickul and Bergmann (2007) suggest that the important notion of continuing support for employees is important for employee reciprocation will lead management to ensure that organisational changes, and their effect on the psychological contract, are clearly explained and understood. This need for explanation is extremely important and also problematic when unfulfilled obligations by management result from situational variables beyond the organisation's control. Under these circumstances, organisations still need to provide support for employees. Environmental uncertainty, leading to such changes as downsizing or restructuring, can result in the erosion of trust and the belief that the organisation cares and shows loyalty to employees. The development of perceptions of employee support will be improved if employees take enough care to ensure that adequate information, about the reasons behind decisions, is communicated to employees. Obviously, this communication will be more effective and believable where management are considered to be credible and then provide legitimate explanations for their decisions.

Relational/Affective Trust

Konovsky and Pugh (1994) argue that relational or affective trust is likely to be developed from the perception of care and concern shown to an employee by the management of an organisation and from the subsequent reciprocal actions of the employee. Where there is a perception that the management are interested in the wellbeing of the employee, then the employee is likely to respond by showing an increased willingness to involve themselves in discretionary extra-role activities. Trust develops from the relational aspects of the interaction between the two parties and operates as a social exchange process (Whitener, Brodt, Korsgaard, & Werner 1998) over and above the terms of the normal commercial employment contract. Blau (1964) argues that this high-quality relationship incorporates the psychological contract elements of trust, goodwill and mutual obligation.

A positive relational/affective trust is likely to lead to improvements in job-related outcomes, such as job performance, according to Dirks and Ferrin (2002), because this trust will create an environment where people will be willing to respond outside the traditional employment relationship. Eisenberger, Fasalo and Davis-La Mastro (1990) argue that the degree of response by an employee will be influenced by that employee's characteristics, their prior work experience and features of the job. Important in an individual's response, according to Shore and Shore (1995) will also be the perception that the care and consideration is given in a discretionary way and that it is given as a form of reward for performance and that it is not given to those whose contribution has been negligible.

The perceived fairness of the decision-making process, as it affects an individual employee, is likely to be an important influence on how that employee assesses the perceived organisational support, according to Tyler and Blader (2000). They argue that people are particularly concerned, in decision-making, about whether employees are seen to have been treated with dignity and whether there is a perception that resources have been distributed fairly. These are considered to be of higher importance than the more practical result of the outcome for the individual, or achieving the result the employee might have liked. This procedural justice aspect is also highlighted by Rhoades, Eisenberger and Armeli (2001) who argue that the social or interactional justice aspects are of prime importance to individuals.

Trust in Supervisors and Managers

Shanock and Eisenberger (2006) suggest that organisations should cultivate perceived organisational support of supervisors, because this is likely to have an effect on lower level employees. Positive perceptions of perceived organisational support by supervisors are likely to lead to supervisors reciprocating this favourable support by increasing their support towards their subordinates. Shanock and Eisenberger (2006) argue that this increased perception, by employees, of better support given to them by supervisors, is likely to increase employee perceptions of organisational support and, as a consequence, increase their in-role performance and extra-role behaviour.

Eisenberger et al. (1986) argue that employees see supervisors and managers as representatives of top management and form perceptions about the organisation, based on the actions of the supervisors and managers. The perceptions they form about the level of care affecting their wellbeing, and the level of appreciation for their efforts given by supervisors and management, will be transposed to a judgment that they have received favourable or unfavourable treatment from the organisation.

According to Amabile (2005), the behaviours by supervisors and managers that best promotes feelings of leader support are: demonstrating a receptiveness to employee's ideas, giving assistance during stressful periods, showing respect for the feelings of employees and refraining from taking action which has the effect of reducing the employee autonomy. This approach is supported by Konovsky and Pugh (1994) who argue that employees may be willing to go beyond their role requirements, provided there is trust that the supervisor or manager is demonstrating appreciation of, and care towards, the employee.

Tan and Tan (2000) found that there was a significant positive relationship between the level of trust and the level of innovative behaviour. They argued for a connection between trust and the amount of autonomy given to employees to explore new ways of doing things. This was also supported by Ross and LaCroix (1996) who found that there was a strong correlation between trust in supervisors/managers and the extent of risk-taking by employees.

Conclusion

The adaptation process of psychological contract development is likely to be both unilateral and reciprocal. Vos, Buyens and Schalk (2003) argue that unilateral adaptation is used by employees to reassess and modify their expectations and obligations under their psychological contract, based on their perceptions of the comparison of promises made to them and employee inducements actually received. They then, in turn, vary their future promises of contributions to the organisation based on what they had contributed in the past.

On the other hand, changes in their understanding of expectations and contributions in the psychological contract can be based on a reciprocal adaptation process. Under this process, employees vary their planned contributions to the organisation based on the level of inducements they receive from their employer.

Employees continually monitor and respond to changes in the level of perceived organisational support and perceived commitment to them, according to Rousseau and Tijoriwala (1998). A perception that the organisation is supportive is likely to be the basis for assessing whether they feel the organisation cares about their welfare and values their contribution. A positive assessment of perceived organisational support is likely to encourage the employee to identify with the organisation and encourage a willingness to commit to the organisational objectives by showing a willingness to engage in discretionary extra-role behaviour. The relational/affective involvement with the organisation, as has been argued, will be the moderator of the level of employee satisfaction in terms of meeting their own needs for recognition, approval and influence, and the expectation that benefits will flow to them from their contribution.

Kerkhof, Winder and Klandermans (2003, p. 627), following research on employees of a Works Council, argued that

> ... a relational model of trust predicts that trust is enhanced when management shows respect and values the Works Council and its members by giving them information on time and by dealing with Council members in a friendly and respectful way.

This chapter has argued that an employee's perception of the support given to them by the organisation will be strongly related to the reciprocation by employees engaging in activities that are directed to assist the organisation in achieving its objectives. The extent of this reciprocation, by the employee, will be based on their assessment of how successfully management communicates to employees that they, the employees, are important and are valued members of the organisation.

References

Amabile, T. (2005, July 12). Creativity: it's all about routine. *The Australian Financial Review*, p. 59.

Aselage, J., & Eisenberger, R. (2003). Perceived organisational support and the psychological contracts: A theoretical integration. *Journal of Organisational Behaviour, 24,* 491–509.

Ashforth, B., & Saks, A. (1996). Socialisation tactics: Longitudinal effects on newcomer adjustment. *Academy of Management Journal, 39,* 149–178.

Axtell, C., Holman, D., Unsworth, K., Wall, T., Waterson, P., & Harrington, E. (2000). Shopfloor innovation: Facilitating the suggestion and implementation of ideas. *Journal of Occupation and Organisational Psychology, 73,* 264–285.

Barney, J., & Hansen, M. (1994). Trustworthiness as a source of competitive advantage. *Strategic Management Journal, 15,* 175–190.

Beccerra, M., & Gupta, A. (1999). Trust within the organisation: Integrating the trust literature with agency theory and transaction costs economics. *Public Administration Quarterly, 23*(2), 177–203.

Blau, P. (1964). *Exchange and power in social life.* New York: Wiley.

Bowen, D., Gilliland, S., & Folger, R. (1999), HRM and service fairness: How being fair with employees spills over customers. *Organisational Dynamics, 27*(3), 7–23.

Cabrera, E. (2003, June). Socio-psychological aspects of knowledge sharing in organisations. In M. Morley (Ed.) *Edited proceedings of International Human Resource Management Conference. International HR Conference,* Limerick, Ireland: University of Limerick.

Cook, J., & Wall, T. (1980). New work attitude measures of trust, organisational commitment and personal need non-fulfilment. *Journal of Occupational Psychology, 53,* 39–52.

Dabos, G., & Rousseau, D. (2004). Mutuality and reciprocity in the psychological contracts of employees and employers. *Journal of Applied Psychology, 89*(1), 52–72.

Deal, T., & Kennedy, A. (1982). *Corporate culture: The rites and rituals of corporate life.* Reading MA: Addison-Wesley.

Dirks, K., & Ferrin, D. (2002). Trust in leadership: meta-analytic findings and implications for research and practice. *Journal of Applied Psychology, 87*(4), 611–628.

Edmondson, A. (1999). Psychological safety and learning behaviour in work teams. *Administrative Science Quarterly, 44,* 350–383.

Eisenberger, R., Armeli, S., Rexwinkel, B., Lynch, P., & Rhoades, L. (2001). Reciprocation of perceived organisational support. *Journal of Applied Psychology, 86*(1), 42–51.

Eisenberger, R., Fasalo, P., & Davis-LaMastro, V. (1990). Perceived organisational support and employee diligence, commitment, and innovation. *Journal of Applied Psychology, 75*(1), 51–59.

Eisenberger, R., Huntington, R., Hutchison, S., & Sowa, D. (1986). Perceived organisational support. *Journal of Applied Psychology, 71*(3), 500–507.

Goulder, A. (1960). The norm of reciprocity: A preliminary statement. *American Sociological Review, 25,* 161–178.

Grover, S., & Crooker, K. (1995). Who appreciates family-responsive HR policies? The impact of family-friendly policies on the organisational attachment of parents and non-parents. *Personal Psychology, 48*, 271–288.

Guest, D. (1994). Organisational psychology and HRM: Towards a European approach. *European Work and Organisational Psychologist, 4*(3), 251–270.

Guest, D. (2002). HRM corporate performance and employee wellbeing: Building the worker into HRM. *Journal of Industrial Relations, 44*, 335–358.

Kerkhof, P., Winder, A., & Klandermans, B. (2003). Instrumental and relational determinants of trust in management among members of works councils. *Personnel Review, 32*(5), 623–637.

Konovsky, M., & Pugh, D. (1994). Citizenship behaviour and social exchange. *Academy of Management Journal, 37*, 656–669.

Lester, S., Kickul, J., & Bergmann, T. (2007). Managing employee perceptions of the psychological contract over time: The role of employer social accounts and contract fulfilment. *Journal of Organisational Behaviour, 28*, 191–208.

McAllister, D. (1995). Affect- and cognition-based trust as foundations for interpersonal cooperation in organisations. *Academy of Management Journal, 38*(1), 24–60.

Masterson, S., & Stamper, C. (2003). Perceived organisational membership: An aggregate framework representing the employee–organisation relationship. *Journal of Organisational Behaviour, 24*, 473–490.

Nahapiet, J., & Ghoshal, S. (1998). Social capital, intellectual capital and the organisational advantage. *Academy of Management Review, 23*, 242–266.

Oldham, G. (2003). Stimulating and supporting creativity in organisations. In S. Jackson, M. Hitt, & A. Denise (Eds.), *Managing knowledge for sustained competitive advantage.* San Francisco: Jossey Bass.

Rhoades, L., & Eisenberger, R. (2002). Perceived organisational support: A review of the literature. *Journal of Applied Psychology, 87*(4), 698–714.

Rhoades, L., Eisenberger, R., & Armeli, S. (2001). Affective commitment to the organisation: The contribution of perceived organisational support. *Journal of Applied Psychology, 86*(5), 825–836.

Robinson, S., & Wolfe Morrison, E. (1995). Psychological contracts and organisational citizenship behaviour: The effect of unfulfilled obligations on civic virtue behaviour. *Journal of Organisational Behaviour, 16*, 289–298.

Ross, W., & LaCroix, J. (1996). Multiple meanings of trust in negotiation theory and research: A literature review and integrative model. *The International Journal of Conflict Management, 7*(4), 314–359.

Rousseau, D., & Tijoriwala, S. (1998). Assessing psychological contracts: Issues, alternatives and measures. *Journal of Organisational Behaviour, 19*, 679–695.

Shalley, C., & Perry-Smith, J. (2001). Effects of socio-psychological factors on creative performance: The role of information and controlling expected evaluation and modelling experience. *Organisational Behaviour and Human Decision Processes, 84*, 1–22.

Shanock, L., & Eisenberger, R. (2006). When supervisors feel supported: Relationships with subordinate's perceived supervisor support, perceived organisational support and performance. *Journal of Applied Psychology, 91*(3), 689–695.

Shore, L., & Shore, T. (1995). Perceived organisational support and organisational justice. In R. Cropanzano & K. Kacmar (Eds.), *Organisational politics, justice and support: managing social climate at work* (pp. 149–164). Westport, CN: Quorum Press.

Shore, L., & Tetrick, L. (1991). A construct validity study of the survey of perceived organisational support. *Journal of Applied Psychology, 76*(5), 637–643.

Tan, H., & Tan, C. (2000). Toward the differentiation of trust in supervisor and trust. *Organisation, Genetic, Social, and General Psychology Monographs, 126*(2), 241–260.

Thomas, D., Au, K., & Ravlin, E. (2003). Cultural variation and the psychological contract. *Journal of Organisational Behaviour, 24*, 451–471.

Tyler, T. (2003). Trust within organisations. *Personnel Review, 32*(5), 556–568.

Tyler, T., & Blader, S. (2000). *Cooperation in groups.* Philadelphia: Psychology Press.

Vos, A., Buyens, D., & Schalk, R. (2003). Psychological contract development during organisational socialisation: Adaptation to reality and the role of reciprocity. *Journal of Organisational Behaviour, 24*, 537–559.

Wayne, S., Shore, L., & Liden, R. (1997). Perceived organisational support and leader-member exchange: A social exchange perspective. *Academy of Management Journal, 40*(1), 82–111.

Whitener, E., Brodt, S., Korsgaard, M., & Werner, J. (1998). Managers as indicators of trust: An exchange relationship for understanding managerial trustworthy behaviour. *Academy of Management Journal, 23*, 513–530.

Zwell, M. (2000). *Creating a culture of excellence.* New York: John Wiley.

Communities of Practice, Clusters or Networks? Prospects for Collaborative Business Arrangements in the Mining and Engineering Sector, Central Western New South Wales

Mark Frost

Judith Crockett

Background

In **December 2001** the local government areas of Orange, Cabonne and Blayney (OCB), located in the Central West of New South Wales, prepared a Local Enterprise Development Strategy, the underlying goal of which was the promotion of sustainable economic development within the OCB region through the expansion of existing business and the attraction of new businesses and investment.

In 2002/03 the OCB received funding under the Commonwealth Regional Assistance Program to undertake research on the regional economy, identify existing industry collaboration and undertake a SWOT analysis of potential cluster models, that is, an analysis of the strengths, weaknesses, opportunities, and limitations of the particular event. The Western Research Institute was commissioned to undertake the study; their report was released in June 2003 and encompassed an overview of the economic performance and trends within the OCB region and a brief macro-level analysis of the environmental services, transport and logistics, and viticulture industry networks.

Additional funding was received from the State and Regional Development Corporation in October 2003 to conduct more specific research into the mining and engineering industry network. This involved the mapping of key network participants, identifying skill strengths and gaps, examining the recruitment and retention of labour, and classifying relationships between sector participants.

In November 2003, the authors were invited to assist the OCB in further investigating a variety of industry network models and to advise on the development and implementation of a preferred model for the OCB region. Preliminary work by the authors included a review of literature on industry collaborative models, and the preparation of a series of discussion papers on potential collaborative projects before the investigation into the viability of a community of practice/network/cluster within the mining and engineering industry network.

Literature Review

The literature abounds with discussions of impediments to regional growth and development in Australia and elsewhere, including a lack of access to skills, especially skilled labour; a lack of awareness of new business opportunities; underdeveloped business skills; a low level of strategic leadership and external business networking in regions; a general failure to identify opportunities that enhance the existing business, which also have multiplier effects to the region; and a lack of supportive infrastructure (Department of Transport and Regional Services [DOTARS], 2002). 'Clusters', 'networks' and, more recently, 'communities of practice' have been identified in much of this work as three forms of collaborative business activity that may assist in overcoming these impediments.

Definitions of a *cluster* vary significantly, but can, for the purposes of this discussion, be summarised as being geographical concentrations of interconnected companies and institutions in particular fields that are large enough to generate externalities such as economies of scale (Porter, 1998, 2001; Rosenfeld, 2005a; DOTARS, 2002). Cluster participants can include suppliers of specialised inputs, specialised infrastructure, extend downstream to channels and customers, extend laterally to manufacturers of complementary products and to companies in industries related by skills, technologies or common inputs (Porter, 1998). A cluster's boundaries are defined by linkages and complementarities across industries and institutions that are most important to competition, for example, they are an alternative way of organising the value chain that results in improved access to suppliers, services and labour markets (Porter, 1998; Rosenfeld, 2005a, 2005b). Theoretically, therefore, the key advantage of a cluster lies in its ability to demonstrate greater gains and incentives than is possible for a business operating in isolation.

Strong social capital is considered pivotal to successful cluster establishment and perpetuation; that is, there must be high levels of trust, reciprocity, cooperation, common interests and values (Braun et al 2005; Porter, 1998, 2000; Romanelli & Khessina, 2005; Rosenfeld, 2005a; Rylatt, 2003). This capital may be historical and already exist between individuals or different firms or may need to be fostered, particularly as new businesses are attracted to the cluster. Links with local educational institutions, particularly universities and vocational training providers (e.g., TAFE NSW) have also been shown to contribute favourably to successful cluster development.

The literature (e.g., Fingleton et al., 2005; Morosini, 2004) also identifies certain costs associated with clusters that sometimes serve as an obstacle to collaboration and the generation of innovation. These include increased competition and congestion in terms of supply and demand, high rates of employee turnover and high rates of noncooperation between firms. Where clusters lack focus, critical mass and social capital, collaboration is unlikely. This failure, at least in an Australian context, has been attributed to initial scepticism and lack of trust among participants (Braun et al., 2005) particularly over the sharing of knowledge.

Networks can be defined as groups of companies joining together to achieve economic goals they would not otherwise be able to achieve (Rosenfeld, 2005a). That is, they 'network to produce more complex goods, extend their market outreach, acquire costly resources or services, or simply reduce costs' (Rosenfeld, 2005a, p. 5) in a structured process that engages industry leaders and active industry players to the extent that they take responsibility for the future of their industry and can develop initiatives to accelerate growth. As with clusters, cooperation is viewed as a key criterion for success. However, in networks these arrangements are often formalised through legally binding arrangements and conditions (Rosenfeld, 2005a, 2005b). The most important trait of a network appears to be a relatively homogenous system of values and views expressing an ethic of work and activity, and of reciprocity and change (Rosenfeld, 2005a).

In contrast to the expanse of cluster linkages and the formality of networks, *communities of practice* (COP) are groups of firms who share a concern, a set of problems, or a passion about a topic and who deepen their knowledge and expertise by interacting on an ongoing basis (Mason, Castleman, & Parker, 2005). A COP may exist for one issue or several issues, on a defined or unlimited basis and have a formal or informal structure. Whatever the structure and function, the outcome will be a 'collective knowledge base' (Brown & Duguid, 1998, p. 96) contributing to significant innovation within the community (Anand, 2007; Lindkvist, 2005; Orr, 1996; Wenger, McDermott, & Snyder, 2002). Members of the COP act as holders of valuable innovation creating tacit knowledge with norms of reciprocity and trust, but their embeddedness prevents this knowledge from being available to outsiders. The turnover of staff between firms ensures that information embodied in one firm is moved to the next and, in the process, enhances the various firms and the wider region (Mason, Castleman, & Parker, 2005), a belief quite contrary to cluster theory.

It is not difficult to see why the difference between clusters, networks and communities of practice are often misused and misunderstood (Rosenfeld, 2005b). All three approaches require trust and reciprocity between participants which builds upon existing social structures and values, although at different levels and intensities.

Clusters and networks represent a means for companies to acquire economies of scale that are external to their firm, characterised by dense collaborative social networks with access to skilled labour and proximity to research centres, yet they exhibit quite dissimilar economic structures and respond very differently to public sector approaches. Clusters are more likely to be concentrations of inter-connected companies and institutions, whereas networks may be spread over a wider geographical area. Networks tend to be the more formalised of the three approaches, while clusters can include both vertical and horizontal integration against the dominant horizontal focus of the other two. On the other hand, com-munities of practice are more focused on knowledge sharing and are more 'fluid' than clusters or networks.

All three collaborative arrangements represent possible opportunities for regional development in Australia. The results that follow explore the viability of the three approaches from the perspective of businesses within the mining and engineering sector in the OCB region.

Project Methodology

Aims and Objectives of Project

The primary objective of the pilot study was to conduct research in the mining and engineering sector of the OCB region that would identify the existence of any economic and social interaction and ascertain the extent to which businesses within the sector saw a need for some form of structured interaction. The research also aimed to determine the potential for mining and engineering industry collaboration, identify a preferred model of collaboration, and establish expectations of potential participants and their perceived drivers of success.

To achieve these outcomes, the project addressed four core questions:

- How far has the mining and engineering sector progressed in such development?
- What is their current level of interest in industry collaboration?
- If such collaborative arrangements were to be established, what would be their preferred structure and function?
- What roles would the various participants, including the councils, local industry bodies and sector businesses, play in the establishment and ongoing growth of the preferred model?

This chapter focuses on the key themes emerging from answers provided to the second and third questions — current levels of collaboration and interaction, preferred structure of future collaborative arrangements, and implications of future collaboration for the respondent's business, for the sector and for the region. Other outcomes of the project are reported elsewhere (Frost & Crockett, 2006).

Methodology

Given the need to obtain an understanding of how the business was operating, together with an in-depth appreciation of the business's interaction with other companies in a hitherto under-researched environment, the project was necessarily of an explorative nature. Bearing this in mind, a survey was developed that asked quantitative and qualitative questions on the nature of the business; current workforce issues; existing industry models; future plans for the business, including impediments to further growth; and perceptions of future networks including advantages and disadvantages, preferred structure and willingness to participate.

The key benefits of the methodology lay in its ability to combine research rigour with the exploration of practical outcomes and recommendations through the identification of key attitudinal and skill drivers, motivators and barriers for successful implementation. The approach also enabled the project team to develop a deeper understanding of the various learning styles, group dynamics and personality types evident within a cluster that could be incorporated into the design of future network formation.

Research Process

Approval for the project was obtained from the Charles Sturt University Human Ethics Committee. Based on the information gained from the existing OCB database, all businesses within the Orange, Cabonne and Blayney shires belonging to the mining and engineering sector were identified — a total of 43 enterprises. A survey was forwarded to each business's manager by post.

Within two weeks of dispatch, the project officer rang the manager and arranged a time to go through the survey over the phone. The project officer subsequently completed the interview, then coded and inputted the data into Microsoft Excel. Completed surveys were received from 13 respondents, thereby providing a 30% response rate.

Results

Overview of Participating Businesses

All businesses involved in this study were engaged in one or more aspects of engineering, with the vast majority located in Orange LGA, the main local regional centre. Sourcing of raw materials, staff and business were also largely domiciled in this centre. The businesses varied in size from sole trader with no staff to those with more than 75 staff. The majority of businesses employed 10 or fewer staff.

Noticeable by their absence were the local mining companies contacted as potential participants and businesses located in Blayney. When asked to assess the level of competition between the respondent's business and other businesses within the sector, participants reported a lack of direct competition between participant businesses in terms of output, but direct competition in terms of labour and resources.

Seventy-five per cent of responding businesses indicated a shortage of labour, particularly skilled labour. The reasons given for these skill gaps were many, the most common being staff moving to other jobs within the mining and engineering sector (notably to the main mining companies). The costs associated with loss of staff included loss of knowledge, loss of experience and cost of training new staff. On the other hand, benefits of innovation and knowledge transfer through new staff were also identified.

Future Plans for Business Growth and Current Impediments

Seventy-five per cent of participating businesses were planning to expand their businesses over the next 5 years within the OCB region and the wider Central West and, to a lesser extent, into the remainder of the state, interstate and overseas. This will have major implications for employment (i.e., it is likely to increase) and continuing difficulties can be expected in sourcing raw materials, particularly within the region.

A number of impediments to growth were identified including competition, lack of capital, lack of skilled staff, pending retirement and lack of access to markets. Competition at various levels of the value chain was the most frequently identified problem.

Participating businesses identified three key areas of assistance that would be of benefit to growing their businesses: changes in government policy, improved education and labour supply, and assistance with marketing. Industry networking was identified as a means of addressing all of these issues.

Current Use of Collaborative Arrangements

A variety of approaches to address local-, regional- and globally-based competitive issues were already in use, with ten businesses engaged in some form of collaborative arrangement with other businesses within the mining and engineering sector or in support industries. All arrangements were related to the supply of goods. The formality of the collaboration varied between businesses, from a 'gentleman's agreement' to formal contracts. Fourteen of these business collaborations (83% of all current collaborations) had been operating for more than four years and were largely related to businesses of a similar size and structure within the Orange district.

Preferred Structure and Function

The majority of respondents (70%) favoured continuation or expansion of ongoing collaborative arrangements but there was no consensus on how such an arrangement should operate in terms of formality/informality, reflecting the different expectations of the potential participants. Those preferring less formality were more likely to wish to belong to a cluster, while those hoping for greater formality believed they may be happier with a networking arrangement.

There was considerable agreement over what future collaboration would actually do, including assistance with marketing, access to communication (as well as the establishment of a database and website), sharing labour, sharing machinery and staff recruitment. Such advantages can be found in both networks and clusters.

There was also considerable agreement over what a community/network/cluster should *not* be like. It was important that the preferred model not take up too much time. Concern was also shown over potential threats to competitiveness, particularly in terms of 'stealing' personnel, products and/or ideas, and what happens if conflict develops between participating businesses. Given that competitiveness and labour shortage were identified as the most likely impediments to further business growth, this result is not unexpected.

External Involvement in Collaboration

Although support for local government involvement in the establishment of collaborative arrangements was given by the majority of respondents, there was little willingness to engage state and/or federal government departments in any initiative. There was some interest in linking business with the local universities and training institutions; however, there was considerable resentment of Technical and Further Education (TAFE) shown in a number of responses.

Perceived Implications of Future Collaboration for Respondent's Business

Respondents were asked in what ways a future network might provide their business with assistance. Responses fell into six main themes — marketing, communication access, lobbying, sharing labour, sharing machinery and recruitment of staff.

The potential value of a future network in terms of enhanced marketing was highlighted in a number of responses. These quotes are typical:

> Making people more aware of what capabilities the firm has.
>
> Knowledge of the mining sector's development strategy . . .
>
> Understanding the market . . .
>
> Information gained before it hits the rest of the market place . . .
>
> The business could be listed on a network — bit like the Yellow Pages® but in a smaller form. Perhaps firm could be listed like the Yellow Pages® under skills . . .
>
> More exposure . . .

The positive implications of a network on alleviating labour and capital shortages were also identified:

> [I'd] hope to reduce imported goods through group support . . .

> [sharing] specialised machinery . . .

> Maybe there are people in this area that could help me out — could get suppliers here in the Central West. Might be able to access other people that we are not currently aware of. [It's an] evolving process. Would like to see something come of the study — strong local production facilities — support in the local area would be good . . .

> Buying materials in bulk — how would this be managed? Shared insurance decreases costs. Would have to be a benefit or not worthwhile . . .

> Reduced duplication of expensive equipment and tools between competitors . . .

In terms of lobbying, a networking group could provide a clear voice to local and state government, while from a perspective of communications and information access, a group might provide shared intelligence. One respondent indicated a networking group should have a role in 'creat[ing] a recruitment strategy for the region...'.

From a more negative perspective, one respondent suggested 'networking would only work if not the same business ... competition if different doesn't help'. It may help with advertising 'as long as business is different ...'. Another observed potential difficulties with 'bitchiness between businesses ...'!

Implications of Collaborative Arrangements for Mining and Engineering Sector

What of the potential advantages of a new networking arrangement for the regional mining and engineering sector? Two key themes can be identified in responses, planning for the future, for example:

> greater overview of the future and the direction the future holds ...

> attract other employers/businesses ...

and sharing workload and other problems.

> bigger work could be done here instead of having to outsource to companies that could handle the larger workload ...

> more efficiency — quality of work completed ...

> a shared approach to solving common problems ...

> it may well offer pooling of resources and more knowledge and use of existing facilities. This could also be a threat if used incorrectly by participants ...

Two respondents identified potential disadvantages of networking for the sector, the 'pooling of knowledge could be used inappropriately', and 'they could steal more of our tradesmen ...'

Implications of Collaborative Arrangements for OCB Region

Several advantages/benefits to the OCB region of establishing a network were identified in responses, all related to improved opportunities for regional development. The following comments are representative of this view:

> Increased turnover ...
>
> More business ...
>
> Labour may move to area ...
>
> Local facilities — support in the area — better to have it locally looked after — build up the region better than outsourcing from Sydney. Sydney still has a big pull on Orange. All materials come from Sydney ...
>
> Infrastructure requirements, increased wealth, increased skills opportunity for school leavers ...
>
> More things happening can only help the region. What happens to the region when the mine closes? ...
>
> Resource sharing could make the region stronger and more cost effective ...
>
> Promoting the region as a great place to live ...

Overall, participants' responses to this question were consistent with the advantages that were identified for the respondents' businesses, including the provision and sharing of specialised machinery, assisting peak workload pressures and when additional technical assistance is required. No regional disadvantages were identified. However, one respondent believed a network would have no regional impact and would not bring in additional work. There was no evidence to suggest that businesses of a particular size were more likely than any other to be in favour of a particular collaborative model.

Discussion and Conclusion

The advantages of collaboration identified by respondents are consistent with those noted in the literature (Braun, McRae-Williams, & Lowe, 2005; DOTARS, 2002; Fingleton, Igliori, & Moore, 2005; Porter, 1998, 2000) including improved marketing, economies of scale and alleviation of labour and capital shortages. These, along with other advantages (including lobbying), suggest that characteristics of all three collaborative models are viewed favourably by the respondent businesses — no model is likely to suffice on their own. It appears that participant expectations of networking are somewhat similar to the theoretical definition and characteristics of networking in that the key requirements of any enhanced association between businesses in the sector are for extending market outreach, acquiring costly resources and cost reduction. On the other hand, other expected outcomes from networking lay in improved access to labour markets and suppliers, and their differing perceptions of the importance of membership, characteristics normally attached to clusters.

The literature suggests that it is difficult to initiate collaborative arrangements between businesses from scratch, particularly networks, unless social and regional embeddedness can be achieved and unless social capital exists. Indeed, Porter (1998) warns that that regional business development policy that targets particular businesses or industries through use of incentives to attract them to less-developed areas is flawed where local expertise and support infrastructure is lacking. This certainly appears to be the case in the mining and engineering sector in OCB, where a lengthy list of concerns related to 'sharing information' is testament to low levels of social capital within the sector. This lack of trust extends to the local vocational training providers, who might, according to the literature, normally be expected to participate closely in successful collaborative arrangements.

The pilot study faced a number of challenges in its implementation, including limited and incomplete information on sector participants. Second, the wide range of business organisations — from sole traders employing no or small numbers of staff, to publicly listed companies — made comparative data analysis difficult. Third, the boundaries of the existing networks were unclear; it was difficult to determine whether a business was a sector participant as opposed to one which provided a service to the sector. Fourth, a lack of participation from mining companies, despite their being dominant participants in the sector, has potentially confounded the results. Their absence was disappointing in that mining businesses were identified in the earlier research by OCB as major employers of labour within the shires, particularly vulnerable to labour shortages, and most likely to draw staff from smaller participants in the mining and engineering sector. Unravelling the complexity of having one or two dominant participants in the sector apparently unwilling to engage in networking, is of likely to be of significance. Finally, it was not easy to determine the extent to which support for networking as a general reference to collaboration was support for 'cluster' development or 'communities of practice'.

Bearing in mind participant responses and the constraints identified above there is much room for further research. Additional work is needed to identify a structure of association that best meets the needs of participants. In this context, it appears that successful networking (perhaps including cluster development) will require, at the very least, an in-depth qualitative study looking at factors underpinning existing conflict within the mining and engineering sector.

Further exploration of other ways in which business owners can be assisted in overcoming key impediments to growth is also required. For example, they may be able to draw upon existing financial capital illustrated in low debt/equity ratios. Further research needs to be undertaken to explore reasons why staff move between jobs; if 'poaching' between businesses is apparent, this is likely to pose a significant threat to the establishment of trust between businesses so essential to successful collaborative arrangements. Clarification of factors underpinning shortage of skilled staff and access to appropriate training is also critical given the key differences that staffing issues play in the collaborative models under consideration.

Where to from here? The development of a medium- to long- term (five to seven year) strategy for achieving cultural change in the mining and engineering sector, incorporating plans to enhance social capital within the sector and in line with the results of the study outlined above, is required. Although key to improving the trust and reciprocity so critical to successful cross-sector collaboration, the establishment of such a strategy is likely to be extremely challenging. It is possible that the OCB councils may have a role to play in enhancing social capital, ideally working with members of the sector.

Whatever model and strategy is decided upon to achieve enhanced collaboration it must acknowledge that a long-term commitment will be required. Change will not happen overnight. There remains much foundational work to be done before it is likely that any innovative collaborative business development approach will succeed in the mining and engineering sector in OCB.

References

Anand, N. (2007). 'Knowledge-based innovation: Emergence and embedding of new practice areas in management consulting firms. *Academy of Management Journal, 50*(2), 406–428.

Braun, P., McRae-Williams, P., & Lowe, J. (2005). Small business clustering: Accessing knowledge through local networks? *Refereed Conference Proceedings, Beyond Cluster—Current Practices and Future Strategies.* Ballarat, Australia: Centre of Regional Innovation and Competitiveness.

Brown, J., & Duguid, P. (1998). Organizing knowledge. *California Management Review, 40*(3), 90–111.

Department of Transport and Regional Services. (2002). *Regional business development literature review.* Melbourne, Australia: SGS Economics and Planning.

Fingleton, B., Igliori, D., & Moore, B. (2005). Cluster dynamics: new evidence and projections for computing services in Great Britain. *Journal of Regional Science, 45*(2), 283–311.

Frost, M., & Crockett, J. (2006, September). *Challenges in using networks and clusters to achieve innovation in contemporary business: A pilot study of a mining and engineering cluster, Orange, Cabonne and Blayney Shires.* Paper presented at 3rd International Conference on Contemporary Business, Leura, Blue Mountains, Australia.

Lindkvist, L. (2005). Knowledge communities and knowledge collectivities: A typology of knowledge work in groups. *Journal of Management Studies, 42*(6), 1189–1210.

Mason, C., Castleman, T., & Parker, C. (2005). Can knowledge management save regional development? *Refereed Conference Proceedings, Beyond Cluster — Current Practices and Future Strategies.* Ballarat, Australia: Centre of Regional Innovation and Competitiveness.

Morosini, P.(2004). Industrial clusters, knowledge integration and performance. *World Development, 32*(2), 305–326.

Orr, J. (1996). *Talking about machines.* Ithaca, NY: ILR Press.

Porter, M. (1998). Clusters and the new economics of competition. *Harvard Business Review, 76*(6), 77–90.

Porter, M. (2001). *Clusters of innovation: Regional foundations of US competitiveness.* Washington, DC: Council on Competitiveness.

Romanelli, E., & Khessina, O. (2005). Regional industrial identity: Cluster configurations and economic development. *Organization Science, 16*(4), 344–358.

Rosenfeld, S. (2005a). Industry clusters: Business choice, policy outcomes or branding strategy. *Journal of New Business Ideas and Trends, 3*(2), 4–13.

Rosenfeld, S. (2005b). Industry clusters: Business choice, policy outcome, or branding strategy? *Refereed Conference Proceedings, Beyond Cluster—Current Practices and Future Strategies.* Ballarat, Australia: Centre of Regional Innovation and Competitiveness.

Rylatt, A. (2003). *Winning the knowledge game: A smarter strategy for better business in Australian and New Zealand.* North Ryde, Australia: McGraw Hill.

Wenger, E., McDermott, R., & Snyder, W. (2002). *Cultivating communities of practice: A guide to managing knowledge.* Boston: Harvard Business School Press.

Time to Take Another Look?
The Mentoring Option
for Work–Life Balance

Pamela Mathews

Stacey Jenkins

The increased complexities and pressures of modern life, combined with attempts to balance both work and life commitments, have culminated in a rethinking of both how to improve the quality, efficiency and commitment of employees and how to provide a more work–life friendly work environment. To date, no one single answer has been able to address these issues. However, through a combination of actions, activities and programs many organisations have been able to improve aspects of work–life balance for their employees. This chapter proposes that the use of mentoring adds a further dimension to the work–life balance repertoire by offering ways to reduce the impact of work issues and concerns.

To accomplish this, this chapter will first discuss the work–life balance concept, the work–life balance approaches adopted by organisations and their experiences to date, and explore the notion of developing further work–life balance approaches. This will be followed by an examination of the concept of mentoring, the perceived benefits of mentoring programs, and provide some examples of organisations that have used mentoring to address specific concerns. The final section will explore the notion that mentoring programs could be used as a means of addressing some work–life balance issues; perhaps even helping to minimise work–life balance concerns that are not able to be adequately addressed by other approaches. It is not intended, within this chapter, to present a model for developing mentoring for work–life balance, but merely to introduce an idea that might be appropriate for discussion and debate. Establishing such a program would involve considerable work and commitment from all those involved, but could serve as a useful means of addressing many organisational and individual concerns.

Achieving Work–Life Balance: Successes and Problems

In 2002, Prime Minister John Howard said 'Nothing is more important than the debate that goes on in the community — I call it a barbeque stopper — about the balance between work and family' (Parliament of the Commonwealth of Australia, 2006, pp.22–23). This area of debate is not just limited to families and the position of carers, as in the past (Hogarth, Hasluck, Pierre, Winterbotham, & Vivian, 2000, p. 100). More recently it has been widened to encapsulate 'everyone' (Edgar, 2005, p.70; Russell & Bowman, 2000, p. 80), with the term 'work–life balance' used to indicate that access to organisational work–life balance practices is not limited to those with family and/or caring responsibilities.

Defining Work–life Balance

This barbeque-stopper debate has also been enlivened by arguments that the term 'work–life balance' (WLB) may be misleading for a number of reasons, the first issue being that the word 'balance' implies that the two parts should be equal, like the scales of justice (Edgar, 2005; Guest, 2001). However, an individual may actually feel satisfied with the scale being tipped more in one direction, due to personal preference and different stages encountered throughout life. The second issue is whether work should include paid and nonpaid work (Guest, 2001; Pocock, 2003). Guest (2001) states, in simple terms 'work' is normally conceived of as including only paid employment. Such issues have therefore resulted in different definitions being offered for the WLB. Essentially though work–life balance is

> ... a self-defined, self-determined state of well being that a person can reach, or can set as a goal, that allows them to manage effectively multiple responsibilities at work, at home, and in their community; it supports physical, emotional, family, and community health, and does so without grief, stress or negative impact. (Canadian Department of Labour, as cited in Bardoel, 2006)

The Need for WLB

'The work/life collision has important effects beyond how we feel: it affects vital economic and demographic trends' (Pocock, 2003, p. 5). According to Campbell and Charlesworth (2004, p. 40) such a collision can affect the ability of workers and families to participate as fully as they might like in the workforce, which can have consequences, such as increased rates of absenteeism, illness, reduced productivity and stress.

Bardoel (2006) highlights three factors that have influenced work–life needs (i) demographic factors that affect the labour force (for example, the significant increase in the participation of women in the workforce resulting in an increased need to balance work responsibilities with life outside of work, such as caring and domestic duties); (ii) labour market trends and changing employment relationships (for example the increasing number of stressed people due to longer hours being worked and the intensity of the work) and (iii) the changes in societal values and attitudes (e.g., men as well as women wanting to play a significant role in their children's development; Bardoel, 2006). Given the increasingly tight labour market and the introduction of legislative measures within Australia such as *The Equal Opportunity for Women in the Workplace Act 1999* (Cth; EOWA), Pocock (2005) believes there is some basis for optimism for the continued development of WLB practices in the longer term.

To respond successfully to these new labour force conditions there is a need for a change in mindset. Organisations must move away from a focus on work–life issues that are reactive to individual concerns to a proactive, strategic approach supported by all stakeholders, to ensure diverse contemporary issues are managed appropriately in an integrated manner that benefits all. The benefits to be derived for two of these major stakeholders, employees and employers, are numerous and the inclusion of benefits common to both allow for a greater chance of a company achieving improved performance and competitive advantage (see Table 1).

Prevalence and Utilisation of WLB Practices

There is vast array of WLB practices that a company can seek to implement to address WLB issues (De Cieri, Holmes, Abbott, & Pettit, 2005; Parliament of Australia, 2006). For example, Bardoel, Tharenou and Moss (1998) identified 100 different work–family practices based on previous studies. From this extensive list they developed 36 types of work–family policies by combining overlapping categories. This allowed grouping into five work–family categories that included: child and dependant care benefits, flexible working conditions, leave options, information services and Human Resource Management (HRM) policies, and organisational cultural issues. Similarly, McDonald, Brown and Bradley (2005) identify

Table 1
Benefits of a Better Work–Life Balance

Organisational	Individual
• reduced turnover	• decreased work–life conflict which leads to
• a positive impact on productivity	◆ decreased absenteeism
• reduced absenteeism	◆ increased overall motivation and satisfaction
• increased return rate	◆ greater organisational commitment
• a positive impact on client customer service	◆ increased productivity
• increase in employee motivation and satisfaction	◆ decreased stress levels
• assist in attracting staff	◆ a positive impacton client customer service
• reduction in induction and training costs	
• reduces stress	
• compliance with legislative requirements	

Source: Dench et al. (2000), Holmes (2005), Mc Donald, Brown & Bradley (2005), Pocock (2005).

three major types of work–life balance policies: (1) flexible work options, (2) specialised leave policies, and (3) dependant care benefits.

The extent to which organisations as a whole adopt work–life balance practices varies, with De Cieri et al. (2005) noting that in the three surveys they examined the most frequently cited WLB practices in order were: part-time work; study leave, flexible starting and finishing times, working from home on an ad hoc basis and job sharing. Noteworthy, however, is that while WLB policies may exist, the actual adoption of them by employees is not necessarily widespread (McDonald et al., 2005; Waters & Bardoel, 2006) and often lags behind implementation. For example, De Cieri et al. (2005, p. 95) found that only 6% of organisations had more than 80% of their employees using available WLB strategies within their organisations.

Thinking Outside the Square: Exploring Other Options

Current Programs Offer Only a Partial Answer

Reasons for the lack of employee uptake of work–life balance policies may be attributed to recent empirical research findings (De Cieri et al., 2005) which demonstrated that some barriers can render the implementation of WLB practices ineffective. For example, barriers listed include: an organisational culture which recognises and rewards long hours; an isolated, unfriendly and unaccommodating workplace for employees with commitments outside of work; a lack of supervisor and manager support; preference of management to recruit people perceived as alike to themselves and a lack of communication and education about WLB strategies (De Cieri et al., 2005). Similarly, Waters and Bardoel (2006) found six emerging themes for barriers to utilisation of work–family practices by employees. These included: poor communication of policies, high workloads, career repercussions, management attitudes, influence of peers and administrative processes.

What Other Factors Need to be Considered?

To overcome such barriers some general implementation, guidelines have been postulated. These include: promote and appoint managers who advocate and practice flexibility, align WLB practices with business goals, ensure there is top management support, develop a multilayered communication strategy, hold managers accountable for the success of the process and ensure it is part of an integrated approach to managing work and the workforce in which formal measures of evaluation are implemented (CCH, 2006; McDonald & Bardoel, 2006). Similarly, Kossek, Dass and DeMarr (1994) advocate that managerial attitudes to work–life balance strategies need to change if innovative and inclusive behaviours and organisational cultures are to be developed to address the changing needs of the current workforce.

What Might be Helpful — Best Practice Examples

Best practice is a term that describes the method of identifying, developing and implementing workplace practices and strategies that will improve business productivity and competitiveness (Wolcott, 1996, p. 23). Best practice principles can be adapted by individual organisations to develop suitable strategies that assist employees in achieving their desired work–life balance.

Results from a longitudinal work–life balance survey of Australian businesses conducted annually for the past 9 years indicate that organisations demonstrating best practice in work–life balance are more likely to have: an implementation strategy that is growing in support and impact; been motivated to implement work–life strategy to attract and retain quality staff; utilised an organisational culture survey and/or work–life questionnaire to identify employee needs; evaluated the results of their work–life strategy; created a supportive work–life balance environment (by means of adopting the above implementation guidelines); taken steps to reduce harassment and discrimination in the workplace; published guidelines for negotiating flexible work arrangements; and accrued bottom line benefits (Holmes, 2005, p. 14). Reported benefits include: turnover reduced by up to 6%, absenteeism decreased by up to 5%, an increased rate of return from parental leave of up to 28%, and increases of up to 16% in employee motivation and satisfaction (Holmes, 2005).

Specifically, since introducing work–life practices Hollywood Hospital in Western Australia (WA) has been enjoying significant cost savings, due to a 95% reduction in the total number of lost days, from 4067 (1994/95) to 203 in 1999/2000 (EOWA, 2006). As Kevin Cass-Ryall, Executive Director of Hollywood Hospital, WA states, 'Seventy per cent of the total operating budget relates to labour costs, so it makes good sense to nurture this resource' (EOWA, 2006).

Mentoring as a Viable Option

Mentoring is well recognised as a method of transmitting acquired knowledge and skills and is traditionally used to prepare employees for current or future positions; particularly in management roles. While its popularity waned for several years due to the increased emphasis placed on formal qualifications (i.e., university degrees) there has been a resurgence of interest in mentoring over the last two decades. This can be attributed to a number of factors, but the primary reasons are associated with the different skills, competencies, qualities and attitudes that can be addressed through mentoring.

Defining Mentoring

There are numerous ways of describing mentoring and the mentoring process. However, in essence mentoring involves 'a relationship which gives people the opportunity to share their professional and personal skills and experiences, and to grow and develop in the process' (Spencer, 1996, p. 5; see Mathews, 2003, for further definitions). While definitions of mentoring are also quite varied it is generally agreed that '(1) a mentor is usually a high ranking, influential, senior member of the organisation with significant experience and knowledge, and (2) the individual is also willing to share their experience with younger employees' (Mathews, 2003, p. 316).

The Resurgence of Mentoring

The revitalisation of mentoring as a popular approach to staff development stems from a recognition of the wide variety of knowledge, skills, abilities, competencies and attributes needed for effectiveness in the 21st century, particularly in relation to business management and leadership (see Mathews and Edwards, 2005, for more details). While universities provide a sound introduction to the tangible knowledge and skills needed, many of these qualities cannot be developed through formal education. This realisation, combined with the general dissatisfaction of many organisations with formal development programs, has served as a catalyst for the search for alternative approaches to staff development that better meet their specific needs; hence the increased use of mentoring.

The question of why mentoring is considered a valuable approach for developing these skills can be seen by simply glancing at the recognised benefits of mentoring programs (see Table 2). Clearly, the staff development potential of mentoring is massive, and one of the most attractive features of such programs is that benefits can be derived for all those involved in the mentoring process: mentees (*protégés*), mentors and the organisation. The versatility of mentoring is also an attraction. Mentoring programs can be targeted to address specific issues or areas of development, or used simply to enhance general staff development.

The increased popularity of mentoring is reflected in the number of organisations introducing such programs and the purposes for which they are being used. Many organisations have adopted mentoring to enhance general staff development and harness some of the recognised benefits. Others have adopted mentoring programs to address specific problems or issues. The strategic benefits of adopting mentoring for specific purposes can be seen through examining the mentoring efforts of selected organisations. For example, Coca-Cola™ foods has used mentoring for many years to improve their competitive advantage by establishing better, more effective links between human resource management activities and staff development (Wachtel & Veale, 1998); the Burlington Northern Santa Fe Railway Co. introduced mentoring to speed up the ability of new employees to acquire relevant company knowledge (Messmer, 1998); and CPA (US) embraced mentoring to enhance professional growth, performance and attitudes (Kleinman, Siegel, & Eckstein, 2001; Siegel, Rigsby, Agrawal, & Lavins, 1995).

However, the benefits gained through mentoring often extend beyond the target issues identified. The CPA (US) found that mentoring had the added benefits of improved job satisfaction, organisational commitment, lower

Table 2

Benefits of Mentoring in the Workplace

Organisational benefits	Mentor benefits	Mentee benefits
1. Improved productivity, performance and service delivery 2. Improved management, communication, and technical skills 3. Better recruitment and retention of skilled staff, retention of corporate knowledge, and support of corporate culture 4. Better assessment, recognition and reward of individual contributions 5. Improved employee development (talent, leadership qualities, challenges) 6. Development of support networks and commitment	1. Intrinsic rewards: personal growth, satisfaction, renewed enthusiasm, self-esteem 2. Opportunity to share knowledge, reflect, test new ideas, acquire information and recognition 3. Exposure to fresh perspectives and ideas 4. Improvement of skills such as communication and leadership	1. Personal growth through the acquisition of skills and knowledge, exposure to corporate culture, improved communication and self-confidence 2. Acquisition of a role model that is supportive, empowering and assists in building networks 3. Expanded outlook that provides opportunities for personal satisfaction, recognition, career mobility and the exchange of information 4. Reduction of stress associated with new positions, roles and responsibilities

Source: Alleman (cited in Carruthers 1993); Carrell, Kuzmits, and Elbert (1992); Spencer, (1996); Lacey (1999); Mullen and Noe, (1999); Rolfe-Flett (2002) and Jassawalla, Asgary and Sashittal (2006).

turnover, less role ambiguity and job burnout and better employee socialisation (Kleinmen, et al., 2001; Siegel et al., 1995); a finding mirrored in an Australian study (Herbohn, 2004) that examined the results of mentoring of female accountants. The Australian CPA mentoring program has also received similar results and is helping to address issues of staff retention and job satisfaction and has the potential to be extended to include more experienced accountants (Mathews & Kent, 2006a, 2006b).

More recently, mentoring has been recognised as one of 'the most effective ways of transferring critical implicit and tacit knowledge from one individual to another' (DeLong, 2004, p. 107), and has been adopted by many major corporations such as, NASA, Quest International®, and the World Bank, who have recognised the potential difficulties associated with 'lost knowledge' as key personnel exit the organisation (DeLong, 2004). At a time when many countries are dealing with the potential problems of an aging workforce, skill shortages, increased employee mobility and increased levels of technology, the retention of critical knowledge (corporate, operational and technical) will become more crucial in the future.

In a major study into the use of mentoring, Hansford, Ehrich and Tennent (2003, p. 224) reviewed 151 different studies and reported that 90% of these identified positive outcomes resulting from their introduction. Considering the range of outcomes reported from using mentoring programs it is not surprising that so many organisations are prepared to try it. Spencer (1996, pp. 24–31) summarises the reported outcomes of mentoring as including increased motivation, skills, self-confidence, job satisfaction, improved resource utilisation, communication, coordination, networking and support between individuals and units, and greater understanding of corporate culture and values.

The achievement of successful results, such as these, is of course dependent upon:

- having a focused program that is realistic and addresses the needs of the organisation and the participants
- the program being properly designed and resourced (including time)
- all parties involved receiving appropriate briefing or training
- the skills and commitment of the mentor and mentee
- effective organisational support and infrastructure for the mentoring program

Addressing Work–Life Balance Through Mentoring: An Integrated Approach

Having briefly reviewed the concepts of mentoring and work–life balance, a degree of similarity or relatedness can be seen. Both types of programs are designed to improve effectiveness, performance, commitment, and so forth, and all organisations are searching for ways to provide staff development and worker-friendly environments in as efficient and cost-effective a way as possible. So, why not explore the possibility of designing a program that will help to address both needs, and what potential benefits might organisations gain by doing so?

The *potential* benefits acquired through the use of mentoring programs and the adoption of work–life balance practices have been well researched and contain many similarities, such as improvements in productivity, staffing, job satisfaction and commitment (refer to Tables 1 and 2), and suggest that the two ideas may work well together. The terminology used and the focus of the benefits may be different but clear relationships can be established. For example, work–life balance practices attempt to reduce stress for both the organisation and individual — an issue also addressed by mentoring through providing insights into corporate culture and unwritten rules, empowerment and improved communication. Similarly, improved employee motivation and job satisfaction, self-confidence and personal growth can be enhanced through both programs.

However, the *actual* benefits acquired through the introduction of work–life balance practices are only just becoming known, as the examples discussed earlier illustrate, and the search is continuing for the most beneficial programs. An examination of the selection of practices in use, presented by Bardoel, Tharenou and Moss (1998), suggests that to date practices have been introduced to address particular concerns or issues experienced by organisations or employees. No attempt has been made to design a single strategy that will encapsulate more than one issue, despite the push for increased efficiency and cost-effectiveness.

If work–life balance practices and mentoring are examined from an holistic perspective, in association with each other and with broader organisational activities, it is clear that both help to address general staffing issues such as attracting, retaining and motivating employees; the primary focus of all human resource activities. The benefits stemming from this interface are in turn reflected in specific staffing areas addressed within both the mentoring and work–life balance literature, such as lower staff turnover, decreased levels of absenteeism, better use of employee skills, and more effective acquisition of skills and knowledge that assist in socialisation.

Developing a holistic, strategic approach that seeks to integrate the overall benefits of both conceptual staff development approaches can present an organisation with several advantages. For example, at the individual level the benefits can result in a happier, more balanced employee who improves their overall work performance and enjoys the benefits that accrue from this, such as greater flexibility in managing conflicting personal and work demands. Likewise, from the organisational level, the overall gains are associated with an organisation's ability to improve its competitive advantage through enhancement of employee skills, improvements in productivity, efficiency and staff stability. These links are illustrated in Figure 1.

The introduction of legislation (i.e., *The Equal Opportunity for Women in the Workplace Act 1999* [EOWA]) that serves to encourage and support the inclusion of WLB programs may stimulate the introduction of new initiatives. Perhaps it is through the EOWA that the integration of mentoring programs and work–life balance policies can, in part, be fostered. For example, by seeking to establish goals that meet the objectives of the Act, organisations could seek to establish mentoring programs that are dependent on the organisation's needs, and help to address work–life balance concerns.

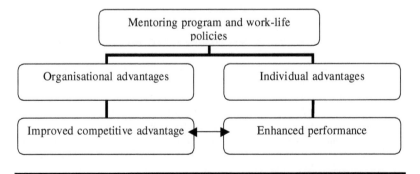

Figure 1

Mentoring and work–life balance framework.

Conclusion

The potential benefits to be gained from both mentoring and work–life balance practices — for organisations, individual employees and the community — are numerous and could serve to improve the culture of the workplace and build stronger relationships between organisations and communities. However, the process of establishing, coordinating and running such an integrated program will not be easy. Commitment from all parties will be essential, and a long-term view must be taken. In this chapter the nature of work–life balance and mentoring and their similarities have been explored. The overlap of several areas of benefit has drawn attention to the possibility of considering whether mentoring could be used to assist organisations in addressing work–life balance issues. At first glance a 'win–win' situation seems to exist — mentoring can be used to provide assistance to organisations and individuals trying to address work–life balance concerns.

At present this is just an idea. The viability and cost-effectiveness of designing or adapting mentoring programs to incorporate issues that need to be addressed in the work–life balance equation needs to be further explored. Many questions still need to be answered — Is it feasible to incorporate work–life balance issues? What work–life balance issues are suited to this form of management? How can the work–life balance concerns be built into mentoring?

Perhaps you cannot make work–life balance issues disappear by 'mentoring them away', but this could be another valuable tool in the fight to maintain better balance in our lives. After all, as the old adage goes, 'A problem shared, is a problem halved'.

References

Bardoel, E.A. (2006). Work–life and HR. In P. Holland & H. De Cieri (Eds.), *Contemporary issues in human resource development: An Australian perspective* (pp. 237–259). Sydney, Australia: Pearson Education.

Bardoel, E.A., Tharenoe, P., & Moss, S.A. (1998). Organisational predictors of work–family practices. *Asia Pacific Journal of Human Resources, 36*(3), 31–49.

Campbell, I., & Charlesworth, S. (2004). *Background report: Key work and family trends in Australia.* Melbourne, Australia:Centre for Applied Social Research, RMIT University.

Carrell, M.R., Kuzits, F.E., & Elbert, N.F. (1992). *Personnel/Human resource management* (4th ed.). New York: Maxwell.

Carruthers, J. (1993). The principles and practice of mentoring. In B.J. Caldwell & E.M.A. Carter (Eds.), *The return of the mentor: Strategies for workplace learning.* London: Falmer Press.

CCH. (2006) Human *resource management.* Sydney, Australia:CCH Australia Ltd.

De Cieri, H., Holmes, B., Abbott, J., & Pettit, T. (2005). Achievements and challenges for work/life balance strategies in Australian organizations. *International Journal of Human Resource Management, 16*(1), 90–103.

DeLong, D.W. (2004). *Lost knowledge: Confronting the threat of an aging workforce.* New York: Oxford University Press.

Dench, S., Bevan, S., Tamkin, P., & Cummings, J. (2000). Family-friendly employment: Its importance to small and medium enterprises. *Labour Market Trends, 108*(3), 111–120.

Edgar, D. (2005). *The war over work: The future of work and family.* Melbourne, Australia: Melbourne University Press.

EOWA 2006, *Business Achievement Award Winners. Equal Opportunity for Women in the Workplace Agency.* Retrieved August 8, 2006, from http://www.eowa.gov.au/Case_Studies/BAA_Winners.asp

Guest, D.E. (2001, March). (The Management Centre, Kings College London). *Perspectives on the study of work–life balance.* Paper presented at the 2001 ENOP Symposium, Paris. Retrieved January 5, 2006, from http://www.ucm.es/info/Psyap/enop/guest.htm

Hansford, B., Ehrich, L., & Tennent, L. (2003). Does mentoring deserve another look? In R. Weisner & B. Millett (Eds.), *Human resource management: Challenges and future directions* (pp. 219–228). Milton, Australia: John Wiley & Sons.

Herbohn, K. (2004). Informal mentoring relationships and the career processes of public accountants. *The British Accounting Review, 36*, 369–393.

Hogarth, T., Hasluck, C., Pierre, G., Winterbotham, M., & Vivian, D. (2000). *Work-Life balance 2000: Results from the baseline study for the department for education and employment.* (Report No. RR249). United Kingdom: The Department for Education and Employment.

Holmes, B. (2005). *Work/Life initiatives: The way ahead: Report on the year 2005 survey.* Roseville, Australia: Managing Work Life Balance International.

Jassawalla, A.R., Asgary, N., & Sashittal, H.C. (2006). Managing expatriates: The role of mentors. *International Journal of Commerce and Management, 16*(2), 130–140.

Kleinman, G., Siegel, P.H., & Eckstein, C. (2001). Mentoring and learning: The case of CPA firms. *Leadership and Organisational Development Journal, 22*(1), 22.

Kossek, E., Dass, P., & DeMarr, B. (1994). The dominant logic of employer sponsored and family initiatives: Human resource managers' institutional role. *Human Relations, 47*(9), 1121–39.

Lacey, K. (1999). *Making mentoring happen: A simple and effective guide to implementing a successful mentoring programme.* Warriewood, Australia: Business and Professional Publishing.

Mathews, P. (2003). Academic mentoring: Enhancing the use of scarce resources. *Educational Management and Administration, 31*(3), 313–334.

Mathews, P., & Edwards, D. (2005). Creating management leadership for the future: An integrated model. *Journal of Academy of Business and Economics, 1*, 147–161.

Mathews, P., & Kent, J. (2006a). Mentoring within the accounting profession: An Australian perspective. *Review of Business Research, VI*(5), 47–54.

Mathews, P., & Kent, J. (2006b, April). Back to the future: Revisiting mentoring within the accounting profession. In L. Beddoe & J. Jesson (Eds.), *Proceedings of the Continuing and Professional Education Conference* (pp. 134–140). Auckland, New Zealand: Faculty of Education, University of Auckland.

Messmer, M. (1998). Mentoring: Building your company's intellectual capital. *HR Focus, 75*(9), s11–s12.

McDonald, P., Brown, K., & Bradley, L. (2005). Explanations for the provision-utilisation gap in work-life policy. *Women in Management Review, 20*(1), 37–55.

Mullen, E., & Noe, R.A. (1999). The mentoring information exchange: When do mentors seek information from the protégés? *Journal of Organisational Behaviour, 20*(2), 233–243.

Parliament of the Commonwealth of Australia. (2006) *Balancing Work and Family.* Canberra, Australia: Commonwealth of Australia.

Pocock, B. (2003). *The work/life collision: What work is doing to Australians and what to do about it.* Sydney, Australia: Federation Press.

Pocock, B. (2005). Work–life 'balance' in Australia: Limited progress, dim prospects. *Asia Pacific Journal of Human Resources, 43*, 198–209.

Rolfe-Flett, A. (2002). *Mentoring in Australia.* Sydney, Australia: Prentice Hall.

Russell, G. & Bowman, L. (2000). *Work and family, current thinking, rresearch and practice.* Sydney, Australia: Macquarie Research Limited.

Siegel, P.H., Rigsby, J.T., Agrawal, S.P., & Lavins, J.R. (1995). Auditor professional performance and the mentor relationship within the public firm. *Accounting, Auditing and Accountability Journal, 8*(4), 3–23.

Spencer, C. (1996). *Mentoring made easy: A practical guide for managers.* Sydney, Australia: Office of the Director of Equal Opportunity in Public Employment, New South Wales Government Publication.

The Equal Opportunity for Women in the Workplace Act (Cth) 1999.

Wachtel, J.M., & Veale, D.J. (1998). Coaching and mentoring at Coca-Cola Foods. *Training and Management Development Methods, 12*(1), 901–904.

Waters, M.A., & Bardoel, E.A. (2006). Work–family policies in the context of higher education: useful or symbolic? *Asia Pacific Journal of Human Resources, 44*(1), 67–82.

Wolcott, I. (1996). *A nice place to work: Small business and workers with family responsibilities.* Canberra, Australia: Work and Family Unit, Department of Industrial Relations.

Marketing Intelligence: How Linguistic Ability and International Experience Impact on an Export Marketing Manager

Jasmine Williams

Troy Heffernan

The development and expansion of international trading blocs such as the European Union, together with an increased interest in the development of bilateral trade agreements (Maur, 2005; Razeen, 2005), are changing the very nature of trading (Paliwoda, 1997). Within this changing environment the international experience and language skills of export marketing managers are increasing in importance (Swift, 1991). So what qualities should small and medium-sized enterprises (SMEs) look for in such managers? This chapter helps to answer this question by exploring the relationship between two sets of managerial characteristics: first, international experience (including language skills), and second, some key export marketing intelligence behaviours; and discusses the extent to which the former may impact on the latter. In doing so, it offers SME employers guidelines on how the backgrounds of applicants for export marketing posts are likely to affect their approach to export marketing information and decision-making, and provides some initial profiles of export decision-makers, based on their international experiences and skills.

The findings presented here are set against a backdrop of prior research into the wider area of export performance, particularly within SMEs, which has identified managerial background and export attitudes/behaviour as two of the main constructs on which export success depends (Leonidou, Katsikeas, & Piercy, 2001; Moini, 1995). In order to develop a comprehensive model of the factors influencing successful export development, it is necessary to investigate the interrelationships between these constructs.

It has long been acknowledged that decision-makers' international and linguistic experience is likely to facilitate speedier access to, and deeper understanding of, information on overseas markets (Swift, 1991). However, the research discussed here is the first to explore the links between these two areas. The findings are based on a two-stage survey of United Kingdom (UK) SME exporters.

Language Skills and International Background

The literature in this area often acknowledges the view, possibly prevalent in the English-speaking business community, that the knowledge and use of foreign languages is not important to international success, as English is the international language of business (Clarke, 1997). A number of empirical studies conducted over the years, however, have questioned the validity of this assumption (Enderwick & Akoorie, 1994; MacDonald & Cook, 1998; Pearson, 1989; Piekkari & Zander, 2005; Swift, 1990, 1991).

Hence, successions of researchers have explored the link between linguistic ability and export performance (e.g., see Cunningham & Spigel, 1971; Enderwick & Akoorie, 1994; Lautanen, 2000; Schlegelmilch & Ross, 1987; Walters, 1990). Though results are mixed, a number of these authors recognise that, in addition to enabling verbal and written communication per se (Henderson, 2005; Swift, 1991), language skills can facilitate more general cultural sensitivity (Zander, 2005) which is seen as an important prerequisite of international marketing success. Linguists may be more likely, therefore, to be employed in marketing than other functions (Enderwick & Akoorie, 1994), where language skills have been credited with enabling a greater grasp of market detail (Swift, 1991).

Moving to the wider area of managers' international experience, a growing body of evidence, gathered over a number of years, and across a variety of countries, has linked the previous overseas life or work experience of decision-makers with their firms' overseas performance (e.g., see Barclays Bank International, 1979; Carlsson, Nordegan & Sjüholm, 2005; Dichtl, Leibold, Koglmeyer, & Muller, 1990; Simmonds & Smith, 1968; White, Griffith, & Ryans, 1999). In addition, there is now evidence that the international experience of managers can be seen as a catalytic agent of change (Shen, 2006). Added to this, the extra resource of international familiarity, personal networks and contacts provided by such overseas experience serves as a vehicle for export information generation (Houman, 2006) as well as improved international performance (Carlsson, Nordegan, & Sjüholm, 2005; Herrmann & Datta, 2002; Yeoh, 2004).

Additionally, studies that have examined the narrower functional definition of managers' experience in exporting have concluded that, on balance, this seems to have little effect on either the export intensity or export growth of companies (Cavusgil, 1984b; Reith & Ryan, 1981). It may, however, have an impact on whether or not companies export at all (Holzmüller & Kasper, 1990).

The evidence to date seems to favour the impact on exporting of living/working overseas over linguistic ability and managers' export experience. At the same time, a number of these studies indicate that international experience and language skills appear to have clearer effects than any of the more general management background indicators of age, education or prior work experience (Leonidou, Katsikeas & Piercy, 2001).

Export Information Collection and Use in Decision-Making

Intelligence generation is the first component of Kohli and Jaworski's (1990) market orientation construct, and the knowledge gained from these activities is seen as being inextricably linked to the adoption of the marketing concept by organisations (Hart & Diamantopoulos, 1993; Kohli & Jaworski, 1990). In addition, market orientation on the part of management is likely to improve performance (Jaworski & Kohli, 1993; Narver & Slater, 1990). More recent investigation has extended and adapted the market orientation construct into an exporting context (Cadogan, Cui, & Li, 2003; Cadogan, Diamantopoulos, & Siguaw, 1999; Cadogan Paul, Salminen, Puumalainen, & Sundqvist, 2001). It follows, therefore, that the collection and use of export market intelligence is likely to be an important element in successful export performance (Diamantopoulos & Souchon, 1998). At the same time, the limited capacity of SMEs to acquire and use market information is seen as a key factor in explaining the poor performance of a number of these companies (Julien & Ramangalahy, 2003).

Despite calls for systematic investigations of the impact of export market intelligence activities on organisations (Wiedersham-Paul, Olson, & Welch, 1978), empirical evidence up to the 1990s was sparse, particularly from SMEs, with much of it centred around the work of one United States academic (Cavusgil, 1984a, 1984b, 1985). In recent years, however, interest in this area has increased (e.g., see Chaudhry & Crick, 1998; Diamantopoulos & Horncastle, 1997; Hart, Webb & Jones, 1994; Souchon & Durden, 2002). This later research has formed the basis for the categories of information sources, collection methods, and decision-making behaviour, developed in the present study (see Appendix A).

Methodology

The fieldwork comprised a qualitative followed by a quantitative study. The aim of the qualitative investigation was to explore the nature and effect of managerial background on export market information collection and use. Groups of export behaviours relating to marketing intelligence were initially derived from previous literature in the area (see Appendix A). These were tested firstly during 15 in-depth interviews with SME export managers in the south and west of England. Transcripts of the interviews were coded as the fieldwork progressed, and sample selection became increasingly more purposeful, using a short telephone pre-interview to establish the degree of export activity in SMEs (10–250 employees). Companies recruited were at least 'experimental exporters' (Diamantopoulos, Schlegelmilch & Allpress, 1990), that is, they were actively committed to exporting. Alternative perspectives on the use of export market information in SMEs were then obtained from interviews with five information suppliers (i.e., market research companies) and four government-funded support agencies.

It soon emerged that, in particular, lack of language skills amongst decision-makers seemed to inhibit direct communication with export markets, at any level. For example, it limited the choice of local representatives to those who spoke English. This, in turn, made companies reliant on second-hand information, which had been both selected and filtered by these — sometimes less than appropriate — representatives. On the other hand, export managers with appropriate language skills exhibited a confidence in developing market contacts and gaining direct market feedback.

For the next, quantitative, stage of the study, it was therefore hypothesised that:

- **Hypothesis 1:** Managers with foreign language skills are more likely to use export market information than are nonlinguists.

There was also qualitative evidence that overseas experience, often obtained prior to joining their present companies, made respondents champions of exporting, leading the search for, and use of, export market information in their companies. From this, it was hypothesised for quantitative testing that:

- **Hypothesis 2:** Export managers with overseas experience are more likely to use export market information than managers without such experience.

In addition, the confidence of the more experienced export managers participating at the qualitative stage seemed to be rooted more in familiarity with export marketing tools than with languages or cultures.

The quantitative study therefore hypothesised that:

- **Hypothesis 3:** The greater the export management experience of decision-makers, the greater the use of export market information.

Shared patterns and frequencies of export information gathering and usage began to emerge during the qualitative fieldwork, as did the need to address connections between attitudes and behaviour (Mishler, 1986). Many studies of export marketing have focused from the start on subjective (e.g., attitudinal) variables, which may be more erratic and less reliable than responses relating to recent actions and behaviour (Joynt & Welch, 1985). In contrast, the focus on behaviour rather than attitudes during the quantitative stage of this research was predicated on the assumption that 'we need to know *what* behaviours people perform before we can explain *why* they perform them' (Peter, 1981, p. 143).

A frequency scale was therefore chosen for the questionnaire. A standard non-parametric scale was developed (Churchill, 1995, pp. 413–420), which a pilot survey confirmed as offering realistic options for all the behaviours tested. The final questionnaire also elicited information on respondents' backgrounds — in particular, their linguistic skills and international experience — using objective measures. These measures are easily answered and verifiable, being less suscepti-ble to change over time than subjective criteria (pp. 336–33). Copies of the ques-tionnaire were mailed to 2000 UK SMEs with fewer than 250 employees. A usable response rate of 21% was achieved, comparing favourably with similar studies (Diamantopoulos & Souchon, 1999).

As a total of 58 activities were measured, some data reduction was desirable in the interests of clarity (Babbie, Halley, & Zaino, 2000). Where this was appro-priate, both factor and cluster analyses were considered as data reduction methods. Following advice from Kline (2000) and Everitt (1980) cluster analysis was chosen as a method of deriving composite variables. This step was taken in the interests of simplification and exploration (Everitt, 1980; Jain, Murty, & Flynn, 1999). Also, given the desire to produce 'classes of behaviours' (Peter, 1981, p. 143) from an exhaustive list, a technique that groups variables according to measures of their similarity or distance, and allows categorisation according to 'natural relationships' (Hair, Anderson, Tatham, & Black, 1998) had considerable appeal. In the event, the clusters identified demonstrated a high level of consis-tency with marketing practice and theory (see Appendix B).

Quantitative Findings

Initially, in the quantitative analysis, a series of Mann-Whitney U tests were run. The first was designed to identify whether or not differences existed between companies where the key export decision-maker spoke a language other than English, and those companies where no foreign language ability existed at this level. The second examined differences between companies where export decision-makers had or had not lived or worked overseas. Sources of export information were examined first. Those who speak at least one foreign language reported greater use of market-related reports, as well as trade fairs, missions and exhibitions, than nonlinguists ($p < .05$); while those with overseas experience used almost all sources more frequently than those without.

Spearman's rank correlation coefficients (Spearman's *rho*, or r_s) were used to measure the extent of associations between exporting experience and export marketing (EM) information gathering and decision-making behaviour. Where significant correlations were observed, Kruskal-Wallis (K-W) analyses of variance, followed up with Mann-Whitney U tests to evaluate pair-wise differ-ences, were conducted, to explore the nature of these relationships (Green, Salkind, & Akey, 1997; Kanji, 1993; Siegel & Castellan, 1988).

Table 1

Export Information Sources: Languages and Overseas Experience

Foreign language?					Lived/worked overseas?		
Gather EMI from:		Mean rank	M-W U	Sig. (2-tailed)	Mean rank	M-W U	Sig. (2-tailed)
Market reports	Yes	199.93	14678.50	.044	208.55	12266.00	.005
	No	177.22			175.48		
Customer/Competitive	Yes	199.90	14835.00	.054	210.06	12206.50	.004
	No	178.13			175.56		
Conferences/Seminars	Yes	193.61	14533.00	.085	200.03	12350.00	.020
	No	175.60			174.30		
Trade fairs/missions/ exhibitions	Yes	197.40	14371.00	.047	198.86	12886.50	.056
	No	175.82			177.05		
Internal company data	Yes	189.46	13853.00	.102	199.07	11449.50	.007
	No	171.84			168.81		
Internet research	Yes	188.05	15041.50	.341	200.40	12076.00	.014
	No	177.79			172.59		
Library research	Yes	194.38	13782.00	.026	195.86	12167.50	.039
	No	171.70			173.56		
Personal interviews	Yes	175.12	14807.00	.690	180.66	13092.00	.562
	No	179.15			174.51		
Telephone surveys	Yes	177.43	15233.50	.633	193.04	12364.50	.040
	No	181.80			173.17		
Focus groups	Yes	183.31	15212.00	.559	195.76	12168.50	.007
	No	178.58			172.67		
Mail questionnaires	Yes	190.40	15341.00	.292	201.75	12431.50	.014
	No	179.52			174.93		

Table 2 indicates that the use of focus groups, trade fairs/missions/exhibitions, as well as internal company data may be related to the number of years exporting experience of decision-makers.

In order to conduct Kruskal-Wallis ANOVA and follow-up paired-sample Mann-Whitney U tests it was necessary to split the sample by categories of exporting experience. To achieve relatively even subsample sizes, respondents were split into three groups: those with up to 10 years' exporting experience; those with 11 to 20 years' experience, and those with over 20 years' experience. These groupings reflect the considerable length of experience of SME export

Table 2

Export Information Sources–Managers' Exporting Experience (r_s)

Market reports	Customer/ competitive	Conferences seminars	Trade fairs/ missions etc	Internal company data	
.038	.068	.101	.142**	.145**	
Internet	Libraries	Personal interviews	Telephone surveys	Focus groups	Mail questionnaires
–.017	.069	.099	.030	.149**	.038

Note: N = 353–369; ** = < 0.01

Table 3
Export Information Sources/Agencies: Managers' Exporting Experience (K-W ANOVA)

Gather EMI from:	Mgt. exporting experience	Mean rank	Chi^2	Sig.
Trade fairs/missions/exhibitions	Up to 10 years	171.77		
	11—20 years	171.13	14.669	.001
	Over 20 years	218.79		
Internal company data	Up to 10 years	164.16		
	11–20 years	174.65	7.621	.022
	Over 20 years	201.45		
Focus groups	Up to 10 years	166.18		
	11–20 years	182.47	7.109	.029
	Over 20 years	192.37		

decision-makers in the sample (mean = 15.71 years) The results are summarised in Table 3.

Mann-Whitney U follow-up tests indicate that, in all three cases where differences were discerned, usage was significantly higher among the most experienced exporters.

Table 4 indicates no differences between linguists (n = 149) and nonlinguists (n = 217) in terms of who they used to collect export market information; though those with overseas experience (n = 116) were more likely to use market research companies, and to hire in temporary staff specifically for this purpose, than those without (n = 248).

The summary of r_s correlations in Table 5, based on managers' exporting experience, illustrates that only in the use of ongoing company staff does a significant (at $p < .01$) relationship appear.

Table 4
Export Information Agencies: Languages and Overseas Experience

Foreign language?					Lived/worked overseas?		
		Mean rank	M-W U	Sig. (2-tailed)	Mean rank	M-W U	Sig. (2-tailed)
Permanent staff	Yes	185.65	15697.00	.689	195.35	12983.00	.109
	No	181.17		176.49			
Govt./professional agencies	Yes	192.27	14342.00	.121	194.85	12835.00	.105
	No	175.09		175.96			
Market research companies	Yes	178.64	1392.00	.332	189.29	11448.00	.008
	No	170.75		166.71			
Marketing consultancies	Yes	172.86	14423.00	.893	176.72	12743.00	.577
	No	173.95		171.96			
Temporary staff	Yes	174.00	14014.50	.603	184.31	11398.50	.006
	No	170.57		165.34			
Universities/ business schools	Yes	177.57	14534.00	.604	181.96	12660.00	.181
	No	174.04		172.42			

Table 5
Those Used to Gather EMI Managers' Exporting Experience (r_s)

Permanent staff	Govt/prof. agencies	Mkt. research companies	Marketing consultants	Temporary staff	Universities/ Bus. schools
.178**	.037	−.055	−.098	.-030	-.004

Note: N = 343–362; ** = $p < .01$

Kruskal-Wallis ANOVA results (Table 6) indicate an highly significant difference here; and Mann-Whitney U tests for pairs indicate that these differences again occur between the most experienced (> 20 years) group and the others.

Moving to export decisions, linguists made more decisions than nonlinguists relating to methods of new market entry, as well as sales organisation, and pulling out of existing markets (though this latter may indicate negative rather than positive export experiences by their companies). They also used information on barriers to entry, on language and translation facilities, and particularly export insurance and finance, more frequently than nonlinguists. These results are shown in Table 7.

As with use of information sources, however, the greatest impact on export decision-making came with overseas experience: all types of export-related decisions were made significantly more frequently by those who had lived or worked overseas; and nine of the thirteen information types were used significantly more in decision-making by those with international experience than those without.

The only impact of management export experience on decision-making was on the frequency with which decisions were made relating to consolidating in existing markets, and sales organisation. As well as having lengthy experience in exporting, decision-makers in the sample had worked with their current companies for a considerable time ($Mean$ = 16.39 years). Thus decision-makers' experience and that of their companies are linked. In those circumstances it is not surprising that companies exporting for a greater period of time are more likely to make decisions relating to operating in current export markets than moving into new ones (though this begs the question of why there are no differences in prioritising existing markets).

Table 6
Those Used to Gather EMI: Managers' Exporting Experience(K-W ANOVA)

EMI gathering by:	Mgt. exporting experience	Mean rank	Chi^2	Sig.
Permanent staff	Up to 10 years 11–20 years Over 20 years	163.00 175.92 218.79	16.168	.000

Table 7

Export Marketing Decisions: Languages and Overseas Experience

Foreign language?					Lived/worked overseas?		
		Mean rank	M-W U	Sig. 2-tailed)	Mean rank	M-W U	Sig. (2-tailed)
Potential of new export markets	Yes	197.10	14783.50	.065	201.17	12901.00	.033
	No	177.50			177.40		
Methods of new market entry	Yes	199.64	13795.00	.009	203.09	12111.00	.008
	No	172.16			173.64		
Prioritizing existing export markets	Yes	191.93	15715.00	.353	211.25	11829.00	.001
	No	181.93			173.44		
Consolidating company's position in export markets	Yes	192.66	15248.50	.232	210.39	11694.50	.001
	No	179.81			172.28		
Organisation of local selling function	Yes	192.54	13098.000	.021	204.67	10546.50	.000
	No	168.08			164.76		
Pulling out of an existing market	Yes	193.04	13999.500	.039	198.61	11957.00	.012
	No	172.54			172.11		
Market information	Yes	201.65	14247.50	.019	210.65	11900.500	.002
	No	175.26			173.72		
Buyer behaviour	Yes	191.76	16042.00	.481	201.43	13224.500	.067
	No	183.76			179.56		
Sociocultural	Yes	192.62	14509.50	.122	198.13	12405.500	.044
	No	175.49			174.52		
NPD opportunities	Yes	181.49	15801.50	.937	185.61	13791.500	.592
	No	182.34			179.56		
Advertising/promotions	Yes	181.67	15693.50	.913	208.19	10826.000	.000
	No	180.53			167.83		
Reports on potential customer	Yes	189.77	15204.00	.324	204.59	11937.000	.005
	No	179.24			172.94		
Barriers to exporting	Yes	194.20	13456.50	.025	200.80	11479.500	.005
	No	170.38			169.55		
Technical standards	Yes	186.95	14933.00	.343	197.74	12057.000	.026
	No	176.77			172.51		
Economic	Yes	187.27	15965.50	.658	190.85	13763.000	.370
	No	182.57			180.83		
Transport/distribution	Yes	186.30	14021.00	.182	186.53	12427.000	.240
	No	172.27			173.43		
Export insurance/finance	Yes	196.84	13121.50	.007	202.45	11205.500	.003
	No	168.19			169.05		
Language/translation facilities	Yes	196.12	13506.00	.014	199.42	11817.500	.012
	No	170.61			171.84		
Customer credit worthiness	Yes	192.48	15632.00	.308	200.98	12936.000	.047
	No	181.55			178.43		

In line with this, Kruskal-Wallis ANOVAs indicate significant differences in EM decision-making frequency for these same two decision-types. Again, the differences appear between more experienced exporters: those with more than 20 years' experience make these decisions more frequently than their less experienced counterparts.

Turning to the types of information used to make these decisions, the only significant relationship appears for the use of sociocultural (politics/legal/business

Table 8

Export Marketing Decisions: Managers' Exporting Experience (r_s)

New market potential	New market entry	Prioritising existing markets	Consolidating company position	Organising selling	Pulling out of markets	
.103	.066	.079	.111*	.147**	.026	

Market reports	Buyer behaviour	Sociocultural	NPD opportunities	Advertising/ promotions	Customer reports	
.099	.071	.117*	.001	.037	.021	

Export barriers	Technical standards	Economic	Transport/ distribution	Export insurance	Language/ translation	Credit worth
.009	.067	.067	–.017	–.051	.067	.009

Note: $N = 351–369$; * = $p < .05$; ** = $p < .01$

practices) information. However, Kruskal-Wallis ANOVA results indicate no significant differences between specified groups based on export experience.

It would therefore seem that experience of living or working overseas has the greatest impact on the frequency with which export market information is collected and used in export decisions.

Conclusion

In summary, the qualitative research highlighted a number of variables likely to impact on export intelligence behaviour, all of which have been previously linked to export development. When the effect of these was tested quantitatively, there was some support for all four hypotheses, particularly hypothesis 2: 'export managers with overseas experience are more likely to use export market information than managers without such experience'. Indeed, experience of living and/or working overseas significantly affected the frequency of both information-gathering and decision-making behaviour by export managers. Linguistic

Table 9

EM Decisions: Managers' Exporting Experience (K-W ANOVA)

Decisions taken:	Mgt. exporting experience	Mean rank	Chi^2	Sig.
Consolidating company's position in export markets	Up to 10 years 11–20 years Over 20 years	175.80 170.15 214.39	11.565	.003
Organisation of local selling function	Up to 10 years 11–20 years Over 20 years	165.47 161.04 215.15	18.602	.000
Sociocultural	Up to 10 years 11–20 years Over 20 years	170.20 176.495.874 203.28	.053	

ability, on the other hand, made little difference to the level of export information gathering and some difference to decision-making behaviour. Experience in the function of exporting had the least effect.

There are some lessons to be learnt here for SMEs needing to recruit export managers, as the nature of these managers' backgrounds seems to influence their style of information-related behaviour. Those with language skills seem more likely to focus on information-gathering activities where these skills can be most used (e.g., market reports and trade fairs), though they demonstrate a limited and conservative approach to market research, using libraries, for example, more frequently than nonlinguists. On the other hand, they seem to take a more versatile approach to export market decisions, being more likely to evaluate new markets and pull out of existing markets than nonlinguists. This is reflected in the types of information they use most, particularly relating to market conditions and barriers to exporting. Their greater use of information about local language and translation facilities may well reflect the importance they attach to languages as keys to market understanding.

Export managers who have had experience of living or working overseas demonstrate higher levels of information-gathering activity, except for trade fairs and the like, and personal interviews, both of which require conversational (and therefore possibly linguistic) skills. They are more likely to employ ad hoc researchers (market researchers and temporary staff) to collect information, and make more export market decisions. On the whole, their incorporation of information in these decisions reflects the greater amount of intelligence gathering they undertake. The exceptions to this are some of the more basic operational types of information (i.e., transport/distribution and economic), as well as information requiring an intricate understanding of customers (i.e., relating to buyer behaviour and new product development opportunities).

Those with longer experience of working in exporting demonstrate the confidence that comes with this in their intelligence-gathering and decision-making styles. Their greater use of trade fairs and similar may indicate a contact, network-driven approach; while their greater use of focus groups suggest greater familiarity with methodologies for market investigations; and their use of internal company data may reflect a reliance on in-company market intelligence which has built up over time. The greater use of permanent staff to collect market information is another indication of the way in which ongoing intelligence-gathering is more likely to be embedded in departments run by experienced export managers. Their greater level of decision-making relating to already existing export markets is also indicative of the length of export experience, while their use of sociocultural information may reflect an importance attached to cultural difference that is born of experience.

From the above, it seems that linguists are likely to be discriminating about the intelligence collected and more innovative in their decision-making, but use information responsibly. Those with international experience are likely to be more active information-gatherers and decision-makers, while length of exporting experience is indicative of a more confident, if rather more conservative, approach. Those responsible for government policies designed to support SME export development may be heartened to learn that their encouragement of the acquisition of language skills could have more wide-ranging implications than those of simple communication. In addition, it seems that such agencies' appreciation of the role of overseas and exporting experience amongst SME export managers should be encouraged.

Limitations and Suggestions for Future Research

This research has relied on a selective use of the variables likely to impact on export performance in SMEs. The interrelationship between other factors in managers' backgrounds, less obviously linked to the export function (such as age and educational experience), which have been shown to have some, direct or indirect, impact on export performance in previous studies (Jaffe & Pasternak, 1994; Schlegelmilch & Ross, 1987), may merit further investigation. In addition, there are factors relating to marketing behaviour, particularly at a strategic level, already discerned as indirectly influencing export performance (Julien & Ramangalahy, 2003; Leonidou, Katsikeas, & Piercy, 2001), that need to be incorporated if a holistic model of export performance is to be developed. Hopefully, the findings presented here will help to stimulate such further research, to assist SMEs in taking advantage of the marketing opportunities provided by today's dynamic international trading environment.

References

Babbie, E., Halley, F., & Zaino, J. (2000). *Adventures in social research: Data analysis using SPSS for Windows 95/98.* Thousand Oaks, CA: Pine Forge Press.

Barclays Bank International. (1979). *The Barclays Bank report on export development in France, Germany and the UK: Factors in international research.* Bromley, England: ITI Research.

Bodur, M., & Cavusgil, S.T. (1985). Export market research orientations of Turkish firms. *European Journal of Marketing, 8* (Spring/Summer), 93–98.

Cadogan, J., Diamantopoulos, A., & Siguaw, J. (1999). *Export market-oriented behaviour, its antecedents, performance consequences and moderating factors evidence from the UK and the US* (Research Paper). Birmingham, England: Aston Business School Research Institute.

Cadogan, J.W., Paul, N.J., Salminen, R.T., Puumalainen, K., & Sundqvist, S. (2001). Key antecedents to 'export' market-oriented behaviors: A cross-national empirical examination. *International Journal of Research in Marketing, 18*(3), 236–282.

Cadogan, J.W., Cui, C., & Li, E. (2003). Export market-oriented behavior and export performance. *International Marketing Review, 20*(5), 493–513.

Carlsson, J., Nordegan, A., & Sjüholm, F. (2005). International experience and the performance of Scandinavian firms in China. *International Business Review, 4*(1), 21–40.

Cavusgil, S.T. (1984a). Organizational characteristics associated with export activity. *Journal of Management Studies, 21*(1), 3–22.

Cavusgil, S.T. (1984b). Differences among exporting firms based on their degree of internationalization. *Journal of Business Research, 12*(2), 195–208.

Cavusgil, S.T. (1985, November/December). Guidelines for export market research. *Business Horizons,* 27–33.

Chaudhry, S., & Crick, D. (1998). Export information providers: Are they meeting the needs of SMEs? *Marketing Intelligence and Planning, 16*(3), 141–147.

Churchill, G.A., Jr. (1995). *Marketing research: Methodological foundations.* Orlando, FL: Dryden.

Clarke, W.M. (1997). The use of foreign languages by Irish exporters. *European Journal of Marketing, 34*(1/2), 80–90.

Cunningham, M.T., & Spigel, R.I. (1971, Spring). A study in successful exporting. *British Journal of Marketing, 5,* 2–12.

Diamantopoulos, A., & Horncastle, S. (1997). Use of export marketing research by industrial firms: An application and extension of Deshpandé and Zaltman's model. *International Business Review, 6*(3), 245–270.

Diamantopoulos, A., & Souchon, A.L. (1998). Information utilization by exporting firms: Conceptualization, measurement, and impact on export performance. In S. Urban, & C. Nanopoulos (Eds.), *Information and management: Utilization of technology—structural and cultural impact* (pp. 112–135). Weisbaden, Germany: Gabler.

Diamantopoulos, A., & Souchon, A.L. (1999). Measuring export information use: Scale development and validation. *Journal of Business Research, 46*(1), 1–14.

Diamantopoulos, A., Schlegelmilch, B.B., & Allpress, C. (1990). Export marketing research in practice: A comparison of users and non-users. Journal of Marketing Management, 6(3), 257–274.

Dichtl, E., Leibold, M., Koglmeyer, G., & Muller, S. (1990). International orientation as a precondition of export success. *Journal of International Business Studies, 21*(1), 23–40.

Enderwick, P., & Akoorie, M.E.M. (1994). Pilot study research note: The employment of foreign language specialists and export success — The case of New Zealand. *International Marketing Review, 11*(4), 4–18.

Evergin, C., Bodur, M., & Cavusgil, S.T. (1993). Information needs of exporters: An empirical study of Turkish exporters. *Marketing Intelligence and Planning, 11*(2), 28–36.

Everitt, B. (1980). *Cluster analysis.* London: Heinemann.

Green, S.B., Salkind, N.J., & Akey, T.M. (1997). *Using SPSS for Windows: Analyzing and understanding data.* Upper Saddle River, NJ: Prentice Hall.

Hair, J.F., Jr., Anderson, R.E., Tatham, R.L., & Black, W.C. (1998). *Multivariate data analysis.* Upper Saddle River, NJ: Prentice Hall.

Hart, S.J., & Diamantopoulos, A. (1993). Marketing research activity and company and company performance: Evidence from manufacturing industry. *European Journal of Marketing, 27*(5), 54–72.

Hart, S.J., Webb, J.R., & Jones, M.V. (1994). Export marketing research and the effect of export experience in industrial SMEs. *International Marketing Review, 11*(6), 4–22.

Henderson, J.K. (2005). Language diversity in international management teams. *International Studies of Management and Organisation, 35*(1), 61–82.

Herrmann, P., & Datta, D.K. (2002). CEO characteristics and the choice of foreign market entry mode: An empirical study. *Journal of International Business Studies, 33*(3), 551–569.

Holzmüller, H.H., & Kasper, H. (1990). The decision-maker and export activity: A cross-national comparison of the foreign orientation of Austrian managers. *Management International Review, 3*(3), 217–230.

Houman, P.H. (2006). Listening to the global grapevine: SME export managers' personal contacts as a vehicle for export information generation. *Journal of World Business, 41*(1), 81–96.

Jaffe, E.D., & Pasternak, H. (1994). An attitudinal model to determine the export intention of non-exporting small manufacturers. *International Marketing Review, 11*(3), 17–32.

Jain, A.K., Murty, M.N., & Flynn, P.J. (1999). Data clustering: A review. *ACM Computing Surveys, 31*(3), 264–323.

Jaworski, B.J., & Kohli, A.J. (1993, July). Market orientation: Antecedents and consequences. *Journal of Marketing, 57,* 57–70.

Joynt, P., & Welch, L. (1985). A strategy for small business internationalization. *International Marketing Review,* Autumn, 64–73.

Julien, P-A., & Ramangalahy, C. (2003). Competitive strategy and performance of exporting SMEs: An empirical investigation of their export information search and competencies. *Entrepreneurship Theory and Practice, Spring,* 227–245.

Kanji, G.K. (1993). *100 statistical tests.* London: Sage.

Kline, P. (2000). *An easy guide to factor analysis.* London: Routledge.

Koh, A.C. (1991). An evaluation of international marketing research planning in United States export firms. *Journal of Global Marketing, 4*(3), 7–25.

Kohli, A.K., & Jaworski, B.J. (1990, April). Marketing orientation: The construct, research proposi-tions and managerial implications. *Journal of Marketing, 54,* 1–18.

Lautanen, T. (2000). Modeling small firms' decisions to export: Evidence from manufacturing firms in Finland, 1995. *Small Business Economics, 14*(2), 107–124.

Leonidou, L.C. (1997). Finding the right information mix for the export manager. *Long Range Planning, 30*(4), 572–584.

Leonidou, L.C., Katsikeas, C.S., & Piercy, N.F. (2001). Identifying managerial influences on exporting: Past research and future directions. *Journal of International Marketing, 6*(2), 74–102.

MacDonald, S., & Cook, M. (1998, November). An exploration of language training in exporting firms. *Local Economy,* 216–227.

Maur, J-C. (2005). Exporting Europe's trade policy. *World Economy, 28*(11), 1565–1590.

McAuley, A. (1993). The perceived usefulness of export information sources. *European Journal of Marketing, 27*(10), 52–64.

Mishler, E.G. (1986). *Research interviewing: Context and narrative.* Harvard, MA: Harvard University Press.

Moini, A.H. (1995). An enquiry into successful exporting: An empirical investigation using a three-stage model. *Journal of Small Business Management, 33*(3), 9–25.

Narver, J.C., & Slater, S.F. (1990). The effect of a market orientation on business profitability. *Journal of Marketing,* October, 20–35.

Paliwoda, S. (1997). *International marketing* (3rd ed.). Oxford, UK: Butterworth Heinemann.

Pearson, M. (1989). Languages in a multinational company. *The Linguist, 28*(5), 146–147.

Piekkari, R., & Zander, L. (2005). Language and communication in international management. *International Studies of Management and Organisation, 35*(1), 3–9.

Peter, J.P. (1981, May). Construct validity: A review of basic issues and marketing practices. *Journal of Marketing Research, 18,* 133–145.

Razeen, S. (2005). Free trade, new century. *Economic Affairs, 25*(4), p.81.

Reith, R.A., & Ryan, E.G. (1981). A study of the perceptions of selected Massachusetts manufactur-ers towards exporting. *Developments in Marketing Science, 4,* 101–104.

Samiee, S., & Walters, P.G.P. (1991). Segmenting corporate exporting activities: Sporadic versus regular exporters. *Journal of the Academy of Marketing Science, 19*(2), 93–104.

Schlegelmilch, B.B., & Ross, A.G. (1987). The influence of managerial characteristics on different measures of export success. *Journal of Marketing Management, 3*(2), 145–158.

Shen, J. (2006). Factors affecting international staffing in Chinese multi-nationals (MNEs). International *Journal of Human Resource Management, 17*(2), 295–315.

Siegel, S., & Castellan, N.J., Jr. (1988). *Non-parametric statistics for the behavioral sciences.* New York: McGraw-Hill.

Simmonds, K., & Smith, H. (1968, Summer). The first export order: A marketing innovation. *British Journal of Marketing, 2,* 93–100.

Souchon, A.L., & Diamantopoulos, A. (1996). A conceptual framework of marketing information use: Key issues and research propositions. *Journal of International Marketing, 4*(3), 49–71.

Souchon, A.L., & Durden, G.R. (2002). Making the most out of export information: An exploratory study of UK and New Zealand exporters. *Journal of Euromarketing, 11*(4), 65–87.

Swift, J. (1990). Marketing competence and language skills: UK competence in the Spanish market. *International Business Communication, 2*(2), 21–26.

Swift, J. (1991). Foreign language ability and international marketing. *European Journal of Marketing, 25*(12), 36–49.

Walters, P.G. (1990). The significance of foreign language skills for initial entry positions in international firms. *Journal of Teaching in International Business, 1*(3/4), 71–83.

White, D.S., Griffith, D.A., & Ryans, J.K., Jr. (1999). Profiling exporting and non-exporting service firms: Critical differences to decision-makers. *Thunderbird International Business Review, 41*(2), 195–213.

Wiedersham-Paul, F., Olson, H.C., & Welch, L.S. (1978). Pre-export activity: The first step in internationalization. *Journal of International Business Studies, 9*(1), 47–58.

Wood, V.R., & Goolsby, J.R. (1987). Foreign market information preferences of established US exporters. *International Marketing Review, Winter,* 43–52.

Yeoh, P-L. (2004). International learning: Antecedents and performance implications among newly internationalising companies in an exporting context. *International Marketing Review, 21*(4/5), 511–535.

Zander, L. (2005). Communication and country clusters. *International Studies of Management and Organisation, 35*(1), 83–103.

Appendix A

Derivation of Export Marketing Behaviours

Sources of marketing information	McAuley (1993), Hart and Diamantopoulos (1993), Hart, Webb and Jones (1994)
Methods of collection	Bodur & Cavusgil (1985), Hart, Webb and Jones (1994), Souchon and Diamantopoulos (1996)
Export marketing decisions	Bodur & Cavusgil (1985)
Information used in export decisions	Cavusgil (1984a), Bodur and Cavusgil (1985), Wood and Goolsby (1987), Koh (1991), Samiee and Walters (1991), Hart and Diamantopoulos (1993), Evergin, Bodur and Cavusgil (1993), Hart, Webb and Jones (1994), Leonidou (1997)

Appendix B

Classification of Export Market Behaviours (From Cluster Analysis)

Sources of marketing information
Published secondary reports (General):
    Trade magazines/journals
    General magazines/newspapers
    Trade/export directories
Published secondary reports (market-specific):
    Country/market sector reports
    International trade statistics
*Trade gatherings:
    Trade fairs/missions/exhibitions
    Conferences/seminars
Competitors and customers:
    Competitors' publications
    Talking to competitors
    Customers' publications
    Talking to customers

Secondary research:
    Internet
    Library

*Primary research:
    Semistructured personal interviews
    Telephone surveys
    Focus groups
    Postal/fax/e-mail questionnaires

Those used to gather information
Government/professional organisations:
    British Trade International/DTI
    Business Link export counsellor/advisor
    Professional/trade association
*Marketing:
    Market research company
    Other marketing consultants

Company:
    Overseas subsidiary/office
    Local agent/distributor
    Company's sales team
    Other permanent in-house staff
*Other:
    Temporary staff hired for the purpose
    Universities/business schools

Export marketing decisions
*Market entry:
    Assessing the potential of new export markets
    Methods of entering new country markets

*Current markets:
    Prioritising existing export markets
    Consolidating company's position in existing export markets
*Ad hoc:
    Organisation of local selling function
    Pulling out of an overseas market

Information used in export decisions
Market conditions:
    Market size/structure
    Sales potential/market growth
    Local competition
    Local agents/distributors
Sociocultural
    Local business practices
    Legal issues
    Political conditions
*Entry barriers
    Potential barriers to entry
    Technical standards

Buyer behaviour:
    How purchasing decisions are made locally
    Local service expectations
    Local price conditions
    Local perceptions of the company
    Customer satisfaction levels
    Product end-uses
**Other
    Customer credit worthiness
    Economic conditions
    Local transport/distribution
    New product development opportunities
    Export insurance/finance
    Language/translation facilities
    Advertising/promotions
    Reports on potential customers

Note: * These clusters were not carried forward to additional analysis as doubts were raised as to their validity (which was established by splitting the sample and comparing the results of each half with the total).
    ** These variables were not included in discrete clusters, and were therefore analysed independently.
    Frequency of behaviour was measured using a 4-point scale from *frequently* (anchored at three or more times a year) to *never*.

Contributors

Anne Ardagh
School of Commerce, Charles Sturt University, Wagga Wagga, Australia.
E-mail: aardagh@csu.edu.au

Parikshit Basu
School of Marketing and Management, Charles Sturt University, Bathurst,
Australia. E-mail: pbasu@csu.edu.au

Zelma Bone
School of Marketing and Management, Orange, Australia.
E-mail: zbone@csu.edu.au

Graham Bowrey
Discipline of Accounting, School of Accounting & Finance, University of
Wollongong, Wollongong, Australia. E-mail: graham_bowrey@uow.edu.au

Estian Calitz
Stellenbosch University, South Africa. E-mail: calitz@sun.ac.za

Judith Crockett
School of Rural Management, Faculty of Science, Charles Sturt University,
Orange, Australia. E-mail: jcrockett@csu.edu.au

Marcelle Droulers
School of Marketing and Management, Charles Sturt University, Bathurst,
Australia. E-mail: mdroulers@csu.edu.au

Roderick Duncan
School of Marketing & Management, Charles Sturt University, Bathurst,
Australia. E-mail: rduncan@csu.edu.au

John (Jack) English

Australian Innovation Research Centre, University of Tasmania, Australia.
E-mail: jack.english@utas.edu.au

Mark Frost

School of Marketing & Management, Faculty of Commerce, Charles Sturt
University, Orange, Australia. E-mail: mfrost@csu.edu.au

Rakesh Gupta

Faculty of Business and Informatics, Central Queensland University, North
Rockhampton, Australia. E-mail:r.gupta@cqu.edu.au

Troy Heffernan

School of Marketing & Management, Charles Sturt University, Australia.
E-mail: troy.heffernan@plymouth.ac.uk

John Hicks

Faculty of Business, Charles Sturt University, Bathurst, Australia.
E-mail: jhicks@csu.edu.au

Mohammad Ziaul Hoque

Department of Accounting and Finance, Monash University, Melbourne,
Australia. E-mail: Mohammad.Hoque@buseco.monash.edu.au

Peter Hosie

School of Management, Curtin University of Technology, Australia.
E-mail: Peter.Hosie@cbs.curtin.edu.au

Kate Hutchings

Department of Management, Monash University, Australia.
E-mail: kate.hutchings@buseco.monash.edu.au

Stacey Jenkins

School of Commerce, Charles Sturt University, Wagga Wagga, Australia.
E-mail: sjenkins@csu.edu.au

Branka Krivokapic-Skoko

School of Marketing and Management, Charles Sturt University, Bathurst,
Australia. E-mail: bkrivokapic@csu.edu.au

Linda MacGrain Herkenhoff

Saint Mary's College, Graduate School of Business, California, United States of
America. E-mail: lherken@stmarys-ca.edu

Robert Macklin
School of Commerce, Charles Sturt University, Wagga Wagga, Australia.
E-mail: rmacklin@csu.edu.au

Pamela Mathews
School of Commerce, Charles Sturt University, Wagga Wagga, Australia.
E-mail: pmathews@csu.edu.au

Brian Murphy
School of Accounting & Finance, University of Wollongong, Wollongong, Australia. E-mail: brian_murphy@uow.edu.au

Grant O'Neill
School of Marketing and Management, Charles Sturt University, Bathurst, Australia. E-mail: goneill@csu. edu.au

Richard B. Sappey
Faculty of Business, Charles Sturt University, Bathurst, Australia.
E-mail: rsappey@csu.edu.au

Peter Sevastos
Department of Psychology, Curtin University of Technology, Australia.
E-mail: P.Sevastos@curtin.edu.au

Robert Sharkie
School of Commerce, Charles Sturt University, Wagga Wagga, Australia.
E-mail: rsharkie@csu.edu.au

Val Siemionow
School of Marketing and Management, Charles Sturt University, Bathurst, Australia. E-mail: vsiemionow@csu.edu.au

Ciorstan Smark
School of Accounting & Finance, University of Wollongong, Wollongong, Australia. E-mail: csmark@uow.edu.au

Andrew Smith
Faculty of Business, Charles Sturt University, Wagga Wagga, Australia.
E-mail: asmith@csu.edu.au

Robert Tierney
School of Marketing and Management, Charles Sturt University, Bathurst, Australia. E-mail: rtierney@csu.edu.au

Rupert Tipples

Agriculture and Life Sciences Division, Lincoln University, Lincoln, New Zealand. E-mail: Tipplesr@lincoln.ac.nz

Clem Tisdell

School of Economics, The University of Queensland, Australia. E-mail: c.tisdell@economics.uq.edu.au

Antonio Travaglione

Faculty of Economics and Business, The University of Sydney, Australia. E-mail: t.travaglione@econ.usyd.edu.au

John Verry

Human Resources Department, University of Canterbury, New Zealand. E-mail: john.verry@canterbury.ac.nz

Ted Watts

School of Accounting & Finance, University of Wollongong, Wollongong, Australia. E-mail: tedw@uow.edu.au

Jasmine Williams

Plymouth Business School, University of Plymouth, United Kingdom. E-mail: jasmine.williams@plymouth.ac.uk

www.ingramcontent.com/pod-product-compliance
Ingram Content Group Australia Pty Ltd
76 Discovery Rd, Dandenong South VIC 3175, AU
AUHW011249130325
408272AU00010B/39